GOD'S CANDIDATE

The Life and Times of
Pope John Paul I

Dedicated to Joyce E. Spackman, who always believed in the project, and to Charles B. Spackman for his comments and advice.

GOD'S CANDIDATE

The Life and Times of Pope John Paul I

Paul Spackman

GRACEWING

First published in 2008 by

Gracewing
2 Southern Avenue,
Leominster
Herefordshire HR6 0QF

ISBN 978 0 85244 187 9

Typeset by Action Publishing Technology Ltd,
Gloucester GL1 5SR

Contents

The author would be grateful for any further information, comments and notification of any factual errors via the publisher for possible inclusion in any future edition.

Preface

Albino Luciani was the first pope to be born in the twentieth century, and also the first to be born of working-class – as opposed to peasant – origins. The primary intent of this work is to detail the course of Luciani's life and reveal the development of his thought and teaching. His papacy, short but undeniably influential, was preceded by much else worthy of consideration.

Luciani was a very private man, but much of his life and thought are accessible through his writings and speeches, and the testimony of close relatives, friends and colleagues. His life spanned a most interesting and vital period in the development of both the Roman Catholic Church and the Italian nation, and in that of the wider socio-cultural and political worlds, and significant parts of these processes and their interrelationship with Luciani's own personal growth have been drawn on. By considering his whole life, with both its continuities and changes, and subsequent events, it is possible to reach a much more comprehensive and balanced view of his essential personality, his papacy and continuing legacy to the Church than has hitherto been possible. His simplification of the papal style is not a surprise to those who know of his childhood and of his approach to life in Belluno, Vittorio Veneto and Venice.

Luciani was a man who took an intelligent interest in the whole world, and who with his own life quietly enriched it. The poor, the young, the disabled, the Third World, and all manner of social, ecumenical and ecological problems received his attention and support, always quietly, with charity and dignity. He was an innovator, and a simplifier of pomp. Ordinary people could readily understand him, and he had a certain quality of gentle, infectious humour that was sometimes intentional, sometimes not. Luciani's personal pastoral practice was also often more liberal and humane than his generally more conservative, traditional doctrine, and in this he was a true northern Italian. Above all, he was what Italians simply call `simpatico'. Many people have been uplifted and drawn nearer to Christ by 'Don Albino', and he would like that. After all, catechesis was his first love.

For a little over a month in the autumn of 1978 a rare atmosphere of vitality and hope was evident in the Vatican, and it set the world aglow. Luciani, newly elected as Pope John Paul I, was a man of such radiant friendliness and obvious humanity that many were drawn to look towards Rome for inspiration. By popular acclaim he quickly became known as 'the smiling Pope'. The people of Rome itself took him to their hearts and called him by the familiar name 'Gianpaolo', just as they would with a personal friend. Pope John XXIII seemed to live again, physically slighter, but more vividly alive even than before. Gianpaolo had the happy knack of making people feel reawakened, spiritually rejuvenated. He tried to shake off the time-encrusted, temporal trappings of the Supreme Pontiff, and adhere more closely to the message of Jesus Christ: the attitude he adopted was that of a pastor, whose parish just happened to be the whole world.

Of course, Gianpaolo's 'new broom' approach and unprecedented popularity did not please everyone, and soon unsettled curial critics in the Vatican were muttering that the pope was out of his depth, taking hours over writing his speeches and spending sleepless nights worrying about his new responsibilities. The wonder is that they actually expected this 'news' to surprise or shock anyone. It had been just the same with Paul VI and besides, what person of Gianpaolo's rather shy, self-effacing and unassuming personality would not experience such feelings for a while after being thrust into the awesome position of being spiritual leader of the world's (then) 750 million Catholics?

Luciani's election as pope was so sudden, and so unexpected (to others at least), that he had no time to adjust and take stock of his new situation. He was immediately immersed in the busy, highly formal Vatican timetable and structure, and cut off from people and normal life. Whilst he was obviously not alone in the Vatican, and indeed had some familiar and friendly faces around him, in a certain spiritual, human sense he was suddenly lonely, detached from familiar experiences. The probably apocryphal story of his walking unannounced out of the Vatican just after daybreak, looking about him, could thus almost be seen as a symbolic act of escape, of getting a breath of fresh air.

With Gianpaolo people dared to hope that honesty, humility, love and peace could prevail in what mankind chooses to call the 'real world'. Millions – Catholics, non-Catholics, non-Christians and those of no faith at all – looked to him. Certainly it would have been an impossible task for him to fulfil all their disparate dreams, but we can be sure that he would have tried his utmost and achieved much. In fact Gianpaolo was uncomfortable with the burden of the papacy, but he did not show it in public. In his humility he continued to give his warm smile, drawing out a reciprocal response in others, making them feel joyful. He, though, was perhaps 'the smiling Pope' almost in spite of himself.

However, we will only ever be able to make an informed estimation of the man's stature as a pope because, almost before it had begun, his papacy was over. A stunned world learned that the Pope was dead. On the day of his funeral it rained heavily in Rome, and this mirrored the emotions of millions of Catholics and non-Catholics alike as they mourned the death of their friend. Unconsciously, his papacy and premature death formed his last ecumenical 'statement', drawing different people together in shared appreciation and sympathy. It is the memory of the man and his inspirational legacy of compassionate love that this book seeks to fix more firmly on the record. We may say of Luciani, as was said of Abel the Just, that 'Though he is dead, he still speaks by faith' (Hebrews 11:4).

My own memories of the time, from television and the press, are quite clear: the white smoke rising from the chimney of the conclave, the expectant crowds, the seemingly tiny figure of the Pope appearing on the balcony of St Peter's, and the immediately evident pure joy of his smile. From that first moment there was a sense of peace and of a new dawn – and then, so soon, he was gone. The British socialist politician Ken Livingstone has said of John XXIII, with whom Gianpaolo had so much in common: 'He made a strong impact on me. His death was the first time I cried for someone who'd died that I didn't know'.[1] The death of Gianpaolo had much the same impact on me, at about the same age, as the death of 'good Pope John' obviously had on Ken Livingstone in 1963.

Researching the life of Albino Luciani has been both a privi-

---

[1] J. Carvel, *Citizen Ken*, Chatto & Windus, 1984, p. 37.

lege and a challenge. It has also been a deeply enriching experience. As always, all responsibility for the opinions expressed
and any factual errors contained in the book rests with the
author. However, I should like to gratefully acknowledge the
kindness of the following people who have helped in the writing
of this work by way of advice, encouragement and information
given:

Pia Basso (née Luciani), for kindly 'fine-tuning' much vitally
important family information; the late George A. Bull, OBE, for
long-term advice and encouragement; Bernard Cartwright, for
timely information on medical aspects; Dr Peter Day, for help
on all matters Orthodox; Dawn Edwards, for early, essential
computer aid; Colonel Alberto Ficuciello, for checking Italian
military records; Richard J. Hardy, for friendship and endless
help with books; the late Peter Hebblethwaite, for helping me
get started on the right track and for leaving me, as he said, 'a
small space' between his seminal papal biographies; Dom
Leander Hogg, OSB, for long-term friendship and invaluable
advice, encouragement, translation, proof-reading, Roman
hospitality at the Monastery of S. Ambrogio . . .; Gemma Jones,
for timely computer assistance; Professor Hans Küng, for kind
permission to quote from his correspondence; Mgr Giorgio Lise,
for important Luciani family information and an introduction;
the late Rev. Preb. Ralph J. C. Lumley, for recounting his
meeting with Luciani in 1978 and for copies of personal photographs; the late Bishop Gerald T. Mahon, MHM, for information
on Vatican II; Sr Mary Joseph McManamon, OSB, Librarian of
the Venerable English College in Rome, for her kind and cheerful assistance; Darren Preston, for patient computer aid; Jane
Roberts, for her support, frequent assistance with the 'percola-
tion process' and many enjoyable forays to bookshops and
libraries, and to Jo Whale of Gracewing Publishing, for her
sensitive and meticulous editing.

Paul Spackman
28 May 2008

Chapter One

Childhood and Seminary Years
1912–1935

Albino Luciani was born at noon on Thursday 17 October 1912 in Forno di Canale,[1] a village with a population of some one thousand inhabitants. Standing 976m above sea level up in the Italian Dolomites at the confluence of the Liera and Biois rivers, the village lies about 135 kilometres north of Venice in the region of the Veneto.

The boy's roots were planted deep in the valley, the family tracing their roots back as far as one Battista Luciani around the year 1580. His grandfather Daniele Luciani was born there on 9 October 1845, marrying local girl Antonia Moè on 12 February 1868. They eventually had ten children, six boys and four girls, although only two boys and two girls survived infancy. Albino's father Giovanni Battista was born on 27 May 1872, part of the first generation to be born in the newly united Italy. Giovanni was also part of the first generation to get some formal education, attending the elementary school for three years.

On his mother's side, the name of Tancon has been traced back to Iacomucius de Tangono in 1440. Albino's grandfather Agostino Tancon was born on 27 June 1853, marrying Maddalena Zus on 4 June 1877. They were to have a more modestly sized family of four children, two boys and two girls, Albino's mother Maria Bortola being born on 19 August 1879.

Giovanni Luciani first married Rosa Fiocco, the happy event taking place on 3 April 1900, in the dawn of the new century.

---

[1] In 1964 the village reverted to its original name of Canale d'Agordo, at the instigation of Luciani's brother Edoardo; by 1978 it had a population of some 1700 inhabitants, of whom almost 70 had the surname Luciani and were related to the new pope. The name Forno di Canale recalled the furnaces used to smelt the copper and iron extracted from the mountains.

The pair were cousins, Rosa's mother Amalia being the sister of Giovanni's mother and marrying Celestino Fiocco. However, deep tragedy was soon to follow. Rosa bore two daughters, Amalia on 27 December 1900 and Pia on 20 November 1902, but both were partially deaf and dumb, learning to speak with a stutter. The poor mother then bore three sons in quick succession, each of whom died after a matter of months. With dogged persistence the parents called each one Albino. Then, less than two months after the loss of the last son, Rosa, worn out with childbirth and loss, died on 27 December 1906, her daughter Amalia's sixth birthday, aged only twenty-nine.[2] It was a bleak winter for the survivors of the little family.

Giovanni did not remarry for nearly five years, the marriage with Bortola taking place on 2 December 1911. The two met whilst they were both working in Venice. Bortola had also had three years of schooling, which was more than most of the other women of Canale, and had worked for eleven years for the Franciscan Tertiary Sisters of St Elizabeth of Hungary ('Elisabettines') at the old people's home of S. Giovanni e Paolo in Venice.[3] Before that she had worked in St Gallen, Switzerland, and for a Lady Ersilina in her private house in Venice. Again, these experiences must have set Bortola a little apart from the average. Her actual name was Bartolomea, but she became known to everyone as Bortola because her name was abbreviated by her two stepdaughters due to their speech difficulties.

Albino's birth was difficult one, the midwife being his aunt, Maria Fiocco; with fears for his life she baptized him at home the same day. All this must have raised terrible shadows in the mind of the anxious father Giovanni when he heard the news of his fourth son's struggle for life. On 19 October Albino's baptism was formalized in the village church of San Giovanni Battista[4] by the curate Don Achille Ronzon. He was so named in memory of a close Bergamesque friend of Giovanni who had been killed in a blast furnace accident while working alongside him in Essen, Germany, another sorrow in his still young life.

On 2 September 1915 another son, Tranquillo Federico, was born, but he was weak and died of broncho-pneumonia on 12 February 1916 aged five months. Tranquillo's death caused Albino some anguish. Edoardo later recalled:

---

[2] Rosa was born on 19 January 1877.
[3] Seabeck, p. 11, and information from Pia Basso.
[4] Baptismal Register n. 22 (1902–1917), entry n. 96, in parish archives of Canale D'Agordo.

With the rigid atmosphere of winter up here, the worry we had was to prevent the cold air from entering the house. Naturally my mother always recommended us to close the door and the windows, so the little child did not take any cold and he did not become ill. I remember to have heard my brother Albino say that in his early years he had suffered a lot, because of the fact that his sisters (of the first mother), Amalia and Pia, reproached him to have made their brother sick like that. He said to me that he often woke up during the night and he thought: 'Perhaps I have been the cause of my little brother's death.' It was the moral suffering that he remembered most.[5]

In the winter of 1915 little Albino himself caught pneumonia, because he ran barefoot out into the snow to play. By the time his mother caught up with him he was dripping wet.[6]

Finally fate smiled on the two hard-pressed parents. Not only did Albino grow up to be healthy, but two more strong children were soon born to them, Edoardo on 26 March 1917 and Antonia on 3 February 1920.

The majority of working-age men in the area had to travel about in search of employment, leaving the village during the summer months largely populated by old men, women and children. It was the same for Giovanni. Before he married Bortola, Giovanni had a very dangerous job on a red lead farm on the island of Murano in the lagoon of Venice. The crystalline powder, toxic when ingested, was used in the manufacture of the lead glass used by the famous glass-blowing industry on the island, giving it weight, lustre and strength. Abandoning this job, Giovanni would leave in spring and return on the onset of winter, working in Austria, Switzerland, Germany (Baden and Westphalia) and in 1923 in France as a bricklayer, engineer, mechanic or electrician! Because of this, he was not even able to be present at Albino's birth.

In 1913 Giovanni emigrated to La Plata in Argentina, in the classic Italian mode of the time, gaining employment as a bricklayer on the aqueduct then under construction. It was a hard existence, but the plan was that when he had saved enough money, Bortola and little Albino would join him.

---

5   Edoardo to Antonio Ugenti, 'The Gift Of Clarity'. Amalia died in 1939. Pia became a nun of the Sacred Heart of Maria in the enclosed convent of Cottolengo di Turino, getting special dispensation from Pope John XXIII to witness Albino's episcopal consecration in Rome in 1958. She died in 1969. Edoardo died on 10 March 2008.

6   A. Luciani, 'Mio Fratello Albino', p. 44.

However, the outbreak of the First World War in Europe in August 1914 led Giovanni to decide to return home.[7] During the war itself the Austrians occupied the valley of the Agordo as far south as the River Piave, but fortunately they did not bother the villagers much, apart from sending out occasional patrols to forage for food.[8]

As a result of his travels and experiences, especially those in Germany, Giovanni came to hold socialist ideas of the old anti-clerical sort, and stood as a socialist in the municipal elections. Looking at a photograph of Giovanni taken at this time, in which he is shown with a pipe and large moustache, Edoardo would later joke with his sister that their father resembled Stalin.[9] Eventually Giovanni's views would become more Social Democrat orientated, but at the time such ideas and actions caused a certain amount of friction with Bortola, who was highly devout. She attended Mass, received Communion and said her Rosary every day, and had at one time considered entering a convent as a nun. Such regular attendance at Mass made a deep impression on little Albino. He later recalled entering his parish church with the organ playing with full voice:

> I forgot my usual poverty and had the impression that the organ was welcoming especially me and my little companions as if we were princes. From this first vague intuition came the strong conviction that the Catholic Church is not only something great, but also makes great the little and the poor, honouring and ennobling them.[10]

Years later Antonia remembered:

> We were poor folk. Our mother was very simple, very Catholic. She knew by heart nearly the whole catechism of Saint Pius X. She taught it to us, for example when she was washing or dressing us. When she was a young girl, she had had the opportunity of meeting Cardinal Sarto in Venice: 'Just think', she told us, 'I saw the man who was to become pope!'.[11]

[7] Edoardo, quoted in *Gente*, 7 September 1978 and *Radiolandia 2000* September 1978, Argentina.

[8] De La Cierva, p. 45.

[9] A. Luciani, 'Mio Fratello Albino', in the Prologue by S. Falasca.

[10] Seabeck, p. 12.

[11] *30 Days*, March 1992, p. 46. Sarto (Pope St Pius X) was Patriarch of Venice from 1893 to 1903, and reigned as pope from then until 1914. He was canonized by Pius XII on 29 May 1954.

Bortola taught the young Albino a simple prayer, one that he remembered and tried to adhere to all his life: 'Lord, take me as I am, with my faults and with my sins, but make me become as You wish'. She was kindly, and being literate she wrote letters for those who were not, but to earn enough to live she had also to go into domestic service. At one stage she worked for a Jewish family, a fact her son later recalled as Pope.[12]

The village of Forno di Canale was founded in the fourteenth century, and is a typical farming community of the region. Centred on its little church and piazza, it nestles amid pine forests and the mountains, which are sharp peaks of magnesian limestone, many rising to over 2500 metres. In summer the temperature can hit 20°C: in winter it can drop to – 17°C, with falls of snow reaching up to 3 metres.

The Luciani home was a grey, three-storey building partly converted from a barn. Its one source of heating was an old wood-burning stove that heated the room where Albino was born. The house had two gardens with common flowers, herbs and vegetables. The family diet consisted of polenta (corn meal), barley, macaroni and any vegetables that were available. Meat was a rare luxury; on special occasions there might be a dessert of carfoni (pastry full of ground poppy seeds). It was not until 1923 that the Luciani family first had white bread in the house; it was brought back up the steep track from the nearby village of Cencenighe with something approaching reverence. Under the guidance of his mother Albino grew the vegetables and aromatic herbs – camomile, mint and absinthe – with which the family supplemented their diet. They also kept a few chickens.

When he became pope, stories and anecdotes concerning Albino's youthful exploits quickly surfaced; all show a normal, healthy boyhood. He was bright, though not exceptional. His sister later remembered him as 'lively and very studious', whilst his brother recalled that from the age of twelve Albino had been 'a master of himself' and that he, Edoardo, had come 'to understand that I should never be surprised by anything he did'.[13]

Like most children, Albino was sometimes sent on errands ('*commissioni*'). In a small copybook that he used as a fourth-grader – and which is still preserved by a relative in Canale – Albino wrote a letter to his mother confessing a lie: 'Dear

---

[12] Hebblethwaite, *Year Of Three Popes*, p. 89.
[13] Dean, p. 5.

Mamma, you sent me to Cencenighe to buy medicine and you gave me 12 lire. On the way I lost two lire and I told you it cost seven lire instead of five. I never had the courage to confess that I lost two.'[14] In the same year, in an essay on his mother, he proudly stated that 'she dresses casually because she is a countrywoman, but she knows how to read and write well and also do counting'.[15]

Bortola was a strong personality, a significant presence and influence on her son and husband. This is shown by the fact that in his home village, even after he became a bishop, he was still called Bortola's Don Albino. And his father was known as Bortola's Giovanni, which was somewhat unusual.[16]

Albino should have begun elementary school in October 1918, but the school, in classrooms in the centre of the former Town Hall building, was still closed because of the war, so his sister Pia taught him to read and write at home. He thus actually began school in October 1919. Edoardo has recalled of his brother:

> In the first years, he was surely anything but a model student. Perhaps with his strong temper, with his kindly, but not less annoying vivacity, he was almost a challenge to his mother and his teachers. Often, his teachers could not do any other than to request his mother, Bortola, to visit the school for a 'chat'. It was not that the boy was bad-mannered or disrespectful to the teachers, or a villain towards his companions but, simply, he could not remain quiet on his bench (. . .)
>
> Sometimes surely, his female school friends incited him to pull their hair; or to jump on benches when he was 'fighting' innocently with his friends; or to sit on the teacher's chair (which was raised on a platform). All things that today seem normal and irrelevant facts of scholastic life, that it would be ridiculous to consider them as problems . . . In times gone by, it was not like that; that's why the boy had a mark in conduct that, if he could see it now, it would-n't live up to him – just as John Paul himself, smiling, confessed to Bellunese pilgrims years later.[17]

[14] Muthig, p. 166.
[15] A. Luciani, 'Mio Fratello Albino', p. 38. The essay was written on 26 January 1923.
[16] Cardinal José Saraiva Martins, 'Albino Luciani: The Smile Of The Christian Life', *30 Days*, no.1, Year XXII, January 2004.
[17] Edoardo Luciani, 'Annoying Vivacity', from *Il Celentone* and *L'Amico del Popolo*, 9 September 1978.

Like many people, Albino himself had mixed memories of his schooldays. He continued to think 'tenderly' and gratefully of his first teachers and could still see himself 'a boy again on the benches' of his village school in youthful awe of their knowledge.[18] However, he later felt that in his day schools had 'exaggerated on the side of rote learning', continuing:

> Some names come back to me: Zenoni (Latin and Greek grammar), Campanini-Carboni (Latin vocabulary), Sanesi (Greek vocabulary). Connected with them I see declinations, paradigms, rules, exceptions, exercises, translated pages in endless number.
>
> History, as recorded in textbooks, seemed to me a distillation of noise, as Carlyle said, all made up of dates, wars, armistices, treaties. In studying a bit of science, I committed to memory series of names, of neuroptera, lepidoptera, coleoptera, diptera, and so on, but I was never sure whether the housefly and the mosquito belong to the order of the diptera, and I was never able to see hymenoptera in the red ants that painfully stung my legs when I sat down in a meadow.
>
> A living school is much better . . .[19]

Once, there was trouble at school, and with Albino the source was a trifle unusual:

> Summer 1922, the final term of the third scholastic year. Another complaint was made to Mrs Luciani about her eldest son. That time, the matter was serious. He had behaved in an intolerable way and the elderly teacher, boiling with indignation, went to Luciani's home. What had happened? Luciani had called her a thief! Why? The explanation was simple: at the beginning of the scholastic year, the teacher had requested Albino to loan a book, which he no longer used, to a poor student. He did so with pleasure but when, at the end of the scholastic year, he had asked the teacher to return the book to him, she had asked him why he wanted that old and worn-out book. More than enough reason for Albino (who was almost nine years old) to call the teacher a 'thief'. It was not only the fact that the book was his, so she could not do what she wanted with it. On the other hand, to demonstrate his generosity towards others, we have the example of the first slice of white bread that he had kept for his little brother, Edoardo. No, even though a book was for him an extremely expensive and precious possession, it was not a determining reason for such a serious accusation. His sense of right and justice had undergone a serious blow because of the teacher's reaction, which was, to him, incomprehensible.

[18] *Illustrissimi*, (US edn), p. 224.
[19] Ibid., p. 202.

The boy doesn't bear partialities and injustices and, when he sees or he thinks to see them, he suffers, moves away locking into himself. In this matter, things that are trivialities for us, acquire an extraordinary importance for the boy.'

(*Crumbs From The Catechism*)

How important this was to make him call his teacher a 'thief'. The teacher reacted without realizing her pupil's indignation, without any pedagogic knowledge and ability to be able to [enter into] the child's psychology, embarassing his mother, Bortola, into taking steps to remedy the matter.[20]

Occasionally Albino, along with his schoolfriend Giulio Bramezza, would miss school altogether. Albino loved birds, and the two boys would climb in the local mountains with birdlime to catch them, in order to raise them and hear them sing. Then they let them go. If they caught goldfinches, the two boys counted their day 'a great success'.

Incidentally, in recounting this memory Giulio made a psychologically interesting comment that illuminates his friend's subsequent career:

We always remained friends. Anyway, it was impossible to argue with him; he always managed to convince me to do what he wanted to do, even if I didn't want to. He had a way of saying things that made one quickly give in to him. He even succeeded in teaching me doctrine and was always there when I needed help. He never changed.[21]

But all the time Albino lived with two constants – poverty and the Catholic Church. He would do farm chores barefoot to avoid wearing-out shoe leather,[22] chores like cutting grass to help boost the family income;[23] only during the long, bitter winter would he generally wear his heavy mountain clogs along with an old cast-off military jacket for warmth. The period at the end of the First World War was one of particular poverty and famine, but Albino remained lovingly conscious of his responsibilities towards his younger siblings, despite his own tender age. It is recorded that

For a job Albino was asked to do, he was given a piece of bread as compensation. On arriving home, despite the fact that he was

---

[20] Regina Kummer, 'Thief', from *Una Vita Per La Chiesa*.
[21] Bramezza, quoted in Seabeck, pp. 13–14.
[22] *Time*, 112, 11 Sept. 1978, p. 47.
[23] Yallop, p. 23.

equally hungry, he gave that piece of bread to his younger brother, Edoardo. While Edoardo ate it, Albino sat near by watching him. Ever since, Edoardo has never forgotten this kind gesture.[24]

Luciani's natural, lifelong sympathy with the poor thus came from lived, personal experience. His links with his place of birth always remained strong, and later on he was still to be seen working in the fields in his cassock during his holidays. Learning was certainly no problem to the boy; he was an avid and precocious reader in a country where adult illiteracy was still nearly fifty per cent. He first read Carlo Collodi's *Le Avventure Di Pinocchio* when aged seven,[25] and went on to read and re-read the works of Charles Dickens, Mark Twain, Sir Walter Scott, the Italian poet and scholar Giosuè Carducci, Christopher Marlowe,[26] Jules Verne,[27] and the Veronese adventure novelist Emilio Salgari.[28] He was also something of a sickly child,[29] and whilst ill and resting he was doubtless still reading!

In late 1918–early 1919 the appalling but now largely forgotten 'Spanish Flu' (H1N1) pandemic hit the world and its war-weary population. One of the deadliest outbreaks of disease in human history, it often killed the young and healthy. Nowhere was immune. Between January and June 1919 it hit the little village of Forno di Canale hard – of a population of no more than a thousand inhabitants, forty-two died, including some of Albino's little friends; Fioretto Faé, Maria Valt and others.[30] As if that were not enough a small earthquake shook the village on the afternoon of 11 October.[31]

As well as being generally poor and hardworking, the people of the Veneto were – and are still – among some of the most devoutly Catholic in Italy. Albino was confirmed on 26 September 1919 by Bishop Giosuè Cattarossi, and took First Communion on 2 March 1923 from Don Filippo Carli, his parish

---

[24] Pia Luciani, 'Albino Luciani', Letter dated 6 February 2003.

[25] Collodi was the pseudonym of Carlo Lorenzini (1826–1890), the Florentine ex-seminarian turned nationalist journalist. Pinocchio was serialized in 1880–81, and first published in book form in 1882.

[26] *Illustrissimi*, pp. 15, 21, 93, 151, 209.

[27] John Paul I, *The Pope Speaks*, p. 326.

[28] De La Cierva, p. 47. Salgari (1862–1911) was the author of over 200 novels.

[29] *The Pope Speaks*, p. 308.

[30] De La Cierva, p. 46. It has been calculated that 'La Grippe' killed 21,642,274 people worldwide.

[31] Serafini, p. 18.

priest since 3 July 1919.[32] He had an early vocation for the priesthood, and in this he was actively encouraged, but never pushed, by his mother and Don Filippo.

The devout Bortola nurtured the desire to have a priest in the family, giving Albino a child's edition of *Introduction To A Devout Life* by St Francis de Sales. Albino was very keen on study: his first reason for wanting to go to seminary was the presence of so many books, the second was his desire to emulate Don Filippo, whom he admired and loved very much.[33] However, Albino had also to obtain the consent of his father, for the cost of his attending the minor seminary at Feltre would be considerable. After discussing the matter with his mother just before his eleventh birthday, he wrote to his father, then in Germany; 'Albino was later to say it was one of the most important letters of his life.'[34] It must have been earnest and persuasive, because fortunately Giovanni duly gave his consent, merely noting that they must make sacrifices. In his letter, which Albino not only kept but proudly carried with him in his wallet for a long time, it is notable that the socialist Giovanni also expressed the hope that when he became a priest, his son would take the part of the poor ones and the workers, as Christ had. The son took these natural words to heart and they became the bedrock of his formation.

During the summer before he was due to enter the seminary Albino took extra lessons in the mornings from a teacher who was staying in the rectory. In the afternoons he would take his books to the field where he had to keep watch on the cow. He would study awhile, then play with the other boys. One day he left his notebook under a tree while he played. When he returned he found that he had left it near the salt lick and that the cow had chewed it. He was in despair, realizing that he would have no homework to show the teacher. He was so worried what the teacher would say that his mother accompanied him to the rectory. The teacher made a rather unthinking joke, saying, 'Since the cow has eaten his lessons, Albino won't be able to go to the seminary.' Poor Albino took him seriously and began to cry. But his kindly priest, who was also present,

---

[32] Bishop Giosuè Cattarossi; born 1863 at Cornale, consecrated 1911, Bishop of Belluno e Feltre from 21 November 1913 untll his death on 3 March 1944. He was known as a zealous pastor and effective orator with an interest in social initiative.

[33] Information from Pia Basso.

[34] Yallop, p. 13.

patted his head and reassured him, 'Now, now, there are other notebooks, and you will be able to go to the seminary.'[35]

So it was that on 18 October 1923, at the age of eleven, Albino started life at the Episcopal Seminary at Feltre, situated in via Garibaldi. Originally founded through the inspiration of Bishop Filippo-Maria Campegio in 1593 and rebuilt by Bishop Zerbino Lugo in 1647, it was not large,[36] but in common with all seminaries at that time it was something of an enclosed, self-contained world. Albino missed the freedom of his village home life. The reading of secular newspapers and periodicals was forbidden, and critical questions were not encouraged: the system was designed to provide answers, not to encourage questions. Albino was possessed of a penetrating intelligence and was endowed with a good memory and enquiring mind, and sometimes he did ask questions. Thus, although his teachers considered him to be generally diligent, they also formed the opinion that he was 'too exuberant. He has such an original personality, only God knows how he will turn out'.[37]

Seminary friend Erminio Scola remembered:

> In the seminary, Luciani was a lively boy; he was strong in Italian and in History ... Luciani also received a punishment from the teacher Troian, during a History lesson, because he was distracted. He wrote poetry on a sheet of paper ... Troian told him off, he ordered him to give the paper to him and he punished him: 'You will stand still for one hour'. Luciani obeyed calm, smiling.[38]

Another friend from that time, Don Felice Tomaselli, recalled that:

> Returning home from Feltre, for Easter holidays, in the third year of secondary school, on the train, they spoke about the last spiritual retreat and they also said, with candour, the promises they had made, while Luciani was silent, watching the landscape from the window of the train.
> 'And you, Albino, what promises have you made?', one of the most curious asked him. He answered thoughtfully: 'I haven't made any, because I am not capable of keeping them'.[39]

---

[35] Seabeck, p. 15, quoting '*L'Amico del Popolo*', 2 September 1978.

[36] In 1922 the two seminaries of the Diocese of Belluno e Feltre had only 46 seminarians; the two sees had been united in 1818. See *Catholic Encyclopedia*, Supp. vol., 1922, p. 94.

[37] Seabeck, p. 17.

[38] Erminio Scola, 'A Punished Poet'.

[39] Don Cesare Vazza, 'Promises ... Didn't Make'.

Albino prospered particularly under the direction of Don Giulio Gaio (1886–1992). He was a diligent pupil; Don Giulio remembered that he 'wrote very long homework, of ten to twelve pages and he showed he had very high intelligence'. In his fifth year, in 1927, Albino obtained marks of 10 for history and geography, 8 for religion, 7.5 for Italian, Latin and Greek, and 7 for arithmetic and French.[40] A typical 'clerical' photograph of the period showing Albino at Feltre seminary still exists; he has an open, questioning, slightly mischievous expression on his face as he pores over a book. A crucifix completes the scene.

The seminary, the 'seed-bed' of learning, is dedicated to the spiritual, moral and intellectual formation of its students. The minor seminary provided training in religion, Latin, the vernacular tongue, and all other subjects necessary to educate the student adequately in his own culture. The major seminary ran courses on philosophy, the humanities and sciences, together with courses on dogmatic and moral theology, canon law, scripture, and auxiliary ecclesiastical studies. Added to this were morning and evening prayers, mental prayer, Mass, and the making of an annual retreat. It was thus quite a rigorous regime.[41]

In the holidays, when not helping in the fields, the young Luciani could be found 're-organizing' Don Filippo's parish library; in summer 1931 he catalogued some 4,000 volumes, the catalogue he produced being still preserved there. However, in line with his naturally vivacious personality, he was not always a model student, as he later confessed when a cardinal.

> One day, at the end of vacation, Don Filippo called me into his room where he was seated, writing something. I stood there, waiting. Every now and then he stopped writing, looked up at me, perplexed, and shook his head. I felt guilty and miserable. Finally he finished writing, signed the letter, sealed it, and gave it to me. 'This letter is for you to give to the rector. I have been very unhappy about you this year, and I am asking him to reprimand you.'[42]

One suspects that Albino's behaviour had not been *that* bad, and that the wily Carli was using the well-worn psychological tactic of a pep talk, laying it on thick to motivate an otherwise promising student!

---

[40] *Tablet*, CCXXXII, 9 Sept. 1978, pp. 876–7; *Clarin*, 27 August 1978, Argentina.

[41] See *Codex Iuris Canonici*, 1917, Lib. III, Pars IV, Tit. XXI, Can.1352–71.

[42] Seabeck, p. 17.

It was Don Filippo who first encouraged him to write for the parish journal *Il Celentone*. Luciani's piece was good but overly intellectual, 'stuffed with much of the fresh knowledge he was gathering from the seminary. Having praised Albino for a job well done, Don Filippo made him note that the less literate parishioners who attended mass every morning might not understand all he had written. He therefore advised him to be simpler in his communications if he wanted to be understood by everyone'.[43] Albino took this excellent advice to heart – with well-known results.

Sometimes during the school term Luciani would receive a visit from his father who, Socialist or not, would always visit the seminary first on his return home from his long working trips abroad.

On 11 February 1929, as Luciani neared the end of his time at Feltre, the Lateran Pacts were signed between the Holy See and the Kingdom of Italy. This naturally had significant consequences for Luciani and his future, and so some consideration must be given here to the vital question of Church-State relations in Italy, and of Fascist influence on church life.[44]

Until 1861 the pope had been a temporal ruler over the very considerable states of the Church, which stretched across central Italy and contained some 3.12 million souls. The breaching of the Aurelian Wall near the Porta Pia and capture of Rome by Italian troops under General Raffaele Cadorna on 20 September 1870 marked the final demise of the power of the oldest sovereignty in Europe, and Pope Pius IX retreated into the Vatican. Nineteen papal and forty-nine Italian soldiers died in the process. Rome was declared the capital of the new, unified Kingdom of Italy on 2 October, after a city-wide plebiscite in which 133,681 voted in favour and only 1,507 against. King Vittorio Emanuele II formally entered the city on 2 July 1871, occupying the Pope's former residence, the Quirinal Palace.

On 13 May 1871 the Italian Parliament passed the Law of Guarantees, by which it proposed to end the 'Roman Question'. Pius rightly rejected this as a unilateral solution that failed to ensure internationally recognized independence for the Pope as pastor of the Universal Church. The pope thus voluntarily became the 'Prisoner in the Vatican', although the frigid atmos-

[43] Pia Luciani, 'Albino Luciani', Letter dated 6 February 2003.
[44] For a masterly treatment of this highly complex subject see Binchy, a very readable book with a much wider interest than its title would suggest.

phere began to thaw from the time of Pope Benedict XV (1914–1922), the 'Pope of Peace', whose wise and conciliatory policies helped to make the eventual solution of the formal *dissidio* possible. Indeed, Benedict has received insufficient recognition from both the Church and from historians for all the tremendous achievements of his troubled pontificate.[45]

Meanwhile, political events in Italy were moving on apace. Following the First World War – which for Italy lasted from 24 May 1915 to 11 November 1918 – and a period of political instability and social unrest, the so-called Fascist 'March on Rome' took place on 28 October 1922. King Vittorio Emanuele III capitulated his responsibilities to his nation and gave in, making the Fascist leader Benito Mussolini the Prime Minister of Italy. To begin with some semblance of parliamentarianism was maintained. However, on 10 June 1924 the Socialist Deputy Giacomo Matteotti, a courageous man who had spoken out against Fascist excesses, was murdered by Fascist thugs. The majority of non-Fascist Deputies, 124 in all, refused to take part in any further parliamentary business and walked out in the 'Aventine Secession'. The die was cast, and Mussolini's hand was forced by outraged world opinion. Within the next couple of years there was a shift from personal authoritarian rule to an all-embracing totalitarianism and the destruction of the existing state structures and liberties. Mussolini became '*Il Duce*'. It is against these trends and Mussolini's need to restore his standing and credibility that his relations with the Church and the eventual signing of the Lateran Pacts must be seen. The Lateran Pacts were crucially important for both parties, but Mussolini's motivation was entirely political. He had firm atheist convictions and only dealt with the Church in its secular manifestations, because he recognized its permanency and influence. Until the overthrow of Fascism the Church was always under siege, sometimes physically as well as intellectually.

After two-and-a-half years of secret and often difficult negotiations the Lateran Pacts were finally signed on 11 February 1929 in the Lateran Palace by Cardinal Pietro Gasparri, Vatican Secretary of State, and Mussolini. They were formally ratified on 7 June 1929, and were really composed of three parts. Article 26 of the Conciliation Treaty declared the 'Roman

[45] Perhaps the accession to the papacy in 2005 of Pope Benedict XVI, who took his name in emulation, will aid his predecessor's restoration to his rightful place in world history.

Question' definitively and irrevocably composed and hence eliminated' and created Vatican City, *lo Stato della Città del Vaticano*, as an independent state of 108.7 acres; what Pope Pius XI called 'the Franciscan minimum'. As an appendix to the Treaty there was a Financial Convention, in which as compensation for the loss of the States of the Church the Holy See settled for 750 million lire in cash and 1 billion lire in 5 per cent negotiable government bonds. In recognition of the economic state of Italy Pius XI settled for considerably less than the amount due to the Holy See, and accepted restrictions and controls on how these funds could be used. Finally, the Concordat attempted to regularize in detail the status of religion and the Church in Italy.

Concerning the Concordat Pope Pius XI declared enthusiastically that 'if not the best that could possibly be made, [it] is certainly among the best that have so far been devised; and it is with profound satisfaction that We express the belief that through it We have given back God to Italy and Italy to God'.[46] He was premature and over-optimistic in his hopeful judgement. The Lateran Pacts were a significant part of the healing process, and marked a great improvement over the situation that had existed before. The Church could scarcely have hoped for better terms under the circumstances, but they could never paper over the 'utter incompatibility'[47] that existed between the 'Doctrine of Fascism' and Christian faith and morals. Fortunately for the Holy See the Pacts proved to be more durable than either the Fascist State or its supportive monarchy, and they were not amended until the signing of the 'Agreement Between the Italian Republic and the Holy See' on 18 February 1984.[48]

That the Pacts were immensely popular in Italy was proved in a vote taken on 24 March 1929. Out of a 9,673,049 electorate, 8,663,412 or 89.56 per cent voted. Of these 8,519,559 were in favour, whilst only 135,761 were against, with 8,092 spoilt papers. Thus, of the total electorate, a staggering 88.07 per cent voted in favour, the highest proportion ever attained in an Italian election. Accordingly, the Chamber of Deputies voted 357 to 2 in favour, the Senate (Upper House) 316 to 6.

During the years of the Fascist Dictatorship the Vatican

---

[46] Holmes, p. 56
[47] Binchy, p. 327.
[48] Ratified by the Italian Parliament on 25 March 1985, effective from 3 June 1985.

pursued its own independent, universalist policies, which were often diametrically opposed to the opportunistic, aggressive policies of Mussolini. Although Italy was now reconciled, there was no over-intimate association between the two sides. Indeed tension, sometimes acute, broke out between them soon after the signing of the Pacts. The Fascist violence against Catholic Action in the summer of 1931 showed 'that the Lateran agreements had given rise to a *dissidio* far more violent in action than that which they had terminated'.[49] Being 'at once personal, universal, and autonomous',[50] Christianity came into conflict with Fascism in all its essential facets. The Fascists claimed to have a respect for Catholicism as *'la religion de l'ordre'*, but only when they felt that it could be subordinated to their own ends. The Church naturally resisted this stifling embrace; Catholicism could never be encompassed within the Fascist State. Nonetheless, a modus vivendi had to be found between Church and State, and with a Latin genius for practical compromise or *combinazione*, this was achieved to a surprising degree. Perhaps inevitably, some members of the Italian hierarchy, notably Cardinal Ildefonso Schuster, OSB, Archbishop of Milan, and Cardinal Adeodato Piazza, OCD, Patriarch of Venice, took this to rather dubious lengths. Schuster in particular initially praised Mussolini, supporting the war against Ethiopia in 1935–36, only disagreeing with the Racial Laws of August – October 1938.[51] Many ordinary priests tended to be anti-Fascist.

A few examples will show the effect of the Concordat on the lives of priests and seminarians. Article 3 stated that all ordained priests and members of religious orders were exempted from doing military service in peacetime. In the event of general mobilization all clerics 'responsible for the cure of souls' were still exempt.[52] This meant that, unlike Angelo Roncalli (later Pope John XXIII) in earlier years, Albino Luciani did not undergo military service.[53] The State finally officially recognized the secret of the Confessional, Article 7 forbidding

---

[49] Binchy, p. 506.

[50] Ibid., p. 336.

[51] Cardinal Schuster was beatified by John Paul II on 12 May 1996.

[52] Binchy, pp. 367–8. Chillingly, the Fascists reasoned that future generations would have had their minds formed by indoctrination in the Fascist youth organizations anyway and perhaps banked on these exemptions being gradually worn away. See Binchy, p. 432.

[53] Confirmed in letter to author dated 12 January 1987 from Italian Military Attaché, London.

judicial and other public officers to 'seek information from ecclesiastics regarding persons or things known to them by reason of their sacred office'.[54] Nevertheless, the authorities retained an unhealthy control over ecclesiastical organization, and a not inconsiderable hold over the ordinary priest (by being able to allege 'grave reasons' as to why he should not be promoted or even continue holding his current benefice). Seminaries thankfully escaped Fascist interference; Article 39 guaranteed the complete freedom of all seminaries 'for the training and instruction of ecclesiastics [from] any intervention on the part of the educational authorities of the Kingdom',[55] although not all Fascists were happy with what they saw as this 'surrender' to the Church.

Let us now return to Luciani. In September 1929 he graduated to the major seminary at Belluno, the Gregorian, founded in 1568 by Bishop Giulio Contarini. In 1797 the seminary had become the headquarters of General André Masséna, one of Napoleon's most able lieutenants in the campaign that drove the Austrians from northern Italy. This was the same campaign, incidentally, that ended over eleven hundred years of independence of the once mighty Venetian Republic – *La Serenissima Repubblica* – the Treaty of Campo Formio being signed on 17 October 1797.

The seminary was reopened and named for Pope St Gregory the Great and himself in 1831 by Pope Gregory XVI (1831–1846), who was born at Villa Cappellari at Mussoi some two kilometres from Belluno in 1765. A Camaldolese monk, in 1799 Mauro Cappellari had written *'Il Trionfo della Santa Sede e della Chiesa contro gli assalti dei Novatori'* ('The Triumph of the Holy See and the Church Against the Assaults of the Innovators'), widely read at the time and advocating absolute papal Ultramontanism. When the author himself became pope, the work was republished in Venice in 1832.

The seminary had a library of great interest, with many manuscipts, codices and incunabula. Of significance to Luciani – as we shall soon see – Pope Gregory had also been a patron of Antonio Rosmini, and had presented a beautifully bound set of his works to the seminary.

A contemporary of Luciani's has recalled his experiences at Belluno:

---

[54] Binchy, p. 368.
[55] Ibid., pp. 491–2.

We were woken up at 5.30 a.m. No heating, indeed the water would often be solid ice. I used to lose my vocation every morning for five minutes. We had thirty minutes to get washed and make our beds.

I met Luciani there in September 1929. He was then sixteen. He was always amiable, quiet, serene – unless you stated something that was inaccurate – then he was like a spring. I learned that in front of him one had to speak carefully. Any muddled thinking and you were in danger with him.[56]

Erminio Scola would agree, remembering a lively discussion with Luciani during a stroll:

We spoke about Popes of the past and I expressed a hard, negative judgement about a Pope. Luciani became infuriated and said: You are wrong, this man was a great Pope ... But I, stubborn, reaffirmed my negative judgement. Luciani then, suddenly, blocked the discussion and told me: 'You are right!' Returned to the seminary, I consulted the History book and I saw that he was 'right', while I was absolutely wrong ... Here I have seen the goodness and the humility of Luciani.[57]

As for the conditions, Scola adds:

I envied Luciani because, in spite of the cold of the rooms, he also managed to fall asleep immediately and snored! While I began sleeping after midnight. One day, I asked him: How can you manage to sleep with this cold? Luciani understood me immediately and he gave me his blankets. What a great pleasure! Finally I also could sleep well.[58]

Luciani did well in history, biblical exegesis and Latin, and was always ready to help his fellow students in these subjects, but he fared less well in mathematics. He loved to sing in the choir, singing with 'gusto' with a characteristic twist of the mouth that sometimes caused his fellow seminarians to tease him.[59]

Another contemporary, Don Constante Pampanin, remembered a serious incident in which Luciani acquitted himself well:

Once, going towards Bolzano Bellunese (it was mid-June, time for examinations) at a certain point, we saw a stable in flames. *L'è fogo! L'è fogo!* (Fire, fire!) I first entered to untie the beasts and,

---

[56] Yallop, p. 16.
[57] Erminio Scola, 'You Are Right'.
[58] Erminio Scola, 'Snores At Night'.
[59] Seabeck, pp. 19–20.

immediately behind me, with plenty of courage, Albino. We managed to save them all.

But we returned late to the Seminary, at about 9.00 p.m. and we had to bear a 'sermon' from the Vice-Director, Don Mario Coletti. Explaining the situation, everything was put right immediately. A few days later, a basket of cherries arrived at our table from the farmers who wanted to thank us.[60]

Another example of Luciani 'in action' is worthy of note. It occurred one summer Sunday afternoon while he was on holiday in Canale. The people had just left the church after Vespers and were milling about the Piazza. A distinguished-looking gentleman climbed on a box and began to harangue them, trying especially to attract the young. He was a Fascist and virulently anti-Catholic. Suddenly Luciani confronted him, talking volubly and gesticulating, telling him in no uncertain terms to leave immediately. The man fled. In the climate of the times it was a brave action to take. After the Second World War the same man became a Franciscan friar.[61]

Luciani continued to read voraciously; he retained his natural incisiveness and managed to avoid narrowness. At the age of seventeen he read the spiritual autobiography of St Thérèse of Lisieux – *'L'Histoire d'une Âme'* ('The Story of a Soul') – and he later wrote that it struck him 'forcibly'.[62] Indeed it did; the serving of God and others with love and humility came to be at the heart of his philosophy. What probably impressed him most was the fact that the *Little Way* of St Thérèse showed how to become holy in ordinary circumstances. That, and the saint's constancy in the face of great adversity.

Another author whom Luciani first read at about that time was Antonio Rosmini-Serbati, (1797–1855), founder of the Institute of Charity, philosopher, theologian, patriot and – of local interest to Luciani – one-time Vice-Rector of the Belluno seminary. Rosmini's most famous and influential work was *The Five Wounds Of The Holy Church*, published at Lugano in 1848.[63] The five wounds were, according to Rosmini: the social

---

[60] Don Constante Pampanin, 'The Fire' from *L'Amico del Popolo*, 1978.

[61] Seabeck, p. 20.

[62] *Illustrissimi*, p. 169. St Thérèse (1873–1897) was canonized on 17 May 1925. Her life and work were very influential in the Church of the time; Pope Pius XI (1922–1939) called her 'the Star of Our Pontificate' at her beatification on 29 April 1923. She was declared a Doctor of the Church on 19 October 1997.

[63] *Delle Cinque Piaghe Della Santa Chiesa* was actually written fifteen years previously, in 1832–33.

remoteness of the clergy from the people; the low standard of education of the priesthood; the disunity and acrimony amongst the bishops; the dependence of clerical appointments on the secular authorities; and Church ownership of property and concern with wealth. Rosmini strove to find a balance between the old and the new by demonstrating how development stems from unchangeable principles, attempting to reconcile Catholic theology with modern political and social thought. He wrote with genuine concern for the Church, and hoped for an improvement of conditions through liberal reform.

However, this was not to be. Rosmini's misfortune was to be before his time and he fell foul of Jesuit intrigue; he was accused of Jansenism, and Pope Pius IX withdrew the offer of a cardinal's red hat. Instead of debate and reform, his book was placed on the Index of Forbidden Books on 30 May 1849. His *A Constitution Based On Social Justice* suffered the same fate.[64] Rosmini submitted and was cleared in 1854, the year before his death. His works appeared again with a *dimittantur* ('without censure'). After his death, however, the accusations continued, a second examination of his works resulting in forty of his propositions being condemned by Pope Leo XIII in 1887–88. Thus *The Five Wounds Of The Holy Church* was still on the Index in the 1930s – and remained on it until the abolition of the Index on 15 November 1966 – but Luciani read the seminary's copy. It had a profound influence on him – in due course he would produce his doctoral thesis on Rosmini, of which more later.

The Church in England, France and especially in Italy due to its proximity to the Holy See and the Roman Curia, was further scarred in the inter-war years by the residual effects of the Modernist controversy under Pope Pius X (1903–1914). In particular, the two diocesan seminaries of Belluno e Feltre had been temporarily closed during the controversy after the Apostolic Visitation of 1908. From 1909 to 1915 the seminary of Belluno was under the spiritual directorship of Don Alfredo Balestrazzi, CSS of the Stimmatini (Stigmatine Missionaries), appointed by Pius.[65] Thus the exclusive, negative and anti-intellectual mentality produced by the *Syllabus of Errors*, which was issued together with the encyclical *Quanta Cura* on 8 December 1864, and which contained eighty errors condemned

---

[64] *La Costituzione Secondo La Giustizia Sociale*, published in 1848.
[65] See L. Bedeschi, 'La Chiesa Bellunese Nel Primo Decennio Del Novecento', Vita Pastorale, n. 2, 2006, pp. 44–6.

by Pius IX, was still prevalent. There was little understanding of non-Catholic opinion in Italy where the vast majority of the population were Catholic.[66] One of Luciani's tutors at Belluno was Professor (later Cardinal) Alfredo Ottaviani, who taught dogmatic theology and preached the doctrine that, where Catholics were in the majority, 'Error had no rights'.

The rigidity of his tutors influenced his own spiritual outlook, until the Second Vatican Council rejuvenated him. But, again, there was always his own inherent level-headedness and his reading. He read the dramas of Carlo Goldoni and the books of French nineteenth-century novelists. He was also deeply influenced by the works of Père Jean-Pierre De Caussade (1675–1751), a Jesuit spiritual writer primarily known for his posthumously published *Self-Abandonment To Divine Providence.*[67]

De Caussade spoke repeatedly of 'the sacrament of the present moment', of willingly surrendering oneself to carrying out God's purpose each and every minute. Each moment brought its appointed task, faithfully to be accomplished, everything was reduced to the purest and simplest commitment to the Will of God in whatever form it might present itself. Its essence was humble submission, expressed in the phrase 'Thy Will be done', whether in joy or suffering. This simple, humble, practical approach to genuinely holy living is clearly reflected in Luciani's own life.

At this time Luciani was gradually progressing towards his cherished goal. He received the tonsure on 31 January 1932, the minor orders of porter and lector on 11 March 1933 and those of exorcist and acolyte on 24 February 1934.[68] He was then ordained into major orders: as sub-deacon on 8 July 1934, and as deacon on 2 February 1935. So deep was De Caussade's influence that he began to think seriously of becoming a Jesuit himself. Two of his close friends, Giuseppe Strim and Roberto Busa, had already been granted permission

---

[66] In the Italian Census of 1931, out of a population of 41,709,851, those returning themselves as being of the Roman Catholic communion amounted to 41,555,604, or 99.63%. See Binchy, p. 570.

[67] *'L 'Abandon À La Providence Divine'* was later compiled from De Caussade's correspondence with the nuns of the Visitation at Nancy, and from notes of conference talks given during the period he was their spiritual director between 1731–40. It was first published in 1860 in popular but much adulterated form, that which Luciani would have read, owning his own copy.

[68] Scopelliti and Taffarel, p. 53. Minor Orders were abolished by Pope Paul VI on 15 August 1972.

by the Rector, Bishop Giosuè Cattarossi, to join the Society of Jesus. Luciani also asked permission. Cattarossi turned down the request, replying 'No, three is one too many. You had better stay here'.[69]

In fact, it was not just a question of numbers. He could not be released to the Jesuits because he was being trained for the Diocese of Belluno through the charity of benefactors, a devout couple, Count Maurizio and Lady Maria Piperno.[70] Maurizio was a wealthy engineer employed by the military, but the couple were childless, so they spent their money on charitable causes. Luciani only found out about the Piperno's kind support just before his ordination, duly writing to thank them deeply on the 30 June.[71]

Canonically, Luciani was too young to be ordained priest, being only twenty-two years eights months and twenty days old, well short of the required twenty-four years. Thus, dispensation had to be requested from Rome. The Vicar-General Mgr Pietro Rizzardini first wrote on 12 January 1935. He got no response. In mid-June Bishop Cattarossi wrote for the third time begging for the dispensation, a mark of the esteem in which the mature young ordinand was held:

> The young man is finishing in these days with laudable success as always in the past the exams for the licence in theology. I confirm his optimum intellectual, moral and religious qualities and his proven vocation for which he is deserving of the grace which he begs; and I declare that if the ordination should be delayed I would not know how to occupy him usefully meanwhile even intellectually. But that which above all renders the ordination of Luciani necessary and urgent are the pressing needs of the diocese.[72]

This last recommendation had the desired effect, Rome acquiesced and Mgr Rizzardini informed Don Bramezza on 25 June that the ordination could proceed.

[69] Yallop, p. 17.
[70] Seabeck, p. 68, and information from Pia Basso. Maurizio died in 1965.
[71] Scopelliti and Taffarel, p. 53.
[72] Scopelliti and Taffarel, pp. 53–4; translation by Dom Leander Hogg, OSB. Don Francesco Taffarel was Luciani's secretary in Vittorio Veneto from 1967–1970.

Chapter Two

Priest 1935–1958

On 7 July 1935 Luciani was duly ordained priest in the ancient Church of San Pietro,[1] Belluno, by his bishop, Mgr Cattarossi. The night before he had got very little sleep in his cell, No.7, in the seminary. The ceremony itself took place before the usual congregation of relations, friends and local priests; they sang the Mass of Lorenzo Perosi and the homily was read by Mgr Angelo Santin.

One person sorely missed was Don Filippo Carli, his friend and mentor having died in hospital in Padua only some nine months before, on 19 October 1934.[2] Don Filippo had been in pain for a while and Luciani had prayed for his health, to no avail. Luciani had returned to his home village from Belluno for the vigil prayers on 21 October, one of the saddest days of his life.

Luciani was appointed to be curate of his home village of Forno di Canale, which suited him well enough. Arriving back home, he was met by virtually the whole village, preceded by the band of the Fire Brigade (to his parents' great satisfaction). The following day he celebrated his first Mass in Forno di Canale; he was entirely happy with his humble position, which after all is the lot of virtually all newly ordained priests.

Luciani worked with the new parish priest, Don Augusto Bramezza, and after six months probation entered the Unione Apostolica Del Clero Diocesano (UAC), an international association of priestly spirituality. Originating in the seventeenth century, finally unified and approved by Pope Leo XIII in 1880, the Union had a simple rule of life intended to foster amongst the secular clergy the spirit of personal sanctification and the

---

[1] San Pietro was built in 1326 and restored in 1750.
[2] Carli died relatively young, having been born at Caviola in 1879.

efficient discharge of their parochial duties. Pope Pius X had himself been a member. Luciani's promise, in his own hand, has been preserved. Written in Latin it states simply:

> I, Don Albino Luciani ... for the greater glory of God and in order to bind myself with greater efficacy to my sanctification and to the salvation of souls ... freely adhere to this Union, and with all my heart I consecrate and offer myself, confiding in the Heart of Jesus and through the intercession of Mary, and promise to observe the Rules of the Union with constancy and fidelity. Amen. The Epiphany of the Lord, 1936.[3]

On 18 December Luciani was transferred as curate to Don Luigi Cappello of Santa Maria Nascente in neighbouring Agordo and named instructor of religion for nine hours a week in the local Technical Institute of Mining; like his father, its pupils often had to migrate abroad in search of work, usually to Belgium.

In July 1937 he was appointed Vice-Rector of the seminary in Belluno, and from that October he began ten years of teaching, at various times, dogmatic theology, philosophy, canon law, the history of art, history, patristics, sacred eloquence (preaching) and catechetics. Again, he was saved from narrowness by being a generalist, and, what is more, by being somebody who had to communicate effectively with a wide range of other personalities in different situations.

The content of his lectures probably differed little from those of his own tutors, but he had a certain freshness of style. Instead of dull repetition, he injected something of his own into his presentation. Years later he recounted advice that he had been given as a young priest on teaching catechetics; good advice that he took to heart and indeed became the living embodiment of:

> The text is merely an aid, a stimulus, not a comfortable armchair in which the catechist settles for a rest ... The text, no matter how well done, remains something dead: it is the catechist who must bring it to life. The lesson is worth only as much as its preparation! ... To children you do not teach so much what you know as what you are; fine words from the catechists mouth are worth little, if other words come from his behaviour to contradict them.[4]

Don Rinaldo Andrich, one of Luciani's students at the time, and

---

[3] Seabeck, pp. 21–2.
[4] *Illustrissimi*, (US edn.), pp. 221–2.

in 1978 himself parish priest of Canale d'Agordo, recalled that 'Don Albino always managed to make the most difficult questions interesting.'[5]

As Vice-Rector, Don Albino's day began at 4.00 a.m. Although he took his job as disciplinarian seriously, he was always 'available' to his students and his office door was always open to them. He was patient and sympathetic, and often took them on long hikes up into the foothills of the Dolomites or on field trips into Feltre to study the abundant paintings, sculptures and architectural features in that culturally rich town. He explained that the artist is trying to create beauty:

> Beauty is not truth, but the radiant expression of truth. One cannot judge the artist only by his technical ability because the artist must have above all, spiritual and moral qualities ... Art must be neither pure realism, nor exaggerated idealism which devalues truth and sacrifices reality ... Nature must be seen with the eyes of a poet ... The artist retouches nature in such a way as to bring it back to that purity and holiness which it had at the beginning of the kingdom of goodness and innocence in which we would all like to live ... entering into the kingdom of art, each one should become better.[6]

On the other hand, he also realized the increasing influence of the communications media, and initiated his students into the techniques of printing, radio and movies to help them understand this tremendous influence, so that they could make good use of them themselves to spread the 'Good News'. He also placed great emphasis on courtesy and good manners, saying they were essential to charity.

It was at this time that Luciani met the saintly Capuchin Fr Leopold Mandic, OFM Cap. The Croatian friar had a special gift for hearing confessions and directing souls, and rarely left his friary in Padua. One day, however, he visited the seminary in Belluno while Luciani was on retreat. Luciani later recounted the meeting:

> One day, my bishop entered the dining room, stopped the reading and said: 'I have come to tell you some good news. Here, at Belluno, we have Father Leopold, a saint. He has agreed to hear your confessions tomorrow if you wish. I recommend that you do not let such an occasion pass. Go to him.' I heeded the advice of my

[5] Hebblethwaite, *Year of Three Popes*, p. 93. Andrich died on 29 June 2001.
[6] Seabeck, p. 24.

bishop. The following day, I went to confession with him, I listened to him and he gave me several pieces of advice.[7]

According to Luciani's sister Antonia the gist of the advice was: 'Stay calm and follow your path.'

By 1938 Luciani wanted to expand his own intellectual horizons and study for a doctorate in theology. Bishop Cattarossi first wrote on 12 September to the Rector of the Lateran University in Rome, Mgr Pio Paschini, on Luciani's behalf. But ten days later he received a negative response.The problem was that while Luciani's superiors thought him highly capable of doctoral work, they wanted him to continue teaching at Belluno whilst undertaking his studies. This suited Luciani, but not the university authorities.

On 21 May 1940 Cattarossi wrote personally to Pope Pius XII, without success, asking that Luciani might study at the Pontifical Gregorian University (*Pontificia Università Gregoriana*) in Rome, 'with dispensation from the obligation of attending classes'.[8] Again, the university authorities insisted on at least one year's obligatory attendance. Founded in 1551 as the Roman College by St Ignatius Loyola, the institution was reconstructed by Pope Gregory XIII in 1572, from which time it gradually became known as the Gregorian University. It is the most outstanding and prestigious of all Jesuit educational institutions, and not unreasonably the authorities were reluctant to grant dispensations too readily.

The impasse was finally broken by the intervention of Mgr Angelo Santin, the new Rector at Belluno, and Don Felice M Cappello, SJ, a renowned canon lawyer who taught at the Gregorian, brother of Don Luigi and distantly related to Luciani.[9] Cappello had spent the summers of 1936–7 on 'holiday' in Agordo and had heard many confessions in the neighbouring confessional to Luciani's. The young priest must have had good opportunities to talk over his ideas with his already revered elder. He must have made a favourable impression, for Pope Pius XII changed his mind and personally granted a dispensation in a letter dated 27 March 1941, signed by Cardinal Luigi Maglione, Secretary of State.[10]

---

[7] Pangyric of Blessed Leopold Mandic, 30 May 1976. Fr Leopold (1866–1942) was canonized in 1983.

[8] Scopelliti and Taffarel, p. 71.

[9] Cappello (1879–1962). The Cause for his Beatification was introduced in 1988 as 'confessore di Roma'.

[10] Yallop, p. 17.

Incidentally, Don Felice gave Luciani the same good advice that their mutual friend Don Filippo had given him: *Sermo brevis e rudis*; to keep his sermons brief and simple, to avoid severity in opinions and decisions, and to 'always find the solution that allows souls to breathe'.[11]

Enrolling as a fourth-year student in theology at the Gregorian in November 1941, Luciani gained his preliminary ecclesiastical *lizenziato* in philosophy with marks of nine out of ten on 16 October 1942.[12] During this period he studied the thought of some of the giants of western philosophy. The Spaniard Francisco Suárez (1548–1617), known as *Doctor Eximius* or Exceptional Doctor, is often considered to be the most prominent Scholastic philosopher after St Thomas Aquinas and one of the foremost Jesuit theologians. An exceptionally erudite and methodical scholar, his principal study in philosophy is the Disputationes Metaphysicae (1597). René Descartes (1596–1650), the French polymath, has been called the Father of modern philosophy; the axiom *Cogito, ergo sum* ('I think, therefore I am') is his most famous formulation. Luciani studied his Discours De La Méthode (1637).

He also studied Immanuel Kant (1724–1804), the German metaphysician who worked on the theory of knowledge, ethics and aesthetics, publishing his famous *Critiques Of Pure Reason, Practical Reason and Judgement* between 1781–90. Important also to the development of Luciani's outlook at this time was his study of the works of Henri-Louis Bergson (1859–1941), the Nobel Prize-winning French thinker whose humanistic 'process philosophy' rejected static values in favour of evolution and development. As well as this, Bergson was also a great literary stylist, having both academic and popular appeal.

Luciani chose as the topic for his doctoral thesis 'The Origin of the Human Soul According to Antonio Rosmini. Exposition and Criticism', for which he studied Rosmini's '*Nuovo Saggio Sull'Origine Delle Idee*', first published in 1830 in Rome in three volumes.[13] In this work Rosmini examined the history of Western thought on the nature of ideas and the possibility of thought. He favoured the Platonic tradition of innatism, inter-

---

[11] S. Falasca, 'Luciani And Confession: His Patience Awaits Us', *30 Days*, no. 3, March 2003.

[12] De La Cierva, p. 119; Seabeck, p. 249.

[13] Translated as *New Essay On The Origin Of Ideas*, 3 vols, 1883–4, by William Lockhart.

preted by Christian philosophy in the works of St Augustine, St Thomas Aquinas, St Bonaventure and others. Rosmini's thought naturally evolved and he made significant changes to his work for the fifth Italian edition (1855, Turin).

The director of Luciani's thesis was the pioneer ecumenist Père Charles Boyer, SJ (1884–1980). Due to the circumstances of the time Luciani did not defend his thesis until 23 November 1946, presenting himself in Hall 'A' of the Gregorian at 11.00 a.m. that morning. He was successful, graduating on 27 February 1947, obtaining a *magnum cum laude* and becoming a Doctor of Sacred Theology.[14] On 3 December of that year Mgr Giovanni Battista Montini, then *sostituto* at the Secretariat of State and future Pope Paul VI, sent a routine enquiry to Bishop Girolamo Bortignon, OFM Cap, Cattarossi's successor, as to the integrity of Luciani's doctrine; Bortignon replied giving 'ample assurances'.[15] The thesis itself, dedicated to his father Giovanni, was not finally published until 4 April 1950, a second revised and much enlarged edition appearing in 1958.

When a man is elected pope the whole of his previous life is suddenly and intensively scrutinized, his every action and motivation examined, often with undue hindsight. Everything is made to point towards his eventual election as if it were inevitable, and it is often not sufficiently appreciated that his life may have been holy, worthwhile and inspirational had he never become pope. Thus it was with Albino Luciani. The official Vatican biography baldly stated for the edification of its readers that he '. . . obtained the doctorate in theology with a brilliant thesis on . . . Rosmini'.[16]

However, more sober judges than *L'Osservatore Romano* have expressed different views. One has described it as 'a competent piece of work'; another, less generous, has stated, 'In my opinion it is worthless. It shows extreme conservatism and also lacks scholarly method'.[17] A third called the thesis 'a mere rehash of out-worn apologetic arguments'.[18] Father

---

[14] Yallop, p. 18. Luciani was the sixteenth pope to be an alumnus of the Gregorian; previous popes included Benedict XV and Paul VI. P. Caraman, *University Of The Nations: The Story Of The Gregorian University*, 1981, Paulist Press, pp. 156–7.

[15] Scopelliti and Taffarel, p. 75. Bishop Girolamo Bortignon, OFM Cap., born 1905, ordained 1928, consecrated 1944, Bishop of Belluno e Feltre 1945–9, Bishop of Padua 1949–82, died 1992.

[16] *L'Osservatore Romano*, n. 35 (544), 31 August 1978, p. 2 (English edition).

[17] Yallop, p. 18.

[18] Hebblethwaite, *Year of Three Popes*, p. 92.

Boyer, aged ninety-three in 1978, could remember nothing about Luciani or his thesis. Too much time had passed by, although he was glad to have taught a future pope.[19]

Scholars and academics are notoriously 'ungenerous' concerning the work of others – especially of students who later achieve greater fame than they – but nonetheless it is obvious that, whilst quite good enough to obtain him his doctorate, Luciani's thesis did not radically enlarge the frontiers of human knowledge. However, like Rosmini, Luciani's thought evolved.

Although it is interesting that he chose to study Rosmini at all, it does not mean that Luciani had at this time arrived at his later more mature, relaxed and liberal outlook. His mind had, in the 1940s, a more traditionalist, reactionary caste, a conditioning imposed by his earlier tutors and the closed seminary world in which he lived. Only later did the experience of practical, pastoral work liberate his true, inner self. His thesis, meanwhile, attacked the liberal Rosmini on the letter, not the spirit, of the latter's writings, trying to demolish him on the grounds of misquotation, superficiality and causistry. But, whatever he thought theoretically of Rosmini's speculative theology, he would later show in a practical way that he had fully absorbed the message of *The Five Wounds of the Holy Church*.

In 1953 Don Clemente Riva completed his doctoral thesis at the Lateran University on 'The Origin Of The Intellective Soul According To Rosmini'. He supported a genuine interpretation of nos. 20–4 of the forty propositions condemned by the Holy Office in 1887. His thesis was also an answer to Luciani's, which not only upheld the condemnation of these propositions, but actually declared it irreversible!

In 1975 Riva was appointed auxiliary bishop for the southern pastoral region of Rome by Pope Paul VI. When presenting himself to John Paul I after the latter's election, Riva confessed his embarrassment at being assistant bishop to a pope whose opinions of Rosmini's teachings he did not share. However, days later, the Pope spoke of Rosmini as:

A priest who loved the Church, who suffered for the Church; a man of vast culture, of integral Christian faith, a master of philosophical and moral wisdom who clearly saw the delays as well as the

[19] Luciani had not forgotten Boyer. During his pontificate he 'sent his former tutor greetings on three separate occasion's; Caraman, p. 139.

evangelical and pastoral inadequacies of the Church. I want to find
an opportunity of speaking about Antonio Rosmini and his work
which I have re-read carefully. First, I shall meet the Rosminian
Fathers and we shall make peace. When I published my thesis on
The Origin Of The Human Soul According To Antonio Rosmini, some
of them did not agree with my thought and my analysis. I want the
doctrinal decree *Post Obitum*, with which the Holy Office
condemned the forty propositions drawn from Rosmini's works, to
be reviewed. We shall do it without haste, but we shall do it.[20]

This shows Luciani's maturing thought and the way in which he
helped pave the way in the re-evaluation of Rosmini's teachings:
today Rosmini exercises special influence through his ascetical
writings, being acknowledged as a man of great sanctity of life. In
1994 the Cause for his Beatification was launched, the
Beatification itself taking place on 18 November 2007. On 1 July
2001, in a most unusual reversal of policy, the Congregation
for the Doctrine of the Faith (CDF) issued a 'Note on the Import of
the Doctrinal Decrees concerning the Thought and Works of
the Priest Antonio Rosmini Serbati'. This stated that the original
'motives for concern . . . can now be considered surmounted . . .
motivated by the fact that the sense of the propositions . . .
does not pertain in reality to Rosmini's authentic position, but
to possible conclusions from the reading of his works'.

Whilst Luciani's life in the early 1940s may have been reasonably stable and settled, for many in the world that was the last
thing that they could claim. After years of tension and abortive
negotiations, the full horror of the Second World War was
unleashed on 1 September 1939 when the Germans invaded
Poland. Despite being a signatory to the 'Pact of Steel' (22 May
1939) Mussolini avoided joining his German allies until 10 June
1940, when the fall of France was imminent. Always unpopular
with the majority of Italians, the war soon became a running
disaster for Italy.

On 19 July 1943 Mussolini had a highly unsatisfactory conference with Hitler at Villa Gaggia, just a few kilometres from
Feltre. It was the thirteenth meeting between the two dicta-
tors; Don Albino's comment on this episode was 'We are in the
hands of two crazy people!.'[21] Just six days later, on 25 July,
Mussolini was ignominiously ousted from power by the Fascist
Grand Council, then deposed and arrested by the King, and

---

[20] Bassotto, 'Il Mio Cuore E Ancora A Venezia', p. 131; Eng. trans in *Witness*,
   7, July 1999.
[21] Serafini, p. 53, '*Siamo nelle mani di due pazzi!*'.

from 8 September the Germans began pouring troops into the country in an effort to secure their southern flank. On 13 October in Rome Marshal Pietro Badoglio declared war on Italy's former allies, and from then until the final surrender of the German forces in Italy on 29 April 1945 the country became the scene of particularly bitter, intense conventional and partisan warfare.

Nowhere was this truer than in mountainous northeast Italy. On 12 September 1943 Mussolini had been spectacularly rescued from captivity in the Campo Imperiale, high on the Gran Sasso d'Italia in the mountainous Abruzzi region, by SS Standartenfuhrer Otto Skorzeny. On 18 September the Germans set the hapless dictator up as the figurehead leader of the Italian Social Republic, based at Salò on Lake Garda. As the fortunes of the Germans and Italian Fascists grew increasingly desperate, so the cruelty meted out by all sides increased. Mussolini and his loyal mistress Clara Petacci were finally shot on 28 April 1945 by communist partisans of the 52nd Garibaldi Brigade in rather mysterious circumstances whilst trying to escape to neutral Switzerland. Their bodies, along with those of a dozen other erstwhile Fascist leaders, were hung upside down in the Piazzale Loreto in Milan to be abused and vilified by the mob.

Thus the war also made its presence felt in Belluno. It is related that Girolamo Bortignon, the tough, bearded Bishop of Belluno who was also a Capuchin Friar,[22] once appealed to the local German SS commander to spare the lives of fifty resistance fighters and hostages who were about to be executed in the Campitello in the middle of the town. His appeal failed and so, in a spirit of true Christian witness, he offered his own life instead. Again his plea was rejected; he personally embraced and blessed all the unfortunates on the scaffold and denounced the executions, which took place on 17 March 1945. The bodies of the hapless victims were left hanging for three days, during which time all shops remained closed in mourning, and the population remained indoors.[23] On another infamous occasion, 20 August 1944, a battalion from SS-Polizei Regiment 'Bozen' killed forty-six people in surrounding villages in retaliation for local partisan attacks.

Like the citizens of all the occupied countries, the priests and

---

[22] Hebblethwaite, *Year of Three Popes*, p. 93.

[23] Ibid., p. 93; Holmes, p. 60; De La Cierva, p. 158; B. B. Carter, *Italy Speaks*, 1947, Victor Gollancz, p. 123. The Campitello was later renamed Piazza dei Martiri in memory of the victims.

seminarians of Belluno were faced with a cruel dilemma; how to oppose the invaders without provoking massive, brutal retaliation? Luciani, like others, walked a tightrope. On the one hand he listened to the confessions of German soldiers – and so incidentally improved his German! Privately, though, he was in sympathy with the Resistance. In the latter part of the war the seminary became a haven for members of the Resistance; discovery by the Germans would have meant death for both the resistance fighters and their Good Samaritans, and there was always the danger of fascist sympathisers in the seminary itself.

More light is shed on this difficult wartime period by the testimony of Luciani's sister Antonia:

> Our family was engaged a lot in the resistance. We have never been fascist. My brother, Edoardo, after 8 September 1943, had constituted one brigade of Catholic partisans. They acted underground. I made the link between them and Belluno; like some kind of courier. Albino gave advice on what way they had to move ... precious information. He was involved a lot. In fact, it wove the threads of the Catholic resistance in our zone'.

When asked if it was true that Luciani saved the life of a Fascist who was ready to be executed by red partisans, she answered:

> Yes, it is true. It was the teacher who had prepared him for the Institute. He was not a true Fascist; but, for reasons of good living, he was very compromised with the Fascist organizations. At night, the communist partisans came and they captured him. The day after, early in the morning, we heard someone knocking at the door. My mother opened it to find a woman kneeling. It was the teacher's wife. She implored: 'Make Albino come to the town, I pray you, only he can save my husband.' Mother soon informed my brother in Belluno, and he did not hesitate to come.
>
> He had a communist cousin, between the partisans. He went to see him. This cousin, at first, said he knew nothing about that story. 'I am not involved with that', he said. Albino insisted. He told him: 'Look, I know, I know you are responsible; I will not return to Belluno until you release the teacher.' Then Albino came back home. The hours passed and the anxiety increased. In the evening, mother asked Albino to return to the cousin, in order to see if there was news. He did it. From the town a courier had left to go to the communist partisans. At dawn, the day after, the teacher could embrace his wife. What times! How many persons were killed for political hatreds, in those years.[24]

---

[24] Antonia Luciani, 'Don Albino And The War'.

Luciani was also able to help his old schoolfriend Giulio Bramezza, who later related

> In 1945, I was a prisoner of war in a German concentration camp. My wife had not heard from me for over a year, and in desperation, she went to Don Albino who was then teaching in the seminary. Shortly afterwards, two German soldiers brought me to a radio and said, 'You may speak. Your wife is listening.' Somehow, Albino had succeeded in finding me.[25]

At the end of the war, members of the Resistance came down from the mountains. Many wanted to dispense their own brand of 'justice' to those they accused of being collaborators of the Germans or Fascists. One night a group erected a gallows and planned to hang twelve such collaborators. Someone quickly informed Don Albino of these grim developments. Exactly what action he took is unknown, but by the following day the gallows had gone and no one was hanged.[26]

The end of the war did not bring an immediate end to upheaval for Italy, as the nation underwent reconstruction and the transformation from monarchy and Fascist dictatorship to republican democracy. King Vittorio Emanuele III formally abdicated on 9 May 1946 in favour of his son Umberto II, who had in any case been exercising power as Lieutenant General of the Realm since 2 June 1944. However, in a referendum held on 2 June 1946 – the first occasion that women had the vote in Italy – 12,718,641 voted for a republic, only 10,718,502 voting to retain the monarchy, with 1,509,735 invalid or contested papers on a 89.1 per cent turn-out. The rule of the House of Savoy was over, and the royal family therefore left the country on 13 June.

The Constituent Assembly approved the new Constitution of the Republic on 22 December 1947. On the issue of incorporating the Lateran Pacts only the Christian Democrats and, incredibly, the Communists supported full integration, the Socialists and lay parties being opposed. The vote went 350 to 149 in favour and the Pacts were incorporated as Article 7 of the Constitution.

In the elections of 18 April 1948 the Christian Democrats won an overall majority. Their leader, Alcide De Gasperi (1881–1954), was thus confirmed in the premiership that he

[25] Seabeck, p. 14.
[26] Seabeck, pp. 24–5.

had exercised since forming a provisional cabinet on 10 December 1945. This was the era of maximum clerical 'influence' in the electoral process, parishioners being warned: 'Stalin cannot see what you do in a voting booth but God can'.[27] By a Decree of 30 June 1949 Pius XII excommunicated those Catholics who belonged to the Communist Party or who published or wrote articles advocating Communism, forbidding priests to administer the sacraments to those who did either of the above. De Gasperi remained as Prime Minister until July 1953; the Christian Democrats retained their dominance, through many shifting coalitions, until April 1992, when they lost power and seriously lost credibility through numerous corruption scandals.

During this period – from 8 March to 4 June, and 26 August to 12 September 1947 – Luciani was twice admitted to the sanatorium of San Gervasio suffering from suspected tuberculosis. Characteristically, he spent his time reading, and the example of St Thérèse of Lisieux and her complete dedication to God comforted him in a moment of weakness. In June 1973 he wrote:

> I remember the time I was ill and sent to a sanatorium, in the days before penicillin and antibiotics, when death awaited pretty well anyone who was sent to hospital. I was ashamed of myself for feeling a little afraid. 'At the age of twenty-three', I said to myself, 'Theresa, who until then had been healthy and full of vitality, was filled with joy and hope when she first spat blood. Not only that, but when her health improved, she got permission to end her fast with a diet of dry bread and water. And you're almost trembling! You're a priest! Stir yourself! Don't be silly!'.[28]

Through his experiences in the latter part of the war and in the sanatorium Albino Luciani came to know himself a little better. Anyway, tests done during both his two spells in the sanatorium proved negative, and the pulmonary illnesses were diagnosed by Dr Gottardi Gottardo as severe viral pneumonia. He made a full recovery, and subsequent tests showed no evidence of a recurrence.[29]

In October 1947 Bishop Bortignon showed his appreciation of Luciani's qualities by appointing him to be Secretary of the

[27] F. Spotts and T. Wieser, *Italy, A Difficult Democracy: A Survey Of Italian Politics*, 1986, Cambridge University Press, p. 120.

[28] *Illustrissimi*, p. 169.

[29] Yallop, p. 242; Seabeck, p. 249.

inter-diocesan Synod of Belluno and Feltre held on 28–30 of that month, the first since 1861, and in November by making him Pro-chancellor of the Diocese. On 15 December Luciani's increase in status was underlined when he was created a Monsignor, one of the *'Camerieri segreti soprannumerari di Sua Santita'.*[30] The increase in responsibility and his interest and ability in the practical, communicable aspects of theology led him naturally into the field of catechetics. On 2 February 1948 Luciani was made Pro-Vicar-General of the Diocese and Director of Catechetics, in which capacity he was made responsible for the Eucharistic Congress that took place in Belluno the following year.

On his being given these appointments, Bortola, now at the very end of her life, asked her son: 'Albino, what are these things they've given you to do?' His simple reply was that he was required to do greater work for the Church, to which his mothers trusting, loyal response was 'If that's how it is, it means I'll pray more for you'.[31]

Luciani drew on his experiences in preparing for the Congress to write a small book called *Catechetica In Briciole* (*Catechesis In Easy Stages* or *Crumbs From The Catechism*). He dedicated it 'To my Mother, my first catechism teacher'. In his typical quiet, practical way Luciani 'condensed' the best material from the Congress: 'In a letter that has been preserved, he declares to the two speakers, Brothers Leone di Maria and Anselmo of the Christian Schools, that he had merely transcribed in popular style what they had said so well in their lectures.'[32] Published in December 1949, the book was at least considered worthy enough to be translated into English the same year. Luciani revised and enlarged it considerably in 1961; it was in its seventh Italian printing by 1978, with a Spanish edition being published in Columbia.[33] Offering advice to religious educators, Luciani referred to the inherent good in children and the skill needed to nurture it in his typically imaginative, anecdotal way. He wrote:

'Michelangelo was asked, "How do you produce statues that are so full of life?" He responded: "The marble already contains the statues; it is just a matter of extracting them". Like marble,

---

[30] *Acta Apostolicae Sedis*, XL, 1948, p. 135.
[31] A. Luciani, 'Mio Fratello Albino', p. 74.
[32] *L'Osservatore Romano*, n. 45 (554), 9 November 1978, p. 5 (English edition).
[33] Muthig, p. 167.

children are rough material: you can extract gentlemen, heroes, even saints'.[34]

Catechetics is that branch of theology that seeks to instruct people, generally children, how to embody Christian values in their everyday lives. A child whose interest is engaged, and who has those values demonstrated by personal example, can, of course, be 'caught' for life. Luciani thus made an excellent and natural catechist, through both his own life and his gift of communication. Yallop assesses his subject correctly when he writes of Luciani that 'he had the simplicity of thought that comes only to the highly intelligent, and added to this was a genuine, deep humility'.[35]

His approach matured gradually; in a 1969 interview with Alberto Papuzzi he said that his main concern was 'the gap between a purely formal and nominal Christianity, based merely on ideas, and an existential Christianity that finds expression in life'.[36] For him, Christianity was about living, not just talking about it.

In 1949 Luciani was appointed assistant to the young women's section of Catholic Action in Belluno, which helped to further broaden his growing pastoral experience. On 9 August of that year he was also reconfirmed as Pro-Vicar-General by Bortignon's successor, Bishop Gioacchino Muccin.[37] In 1951 Luciani collaborated closely with Bortignon, now Bishop of Padua, at the *Certosa* (Charterhouse) of Vedana in organizing the third Council of the Veneto Province. In between preparing and studying Synod documents he participated in the prayers of the Carthusian monks.[38]

Through the 1950s Luciani made steady progress, deepening his pastoral experience and continuing to gain modest recognition. In 1950 he wrote a study in Latin about the privileges conferred on the *comune* of Agordo in the time of Bishop Salvatore Bolognesi, Bishop of Belluno 1871–1899. On 6 February 1954 he was nominated Vicar-General of the Diocese. Bishop Muccin said in praise of him 'Luciani is a priest who lives and breathes his faith and his mission; he feels and communicates a religious, human warmth of a pastor.'[39] On 30 June 1956 Luciani became Canon of the Cathedral. Also in 1956,

[34] *Time*, 112 11 September 1978, p. 46.
[35] Yallop, p. 19.
[36] Hebblethwaite, *Year of Three Popes*, p. 93.
[37] Seabeck, p. 249.
[38] Vian, p. 675; Serafini, pp. 54–5.
[39] Scopelliti and Taffarel, p. 77.

whilst he helped in the preparation of the upcoming Congress for the Eucharistic Year, held on 9–16 September, Muccin nominated Luciani to be elevated to the episcopate, but the time was not yet ripe. The Consistory in Rome turned Luciani down, on the grounds of 'precarious health and a weak voice'![40] Muccin protested Luciani's case, attesting to his hard working nature, but to no avail.

One event that made a big impact on Luciani during this period was the solemn canonization ceremony performed by Pope Pius XII for his predecessor Pius X on 29 May 1954. Mgr Luciani went to Rome to be present personally at what proved to be something of a high-water mark of Roman pageantry, some 800,000 people witnessing the spectacle. On his return to Belluno, he had a small article published in *L'Amico del Popolo*, in which he wrote 'I saw the Pope, the cardinals, the bishops, an immense crowd. I saw the living Faith, the pulsating Church, with all their manifest signs of catholicity and holiness'.[41]

By 1958, when he reached the age of forty-six, Luciani was reasonably settled in life. His mother had died on 2 March 1948 and his father on 9 January 1952, but he kept in close touch with his brother and sister. Having seen military service from 1938 to 1943, including the war in Libya where he was wounded by a mine outside El Alamein, Edoardo had become an elementary school teacher and three times Christian Democrat Mayor of Canale d'Agordo, married Antonietta Marinelli on 9 August 1944 and was living in the family home, No. 8 via Rividella. His sister Antonia, known as 'Nina', had worked for a time in Switzerland before settling with her bricklayer husband Ettore Petri and two children in Santa Giuliana di Levico, near Trento.

Luciani was fulfilled: he had his work and his books. Exercise he got by cycling around the diocese and climbing the local mountains. What is more, he was popular in the parish, and everyone knew him simply as Don Albino.

However, a brisk series of events in the outside world, events over which Luciani had no control, were to initiate big changes in his life. At 3.52 a.m. on 9 October 1958 Pope Pius XII died in a coma at Castel Gandolfo, the papal summer residence in the Alban Hills some 20 kilometres from Rome. After reigning for nearly twenty years, the eighty-two-year-old pope had been in poor health and increasingly isolated for some years; two

---

[40] Vian, p. 675.
[41] Luciani, *Opera Omnia*, vol. 9, pp. 447–9. Pius was the first pope to be sanctified since the seventeenth century.

strokes finally broke even his constitution. Shortly before his death, Pius had confided prophetically to a European diplomat: *'Apres moi, le deluge'.*[42]

On 25 October the conclave to elect his successor got under way, fifty-one cardinals attending, of whom seventeen were Italian. On 28 October Angelo Giuseppe Roncalli, the Patriarch of Venice, was elected pope on the eleventh ballot after a hard-fought, see-saw contest, taking the unexpected name of John XXIII – unexpected because the name had already been used by an anti-pope of 1410–15. On 4 November the new pope was crowned. Portly and already aged nearly seventy-seven when elected, Roncalli was expected by many to be little more than a 'transitional', caretaker pope. He proved, of course, to be anything but that.

Pope John's election caused a domino effect in episcopal appointments. Giovanni Urbani was moved to Venice to replace Roncalli, and Giuseppe Carraro was moved to Verona. Who could fill the vacancy in Vittorio Veneto? One evening Pope John asked his friend Girolamo Bortignon to supper and asked him for suggestions. Bortignon put forward as a candidate 'a little priest, a certain Luciani, who is all over the place, one moment here, one moment there'.[43] Pope John smiled. 'I know him. I know him. He will do me fine.'[44] Luciani was genuinely surprised at his nomination, declaring after his appointment with typical modesty, 'I have taken a couple of train journeys with him, but he did most of the talking. I said so little he could not have got to know me.'[45] The two men had met in the summer of 1956, when Luciani had helped to arrange the then patriarch's vacation to San Vito di Cadore in the mountains: behind Pope John's kindly old peasant face lay a very shrewd brain, a fact of which the world was soon to become aware.

Luciani first found out about his appointment on 9 December while he was teaching a class in the seminary in Belluno. The bell rang and Bishop Muccin summoned him and all the students to make the popular announcement. His sister Antonia only knew when she spotted a copy of *Il Gazzettino* on a news-stand saying 'Albino Luciani new bishop of Vittorio Veneto'.[46]

[42] Murphy, p. 13.
[43] Greeley, p. 133.
[44] Yallop, p. 19.
[45] Yallop, p. 19.
[46] Scopelliti and Taffarel, pp. 81–2.

Pope John formally declared Luciani's appointment in the secret consistory of 15 December.[47] The same day Luciani travelled by train to Rome, accompanied by Mgr Ausilio Da Rif. For eight days he followed a course of spiritual exercises in preparation. Pope John also insisted on consecrating Luciani himself.

> On his patronal feast, St. John's day [27 December], the Pope conferred episcopal consecration on the altar of the Confession in St. Peter's upon [amongst others] ... Monsignor Albino Luciani, Vicar General of the diocese of Feltre e Belluno, near Venice ... Co-consecrators with the Pope were the Bishops of Padua and Feltre e Belluno.[48] Those present in St. Peter's included the Italian Prime Minister [Signor Amintore Fanfani] and the Mayor of Rome [Signor Urbano Cioccetti].[49]

At the consecration Pope John read an apt passage from the fifteenth-century devotional work *De Imitatione Christi* (*The Imitation Of Christ*), commonly attributed to Thomas à Kempis:

> Strive, son, to do another's will rather than your own. Choose always rather to have less than more. Seek always the lower place and to be subject to all. Desire always and pray that the will of God may be completely fulfilled in you. Look, such a man treads the frontiers of peace and rest.[50]

From Luciani's point of view, there was only one small hitch. The secretary bearing his cloak was delayed in entering the Vatican by the throng of pilgrims, and was late in arriving in the audience room after the ceremony. For the official photographs with Pope John and the other newly consecrated bishops Luciani had therefore to borrow one from Mgr Giuseppe Micossi, prevost of Serravalle, who was much taller than him. Luciani took it in good part, but the result was faintly absurd, as he did his best to look grave in the voluminous garment![51]

At any rate the appointment had come with unusual speed, the see having been vacant for a mere fifteen days. Pope John praised his new bishop warmly, but as usual Luciani showed his transparent humility, maintaining that the merit of his little achievements were wholly through God's grace. To the townspeople he responded:

---

[47] *Acta Apostolicae Sedis*, XXV, 1958, p. 989.
[48] Girolamo Bortignon and Gioacchino Muccin (1899–1991), Bishop of Feltre e Belluno 1949–1975. Luciani left Muccin his episcopal cross in his will.
[49] *Tablet*, CCXIII, 3 January 1959, p. 20.
[50] Book III, ch. 23, 'On Four Sources Of Peace'.
[51] Frs Francesco Taffarel and Ausilio Da Rif, 'Humilitas' (1984–5).

The Lord does not like to write certain things on bronze nor on marble but simply on dust, so that if the writing remains, not disturbed, not blown away by the wind, it becomes clear that such is the work of the Lord only. I am the pure and poor dust; on this dust the Lord has written.[52]

This is indeed true – sometimes such work is the most lasting.

---

[52] Pia Basso (née Luciani), 'Albino Luciani', Letter dated 6 February 2003.

Chapter Three

Bishop 1958-1969

Bishop Luciani entered his new diocese on 11 January 1959, arriving simply, by train. Vittorio Veneto, named in honour of King Vittorio Emanuele II in 1866, was the town that gave its name to the final victory of the Italians over the Austro-Hungarians in the First World War, during the period 24 October – 4 November 1918. By 1958 it had a population of some twenty-five thousand inhabitants, consisting of the lower industrial quarter of Ceneda and the medieval walled town of Serraville with its many old houses and churches. Luciani occupied rooms in the Castle of San Martino, of eighth-century Longobard origin and now the Bishop's Palace.

The new bishop chose familiar images from the locality for his episcopal coat of arms: symbolic mountains of Agordo with three stars (faith, hope and charity), all on an azure background; the lion of St Mark was added when he became Patriarch of Venice. His motto, *Humilitas*, was borrowed from St Carlo Borromeo (1538-1584). 'Humility' and all its implications meant something tangible to Luciani. His Vicar General said of him

> He united strength with gentleness and paid no heed to the criticisms levelled at him; the saints look to God and not to themselves. 'It is enough that God is content with me,' he would say. 'What I imagine myself to be must be cut down to size. What others think of me is of no importance. What God thinks of me is important.[1]

Borromeo was one of the great leaders of the Counter-Reformation; in the last sessions of the Council of Trent he took a prominent part in drafting the Roman Catechism, Missal and

[1] Seabeck, p. 34.

Breviary, promulgated in 1566. He undertook radical reform in his see of Milan, establishing for the first time sound curricula and seminaries for the training of the clergy. His reforming zeal was not always popular; in October 1569 a priest of the corrupt Humiliati brethren attempted to assassinate him. Borromeo merely redoubled his efforts. He patronized the Jesuits and the Barnabites, founded a Confraternity of Christian Doctrine for instructing children, took great personal interest in the poor and the sick and was a patron of learning and the arts. In 1610 he was canonized as 'the model of a bishop according to the Council of Trent'. It is not difficult to understand why Luciani should feel inspired by this holy bishop: it was to Borromeo that Pope John devoted a lifetime of study and writing.

Luciani celebrated his inaugural Mass with Mozart's Mass in D Major, written in 1774 for four voices.[2] When he first preached to his congregation he gave them an eloquent insight into the mind and qualities of their new pastor:

> With me the Lord uses yet again his old system. He takes the small ones from the mud of the streets. He takes the people of the fields. He takes others away from their nets in the sea or the lake, and he makes them Apostles. It's his old system.
>
> As soon as I became consecrated a priest I started to receive from my superiors' tasks of responsibility and I have understood what it is for a man to be in authority. It is like a ball that is pumped up. If you watch the children who play on the grass outside this Cathedral[3] when their ball is punctured they don't even bother to look at it. It can stay with tranquility in a corner. But when it is pumped up the children jump out from all sides and everyone believes that they have to right to kick it. This is what happens to men when they move up. Do not therefore be envious.[4]

He now had four hundred priests in his charge, and some of these had sought to present their new bishop with gifts and money on his arrival in the diocese. He graciously declined these and attempted, at a general gathering, to explain his reasons:

> I come without five lire. I want to leave without five lire . . . My dear priests. My dear faithful. I would be a very unfortunate bishop if I didn't love you. I assure you that I do, and that I want to be at your

[2] De La Cierva, p. 190.
[3] Duomo of Santa Maria Nuova (Assunta), rebuilt between 1740–1773 in Neo-Classical style by Domenico Schiavi Di Angelo (Tolmezzo), (1718–1795).
[4] Yallop, p. 20.

service and put at your disposal all of my poor energies, the little that I have and the little that I am.[5]

In fact, the new bishop had considerable energy and put it to good practical use. During his relatively brief time in Vittorio Veneto 'He modernised the House of Retreats, completed the seminary, opened new churches and inaugurated various parochial works, organised the Diocesan Archives, and reno-vated the printing equipment at the seminary.'[6]

Above all Luciani was accessible, both to his priests and to his flock, making frequent visits to families, the sick and the poor all over his diocese, often quietly leaving little monetary gifts. He began his pastoral visitation promptly, on 17 June: eventu-ally he would make at least two pastoral visitations to all of the 180 parishes in his care. His Senate of Priests was elected entirely without nominations from its bishop, a form of democ-racy most unusual in the pre-conciliar Church. When the Senate recommended the closure of a particular minor semi-nary against his better judgement, he nevertheless consulted his parish priests. It became obvious that a majority favoured closure and so he authorized the decision. The pupils went to state schools and he later stated publicly that the majority view had been right and his own wrong.

Luciani could also be forthright in putting forward his own views. On 4 February 1960 he wrote a piece in the diocesan bulletin about Francesco Forgione (1887–1968), better known as Padre Pio of Pietrelcina, the famous Capuchin stigmatic and mystic. Many uncritically adored Padre Pio; some, like Girolamo Bortignon – himself a Capuchin – denounced him vehemently. Luciani made his own measured criticisms, likening Padre Pio's ministry to 'an indigestible dainty' and expressing his concern that he appealed to people with an 'exaggerated craving for the supernatural and the unusual'. He continued: 'The faithful have need for solid bread (the Mass, the catechism, the sacra-ments), which nourishes them, not chocolates, pastries, and sweetmeats that burden and beguile.'[7] Luciani, always wary of 'personality cults', was especially concerned about the pilgrim-ages to Padre Pio at San Giovanni Rotondo, particularly those organized by post.

[5] Yallop, p. 20.
[6] Seabeck, pp. 29–30.
[7] C. Bernard Ruffin, *Padre Pio: The True Story*, 1982, Our Sunday Visitor Inc., p. 286. John Paul II beatified Padre Pio on 2 May 1999, and canonized him on 16 June 2002.

In 1961, in an address to the clergy of Belluno on priestly vocations and training, he recalled Döllinger, Renan and Passaglia, whose 'dissident' theological views had threatened schism in the Church in the late nineteenth century. In doing so he revealed the pastoral core of his own approach towards being a priest, asserting of the aforementioned men: 'They were lost through too much theology. They were too much theologians and too little pastors of souls . . . Theological learning ought to put itself at the service of the pastoral ministry.'[8]

In his own diocese, priests never had to make appointments to see their bishop; if they came, they were seen. Luciani was making a great impression, in his own quiet, unassuming way, without even realizing it. One man made an astute comparison between Luciani and Pope John, who had consecrated him:

> It was like having your own personal Pope. It was as if Papa Roncalli [John XXIII] was here in this diocese working alongside us. His table usually had two or three priests at it. He simply could not stop giving of himself. One moment he would be visiting the sick or the handicapped. They never knew at the hospitals when he was coming. He would just turn up on a bike or in his old car leaving his secretary to read outside while he wandered the wards. The next moment he would turn up in one of the mountain villages to discuss a particular problem with the local priest.[9]

On one of Luciani's travels round his diocese, his car was involved in a near miss with a farmer's tractor. How he responded to the incident was typical of the man. Years later, the farmer still vividly recalled the mishap: 'I swerved and some hay fell off the wagon I was pulling. But in an instant the bishop was down there throwing the hay back on.'[10]

However, Luciani's life in Vittorio Veneto was not always one of simplicity and contentment. In early August 1962 the vice-director and treasurer of his diocesan administrative council, Don Guerrino Cescon, came to him with a confession. Together with another member of the council, Mgr P. Stefani, he had become involved with a sales representative from Treviso who speculated in property, one Carlo Luigi Antoniutti. Antoniutti's

---

[8] *Tablet*, CCXXXII, 2 September 1978, p. 838. Johannes von Döllinger (1799–1890), theologian and historian, a leader of the Old Catholics in Germany from 1870; Ernest Renan (1823–1892), orientalist and philosopher; Carlo Passaglia (1812–1887), former Jesuit, theologian.

[9] Yallop, p. 21. Yallop does not name his source, presumably a priest.

[10] *Tablet*, CCXXXII, 9 September 1978, p. 876.

speculations failed and, becoming bankrupt, he had committed suicide in the house of one of his 'partners', Dr Roberto Dacomo, on 17 June 1962. The two priests had joined in his schemes, disastrously, the outcome being that more than 283 million lire of parish funds were missing.

Luciani had very firm opinions on ecclesiastical wealth; he believed in a Church of the poor, for the poor, a Church that should be materially poor and seen to be so. First, he twice tendered his own resignation to the Pope, but John wisely refused to accept it. Next, concerned to limit the scope of the scandal, he appealed to the editor of the Venice newspaper *Il Gazzettino* to treat the story in a fair, rational manner. Then, he called his four hundred priests together. He refused to follow the usual path of claiming clerical exemption from civil action; that would be to perpetuate injustice. Gently but firmly he spoke to the gathered assembly:

> It is true that two of us have done wrong. I believe the diocese must pay. I also believe that the law must run its due course. We must not hide behind any immunity. In this scandal there is a lesson for us all. It is that we must be a poor Church. I intend to sell ecclesiastical treasure. I further intend to sell one of our buildings. The money will be used to repay every single lira that these priests owe. I ask for your agreement.[11]

Luciani got their agreement, and his standing was increased in the eyes of the majority, although some considered him almost too moral. After the ensuing trial, on 14 July 1965 Don Cescon was sentenced to a sixteen months prison sentence, while Mgr Stefani was acquitted and left the diocese.

Whilst allowing his priests to be prosecuted, Luciani characteristically tried to protect the men from further public condemnation. He exhorted his diocese to practice Christian charity, particularly in a letter he wrote on 9 August 1962.

> Where should a priest go if he wants to avoid indiscreet and painful curiosity at such a bitter moment for him, if not a monastery? You have already pointed out five or six times that Mgr Stefani is in the monastery of Follina! So leave him in peace if you have nothing new to say to him.[12]

Meanwhile, great events had been taking place in Rome,

---

[11] Yallop, pp. 23–4.
[12] Kummer, pp. 280–1; *Opera Omnia*, 2, pp. 465–6.

events that would be of immense significance for both Luciani and the whole Catholic Church. In a consistory held on 25 January 1959 Pope John had made three proposals: a diocesan synod for Rome,[13] a revision of the Code of Canon Law,[14] and, most unexpected and startling of all, an ecumenical council for the universal Church.

Historically, such councils have been associated with great crises in the life of the Church. From the very beginning John saw *his* council, the twenty-first in a line stretching back to Nicaea in 325, as having a profound objective. In his first encyclical, *Ad Petri Cathedram* of 29 June 1959, he stated that the Council's work would be chiefly concerned with the encouragement of Christian unity. A key problem, widely recognized, was the remoteness of authority from everyday life. What was needed was reform of the Church's internal power structure *and* revision of the relationship between the Catholic Church and the modern world. This would prove to have far-reaching political as well as theological implications, bringing about new orientations.

On 11 October 1962, after much preparation and anticipation, the opening ceremony of the Second Vatican Council took place in St Peters, 'some 2,381 Council Fathers'[15] being present. Bishop Luciani was one of them. To a degree he had already anticipated the Council in his own diocese, but that does not mean that the sessions of the Council were not a period of great importance in his personal development. The four sessions of the Council ran 11 October–8 December 1962; 29 September–4 December 1963; 14 September–21 November 1964; 14 September–8 December 1965. During this considerable length of time he had ample opportunity to read, think and discuss ideas with others.

In his opening address Pope John stated that 'authentic doctrine has to be studied and expounded in the light of the research methods and the language of modern thought. For the substance of the ancient deposit of faith is one thing, and the way in which it is presented is another.'[16] He repudiated the closed, defensive-mindedness of the pessimists. Initially the conservative, curia-set agenda dominated, emphasizing the

---

[13] The first; it was held on 24–31 January 1960, decrees effective from 1 November 1960.
[14] Finally promulgated on 25 January 1983, effective from 27 November 1983.
[15] Kaiser, p. 79.
[16] Hebblethwaite, *John XXIII*, pp. 431–2.

juridical aspects and the hierarchical structure of the Church. The Curia had considerable organizational resources behind them, being on home territory. Most of the visiting Fathers initially had a passive attitude – their 'revolution' came largely as a surprise to most of them, the evolving, maturing fruit of new dialogue and novel contacts and exchanges, just as John had intended. George Bull identified the process very neatly:

> The key to the transformation is to be found in the revolution in communications that took place among the Fathers of the Council (between themselves, with progressive theologians and prelates, and with the outside world) and, simultaneously, the development of a rudimentary but effective sense of group solidarity. From a psychological rather than sociological standpoint, the key to the transformation was the exposure and, as it proved, vulnerability away from home of men on the whole little accustomed to criticizing their superiors, or being criticized by their own lower ranks, to new thought, new faces, and freedom of speech.[17]

In the event the tide at the Council, encouraged by John, ran strongly in favour of reform – though not without setbacks. The trend was towards initiative, to empower bishops to use their own pastoral experiences to bring about renewal, *aggiornamento*. Concerning the Roman Curia, John, by summoning his Council, 'brought about a palace revolution, to depose not the king but the courtiers'.[18] Crucially, the Council also raised questions of the freedom of inquiry and expression of Catholic scholars.

Luciani himself never spoke publicly at the Council – perhaps indicative of his rather self-effacing nature and meagre assessment of his own abilities, although in fact only about ten per cent of those gathered spoke on the Council floor. Cardinal Wojtyla was one of those: he spoke on twenty-four occasions. However, Luciani did submit a written intervention on Collegiality.

In his text Luciani spoke in conventional terms of the power received by Peter and the apostles, and therefore by the pope and the bishops, from Christ as recorded in the Gospels. Sometimes this power is exercised by the whole college of bishops, at other times by the pope alone. The college of bishops consists only of the successors of the apostles, with the pope as necessary centre and head, and does not function

---

17 Bull, *Vatican Politics*, p. 96.
18 Ibid., p. 33.

separated from the pope. In the course of the centuries the collegial power has been exercised parallel to the power of the pope.

Thus far his comments on the double exercise of power were important but routine. But before he reached his natural, concluding observation that all present at the Council recognised the primacy of the pope, he gave a personal insight:

> How can the bishops be at the same time under the Roman Pontiff's power, and with him administer the supreme power? I must confess that I have not found any full explanation for such a problem. Faith supplies me with two issues: the bishops together with the Pope share the supreme power and, above them, the Pope has this same power. Faith does not say how these two statements are compatible. This is not new nor extraordinary in the theological field, and once again this invites us to go beyond the realm or categories of political things, and so to build up a quite unique concept of 'power', not at all devoid of mystery.[19]

As so often, Luciani had managed to penetrate to the essential heart of a dilemma and to explain it in relatively simple terms.

On 11 August 1964 Luciani also delivered an address at Verona to the Cardinals, Archbishops and Bishops of the Lombardy – Veneto regions, entitled *'La Beata Vergine Maria nel Mistero di Cristo e della Chiesa'*, which fed into the debate on Chapter VIII of *Lumen Gentium*. Neither of his interventions attracted much attention at the time, but this is not particularly surprising given the number of Fathers and topics involved. In other words, Luciani spent his time developing his own thoughts rather than trying to influence those of others. He kept out of the intrigues that many of the Italian bishops were involved in, and spent his evenings studying draft texts. He tended to be, when not actually in the Council meetings, a little isolated in his room in the Roman minor seminary near the Vatican. From his window, during the first session, he could sometimes catch sight of Pope John reading his breviary on the terrace of the Torre di San Giovanni.[20]

However, this is not to say that he made no friendships as the Council progressed. He made contacts with Belgian theologians

---

[19] Original Latin in *Acta Et Documenta Concilio Oecumenico Vaticana II Apparando – Periodus II*. Animadversiones Scriptae – Cap. II De Ecclesia. No. 91, pp. 798–802. Quote from p. 801, para. 2; I am indebted to Dom Leander Hogg, OSB for the translation.

[20] Hebblethwaite, *Year of Three Popes*, p. 95.

and with the Germans, whose language he was best at. He also made some friendships for life. He was a friend of Cardinal Giacomo Lercaro,[21] who was a friend of Pope John and a leading 'liberal', in favour of liturgical reform and collegiality. Lercaro had turned his episcopal palace in Bologna into a home for orphans and had a working relationship with local communists. With Cardinal Pierre-Marie Gerlier of Lyons, the Brazilian Bishop Helder Câmara, and, as its theologian, the French Dominican Père Yves Congar, OP he founded an informal movement of Council Fathers called 'the Church of the Poor'. Lercaro took his cue from Pope John's broadcast of 11 September in which he had said: 'Faced with the developing countries, the Church presents herself as she is and as she wishes to be, as the Church of all and especially the Church of the poor'.[22]

On 6 December Lercaro made an impassioned commentary on John's definition of the Church.

[He] showed that this is true in all fields, theological, pastoral, ascetic and disciplinary. The characteristic note of the incarnation, he said, is in fact poverty; but the Church is the projection in time of that mystery, and the poverty of its leader becomes a law for its members. As for the poor, they have been given a new dignity in the Gospel, and today the Church finds itself in a world where two-thirds of the inhabitants are not only poor but starving: its apostolate cannot therefore disregard this tragic fact. Finally, in order to realise its vocation as a Church of the poor, the Church must demonstrate its own poverty in its institutions, manifestations, and individual members.[23]

As Congar emphasized, the exercise of *authority* in the Church was for *service*. Though the movement did not have great impact on the Council itself, its concerns have become increasingly relevant and significant in the post-conciliar Church.

Other friendships that Luciani made at this time included men of the calibre of Cardinal Leon-Joseph Suenens, Archbishop of Malines-Brussels; Cardinal Stefan Wyszynski, Archbishop of Gnienzo and Warsaw; Karol Wojtyla, Archbishop of Krakow; François Marty, Archbishop of Rheims; and Hyacinth Thiandoum, Archbishop of Dakar. Years later, at a meeting of

---

[21] Cardinal Giacomo Lercaro. Born 1891, Archbishop of Bologna 1952–1968, cardinal 1953, died 1976.

[22] Hebblethwaite, *John XXIII*, p. 463.

[23] C. Falconi, *Pope John And His Council*, 1964, tr. M. Grindrod, Weidenfeld and Nicolson, p. 326.

the Synod of Bishops, Luciani said to Wojtyla 'I remember that during the Council we were sitting fairly near each other, and you never stopped writing'.[24] What Luciani didn't know was that he was making notes for a new book, not taking notes of the speeches. However, that didn't stop Wojtyla taking a very active part in the debates!

Pope John died of intestinal cancer aged eighty-one on 3 June 1963, after the First Session of the Council. John died in his bed in his Vatican apartment at 7.49 p.m.; outside, in St Peter's Square, Cardinal Luigi Traglia was saying a Mass for the dying man before a large crowd. John expired at the very moment that he spoke the formal words of dismissal *'Ite, Missa Est'* ('Go, the Mass is ended'). He was much mourned, and there was considerable speculation concerning the Council's continuation.

John's successor was Giovanni Battista Montini, the Cardinal Archbishop of Milan, who was elected on the sixth ballot on 21 June 1963, taking the name Paul VI. The very next day Paul promised that not only would the Council continue, but that he would dedicate his entire pontificate to it. Most important of all, he would 'guide' it in very much the same direction as Pope John, encouraging 'awareness, renewal, dialogue' in the life of the Church. The future seemed promising.

Paul has been accused of being vacillating, and to an extent it was true; he was more intellectually and emotionally angst-ridden than John, more prone to being swayed by differing opinions. However, it needs to be remembered that Paul inherited a fast-changing Church, unlike the apparently stable edifice that John had inherited only five years before. For one thing, criticism was much more freely expressed, including that aimed at the Pope. Paul gave more importance to the papal office than John had done, seeing it as the personification of Church unity. His attempts to always reconcile the progressive majority and conservative minority slowed done the pace of the Council, and indeed unduly watered down many of its reforms, to the dismay of the progressives. Many of them believed that Paul inaugurated 'reformed Romanism' by his reassertion of papal authority. Paul himself was to say in 1967 'The Pope – as we all know – is undoubtedly the gravest obstacle to the path of ecumenism.'[25]

---

[24] M. Malinski, *Pope John Paul II: The Life Of My Friend Karol Wojtyla*, tr. P. S. Falla, Burns & Oates, 1979, p. 42.
[25] Hebblethwaite, *Paul VI*, p. 9.

For Luciani, then, the Council was a period of opportunity, spiritual renewal, 'conversion and going back to school'.[26] His greatest difficulty with his process of rejuvenation was with the Council's declaration On Religious Liberty (*Dignitatis Humanae Personae*). One of the major innovations of Vatican II had been defined in Pope John's opening address, John directing that at his Council there should be no sterile condemnations as in the past, but rather positive, forward-looking measures designed to make the Church and its teaching relevant to the world. John had stated unequivocally that the Church had always been opposed to errors: 'it has often condemned them with the utmost severity. But now the Bride of Christ prefers to use the medicine of mercy rather than of severity. She believes that the needs of today can best be met by showing the validity of her doctrine rather than by further condemnation'.[27]

This new, enlightened approach was nowhere more in evidence than in such declarations as On Religious Liberty, which came to be seen as one of the touchstones of the 'Council's relevance and sincerity'.[28] It went directly against the beliefs of those like Cardinal Alfredo Ottaviani, Prefect of the Holy Office, who held that 'error had no rights', a theory that, as he freely admitted afterwards, Luciani had also been teaching his own pupils 'for years'.[29] The *natural* instincts of both John and Luciani were to find and concentrate on areas of agreement, not conflict, and thereby hope to make some progress, trusting in Divine Providence.

In summary, On Religious Liberty asserts the following:

Part 1 of the declaration, 'The General Principles of Freedom', states that the human has a right to immunity from coercion on the part of individuals, special groups, or any human power. Government should respect and favor the religious life of the citizenry but should not command or inhibit religious acts; in preventing abuses, it must act according to juridical norms for the preservation of public order. Part 2, 'Religious Freedom in the Light of Revelation', asserts that man's response to God in faith must be free. The Church must enjoy freedom and independence. The Council denounces and deplores the oppressive policies of some governments and emphasizes the

---

[26] Hebblethwaite, *Year of Three Popes*, p. 95.

[27] C. Falconi, *Pope John And His Council*, p. 152. It did not stop 454 'conservatives', – a minority, but a sizeable one – in the Fourth Session after Pope John's death, from trying to get the Council to condemn Communism. They failed.

[28] Bull, *Vatican Politics*, p. 86.

[29] *Time*, 112, 4 September 1978 p. 10.

necessity of religious freedom, which should everywhere be provided with an effective constitutional guarantee.[30]

Luciani himself later explained, simply and disarmingly, how he changed his mind: 'I studied the question in depth, and reached the conclusion that we had been wholly wrong'.[31] His own prudent approach to error in future can be seen from this passage which he subsequently published in an article: 'If you come across error, rather than uprooting it or knocking it down, see if you can trim it patiently, allowing the light to shine upon the nucleus of goodness and truth that usually is not missing even in erroneous opinions'.[32]

The first schema (draft text) of the declaration had been presented to the Council Fathers by the Secretariat for Promoting Christian unity on 19 November 1963. After much debate and redrafting the vote to accept the schema as a whole was taken on 19 November 1965. Of a total of 2,216 Fathers present, 1,954 voted *Placet*, 249 voted *Non placet*, whilst 13 papers were invalid. Pope Paul VI promulgated the Declaration on 7 December 1965, the only conciliar document addressed to the whole world.

The Council had also prepared a strongly worded statement on the armaments race in its Pastoral Constitution on the Church in the Modern World (*Gaudium Et Spes*).[33] It stated that 'While extravagant sums are being spent for the furnishing of ever new weapons an adequate remedy cannot be provided for the multiple miseries afflicting the whole modern world'.[34] This simple truth did not please all the Fathers, especially those from nations that perhaps had cause to have uneasy consciences. This was, of course, the time of increasing US involvement in Vietnam, and it prompted Luciani to comment: 'No doubt Cardinal Spellman saw in this an attack on US policy, but today the Church cannot refuse to commit itself on this question'.[35] Most of the Fathers, Luciani included, did not refuse to commit themselves. In the final vote of 6 December

---

[30] NCE, vol.14, pp. 571–2. Full text and notes in Abbott, pp. 672–700.

[31] Hebblethwaite, *Year of Three Popes*, p. 96.

[32] Yallop, p. 22.

[33] For full text and notes see Abbott, pp. 183–316.

[34] Abbott, p. 295; Pt. II, ch. V, para. 81.

[35] Hebblethwaite, *Year of Three Popes*, p. 96. Cardinal Francis J. Spellman (1889–1967), Archbishop of New York; militant anti-Communist dubbed by the Russians as 'the archangel of atomic war', active supporter of the Vietnam War. The US bombing campaign in Vietnam had begun in February 1965.

1965, with 2,373 Fathers present, 2,111 voted *Placet*, 251 *Non placet*, whilst 11 papers were invalid. Pope Paul promulgated the Pastoral Constitution on 7 December 1965.

Importantly, one vital issue had been removed from the schema in late October 1964, with immense repercussions later. Cardinal Gregory Agagianian announced that there would be no public discussion on the Council floor of 'certain points' arising in the schema – namely, contraception. Pope Paul had reserved to himself the responsibility for deciding on the lawfulness of use of the pill. The removal of even the competence to properly discuss this vital issue on the Council floor was perhaps the biggest single lost opportunity of the Council. Despite this, on 29 October Cardinal Léger, Cardinal Suenens and Patriarch Maximos IV Saigh discreetly but clearly underlined in their interventions the momentous changes in attitudes to sexual problems taking place in the Catholic world.

Maximos, the bearded, lithe eighty-seven-year-old Melkite Patriarch of Antioch, particularly hit home when he stated that he considered it the 'pastoral duty' of the Council to find a practical solution to the demographic pressures condemning 'hundreds of millions of human beings to a misery that is unworthy and without hope . . .'[36]

Maximos was outspoken. What is more he spoke in French, not the official Latin, on the grounds that he was an 'Oriental' Christian, not a Latin one. He spoke passionately of one of the Church's greatest scandals, what he called the disparity between official doctrine and 'the contrary practice of the immense majority' of Christian couples. 'The faithful find themselves forced to live in conflict with the law of the church, far from the sacraments, in constant anguish, unable to find a viable solution between two contradictory imperatives: conscience and normal married life. The council must find a practical solution. This is a pastoral duty. We must say if God really wishes this enfeebling and unnatural impasse.'

He developed his point with sensitivity and real insight. 'In marriage, the development of personality and its integration into the creative plan of God are all one. Thus, the end of marriage should not be divided into "primary and secondary".' To general astonishment, he then challenged his audience:

And are we not entitled to ask if certain positions are not the outcome of outmoded ideas, and perhaps, a celibate psychosis on

---

[36] Bull, *Vatican Politics*, p. 108.

the part of those unaquainted with this sector of life? Are we not, perhaps unwittingly, setting up a Manichean conception of man and the world, in which the work of the flesh, vitiated in itself, is tolerated only in view of children? Is the external biological rectitude of an act the only criterion of morality, independent of family life, of its moral, conjugal and family climate, and of the grave imperatives of prudence which must be the basic rule of all our human activity?

Far from me to minimize the delicacy and the gravity of the subject, or of eventual abuses: but here, as elsewhere, isn't it the duty of the church to educate the moral sense of her children, to form them in moral responsibility, personal and communitarian, profoundly rooted in Christ, rather than to envelop it in a net of prescriptions and commandments, and to demand that they purely and simply conform to these with their eyes closed?

Maximos concluded with a plea for a new maturity and understanding: 'Let us see things as they are and not as we would like them to be. Otherwise we risk speaking in a desert. What is at stake is the future of the mission of the church in the world'. He quoted Paul VI's statement from the opening of the Council's second session, reminding his listeners of the commitment that had already been made to the people of God, who were living in a world God loved: 'Let the world know this: the church looks upon the world with profound understanding, with a sincere admiration, with a sincere intention not to subjugate but to serve it, not to despise it but to appreciate it, not to condemn it but to support and save it'.[37]

It was an astonishing performance, and won great applause. It raised many issues, chiming closely with Luciani's own developing ideas.

Before the Council had even begun Luciani had to some extent anticipated its spirit and aims in a pastoral letter, 'Notes on the Council', dated 18 April 1962, which he issued to prepare his flock for the upheaval that he foresaw ahead. Once the Council was in session the changes that he had already introduced in his diocese were accelerated. He urged his seminary teachers to renew their theological thinking, to abandon their old manuals and consult instead such relatively progressive journals as *Nuova Teologia*: in this regard he set a personal example, as we have seen. He discussed the issues raised by 'Pope John's revolution' over the dinner table with not only

---

[37] R. Kaiser, *The Encyclical That Never Was: The Story Of The Commission On Population, Family And Birth, 1964–66*, 1987, Sheed & Ward, pp. 97–8.

priests but seminarians as well; after all, they were the next generation who must consolidate the gains. He wrote on a weekly basis to all his priests, sharing his ideas and plans with them. Monsignor Mario Ghizzo, who worked with him, commented that Luciani 'totally absorbed Vatican Council II. He had the Council in his blood. He knew the documents by heart. Further, he implemented the documents'.[38] He was in full agreement with those who saw Vatican II as 'merely the opening phase in a long educational campaign' for clergy and laity alike, both internally and in the Church's 'endeavour to change the attitudes of the Church towards the modern world'.[39]

In January 1965, just after the third session of the Council had ended, Luciani gave a course of spiritual exercises to priests from various dioceses in the Veneto under the general title of *Historia salutis*. One participant tape-recorded these retreat talks then typed them out for his own use. Not being edited, Luciani's words retain their colloquial directness. He took as his starting point the well-known parable of the Good Samaritan (Luke 10:25–37), saying 'The Good Samaritan is Jesus, the unlucky wayfarer is we ourselves.'

> He recognized human frailty, of our need to help ourselves and eachother, with God's help, telling a charming little parable of his own to illustrate his point:
> Paradise is a bit above our heads and we struggle to get there. Well, we're in the situation of a little kid, of a little girlie who's seen the cherries, but can't manage to get hold of them; so her daddy has to come, hoists her and says: up, little one, up! Then yes, he lifts her and she can pluck and eat the cherries. That's how we are: Paradise allures us, but it's too high up for our poor efforts. Woe to us if the Lord doesn't come with his grace![40]

Luciani's concern for the poor and his whole-hearted sympathy with the new social drive of the Church lead naturally into a concern for the Third World. So it was that Vittorio Veneto adopted the small diocese of Ngozi in the north of Burundi, which Luciani visited from 16 August to 1 September 1966 along with Mgr Luigi Morstabilini, Bishop of Brescia, who was visiting his diocesan mission at Kiremba, and Dr Italo Fantin,

---

[38] Yallop, p. 24.
[39] Bull, *Vatican Politics*, p. 140.
[40] S. Falasca, 'His Patience Awaits Us', *30 Days*, no. 3, 2003. After the pope's death the talks were published in 1980 under the title *Il Buon Samaritano*.

senior doctor at the Hospital of Pieve di Soligo and representative of the diocesan committee *'Un Pane Per Amor Di Dio'*. There he had already founded, in 1962, a mission of three priests – Don Luigi Sgargetta, Don Vittorio De Rosso and Don Giuseppe Zago – from his diocese, and also a dispensary and a maternity clinic. Luciani met Dr Cyprien Henehene, the Minister of Health, in the hope of facilitating help with the practical details of these projects.

Luciani's visit came at a particularly troubled time. On 15 January 1965 the moderate Hutu Prime Minister Pierre Ngendandumwe had been assassinated; severe tribal disturbances followed with the subsequent execution of virtually all the leading Hutu politicians. On 8 July 1966 the Crown Prince – a Tutsi – deposed his father Mwambutsa IV, suspended the constitution and appointed Captain Michel Micombero as Prime Minister. On 1 September he was enthroned as Mwami Ntare IV; on 28 November Micombero declared Burundi a republic with himself as President. The Mwami went into exile, only to be killed on 29 April 1972 on his return in an attempted *coup d'état*.

The 1963 figures show that of a population of 2,644,000, Catholics formed 1,460,000 or 55.2% of the population of Burundi, whilst catechumens formed another 133,600 or 5%.[41] Almost all education took place in Catholic schools, which had 90,000 students. There was one major seminary and six minor ones. The population was well disposed towards Catholicism, and an active lay apostolate worked closely with the hierarchy. The faith and the Belgian-dominated Church could thus fairly be said to be flourishing, as Luciani saw on his visit to Ngozi.

Indeed, Burundi and its people made a powerful impact on Luciani, as he recorded in a thirty-page document entitled *'Quindici Giorni In Africa: Ho Lasciato Una Parte Del Mio Cuore Nelle Missioni'*. He wrote

> The missionaries brought home to me most forcibly the love of God, Who loves all men and wants all to reach salvation. He who encounters the missions encounters the Father, and also the Son, the First Missionary. A true Christian cannot but feel the problem of the missions.[42]

---

41 *New Catholic Encyclopedia*, vol. 2, pp. 906–7. 'Catechumens' are those who are being instructed and prepared for baptism, the catechumenate lasting four years. By comparison there were 820,000 Animists, 111,000 Protestants and 25,000 Moslems. Tribally, 84% of the population were Hutu, 15% Tutsi and 1% pygmoid Twa Bemba.

He found the spiritual life of the people, under their Bishop, Mgr André Makarakiza M.Afr. of Kitega, to be excellent. Makarakiza wanted Luciani to inaugurate the new church in Kitega, which had been built largely with the help of money donated by the faithful of Vittorio Veneto. He asked Luciani to preside over the proceedings, but Luciani gently but firmly declined, saying 'Not for the world! You are the bishop here; we are only here to give you a helping hand'.[43]

However, Luciani also could not fail to note the prevalent poverty, strife and disease of the area, and be moved by it.[44] Luciani saw a lot of the diocese in his relatively short time there; at one point the car in which he was travelling got stuck in the mud; the bishop got out to push along with the rest. He did indeed 'leave a part of his heart with the Missions'; the impressions imprinted on his memory were stored to lend weight to future arguments.

One thing that struck Luciani during his time in Burundi was the high birth-rate and the high infant mortality rate. Questions concerning the population explosion and the attendant issues of birth control and abortion were becoming increasingly prevalent in the 1960s amongst both Catholics and non-Catholics. As those issues were – and continue to be – crucial to the life of the Church and the world, and the fact that Luciani played a large, hitherto undervalued role in events and that they indirectly contributed to his subsequent elevation, it will be as well to consider them in some depth.

In March 1963 Pope John had set up an advisory Pontifical Commission on Population, Family and Birth. 'Artificial' Birth control – as it was called in Catholic circles, as against the 'natural' rhythm method – was one of the major issues that it was to study. Pope Paul enlarged the Commission from its original six (all male) members until it had sixty-eight members and a considerable number of 'consultants', still overwhelmingly male in composition but at least including a handful of married couples. One of the papal appointees nominated in spring 1966 for the fifth session of the commission was Karol Wojtyla, then Archbishop of Krakow, but he did not attend a single meeting. Many Catholics, encouraged by the reforms of

---

[42] Seabeck, p. 31.

[43] Ibid., p. 30.

[44] For a summary of Burundi's subsequent religious and political problems see B. Harden, 'Vendetta On Church In Divided Burundi', *Guardian*, no. 43,814, 28 July 1987, p. 8. See also *World Christian Encyclopedia*, 'Burundi', pp. 205–7.

the Second Vatican Council, confidently expected liberalizing changes in attitudes and methods, not least in the area of liberty of conscience. Some began to practise birth control in the expectation of change.

On 26 June 1966 the Commission's majority report, *Responsible Parenthood*, was produced, backed by sixty-four of the sixty-eight members, an overwhelming majority. It 'favored leaving the method of birth regulation to the consciences of individual married couples, provided that selfishness were excluded and the conjugal life taken as a whole were open to procreation'.[45] The four dissenting priests who formed the minority also produced a report at the behest of Cardinal Alfredo Ottaviani, despite the fact that their opinions had been represented in the majority report.

Pope Paul wavered, unsure as to which direction to go in. The Commission was immediately disbanded, and its wealth of accumulated experience lost. Initially attracted by the majority report's conclusions, Paul soon worried about what he percieved as their implications for papal authority, in that any authoritative statement he made based upon them could be seen as breaking the continuity of the magisterium and contra-dicting the encyclical of Pius XI, *Casti Connubii* (On Christian Marriage), promulgated on 31 December 1930. Unfortunately, he gave too much consideration to scientific data and a 'sea of documents', and not enough to psychological experience and the 'human dimension'.

Eventually, he took the matter entirely into his own hands, but took so long that the Commission's report leaked, being published by the *National Catholic Reporter* of Kansas City on 16 April 1967, and by the London-based *Tablet* on 22 April. Paul retreated to Castel Gandolfo to work upon his encyclical. Of the many reports and studies available to him on which to base his final judgement were some from the various regions of Italy. One such was from the Veneto diocese. The Patriarch of Venice, Cardinal Giovanni Urbani, called a meeting of the Triveneto Episcopal Conference, of which he was President: after a day's debate it was decided to make Luciani responsible for producing their report.

The decision to give Luciani the job was a sound one, for he had been studying the problem for a number of years, during which time he had consulted with doctors, sociologists, theolo-gians and, above all, married couples, some of whom he

---

[45] *New Catholic Encyclopedia*, vol.16, p. 215.

believed, as he wrote in the diary he kept during the Council, to be suffering a 'spiritual trauma' and a 'laceration of conscience'. Among the latter group was his own brother Edoardo, who eventually fathered nine children; Luciani baptized all nine and celebrated wedding Masses for two of the sons and three of the daughters.[46]

Already, back in January 1965, Luciani had given a retreat for the pastors of the Veneto, during which he had recalled the following:

> A Capuchin bishop told me at the council, 'Sometimes I thank God that I'm a bishop for only one reason, not for anything else. The reason is that I don't have to hear confessions at Easter, dealing with painful, difficult cases that are hard to resolve. These blessed Christian couples simply don't want to convince themselves that the use of contraceptives is a sin. At the end I never know what to say ... What could I say to a young father who already had six children and he was the sole support of the family? I knew that he was a good young man and in every other way obeyed the law of God.'
>
> I assure you, [Luciani told the pastors] the bishops would be extremely happy to find a doctrine that would declare licit the use of contraceptives under certain conditions ... If there's only one possibility in a thousand, we have to find this possibility and see if maybe with the help of the Holy Spirit we can discover something that previously escaped us.[47]

Characteristically, Luciani recognized the bishop's difficulties but did not want to side-step the issue, being determined to tackle the issue head-on for everyone's benefit, especially the struggling parents. Indeed, so well known was his stand on the issue by this time that some Italian wits referred to him as 'the bishop of the pill'. Thus, when the Pope sent his personal theologian Mgr Carlo Colombo to sound out the bishops of the Triveneto, in a closed-door session, Luciani argued that Colombo's position was 'too abstract' and did not take account of couples real-life difficulties.[48]

Luciani could not emphasize enough the importance of the issue, or the need for its prompt and sympathetic resolution. In the spring of 1968 he gave a series of presentations in parishes. His position on birth control was made perfectly clear on an audio recording made at Mogliano Veneto:

[46] *Tablet*, CCXXXII, 2 September 1978, p. 854.
[47] J. L. Allen Jr., 'Pope John Paul I And The Pill', *National Catholic Reporter*, vol. 3, no. 2, 5 September 2003. Was the 'Capuchin bishop' his friend Bortignon?
[48] Ibid.

For me, this is the most serious theological question that has ever been dealt with by the church. In the age of Arius and Nestorius, the issue was the two natures of Christ, and these were serious questions, but they were understood only at the very top of the church, among theologians and bishops. The simple people understood nothing of these things and said, 'I adore Jesus Christ, the Lord who has redeemed me', and that was it, there was no danger. *Here, on the other hand, it's a question that no longer regards solely the leadership of the church, but the entire church, all the young families, the young Christian families. It is a truly central point that they are still studying.*[49]

By April 1968 Luciani had written and submitted his report, which met with the full approval of the Conference. Cardinal Urbani had signed it and sent it directly to Pope Paul. That summer, Urbani saw the pope at Castel Gandolfo; 'after the audience he said that Paul VI had had Luciani's document on his desk and had expressed great interest in it. Cardinal Urbani said that Pope Paul seemed oriented in the direction of the document – which certainly was not the direction of *Humanae Vitae*.[50] Paul told Urbani that he valued the report greatly, so much so that Urbani called in at Vittorio Veneto personally to tell Luciani of the pope's gratitude and esteem.

In his report Luciani recommended to the pope that the Church should approve the use of the anovulant pill developed by the American biologists, Professors Gregory Pincus and John Rock (a devout Catholic); in effect, that it should become the *Catholic birth control pill*. On 13 April 1968 Luciani raised the issue in a sermon to the people of Vittorio Veneto, referring to the subject with his characteristic delicacy as 'conjugal ethics'. Having loyally observed – and loyalty to the pope, whatever his own opinions might be, was another characteristic of Luciani's – that priests in speaking and in hearing confessions 'must abide by the directives given on several occasions by the Pope until the latter makes a pronouncement',[51] he went on to make three important statements which clearly show the forward-looking moderation of his views and warm humanity:

1. It is easier today, given the confusion caused by the press, to find married persons who do not believe that they are sinning. If

[49] Ibid., my emphasis.
[50] Fr Mario Senigaglia, secretary to both Urbani and Luciani during their periods in Venice, quoted in Withers, p. 233.
[51] Yallop, p. 30.

this should happen it may be opportune, under the usual conditions, not to disturb them.

2. Towards the penitent onanist, who shows himself to be both
   penitent and discouraged, it is opportune to use encouraging
   kindness, within the limits of pastoral prudence.

3. Let us pray that the lord may help the Pope to resolve this question. There has never perhaps been such a difficult question for
   the Church: both for the intrinsic difficulties and for the numerous implications affecting other problems, and for the acute way
   in which it is felt by the vast mass of the people.[52]

Pope Paul's encyclical letter *Humanae Vitae*, on 'The Right
Ordering of the Procreation of Children', was published on 25
July 1968. It caused great controversy throughout the Catholic
and non-Catholic world. Having consulted his experts and
bishops – people like the members of his commission and
Albino Luciani – Pope Paul then totally rejected their advice.
The only methods of birth control that Paul considered to be
acceptable were 'chastity' and the rhythm method. No artificial
method of contraception could be allowed as it was 'absolutely
required that *in any use whatever of marriage* there must be no
impairment of its natural capacity to procreate human life'.[53]
Further, in consideration of the sacredness of human life, Pope
Paul specifically declared to be unlawful: 'the direct interrup-
tion of the generative process already begun and, above all,
direct abortion, even for therapeutic reasons'; 'direct steriliza-
tion, whether of the man or of the woman, whether permanent
or temporary'; 'any action, which either before, at the moment
of, or after sexual intercourse, is specifically intended to
prevent procreation – whether as an end or as a means'.[54] A
distinction was also drawn between sexual intercourse during
infertile periods and that employing contraceptive methods: 'In
reality, these two cases are completely different. In the former
married couples rightly use a facility provided them by nature.
In the latter they obstruct the natural development of the
generative process'.[55]

Such emphatic statements left little room for debate or 'interpretation', although theologians like Karl Rahner, SJ and Bernard

---

[52] Ibid., p. 30.
[53] *Humanae Vitae*, CTS, Do411, p. 13.
[54] Ibid., p. 15.
[55] Ibid., p. 17.

Häring, CSSR claimed that *Humanae Vitae* was not infallible and could therefore be reversed.[56] Many considered that the encyclical undercut the realistic, relevant tone set by the Council, whilst also undermining papal authority, as many Catholics either left the Church or continued practising contraception. Some considered that Paul should have concerned himself more with the potentially graver implications of abortion.

What was Luciani's response to *Humanae Vitae*? Ten years later, when he became Pope, the Vatican would assert that his response had been 'Rome has spoken. The case is closed'. This was far from the truth. His real feelings are shown in a pastoral letter to his diocese, 'On Reading The Encyclical', dated 29 July, just four days after the publication of Pope Paul's encyclical. He admitted his disappointment, noted that 'never, perhaps, [had] there been such a difficult issue facing the church', then continued:

'I confess that *in my heart I hoped that the very serious existing difficulties could be overcome*, and that the [Magisterium's] reply ... *might coincide, at least in part, with the hopes raised in so many couples* after the establishment of a special pontifical commission to examine the issue'.[57] He acknowledged the amount of care and consideration the pope had given to the problem; 'He knows that he will be a cause of bitterness to many; he knows that a different solution would probably have brought him more human applause;[58] but he places his trust in God and, in order to be faithful to His Word, reproposes the constant traditional teaching ... in all its purity. Recent scientific discoveries? The social evolution of our epoch? The growing need for 'responsible parenthood'? The necessity of harmonizing this 'responsible parenthood' with the demands of conjugal love? All these things are kept in mind, but they do not solicit a new doctrine'. Looking ahead, Luciani wrote:

> The thoughts of the Pope, and mine, go especially to the sometimes grave difficulties of married couples. May they not lose heart, for goodness sake. May they remember that for everyone the door is narrow and narrow the road that leads to life (cf. Matt. 7:14). That the hope of the future life must illuminate the path of Christian

---

56 Holmes, p. 235.

57 Withers, pp. 233–4. My emphasis.

58 This was true, and Paul had said as much. See *Humanae Vitae*, CTS Do411, p. 19. For Paul's feelings during the writing of *Humanae Vitae*, see *The Teachings of Pope Paul VI*, vol. I, 1969, pp. 115–19. He never produced another encyclical.

couples. That God does not fail to help those who pray to Him with perseverance. May they make the effort to live with wisdom, justice and piety in the present time, knowing that the fashion of this world passes away (cf. 1 Cor. 7:31) ... 'And if sin should still have a hold on them, may they not be discouraged, but have recourse with humble perseverance to God's mercy through the sacrament of Penance'.[59]

This last quotation, taken from *Humanae Vitae*, offered some comfort for those like Luciani who had hoped for some reform. Trusting that he had his flock with him in a 'sincere adhesion to the teaching of the Pope', he gave them his blessing: Luciani, with his taste for progress through compromise between as many people as could be brought into agreement, pursued a more subtle policy than those priests in other countries who took an openly hostile line or left the priesthood altogether.

Thus in January 1969 he took up the topic again, having become aware that some of his priests were denying absolution to married couples practising contraception, whilst other priests were readily absolving what Pope Paul, reaffirming the traditional teaching of the Church, had deemed a sin. In dealing with this problem, Luciani quoted from the response issued on 10 September 1968 – and which he had helped to draft – from the Italian Bishops' Conference to *Humanae Vitae*. It concentrated on the spirit, not the letter, of the law. Priests were recommended to show 'evangelical kindness' towards all married people, but especially as Luciani pointed out, towards those 'whose failings derive ... from the sometimes very serious difficulties in which they find themselves. In that case the behaviour of the spouses, although not in conformity with Christian norms, is certainly not to be judged with the same gravity as when it derives from motives corrupted by selfishness and hedonism'.[60] He also urged those in trouble not to feel 'an anguished, disturbing guilt complex'.

Luciani continued to wrestle with the problem; in February 1974 he gave an interview to the Venetian daily *Il Gazzettino* in which he made a statement that would have had incalcuable implications had his papacy not been cut short. He reminded Catholics that they were obliged to abide by *Humanae Vitae*, then added: 'However, the practical difficulties remain. When the faithful tell me about them, I understand them very well. If

[59] Yallop, pp. 31–2.
[60] Yallop, p. 32.

I were the 'divine master of the law', I would abolish the law'.[61]
Mario Senigaglia, his secretary from 1969 to 1976, later
confirmed this view: 'He would have reexamined 'Humanae
Vitae', not to condemn it, because that wasn't his style, but to
find a possible way out. He always looked for the encyclical's
mitigating clauses, and he was very aware of the pastoral difficulties [it caused]'.[62]

Luciani's loyalty at this difficult time was not lost on Pope
Paul. The Pope had appreciated Luciani's report, and his subsequent loyalty to the Pope and his encyclical impressed Paul. A
sensitive man, he knew the personal cost to Luciani, and
observed to his Under-Secretary of State Monsignor Giovanni
Benelli, 'In Vittorio Veneto there is a little bishop who seems
well suited to me'.[63] Benelli was astute enough to establish a
friendship with Luciani: it was to prove genuine and subsequently have far-reaching consequences.

In late 1966 another crisis had arisen within Luciani's diocese
of a somewhat unusual nature, one that ultimately even his
talent for conciliation could not solve. On 13 December of that
year Mgr Giuseppe Faè died. He had been the parish priest of
Montaner, an outlying hamlet of the *Comune* of Sarmede, since
1927. He had been an energetic, devoted and popular priest,
active in the Resistance from 1943 to 1945. Arrested for anti-
Fascist activity in March 1944 he had only escaped death
through the intervention of Gioacchino Muccin, then Archpriest
of Pordenone. His sister, Giovanna Faè, was sent to a concen-
tration camp and never returned.

In his later years Mgr Faè had been ably assisted by his chap-
lain, Don Antonio Botteon. When he died, aged eighty-one, Mgr
Faè was widely regarded locally as a saint. Luciani was himself
present at the funeral on 16 December 1966.

Running alongside this feeling was the growing desire in
Montaner for greater political autonomy from the 'parent'
Comune of Sarmede. Times were hard, with the community
suffering from considerable emigration, particularly amongst
its male workface. So strong was opinion that in 1964 all the
political parties represented, from the Christian Democrats,
Communists and Socialists to the Neo-Fascists, had formed a
coalition, the *Unione Democratica Montanerese*, to campaign
for their cause.

[61] Withers, p. 234.
[62] Ibid., p. 233.
[63] Yallop, pp. 32–3.

So, when the Diocesan Curia of Vittorio Veneto overrode local feeling and nominated Don Giovanni Gava to be Mgr Faè's successor instead of Don Antonio, trouble boiled over. The parishioners wanted 'their' man, while the Curia insisted on the Bishop's right under Canon 455 of the 1917 *Code of Canon Law* to nominate a priest for the post. They felt that Don Antonio was too young. Positions hardened as both sides saw basic principles at stake. On 1 February 1967 Montaner sent a delegation to Luciani, backed by 388 out of 403 families, to no avail. A delegation to Rome on 9 February met with a similarly negative response from the Secretariat of State. Representatives from the Protestant and in particular the Orthodox Churches began to appear in Montaner and the dispute gradually took on the nature of a rebellion against the institution of the Catholic Church itself, the women of the community playing an especially active role.

Soon the citizens of Montaner split into two rival factions. The majority, despite their opposition to the authorities and what they saw as an 'imposed' candidate, wished to stay within the Roman Catholic Confession. The minority faction sought sanction for their demands elsewhere, ignoring Luciani's attempts to find a compromise candidate, including the proposal to send a Capuchin Friar as priest for an interim, six-month 'cooling off' period. A pastoral visit by Luciani himself on 12 September 1967 was to no avail either. On Christmas Day he named Don Lorenzo De Conto as parish priest, and for the faithful that was the end of the matter.

As for the dissidents, their decision fell upon the Orthodox, largely due to the presence of a charismatic Orthodox priest, a local convert from Roman Catholicism to Orthodoxy, one Bruno Vettorazzo, Padre Claudio, who came to Montaner in June 1969. The construction of the Orthodox Church of La Trasfigurazione was begun only fifty metres from the Catholic one of San Pancrazio Martire: it was consecrated on 7 September 1969 in the presence of Archbishop Anthony Bloom of Sourozh, Exarch of the Moscow Patriarchate in Western Europe. Though subsequently passing through various Orthodox rites and allegiances, the small community remains in existence, testimony to the depth of the grievances that could not be solved in the turbulent years of the late 1960s.[64]

[64] For full details of this strange affair see Valentina Ciciliot *Il Caso Montaner (1967–69): Un Conflitto 'Politico' Tra Chiesa Cattolica E Chiesa Ortodossa*, 2005. Laureate Thesis in History. Faculty of Literature and Philosophy. Universita Degli Studi Di Venezia-Ca' Foscari.

The Second Vatican Council had created a spirit of renewal and exuberance in the Church, but also – and this was especially so after the publication of *Humanae Vitae* – some problems of confusion and dissension in some quarters. Vittorio Veneto was not exempt from these pressures, but Luciani remained confident. This attitude was evident in an interview with the distinguished Vaticanologist Giancarlo Zizola in 1969:

'The remedy is to proclaim the truth but in a positive way, stressing the essential, expressing it in a way that will make sense for contemporary people, and remaining in touch with modern culture. There is usually a grain of truth and goodness even in false opinions'.[65] In this he was echoing Pope John's opening speech to the Council, refuting the 'prophets of doom' and insisting on dialogue with, and a non-judgmental approach towards, the modern world.

Luciani's political outlook was rather more complex. From having a reasonable working relationship with the communists in the 1950s he shifted gradually rightwards – as is not uncommon with men as they get older and get positions of greater responsibility – until his politics became those of the centre, the politics of compromise. This was entirely consistent with his personality, and never led him to abandon the fight against economic poverty.

He thought that a bishop should be primarily a 'religious' figure, and posed this question in his interview with Zizola: 'Can you see me manipulating votes or managing affairs? I'm not that sort of chap. I leave financial questions to others, to experts. A bishop has other things to do, he has the Gospel ...'[66]

Luciani had seen a change in public opinion concerning the role of the clergy in politics, and in an interview with Alberto Papuzzi, in the same year (1969) he explained why he was not entirely pleased with this development:

People used to say that the hierarchy should steer clear of politics; now they are beginning to demand that priests should have the right to commit themselves – just like any other man – and take positions of responsibility in political parties. This does not seem to me to square with the logic of the Council. The priest is – normally – a man for all: he cannot be the man of a party or a faction. Exceptions are always possible: I am thinking of Don Sturzo and

[65] Hebblethwaite, *Year of Three Popes*, p. 97.
[66] Ibid., p. 97.

Ignatius Seipel.[67] But we have to beware of deceiving ourselves: in time politics tends to devour those who go in for it.[68]

Luciani strongly approved when Cardinal Urbani condemned the *Comitati Civici* ('civic committees') of the Venetian Professor Luigi Gedda, head of Catholic Action 1952–58, who had attempted to turn Catholic Action into an arm of the Christian Democratic Party and, far worse, into an ally of the Neo-Fascists.[69] Through these 'civic committees', a thinly veiled front organization of clericalist outlook, the hierarchy had been able to exercise some considerable control over the political activities of Catholics. Now they were taking a more neutral stance. However, Luciani was realistic enough not to project the Italian experience onto the rest of the world. Alberto Papuzzi asked him for his opinion of Camilo Torres (1929–1966), the aristocratic Columbian priest and sociologist turned revolutionary killed by government troops whilst fighting with the Army of National Liberation (ELN) guerillas. Luciani thought carefully before answering that 'in Brazil and Columbia it was true that a few families had everything while many others went hungry'.[70] Then he saw his visitor out.

On 17 September 1969 Cardinal Urbani died unexpectedly in Venice at the age of sixty-nine following a heart attack. The choosing of his successor proved to be difficult and controversial. Initially Pope Paul's choice fell on his 'little bishop', Luciani, who was both 'a local man' from the Veneto, and a by now well-known and active member of the doctrinal commission of the Italian Conference of Bishops (CEI). It was while he was in Rome from 19 to 22 November on work for this body that he was informed of Pope Paul's wishes.[71] But Luciani was reluctant

---

[67] Luigi Sturzo (1871–1959) and Ignaz Seipel (1876–1932) were two priests who were active in the inter-war years, in Italy and Austria respectively, in the field of democratic Christian political and social action. Sturzo founded the Partito Popolare Italiana (PPI), the forerunner of the Christian Democrats, in 1919.

[68] Hebblethwaite, *Year of Three Popes*, p. 98.

[69] Movimento Sociale Italiano (MSI). That Cardinal Urbani should condemn this trend was noteworthy, as he himself was noted as 'a mainstay of the conservative wing of the Church and particularly so among the Italian bishops': *Tablet*, vol. CCXXIII, 27 Sept 1969, p. 961.The committees were at their height in the 1950s, having some 2 million members. Gedda (1902 – 2000).

[70] Hebblethwaite, *Year of Three Popes*, p. 98.

[71] Scopelliti and Taffarel, p. 184.

to move, and said so. 'I am not in good health and my voice gets weaker daily' he explained, but Pope Paul merely replied 'A microphone will help your voice, while as for your health, trust in God'.[72] Next the idea of appointing the conservative Cardinal Antonio Samorè or Mgr Franco Costa, the general assistant of Catholic Action, was mooted. However, a group of a hundred Venetian laity wrote to Pope Paul to protest at the way the local Church had been excluded from the process of choosing a new patriarch. They claimed that 'all the members of the Church should take part in the choice of a bishop'.[73] Interestingly, this argument showed definite Rosminian influence: in answer, Pope Paul consulted widely, though in secret. Once more Luciani became the favourite candidate and this time, reluctantly and under pressure, he had to accept. He was appointed as Archbishop and Patriarch of Venice on 15 December 1969;[74] Venice celebrated, unaware that Luciani would rather have remained in Vittorio Veneto.

---

[72] *Tablet*, CCXLII, 24 September 1988, p. 1089.
[73] Hebblethwaite, *Year of Three Popes*, p. 99.
[74] AAS, LXII, 1970, p. 6.

Chapter Four

Patriarch of Venice and Cardinal 1969–1978

Before he left for Venice, the people of Vittorio Veneto made Luciani a donation of one million lire. He gently declined the gift and suggested that the people should donate the money to their own personal charities, explaining: 'I came to you owning nothing, and I want to leave you owning nothing'.[1] He did, however, accept the honorary citizenship of Vittorio Veneto, bestowed on 1 February 1970.

On 14 January Luciani had been elected as President of the Episcopal Conference of the Triveneto,[2] and on 8 February he entered the city of Venice as Patriarch, the forty-fifth since the title was established in 1451. Traditionally, the entry into the city of a new patriarch took place amongst a procession of gondolas and much pomp. Luciani disliked, and was a little embarrassed by, such ostentation, and so he cancelled the ritual welcome. After being greeted by the mayor, Signor Favaretto Fisca, on the jetty of St Mark's Square, he made a speech that immediately established his personality in the minds of his listeners:

I am a child of the mountains who knew Venice only in imagination and as though in a dream. I thought to myself in Venice the canals are alive with gondolas, and the gondolas are moored along them just as naturally as we tether beasts to a tree. There, among the many houses and churches, rose a tower, so meek and gentleman- ly that when it decided to fall down, it took care not to hurt anyone[3] ... As student and professor I came to know Venice through books. A Venice first of all built on piles in the lagoon, then much threat-

[1] Hebblethwaite, *Year of Three Popes*, p. 100.
[2] Vian, p. 676.
[3] A reference to the campanile of San Marco which collapsed in 1902 and was rebuilt in 1903–1912.

ened, then a royal city, then the powerful Serenissima, and finally declining into a provincial capital: but all the time a unique city that could attract the admiration and the attention of the world and draw visitors to it from everywhere.

As Bishop of Vittorio Veneto I came to know it through the workers who every day 'migrated' from the diocese down to Mestre and Marghera: this was the 'other' Venice, with few monuments but so many factories, houses, spiritual problems, souls. And it is to this many-faceted city that Providence now sends me.

Signor Mayor, the first Venetian coins, minted as long ago as AD 850, had the motto 'Christ, save Venice'. I make this my own with all my heart and turn it into a prayer: 'Christ, bless Venice'.[4]

Luciani had neatly encapsulated the various facets of Venice; old and new, sacred and profane, rich and poor, and with the diocese covering a population of some 365,000, the city was a very different proposition from rural Vittorio Veneto. Venice shows little outward sign of change since the time of Antonio Canaletto (1697–1768). There are no modern buildings, except at the western end of the city, around the Piazzale Roma and the Rio Nuovo. The Venetians themselves retain their sense of independence and their love of pageantry, reflecting their rich history. Their city is one of the most beautiful on earth, but it wears an air of slightly melancholy, decayed splendour. It also, now as then, suffers from a declining population as the young look for work in the mainland industrial towns of Marghera and Mestre; by 1970 the resident population of the *centro storico* was already down to 111,550. The popular image is of Venice in the sun, full of tourists; during the winter it is much quieter and subject to floods, fogs and snow. A city of endless, fascinating contrasts indeed – and, as a diocese, one acknowledged to be difficult to control.

People, however, found Luciani's personality refreshing: they were 'struck by his directness, simplicity and humour'[5] and largely responded. Thus he made an equally good impression later the same day when he delivered a homily in the packed Basilica of St Mark's. Inevitably, he made deferential reference to his two predecessors who had become popes in this century. He quoted the inaugural sermon of Giuseppe Sarto (later Pope St Pius X): 'Though I have never seen you before, I already carry you in my heart: you are my family and will remain in my love'.[6]

---

[4] Hebblethwaite, *Year of Three Popes*, pp. 100–01.
[5] Ibid., p. 101.
[6] Ibid.

Luciani had the ability to naturally, almost unconsciously establish personal links with people, whether individually or in a crowd. Effortlessly, his personality, his message, communicated itself directly to each of his listeners. It is a gift that cannot be learnt; often the subject is scarcely conscious of it. Luciani made Sarto's words his own. He was fully conscious of the fact that his mission must be directed at his whole flock and also at every individual within it. Aware of the enormity of this task, and also of his own human frailty, he quoted from Ezekiel 34 and admitted that this was an easier attitude for God to take than for his bishops.

Luciani also quoted Angelo Roncalli[7] (later Pope John XXIII), who had said to Luciani when ordaining him bishop in 1958: 'You have come to the episcopacy from teaching theology. That is an excellent thing. But it is not learning, not exquisite and abstruse language that make a good pastor, but rather complete availability to God and to men'.[8] These sentiments had indeed always been at the heart of Luciani's ministry; he had always been accessible to his priests and the people. Luciani drew no anti-intellectual conclusions from Pope John's words, but rather called for a mature, questioning faith, a brave start in traditionalist Venice:

> Today science has developed tremendously and purified our knowledge from a thousand defects and *naïvetés* of the past; our religious knowledge, likewise, has to be cleansed of certain *naïvetés* which science contradicts and which were not, anyway, part of the authentic Christian revelation. The language and intellectual attitudes of men today have changed: and we should have the courage to change our style, offering the truth in fresh language, adapted to the new attitudes. There is today a tendency to think that religious life consists merely in worship and a few moral acts. We must, rather, make room in our whole being for the truth, and let it become the centre of our thinking so that it can direct our entire life.

---

[7] Roncalli was Patriarch of Venice from 1953 to 1958, and reigned as pope from then until 1963. The process for his beatification was initiated by Paul VI on 7 December 1965 at the end of the Council. Bishop Luigi Bettazzi had already called for his canonization by acclamation at the Third Session in 1964. However, Paul cautiously 'balanced' this popular act by simultaneously initiating the cause for Pius XII. John was beatified on 3 September 2000.

[8] Hebblethwaite, *Year of Three Popes*, pp. 101–02.

He concluded his homily:

> You are all brothers', says the Lord. And Patriarch Roncalli liked to say: 'I am your brother Joseph.' The glory of the diocese of Venice will not be based on its magnificent churches or its splendid past, but on the efforts we make to realize fraternal union among ourselves.[9]

This hopeful, open-minded homily, in essence a summary of Luciani's approach towards his ministry, found an appropriate context in the liturgy. Over a hundred priests of the diocese concelebrated and the bidding prayers or 'prayer of the faithful' were led by a young woman, a nun, and two young men. When Mass was over, the boys of the Capella Marciana – the choir school of the Cathedral – spread throughout the congregation in groups of four and sang a *Te Deum* in harmony with men situated in the organ loft. It was a Venetian festival, celebrated with organs and bells.

The very next day, however, Luciani plunged himself into the practical work of his ministry, what he loved most. Declining various social engagements, and accompanied by his new secretary, Father Mario Senigaglia, he paid a respectful call on the elderly mother of his predecessor, before visiting the seminary, the women's prison of Giudecca, the men's prison of Santa Maria Maggiore, finally celebrating Mass at the Church of San Simeone. And it was fortunate that the new patriarch was showing himself to be pastorally active, for attendance in the churches of the 127 parishes was very low, containing more tourists than faithful. He began his pastoral visit on 25 October.

Luciani himself lived on the fifth floor of the patriarchal palace, a relatively modest building next to St Marks, built between 1837 to 1850 and giving onto the Piazzetta del Leoncini (rather unsuccessfully renamed Piazza Giovanni XXIII). In his room was an oval table covered with books and papers, a sofa and two armchairs with ochre-coloured covers, and a Byzantine icon of Our Lady given to him by Pope John. In one corner were precious bone fragments, relics of the first Patriarch of Venice, St Laurentius Giustiniani, Patriarch from 1451 to 1456. The reception room was like all such places: red chairs arranged around a big conference table, uninspiring pictures on the walls. As one of the Sisters of Maria Bambina who looked after

---

[9] Hebblethwaite, *Year of Three Popes*, p. 102; 'I am your brother Joseph': Genesis 45:4.

Luciani explained, 'He always said that the best pictures of Venice were those one saw through the window'.[10] On the door of his chapel, a tiny place with room only for two kneelers, was his episcopal coat of arms.

Luciani watched little television, apart from the news and dramatizations of the works of Goldoni: for relaxation, apart from his books, he derived especial pleasure from listening to the works of the Venetian baroque composer Antonio Vivaldi,[11] along with those of J. S. Bach, Mozart and Beethoven. He was inspired by the paintings of Giotto and Fra Angelico, possessing a fine reproduction of the latter's 'Madonna'. He would often be in bed by nine o'clock and be up again by five in the morning, and admitted himself that he ate 'like a canary', being satisfied in the evening with coffee and a brioche. On some evenings, as Sister Vincenza would later reveal, Luciani would quietly go to his favourite restaurant in Venice, dressed as an ordinary priest, to eat seaweed pizza.[12]

As usual, Luciani encouraged all those in need to call on him. His availability and generosity meant a constant and, for his secretary, sometimes exasperating stream of unfortunates, the poor and unemployed, the lonely, ex-prisoners, ex-prostitutes, alcoholics and addicts. All received a welcome, quietly and without fuss.

Sometimes his anonymity could be dangerous, but Luciani typically took it in his stride. Mgr Giovanni Ronchi rather quaintly relates that:

> In Venice, his outer modesty could be touched by the hand: the Patriarch used to go for a walk in the evening, alone, by the narrow, romantic streets of the city of the lagoon. Nothing distinguished him from a simple Priest. One night, he arrived at his residence with a swollen cheek. 'What happened?', asked the frightened nuns who came to him. 'Oh, nothing in particular – the Cardinal answered – I met a drunkard, "a Priest-eater". He hit me on my face. And here I am'. The Police investigations did not give any result.[13]

---

[10] Ibid., p. 103.

[11] *Time*, 112, 4 Sept 1978, p. 8. Antonio Vivaldi (1678–1741), received the tonsure from the Patriarch of Venice in 1693, and was ordained in 1703. Because of his red hair he got the nickname of the 'Red Priest', although soon after his ordination he gave up saying Mass, and became a simple abbé with no pastoral duties. He is probably best known for the violin concertos that make up 'The Four Seasons', published in about 1725.

[12] Thomas and Morgan-Witts, p. 335.

[13] Mgr Giovanni Ronchi, 'A Punch In The Face'.

For his annual holidays, never longer than a week, Luciani always stayed in the convent of the Madonna of Pietralba, run by the Servants of Mary, situated 1,521 metres up in the beautiful Alto Adige near Bolzano (Bozen), a shrine he once walked to as a boy with his mother on pilgrimage – a distance of some sixty kilometres. Bortola had carried flour with her so that she could make polenta and feed her children along the way. The popularity of the Sanctuary as a place of pilgrimage since its foundation in 1553 is attested to by the large number of ex-votos left by the pilgrims.

Luciani was not tempted by monastic life, however; for lunch he would go to a trattoria in the village and enjoy talking with the locals, followed by a quiet game of bowls (*bocce*). He loved also to walk in the woods, listening to the singing of the birds. Between 1972 and 1977 he was accompanied by Don Mario, and the pair would climb the nearby Corno Bianco (Weisshorn), 2,316 metres, at a steady pace.[14]

A valuable glimpse of Luciani's more personal life and qualities at this time was given in an interview with John Cornwell by Dr Lina Petri, Luciani's niece:

> My uncle was very fond of me, because I was the only daughter of his sister. He was very close to her. We were a close family and we saw a lot of him. When he was in Venice I used to stay with him four or five times a year, and when I came to study medicine in Rome [at the Policlinico Agostino Gemelli] I used to see him every two months when he came down to the Episcopal Conference. He was thought to be a bit naïve, you know, the 'smiling' Pope, but actually he was strong. He was shy, but he knew what he wanted and how to get it. He was humble, but he was quite determined. Don't forget he was a Patriarch and a Cardinal.
>
> When I was sixteen years old, in the fifth year at the Ginnasio, I stayed with him on my own, without the rest of the family, during the Christmas holidays in Venice; he had two little guest rooms in the house. I spent a lot of time with him, especially at lunch and at supper. He would tell me where to go in Venice, he paid a lot of attention to me, just like a father or mother.
>
> He gave me money to buy new clothes. He even did this when I was here in Rome. He said to me, 'Here, take this money and go and buy yourself a new dress.' I was just a student; it meant a lot to me. He knew that the family on my mother's side was poor, and he had it on his conscience that my mother didn't get an education because she had to start work at the age of eleven to help pay for

---

[14] Muthig, p. 170; Hebblethwaite, *Year of Three Popes*, p. 104; Yallop, p. 244; Seabeck, p. 49.

him to go to the seminary. Whenever he gave me money he used to say, 'Listen, Lina, this isn't the Church's money, this is my own money given to me personally as a conference fee. I can use it how I wish, and *you* are the very first of my poor.' He was always scrupulous like that. And he always told me that he would be deep in debt to my mother for the whole of his life.

He and my mother were really close. When it was announced on TV that he was Pope she collapsed on the ground, not with joy or happiness, but with sheer pity for him, because of the huge burden he would have to bear. Nobody thought for one moment that he would be made Pope. We have a photo of him that we all keep and cherish. He's holding her face in his hands after he had become Pope. They were on their own at the beginning of the audience with the family, and she said to him, 'Just think, Albino, if only mama were here!'.[15]

When he had guests Luciani gave them a warm welcome. From 21 to 28 September 1970 the second meeting of the Anglican-Roman Catholic International Commission (ARCIC) met in Venice, hosted and paid for by the patriarch. After one dinner at the palace given for the Commission one of the Catholic delegates, Mgr Philippe Delhaye of Louvain, joked 'we must put off the day of reunion for as long as possible if it enables us to have meals like that'.[16] In actual fact the meeting produced useful working papers on the Eucharist, Ministry and Authority. During his time in Venice Luciani would sponsor further ecumenical meetings between Catholics and members of the World Council of Churches, Pentecostalists, Jews and Anglicans.

Besides this congenial activity, Luciani was rapidly plunged into the more problematic concerns that came with his high office. In 1970 there were violent strikes and demonstrations at Mestre and Marghera on the mainland. Luciani made pleas for patience and 'negotiation round a table', but this moderate advice did not find favour with the politically conscious workers of the Socialist and Communist unions. He strongly criticized their militant activity, but also faulted the Church because it had 'sided with interests of management, swallowing the violence engendered by the police,'[17] an unusual statement from a senior member of the Italian hierarchy!

In 1971 he tried to intervene in a conciliatory way when 270 workers at the SAVA alumina and aluminium plant were made redundant. He urged the employers 'never to forget the dignity

[15] Cornwell, *A Thief in the Night*, pp. 238-9.
[16] Hebblethwaite, *Year of Three Popes*, p. 103. Delhaye (1912-1990).
[17] *Tablet*, CCXXXII, 2 September 1978, p. 854.

of their workers' and exhorted the workers to 'seek for a nego-
tiated solution'. Luciani was quickly attacked from both sides
for his trouble, and it could be that the pain these two incidents
caused him contributed to his mild doctrinal drift rightwards
during his time in Venice. In 1898 the young Angelo Roncalli
had recorded the words of Cardinal Giuseppe Sarto: 'I was
much more fortunate and lived much more happily when I was
a simple country curate than now when I am seated on the
Patriarchal throne of Venice'.[18] Albino Luciani would have
agreed profoundly with these sentiments!

Another problematical issue still alive at this time, in which the
patriarch became peripherally involved, was that of the 63,654
Italian soldiers who had been listed as missing in the Soviet Union
at the close of the Second World War. Some 40,000 of these men
were still unnaccounted for, despite spasmodic indications that
some of them at least were very much alive. One such indication
came when several weekly picture magazines published a photograph taken at a food pavilion at a recent Moscow Fair. In the
picture was a clear head shot of Private Nello Magnabosco, a truck
driver with the Pasubio Division on the Russian Front in 1941,
recognized by many in his home town of Chioggia. His brother
tried for several years, without success, to get an entry visa for
the Soviet Union. Finally he took his case to Albino Luciani, who,
because of its importance, brought it to the attention of the Pope.
Paul duly passed the case on to Padre Werenfried Van Straaten –
the 'Bacon Priest' – founder in 1964 of 'Aid to the Church in Need'
and famous for his undercover activities behind the 'Iron
Curtain'.[19]

On 27 January 1971 Luciani visited Paris with a Venetian
delegation to attend a benefit for the preservation of the city of
Venice. Whilst there, he called on Cardinal François Marty, the
Archbishop of Paris.

From 12 to 14 June Luciani made a pastoral visit to Basle and
Muttenz in Switzerland, visiting immigrant Italian workers and
recalling his own father's travels. He returned home by way of
Annecy, capital of the Haute-Savoie *departement* of France, in
order to visit the shrine of St Francis de Sales.

From 29 June to 6 July Luciani headed a diocesan pilgrimage
to the Marian shrine at Lourdes in the Hautes-Pyrénées, the
scene, between 11 February to 16 July 1858, of numerous

[18] Pope John XXIII, *Journal Of A Soul*, 1980 (rev.), Geoffrey Chapman, p. 436.
[19] Lo Bello, pp. 114–15. Van Straaten (1913–2003).

visions of the Virgin Mary by St Bernadette Soubirous (1844–1879). The Virgin revealed her identity with the words 'I am the Immaculate Conception'. Bernadette's visions were declared to be authentic in 1862 by Pope Pius IX; the underground spring of the Massabielle grotto was declared to have miraculous healing properties and the cult of Our Lady of Lourdes was authorized. The site soon became a major centre of pilgrimage, especially for the sick and disabled, and a basilica above the grotto was consecrated in 1876.

Luciani penned a pastoral letter on his return.[20] He wrote of the Madonna's aversion to sin, but also of her tenderness for sinners. He wrote of eternal salvation, prayer and respect for authority, balancing this last with the statement: 'Woe to the bishops before God if by their pusillanimity and laziness they fail to make good use of their authority.' He concluded:

> While I was at Lourdes, I meditated on these points. On one hand I had before my eyes priests, doctors, ladies, stretcher-bearers, many of whom were very young, all lavishing their care day and night on the sick, the heart and centre of our pilgrimage; and on the other hand, there were the sick themselves who won our hearts with their resignation and gratitude. Then I told myself: *How beautiful is the Christian community when its members love and help each other, when they pray, when they are calm and their souls are at peace, and when they do not wear themselves out in endless arguments!*

Later the same year Pope Paul gave a further demonstration of his confidence in Luciani, nominating him as one of the non-elected members of the Synod of Bishops. This had come into being on 15 September 1965 with the publication of the Motu Proprio *Apostolica Sollicitudo* of Pope Paul. In keeping with the new conciliar spirit of collegial responsibility – an interest of Luciani's at the Council as we have seen – the Synod was constituted as a permanent body of bishops whose function was to *advise* the Pope on matters that were of importance to the whole Church. However, the Pope reserved the right to make the final decisions and, whilst necessary and useful, the Synod has not as yet proved to be an outstanding success. One of the unintended benefits of the Synod is that it has been a useful meeting place for cardinals and possible future cardinals to exchange ideas, get to know each other and gain confidence and experience for conclaves.

---

[20] This was actually his second visit, having been on a pilgrimage with sick Italian priests in July 1964.

The Second General Assembly of the Synod, held in Rome from 22 October to 6 November, had as its themes 'Justice in the World' and 'The Priestly Ministry'. Two hundred and ten bishops participated in this Synod, the first to be held in the custom-built auditorium above the Nervi Hall.They had a less ambitious agenda than those of the First General Assembly of 1967 and the Extraordinary Assembly of 1969, and eventually left even the final drafting of its recommendations to specially appointed commissions. At the Synod, however, Luciani showed his true concern for the poor, especially those of Third World countries like Burundi, when he made this statement:

> I suggest, as an example of concrete help to the poor countries, that the more fortunate churches should tax themselves and pay one per cent of their income to the Vatican aid organizations. This one per cent should be called the 'brothers' share' and should not be given as charity, but as something that is owed, to compensate for the injustices being committed by our consumer world against the developing world, and to make up in some way for social sin, of which we should all be aware.[21]

Although Luciani was 'positive' about the Synod as a forum for discussing issues of current concern to the Church, he kept firmly in mind its purely advisory nature, remaining loyal, in a perfectly genuine way, to the person and position of the Pope.[22] Thus concerning the Synod he wrote:

> Some have gone so far as to suggest that decisions at the Synod should be taken on the basis of a majority vote. But that would be to apply democratic methods to the Church. The Church, however, is different, and the Synod is not a parliament. The fathers are neither legislating nor decision making -they are the consultative organ of the pope.[23]

In the summer of 1972 Luciani became involved in the controversy over the Banca Cattolica del Veneto, founded in 1892 and known as 'the priests' bank'. Until then the bank had loaned money to the clergy at very low interest rates, in order to help them carry out their priestly ministry and charitable works. Now, the low interest loans ceased; the clergy of the Veneto

---

[21] Yallop, p. 36.

[22] *L'Osservatore Romano*, n. 39 (548), 28 September 1978, p. 5 (English edition).

[23] Hebblethwaite, *Year of Three Popes*, pp. 109–10 (from *L'Osservatore Romano*, 7–8 January 1972).

would have to pay the full rate of interest, limiting the amount of good works that they could carry out. What had happened?

Since 1946 the majority shareholder in the bank had been the Istituto per le Opere di Religione (IOR) – often, if inaccurately, known as the 'Vatican Bank'. In early 1972 its holding was 51 per cent. The various dioceses of the Veneto also had small shareholdings amounting to less than 5 per cent of the total. A clear understanding existed that the IOR's holding was an insurance against any potential takeover by a third party.[24]

On 30 March 1972 the new President of the IOR, Archbishop Paul Marcinkus, acting with the full assent of Pope Paul VI, sold – via various holding companies – to Roberto Calvi, Managing Director of the Banco Ambrosiano of Milan, 37.4 per cent of the total shares, retaining only 5 per cent and making Calvi the majority shareholder. For this Calvi paid 27 billion lire, or about $45 million. It was a brilliant investment on his part, for the Banca Cattolica was one of the wealthiest and most profitable in Italy, flush with the savings of the faithful.[25]

However, the bishops of the Veneto were indignant, because the sale had taken place without any consultation: quite rightly, they felt they had a moral right to have had some say in what happened to 'their' bank. They communicated this frustration directly to Luciani, face-to-face, in his patriarchal palace. Luciani studied the matter, then complained personally to Marcinkus in his office in the Vatican. Although Marcinkus would later deny that any ill will occurred between him and the patriarch, in any event it is evident that Luciani did not receive a sympathetic hearing; one report had Marcinkus reply to the patriarch: 'Eminence, don't you have anything better to do?'.[26] Luciani returned to Venice. There was little else he could do; the deed was done, and in strict legal terms the Veneto clergy did not have a case.[27]

---

[24] Yallop, p. 37.

[25] R. Cornwell, *God's Banker*, 1984, Unwin, p. 61; Yallop, pp. 38–9, 142–3; L. Gurwin, *The Calvi Affair*, 1984, Pan, p. 19. The exact details of the 'mechanics' of the deal have been much simplified here. In 1971 the Banca Cattolica's capital was 3 billion Lire; C. Pallenberg, *Vatican Finances*, 1973, Penguin, p. 116.

[26] Gurwin, p. 21, quoting Italian magazine *Panorama*, 5 July 1982.

[27] R. Cornwell, p. 62; J. Cornwell, *A Thief in the Night*, pp. 104–5; Gurwin, p. 21. It was later claimed that on 11 November 1972 Calvi had received $3.3 million as a *personal commission* on the transaction; R. Cornwell, p. 84. The man who uncovered these facts, Milanese lawyer Giorgio Ambrosoli, was murdered outside his home on 12 July 1979; Gurwin, p. 45.

In protest, however, Luciani and many of his bishops closed their accounts with the Banca Cattolica; Luciani moved the official diocesan accounts of Venice to the small Banco San Marco.[28] Further, he tried to get the word *Cattolica* removed from the bank's title, without success. Apart from any other consideration, he felt that Calvi was tainted: he would, of course, soon be proved right, though only after his own death.

Roberto Calvi – 'God's Banker' – was by all accounts a cold, insecure man, isolated and obsessively secretive, impressed by aristocratic titles, secret societies and *potere occulto* ('hidden power'), a man full of fear and conspiratorial intrigues. All this eventually caught up with him in mysterious circumstances.

In 1981 he was convicted of currency violations, but bailed pending appeal. On 11 June 1982 he left Italy on a false passport with a suitcase full of crucial documents on Banco Ambrosiano's activities. On 17 June Calvi's secretary Graziella Teresa Corrocher, aged fifty-five, jumped from the fourth floor of the bank's Milan Headquarters. She left a suicide note condemning Calvi for the damage he had done to the bank and its employees. On the morning of 18 June Calvi's body was found swinging from scaffolding under Blackfriar's Bridge in London, the Coroner reaching an open verdict on the cause of death after a second inquest. However, in December 1998 his body was exhumed and re-examined, advances in forensic techniques showing that he had in fact been murdered. On 18 April 2005 five people accused of the crime were formally charged with murder, the trial opening in Rome on 5 October. However, on 6 June 2007 the presiding judge found all five innocent on the grounds of 'insufficient evidence', but did rule that Calvi's death was murder, not suicide. The mystery therefore continues, with about a dozen people still being investigated.

At any rate, Calvi had finally over-reached himself, thinking he could swindle even the Mafia, which used the Ambrosiano to launder its money from the drugs trade. A fall in the stock market exposed him: his fraudulent financial empire, including the Banco Ambrosiano, collapsed, with the destruction of many careers, fortunes and reputations. The bank went into compulsory liquidation on 6 August, with its liabilities exceeding its assets by 480 billion lire. Its collapse – Italy's biggest private banking failure – was due largely to bad loans of $1.287 billion (£812 million) to ten shell-holding companies in Panama, Luxembourg and Liechtenstein, backed by 'letters of patron-

[28] Yallop, p. 40.

age' dated 27 August 1981 from the IOR. The 'letters' were useless as Calvi, unknown to anyone else at the Ambrosiano, had given Marcinkus a letter in return cancelling the guarantee.

Although *most* of the money – except $40 million embezzled by Calvi – was subsequently recovered, the Vatican never acknowledged responsibility. However, on 30 June 1986 the IOR paid Banco Ambrosiano's 119 creditors $240.82 million 'on the basis of non-culpability' but 'in recognition of a moral involvement'.[29] Many concluded that the payment was, at least in part, the 'price' for securing the amicable renegiotiation of the Concordat between Italy and the Holy See.

On 25 February 1987 Milan magistrates issued warrants for the arrest of Marcinkus, the IOR's Managing Director Luigi Mennini and Chief Accountant Pellegrino De Strobel, alleging them to be 'accessories to fraudulent bankruptcy'. However, no progress was made with these proceedings, as the Holy See invoked immunity under the terms of the Concordat. Only on 21 June 1989 did Pope John Paul II belatedly accept the resignation of Marcinkus from the IOR, who then returned to the US the next year, dying on 20 February 2006.

Pope Paul continued to look on Luciani with favour and to appreciate his moderation and loyalty. In an audience granted to Venetian priest Father Mario Ferrarese, Pope Paul declared three times, 'Tell the priests of Venice that they should love their Patriarch because he is a good, holy, wise, learned man'.[30] Recommendations come no higher, and during the week 12–17 June 1972 Luciani was elected vice-president of the Italian Episcopal Conference – *Conferenza Episcopale Italiana* (CEI) – a position he held until 2 June 1975. On 16 September 1972 Pope Paul stayed at the patriarch's palace in Venice on his way to the Italian National Eucharistic Congress in Udine. In his first Angelus address on becoming Pope, Luciani recalled that

On the wide footbridge in St Mark's Square, he [Pope Paul] made me blush to the roots of my hair in the presence of 20,000 people, because he removed his stole and placed it on my shoulders. Never have I blushed so much!'[31]

---

[29] For more detail see C. Raw, *The Money Changers*, 1992, HarperCollins. Raw calculates the *real* loss to the Holy See to have been $513 million.

[30] Yallop, p. 40. It should be noted that after the pope, one of whose titles is 'Primate of Italy', the Patriarch of Venice is the most senior priest in the Italian Hierarchy.

[31] *The Teachings of Pope John Paul I*, p. 3; Angelus address of 27 August 1978. See also *The Pope Speaks*, p. 312.

Pope Paul did not make a practice of insignificant public gestures, and here he clearly showed his regard and esteem for Luciani.

Luciani's detestation of publicity sometimes caused problems. On 2 February 1973 Mgr Oreste Rauzi, the eighty-five year-old Auxiliary Bishop of Trent, died. Luciani was driven to Trent for the funeral by Don Mario in a grey Flavia belonging to the diocese. As the pair left the autostrada they saw a contingent of *carabinieri* and police obviously waiting to escort them into Trent. 'Drive straight ahead,' said Luciani, 'and let's see if we can give them the slip'.[32] The *carabinieri* paid no attention to the two ordinary-looking priests; the problems occurred when they arrived in Trent and were not at first recognized because the local clergy had expected their patriarch to arrive surrounded by a full motorcycle cavalcade!

Meanwhile, Pope Paul had not finished honouring his loyal and humble patriarch. At the consistory of 5 March 1973 Luciani was created a cardinal priest, the first amongst thirty prelates to receive the red biretta from the hands of Pope Paul that day.[33] His titular church in Rome was the Basilica of San Marco adjoining the Piazza Venezia, which once formed part of the Venetian Embassy. In his speech Luciani made the perceptive, accurate observation that 'Vatican Council I has many followers and so has Vatican Council III. Vatican Council II, however, has far too few'.[34] He wanted to consolidate the gains – and heal the wounds – created by the Second Vatican Council before leaping further into the unknown.

The same spirit infuses the homily he gave on 'Christ the Liberator' on 7 March back in Venice:

> 'New theology?' And welcome! At times, however, it's not a matter of a new theology, but of old Gnosis. The presumptious mentality of the old gnostics often re-surfaces: 'We give explanations at the highest level of science; we eat up the poor, obsolete and bygone explanations of the Magisterium!'. The method of Gnosis is also coming back, that of taking the arguments and terms of the Catholic faith, but only partially, usurping the right to sift them and select them, to understand them in one's own way, to mix them

---

[32] Hebblethwaite, *Year of Three Popes*, p. 104.

[33] *Acta Apostolicae Sedis*, LXV, 1973, pp. 165, 203. There are three Orders of cardinals: bishops, priests, deacons.

[34] Yallop, p. 41. Vatican Council I was held 8 December 1869 – 1 September 1870. 'Vatican Council III' is the hypothetical next Council called for by some progressive theologians.

with extraneous ideologies and to base adherence to the faith no longer on divine authority but on human motives; on this or that philosophical opinion, for example, on the match between a particular argument and predetermined political choices adopted earlier.

On 22 November *L'Osservatore Romano* published an article of Luciani's entitled 'The Identity Of The Priest' in which, speaking from the heart, he outlined the simple, practical, theological focus and justification of the priesthood. In essence, he decried the 'watering-down' of the position of God in pastoral action. Priests should preach social and political liberation as one of the elements constituting the Gospel, not as the one constituent of the Gospel: the latter would neglect the salvation of individuals.

Luciani reminded his readers of the basic Article of Faith that the Son of God became man, while remaining true God. A priest participated in 'the priesthood of a Christ who is mediator and saviour, because he is God become man'. Therefore, there could be no denial of the divine nature of Christ without abandoning the whole *raison d'être* of the priesthood. Luciani had now arrived at the crux of his argument, the nature of the priesthood as revealed by Christ's personal example:

> It is not so much a question of defining our priesthood as of living it. We have the example of Christ before us; he was meek and humble, chaste, poor and obedient. He prayed intensely, keeping in continuous touch with the Father, and taught people to pray. He was extremely anxious to be a teacher, a plain, popular teacher; of him his hearers said: 'Nobody has ever spoken as this man speaks' (Jn. 7:46). He gave himself entirely, generously for the spiritual and material needs of men. He sacrificed himself, offering his life for all and ordering the apostles to repeat it until his return. There we have all we want: to imitate him, to aim at a holiness perfected day by day by the generous exercise of the ministry and of charity, to live with him a life of intimacy, bound to him by trusting love and intense prayer, that is the important thing for us.[35]

Luciani believed that it might be beneficial for priests to join together in associations such as the Apostolic Union that he himself had joined in 1935. Again, he did not miss the opportunity of advocating loyalty to the Pope in 'these difficult times', adding that the Apostolic Union, with its renewed statutes,

[35] *L'Osservatore Romano*, n. 47 (295), 22 November 1973, p. 11 (English edition).

could help its members 'to adapt themselves within proper limits to the new times and to the true and good elements that exist in the ferments pervading the world today'. In language quite radical for a senior member of the hierarchy, he responded to the call for a more biblically based piety:

> Let us remove from popular devotions the superfluous incrustations, let us see to it that the people are, and feel that they are real participants, especially in Holy Mass.

Further, Luciani stated that priests were bound to 'shed the light of the Gospel – in appropriate and due measure – on the burning human problems of the day'. There were 'grave injustices' in the world that priests should strive to remove. The field of education was another contentious issue. He summarized some of the issues being hotly debated, concluding:

> Since not everything is false and evil in this medley of ideas, we must keep ourselves well informed, support or at least not oppose what is not bad, try to use new methods in the religious instruction of the children, stimulate the parents to play their part with clear and correct ideas and the determination to act.

Luciani realized that his brief overview did not begin to answer all the dilemmas faced by priests, and concluded with a few words of comfort and warning:

> Of Christ, the perfect priest, and the model for all priests, St Paul wrote: 'For Christ did not please himself; but, as it is written, "The reproaches of those who reproached thee fell on me"' (Rom. 15:3; Ps. 69:10). Again, it is from St Paul that the words applied to St Francis in the Liturgy are taken: 'Far be it from me to glory except in the cross of our Lord Jesus Christ, by which the world has been crucified to me, and I to the world' (Gal. 6:14). These two thoughts of St Paul may help us in two situations: when we have the the impression that we – as priests – are outdated and useless instruments, while we would like to see the tangible results of our work; and when, in order to embody ourselves better in the world, we might be tempted to laicize ourselves or become more mundane than we should.[36]

However, 1974 was a year in which pressing social and political concerns began to crowd in on Luciani, and one of the most

---

[36] *L'Osservatore Romano*, n. 47 (295), 22 November 1973, p. 11 (English edition).

controversial of these was the issue of divorce. It could well be described as the biggest policy crisis of his patriarchate. Divorce had become legal in the Italian State on 18 December 1970 with the passing of the Fortuna-Baslini law by a small majority, despite the intense opposition of the Church. In the spring of the year in question the right-wing of the Christian Democrats and their Neo-Fascist allies called for a referendum on the subject in an effort to bring down the Centre-Left coalition government. Setting up a National Committee for a Referendum on Divorce (CNRD) under Dr Gabrio Lombardi, they collected 1,370,134 signatures, far more than the 500,000 needed to demand a referendum as a constitutional right.[37] Luciani was deeply opposed to the referendum: he was convinced that it would divide the Church and result in the majority voting to retain the divorce laws unchanged. This would underline the defeat of the Church's position. On the nature of divorce itself he had this to say:

> I think that matrimonial love is giving of oneself to another, but so intimate and noble, so loyal and trustful, that in a way it claims everything, and in another it excludes everyone. That love is a decapitated love if we admit reservations, a temporary nature, and rescindability. So that divorce is the sword of Damocles hanging over conjugal love: its presence generates uncertainty, fear, suspicion.[38]

Others, perhaps less idealistic and more pragmatic, took other views. Archbishop Benelli was convinced that the Church could win the debate and the referendum. The debate itself, both within the Church and throughout Italy, became intense. On 16 April, shortly before the referendum was due to take place, the local branch of FUCI,[39] the student group organized by a priest in San Trovaso[40] in Venice, produced a forty-page pro-divorce statement entitled 'Pastoral And Political Reflections On The Occasion Of The Referendum'.[41] They printed five hundred copies and sent one to every bishop in the Veneto region. Luciani read and considered the document carefully that same night. He had tolerated the students 'radical experiments in

---

[37] Hebblethwaite, *Paul VI*, p. 619.
[38] *Time*, 112, 11 Sept 1978, p. 46.
[39] Federazione Universitaria Cattolica Italiana, affiliated to Azione Cattolica Italiana.
[40] Venetian dialect corruption of Santi Gervasio e Protasio.
[41] Reproduced at www.bibliosofia.net/files/FUCI.htm.

liturgy and biblical research':[42] now they had gone too far. The next morning he simply withdrew the students' spiritual counsellor, Don Napoleone Barbato, also warning twenty of his priests that if they persisted in participating in pro-divorce rallies, he would suspend their right to say Mass. Contrary to popular belief he left the student group intact.

Luciani's action made national headlines. Many in the Church saw it as an act of courage, whilst many secular commentators attacked what they saw as another instance of bigotry on the part of the Italian Church hierarchy. What had outraged Luciani was not so much the students' pro-divorce statements, based on 'their argument that Italy had become a pluralist society',[43] but the fact that they had added force to their ideas by quoting extensively from a wide selection of church authorities, leading theologians and several documents of the Second Vatican Council. Regarding the use of the latter in such a way, Luciani held that it was a twisting of church teaching. He almost felt protective towards the great social documents of the Council in which he had played a part, and although it was now accepted that error had rights in the modern Church, there had to be limitations to those rights.

Thus the students quoted from *Dignitatis Humanae* extolling the rights of the individual:

> Protecting and promoting the inviolable rights of man is the essential duty of every civil power. The civil power must therefore guarantee to every citizen, through just laws and through other suitable means, the effective protection of religious liberty.[44]

These noble sentiments were used as a peg on which to hang the statement that followed:

> On other occasions the Church has found itself confronted by serious situations in society against which the only reasonable possibility was obviously not the use of repressive methods but the adoption of moral criteria and juridical methods which favoured the only good which was then historically possible: the lesser evil. Thus Christian morality adopted the theory of the just war; thus the Church allowed the legalization of prostitution (even in the Papal States), while obviously it remained forbidden on a moral level. And so also for divorce . . .[45]

[42] *Time*, 112, 4 Sept. 1978, p. 9.
[43] Hebblethwaite, *Year of Three Popes*, p. 106.
[44] Yallop, p. 51.
[45] Yallop, pp. 51–2.

'Expediency' was an unacceptable argument as far as Luciani was concerned, and he naturally and rightly felt that the Council documents had been quoted out of context and with a meaning alien to their original ones. This alone destroyed the validity and credibility of the argument, whatever it's other merits. However, in the field of divorce as in others, Luciani's personal belief was more generous and liberal – one might say charitable and Christian – than his public doctrine, as Mario Senigaglia later testified:

> It was more enlightened than popular comment would have it. He could and did accept divorcees. He also easily accepted others who were living in what the Church calls 'sin'. What outraged him was the biblical justification.[46]

Meanwhile, Luciani's conviction proved to be correct: the referendum, held on Sunday 12 May 1974, resulted in a 59.1% to 40.9% majority for the pro-divorce lobby, a wider margin than most expected.[47] Few regions voted to repeal the 1970 Law, and then only by small majorities, while industrial cities like Turin voted for divorce with majorities nearing 80%. In Venice the pro-divorce vote was 70.8%. Over forty priests who had advocated pluralism in Italian society were suspended by the hierarchy. The Church was divided – Pope Paul publicly expressing his 'astonishment and grief' at the outcome – and a dilemma was created for those who had to try to reconcile the differences between Church and State.

Of equal contentiousness at this time was the growing crisis over abortion. According to World Health Organization estimates, by the mid-seventies Italy had the highest rate of illegal abortions in Western Europe, with the correspondingly highest number of accidental deaths. Many other women simply went abroad for the operation. Luciani of course joined in this passionate national debate. Using the disarmingly innocuous medium of an imaginary letter to the eighteenth-century Venetian dramatist Carlo Goldoni, in November he published his most forthright views in the *Messagero di Sant' Antonio* of Padua.

He wrote partly in response to a 25 July press conference statement by a woman Deputy of the Italian Parliament, whom he identified only as Signora N, who proposed the liber-

---

[46] Yallop, p. 52.
[47] *Tablet*, CCXXVIII, 18 May 1974, p. 489; Castelli, p. 24, n. 16.

alization of abortion, declaring: 'The right to live one's own sexuality is today restricted by the sense of sin ... There exists the woman's right to live her own sexuality not only within a family or with reference to a future family'.[48] Luciani pondered on how many women agreed with the Deputy's thesis; if numerous, he considered that it would constitute *'not so much an advance of 'feminism', but a collapse of femininity and of humanity'.*[49]

Then he outlined his own views in a vigorous, almost combative style that reads like the manifesto it is:

> You heard the woman parliamentarian: liberalized abortion and new regulation for the advancement of women.
>
> But will it be real advancement? Investigations by Japanese, English and Hungarian physicians into abortions, even those carried out under the aegis of the law and in specialized hospitals, show that such abortions are always a trauma for the woman's health, for later child-bearing, and for later children. Psychologists and psychiatrists, furthermore, indicate other bad consequences: these, they say, perhaps generally lie dormant in the unconscious mind of the woman who has had the abortion, but they surface later, in moments of crisis.
>
> We have said nothing of the moral aspect: abortion not only violates the laws of God, it goes against the deepest aspirations of woman, troubling her greatly.
>
> In many cases, too, the abortion does not free the woman so much as it frees her partner, whether he be her husband or not, from nuisances and irritations, allowing him to give free rein to his sexual desires without assuming the obligations involved: it is a retrocession, rather than an advance, for women with regard to men.[50]

Having outlined the effects of abortion, Luciani now attacked the defences of the pro-abortionists and their allies, denying that regulation was a lesser evil, preventing illegal abortions and the deaths of numerous young women:

> But the experience of other countries proves that illegal abortions do not diminish at all with the advent of legalization, unless this permits *any* abortion. The number of the young victims of illegal operations is, besides, often exaggerated, for propaganda purposes. 'Other civilized nations have legalized abortion: why not Italy?'

---

[48] Luciani, *Illustrissimi*, (US ed.), p. 243.
[49] Ibid., p. 244. My emphasis.
[50] Ibid.

I reply: If legalizing abortion is an error, why should we also err? A disease imported into Italy from outside does not become health just because it is imported; it becomes infection, epidemic.

In defence of abortion an even more specious line is beginning to be heard. 'What is important,' they say, 'is the twelfth week'.

Yes, because that is the moment of the *two lives* of the foetus in the maternal womb. The first life is *human*, still vegeto-animal; the second is *humanized*, but humanized on one condition. Namely, on the condition that the parents, the moment the presence of the new little being has been perceived, 'call it to be born', want it, recognize it, create a bond of love with it, thus conferring on it the 'right to be'. And they add: as a rule, the parents have to make this call; if, however (a very ugly *however*), there is a motive, the parents can, without sin, reject the child and expel it. At most, to avoid abuses, so that it will not be too easy to expel, they should consult doctors or magistrates before deciding.

Alas, . . . those 'two lives' exist only in the heads of some theologians. Outside those heads, in the mother's womb, concretely, there is only one life to make its imploring appeal to parents and to society. These theorists suppose that, after the famous twelfth week, it is up to the parents to create rights in the new being. The opposite is true: it is the new being that, from the very beginning of his development, creates duties in the parents.

And, beyond the new creature, there is God, who has commanded: 'Thou shalt not kill!' 'Life', Vatican Council II wrote, 'must be protected with the greatest care from the moment of conception; abortion, like infanticide, is an abominable crime' [*Gaudium Et Spes*, Pt. II, Ch.I, Para.51].[51]

This was a blunt Luciani who had lost the more nuanced sensitivity he had shown over the issue of birth control. What, for instance, was to happen in cases of pregnancy after rape? Or in cases where the mother's life was in grave danger? Or in cases where the foetus was recognized to be severely deformed?

However persuasive his arguments, Luciani was running counter to opinion in Italian society, as he himself undoubtedly realised. Pressure grew. A pending referendum on abortion in 1976 led to a national political crisis forcing elections. Finally, Parliament passed a law, one of the most liberal in Western Europe, just prior to the deadline for holding another referendum. On 14 April 1978 the Chamber of Deputies signified its approval of state-subsidised abortions by a vote of 308 to 275. On 18 May the Senate also voted 160 to 148 in favour and it duly became law on 6 June.

---

[51] Luciani, *Illustrissimi*, (US edn), pp. 245–6.

The new Law 194 permitted abortion on demand for any woman aged eighteen years or over if she decided that childbirth would endanger her physical or mental health. Women under the age of eighteen needed the consent of a parent or guardian. After the first trimester (three months) a medical certificate was required to terminate a pregnancy. The implementation of the new law initially caused problems in many of Italy's overcrowded hospitals and clinics as many physicians – mostly male and Catholic – took advantage of a clause allowing them to withdraw from the state abortion scheme on grounds of conscience.

The statistics proved Luciani to be wrong in thinking that the illegal abortion rate would not drop, or that abortion was considered by some as an 'easy', permissive option. After legalization ... there was an initial increase in incidence, with a peak of 234,000 abortions performed in 1982 ... (380.2 per 1,000 live births). Subsequently, there has been a steady decline, with 139,000 abortions performed in 1999 ... (266.9 / 1,000). From 1983 to 1998 it is estimated that illegal abortions dropped proportionately even more from 100,000 to 27,000. Further, '*it has been observed that in most cases, abortion is not considered to be the contraceptive method of choice but instead results from the failure to control fertility using other methods*'.[52] The status quo was maintained when, on 17 May 1981, in two referenda, Italians voted overwhelmingly to leave the abortion law as it stood. Despite John Paul II's vehement opposition to abortion only 30% supported his position.

To return to our chronological narrative: from 27 September to 26 October 1974 Luciani attended the Third General Assembly of the Synod of Bishops, held in Rome and having as its theme the 'Evangelization of the Nations'. It was the first Synod to concentrate on the Church's mission to the World, reflecting a more outward-looking approach than previously. Two hundred and nine bishops participated, about half of them from the developing world, and forming altogether about 1 in 15 of the total world number. However, despite being the best prepared Synod to date, once again it proved to be a disappointment and ended without promulgating any definitive document, merely a hastily drafted general message and a list of major concerns.

One of the principal points of debate concerned the relation

[52] A. Spinelli and M. Grandolfo, 'Abortion In Italy', *BEN-Notiziario ISS*, vol.14, no. 4, April 2001. My emphasis.

between faith and political commitment. Some bishops, mainly Latin Americans, demanded a 'theology of liberation', with salvation coming from liberation from injustice and oppression. Eventually a final text was agreed on that emphasized that, amongst other things, the faith needed to be adapted to local customs and usages, whilst maintaining unity with Rome. However, in his closing address Pope Paul firmly opposed any divergence in theology and strongly restated his primacy.

Thus, although the discussion sessions were largely conducted in a spirit of lively realism, some voiced the opinion that the Synod was in danger of merely becoming a formal and routine exercise. Luciani called for greater unity and responsibility among the members of the Church. Whilst agreeing that the whole community had the task of evangelization, he stressed that Christ's words 'He who hears you hears me' were addressed to the bishops specifically. He continued, saying that: 'There is a lot of superficial writing around today from people who act as though they were teachers in the Church, without bothering to receive a mandate from the *magisterium* or even trying to be in harmony with its teachings'.[53]

Luciani kept up his personal contacts: as did other cardinals, he would visit Karol Wojtyla in his room at the Polish College (*Pontificium Collegium Polonorum*) in Rome, in order to continue debating points of mutual interest.[54]

Also in 1974, Albino Luciani attended a very different sort of conference – though of equal importance – this time one in Venice on the environment and the use of world resources. Here again he showed his concern for the world around him. He said that its resources should not be used without thought of the consequences. 'Man has the power to change the world in a thousand ways: he should not use this power to harm what God has created'.[55] It was this conference which has provided us with one of the best 'Luciani anecdotes' (many of which are amusing and have an attractively naive edge to them). At this conference Luciani became engrossed in talking with one of the foreign participants. Still having much to discuss when the time came for him to leave, Luciani invited the ecologist to call on him at home. 'Where do you live?' asked the ecologist. 'Just

---

[53] Hebblethwaite, *Year of Three Popes*, p. 110.

[54] G. Blazynski, *John Paul II: A Man From Krakow*, 1979, Weidenfeld and Nicolson, p. 127. 'When Luciani had been elected Pope John Paul I, Wojtyla would point out the chair in which he had sat'.

[55] Dean, p. 9.

next door to San Marco' responded Luciani. 'Do you mean the Patriarch's Palace?' 'Yes.' 'And whom do I ask for?' 'Ask for the Patriarch'.[56]

The patriarch also took a keen interest in his local environment. Whilst on one of his informal tours around Venice, he stopped to congratulate the restorers of the Church of San Nicolò dei Mendicoli connected with the British Venice In Peril Fund, essaying 'a few words in his halting English'.[57]

In November Luciani was in Austria, visiting the Hofkirche in Innsbruck. Built between 1553 to 1563 and originally Franciscan, it is the church in which Queen Christina of Sweden famously abjured Protestantism on 3 November 1655 whilst on her way to Rome. Of immediate interest to Luciani, to the left of the main door, were the tombs of the Tyrolean patriot and hero Andreas Hofer (1767–1810) and his fellow partisans Joseph Speckbacher and Joachim Haspinger, OFM Cap. Hofer was a brave fighter and convinced Christian; he was finally betrayed and executed by a French firing squad in Mantua. Luciani was inspired by Hofer's 'Christian faith ... and the close-knit quality of [his] people': he wished to channel such faith and strength to 'restore the unity of souls, the unity of the Church and of the country'.[58]

Pope Paul declared 1975 to be a Holy Year, keeping to the tradition that there should be one celebrated every twenty-five years. Obviously the 'main event' was in Rome, although the crowds attending were not as large as had been hoped for. Venice, fittingly, took as its role the portrayal of the religious aspects of Italian culture.

Besides attending events in celebration of Holy Year, Luciani continued to be engaged in ecumenical work, work that would be remembered after his death. Thus, in 1978 Rabbis Saul I. Teplitz and Henry Siegman of the Synagogue Council of America sent a telegram to the Vatican on that sad occasion, which read in part:

> His passing is a loss to the Church and to mankind. In his all too brief ministry he symbolized a hope for reconciliation between people ... We are particularly mindful of the Pope's warmth for the Jewish people. His inspiring words in a meeting with Jewish leaders in Venice in 1975 gave us hope that he would carry forward the

---

[56] Hebblethwaite, *Year of Three Popes*, p. 104; Yallop, p. 50.
[57] C. Hibbert, *Venice: The Biography Of A City*, 1988, Grafton, p. 326.
[58] Luciani, *Illustrissimi*, pp. 276, 279.

work of Catholic/Jewish understanding. We are moved too by the prayer he uttered for peace in the Middle East and his expressed recognition that Israel's security was a necessary prerequisite for that peace.[59]

On Sunday 15 June municipal elections took place in Italy, with most areas holding provincial and regional elections at the same time. In common with most of the Italian hierarchy Luciani spoke out against the Communists. In doing so he gave evidence of his rightward drift since his days in Belluno and Vittorio Veneto. He publicly declared that Christianity and communism were incompatible. He said that these priests who suggested that it was permissible for Catholics to vote for left-wing candidates were advocating a *scelta di classe*, an option for the working class, and were thereby placing the liberty of Italy at risk.[60] In the event the Communists made great gains and came within 2.5% of becoming Italy's largest single party. The whole episode – and his similar comments in October 1977 – showed why so many people, who only knew him from his public face during his Venice years, wrote him off as a conservative. When be became Pope, responsible only to God, Luciani could shed this image and reveal his true, more liberal one. Thus, what appeared 'new' in him to many people, had in fact been part of his beliefs and personality for a long time. Just like Pope John XXIII before him, he would surprise the world-weary pundits with his vitality and humane love. In other words, his election freed him from conformity and he reversed the trend of his recent years and returned to his roots.

To return to 1975: on 30 September he was named – along with, amongst others, Cardinals Paulo Evaristo Arns, OFM, Pericle Felici and Karol Wojtyla – as a member of the Congregation for the Sacraments and Divine Worship.[61] This was to be Luciani's only slight involvement with the Roman Curia before his election as Pope. Again this meant that he was virtually unknown in some circles, whilst being rather better known to his fellow cardinals and bishops.

Luciani was also better travelled than many knew, principally because he kept quiet about his activities and, through genuine humility, kept a low profile, unlike some prelates. Cardinal Sebastiano Baggio, Prefect of the Congregation for Bishops,

[59] *Acta Apostolicae Sedis*, LXX, 1978, p. 853.
[60] Hebblethwaite, *Year of Three Popes*, p. 106.
[61] AAS, LXVII, 1975, p. 601.

gradually acquired for himself in Rome the nickname 'Viaggio Baggio' or 'Baggio the traveller' due to the nature of his power play for the papacy as Pope Paul became increasingly obviously near death.[62]

In 1975 Luciani made two visits abroad, first to Germany and, later in the year, Brazil. The first visit, on 18 May, had a duel function. As the guest of Cardinal Hermann Volk of Mainz, he participated in the thousand-year celebrations of the cathedral in that city. His other purpose was to make a pastoral visit to various Italian immigrant communities in the area. This journey led to an incident of the type of which we are becoming familiar. Motoring through Germany with Father Senigaglia Luciani arrived at Aachen. Luciani particularly wanted to pray at a very ancient altar in the cathedral. Senigaglia watched as Luciani was informed, rather peremptorily, by the cathedral officials that the altar was closed and that he should return another day. Back in the car Luciani translated this conversation for Senigaglia's benefit. Enraged, Senigaglia burst from the car, ran to the cathedral and gave the dignitaries a piece of his mind in voluble Italian. They understood enough to realize that the little priest they had turned away was the Patriarch of Venice. Now it was Luciani's turn to get angry with his secretary as he was virtually pulled from the car by the German priests. As Luciani entered the cathedral one of the still apologetic priests murmured to him, 'Eminence, a little bit of red, at least, could be useful'.[63]

From 6 to 21 November he spent time with his friend Cardinal Aloisio Lorscheider, OFM, the popular Archbishop of Fortaleza, Brazil. Whilst there Luciani visited the numerous Italian parishes to help deal with their pastoral problems, having been invited by the government to participate in events marking the centenary of Italian – and specifically Venetian – migration to Brazil; many of the original migrants descendants still spoke in Venetian dialect. He also studied the widespread phenomenon of *communidades de base* – basic communities, grass-roots experiments in practical Christianity – and other evangelical projects.[64] Once again he came into close contact with grinding Third World poverty.

During this visit he was given the degree *honoris causa* from

---

[62] Greeley, p. 86. In contrast Greeley noted, p. 252, n. 2(d), in typically colourful language, that Luciani 'apparently avoids Rome as though it were a contagious disease'.

[63] Yallop, p. 50.

[64] Murphy, p.167.

the State University of Santa Maria a Rio Grande do Sul, having presided over the great Marian pilgrimage in that city on 9 November. With characteristic thoroughness Luciani had learnt some Portuguese from two Franciscan Sisters of Christ the King in Venice, Edith Onghero (a Brazilian) and Valentina Kanton (an Italian usually resident in Brazil), in order to be able to preach to the Brazilian crowds in their own language.[65] Lorscheider later said of his visit: 'On that occasion many people hazarded the guess that one day the Patriarch of Venice could become pope.' The esteem was mutual: on his return from Brazil Luciani confided in a Venetian priest that he would be happy to see Lorscheider as pope, saying of him 'He is man of faith and culture, and he has a good knowledge of Italy and of Italian'. He added: 'The time has come to choose a pope from the third world'.[66] That Lorscheider was also a man noted for speaking out against the political violence and oppression that then beset his country is noteworthy.

Early in 1976 Luciani was in Rome, attending another Italian Bishops' Conference. Apart from making pronouncements underlining its hardening position against Communism, the conference discussed the serious economic crisis that Italy was then facing. More privately the bishops discussed how much the Vatican had lost in the wake of the collapse of Sicilian financier Michele Sindona's Banca Privata Italiana – *Il Crack Sindona* – in September 1974;[67] some estimates put the amount at $30 million. On his return to Venice Luciani wrote an article which was published in the next edition of the diocesan magazine under the title 'A Loaf of Bread For The Love of God'. He began by authorizing a collection in all churches on Sunday 29 February in aid of the victims of the Guatemalan earthquake disaster of 4 February, which had killed some 23,000 people, left another 80,000 injured and a million homeless. Then he commented on the state of the Italian economy, advising his readers that the Italian bishops and their ecclesiastical

---

[65] *Esquiú*, 17 September 1978, (Argentina).

[66] Hebblethwaite, *Year of Three Popes*, p. 80. In the 1978 conclave Luciani consistently voted for Lorscheider – and vice versa.

[67] Sindona was an 'associate' of Roberto Calvi and Licio Gelli, 'Venerable Master' of the 953 member illegal P2 masonic lodge. Extradited from the US, he died in hospital in Voghera on 22 March 1986, four days after being sentenced to life imprisonment by a Milan court for hiring William Aricò to murder Giorgio Ambrosoli in 1979. He had drunk coffee containing potassium cyanide in his Milan prison cell; whether it was suicide or murder remains unproven, though the initial Inquest's verdict was suicide.

communities were committed to showing practical signs of understanding and help. Further, he deplored:

> The situation of so many young people who are looking for work and cannot find it. Of those families who are experiencing the drama or prospect of sacking. Those who have sought security by emigrating far away and who now find themselves confronted by the prospect of an unhappy return. Those who are old and sick and because of the insufficiency of social pensions suffer worst the consequences of this crisis . . .
>
> I wish priests to remember and frequently to refer in any way they like to the situation of the workers. We complain sometimes that workers go and seek bad advice from the left and right. But in reality how much have we done to ensure that the social teaching of the Church can be habitually included in our Catechism, in the hearts of Christians? Pope John asserted that workers must be given the power to influence their own destiny at all levels, even the highest scale. Have we always taught that with courage? Pius XII while on the one hand warning of the dangers of Marxism, on the other hand reproves those priests who remain uncertain in [the] face of that economic system which is known as capitalism, the grave consequences of which the Church has not failed to denounce. Have we always listened to this?[68]

Luciani then demonstrated his own distaste for Church wealth – in the spirit of practical help that he had earlier recommended – continuing:

> I have urged and authorized parish priests to get rid of gold plate, pearls and rings offered by the faithful as ex votos. I want to set an example myself by offering the golden chain which used to belong to Pope Pius XII and which was given to me by Pope John XXIII when he ordained me bishop. It is not much in view of the immensity of the needs. But perhaps it will help to make it understood that the real treasures of the Church are [as St Lorenzo said] the poor, the disinherited, the weak, and that they should be helped, not by occasional almsgiving, but in such a way that they can rise to the standard of life and the level of education to which they have a right.[69]

Luciani also stated that he intended to auction a valuable pectoral cross with gold chain and the ring of Pope John, which had both been given to Venice by Pope Paul during his

[68] Yallop, p. 55.
[69] Hebblethwaite, *Year of Three Popes*, p. 111.

September 1972 visit. The proceeds from all these activities were to go to the Centro Don Orione for mentally handicapped children.[70] Luciani himself raised the equivalent of £8,000 just by selling gold plate belonging to the patriarchate.[71] Later in his article he developed his theme that Christianity should be both caring and practical, by quoting two Indians. Firstly, Mahatma Gandhi: 'I admire Christ but not Christians'. This he followed by expressing the wish that perhaps one day the profound words of the great Christian missionary Sadhu Sundar Singh (1889–1929) would no longer be true:

> One day I was sitting on the banks of a river. I took from the water a round stone and I broke it. Inside it was perfectly dry. That stone had been lying in the water for a very long time but the water had not penetrated it. Then I thought that the same thing happened to men in Europe. For centuries they have been surrounded by Christianity but Christianity has not penetrated, does not live within them.[72]

Luciani's vision of the Church was thus one of a community of caring and concern: 'the combination of doctrinal rigour and social open-mindedness is not uncommon among Italian churchmen'.[73] The response to his article was naturally mixed. Some applauded him, whilst some of the traditionalists of Venice attacked him for, as they thought, betraying the heritage of the city. A deputation of this latter group came to see him in his office. Having listened to their grievances, he replied simply:

> I am first a bishop among bishops, a shepherd among shepherds, who must have as his first duty the spreading of the Good News and the safety of his lambs. Here in Venice I can only repeat what I said at Canale, at Belluno and at Vittorio Veneto.[74]

The divisions becoming increasingly apparent within the Italian Church at this time, as old certainties began to break down in a fast-changing society, disturbed Luciani. What he viewed as priestly indiscipline particularly grieved him, and this is reflected in an Easter sermon that he gave:

---

[70] Don Luigi Orione (1872–1940) was the founder of the Little Work of Divine Providence (Piccola Opera Della Divina Providenza) for the care of orphans, the elderly and the needy. Canonized 16 May 2004.

[71] Dean, p. 8.

[72] Yallop, p. 56. Singh uttered these words in 1920.

[73] Hebblethwaite, *Year of Three Popes*, p. 111.

[74] Yallop, p. 56.

Some are in the Church only as troublemakers. They are like the employee who first moved heaven and earth to get into the firm but once he had the job was perpetually restless and became a pestilential hair shirt on the skin of his colleagues and his superiors. Yes, some people seem only to look at the sun in order to find stains on it.[75]

On 14 July Pope Paul wrote to Luciani to mark the quatercentenary of Titian's death.[76] In his letter the Pope expressed the hope that the celebrations might be a cause of inspiration to mankind to honour religion with the beauty of his art and to preserve for this and future generations the high ideals of the Christian and human spirit that are expressed and transformed by art. He pointed out that from his earliest days, Titian had always given attention to sacred subjects and displayed an intense religious awareness. Titian, Pope Paul said, bore a continuous witness to the reality and vitality of the religious experience.

Further, that Titian's many paintings of the Mother of God bore witness to his faith in the salvation accomplished by Christ the Redeemer and to his reverence for his Mother ... What the Holy Father was, above all, drawn by, however, were those works that evidenced a delicate but vigorous personal faith, works whose genius of colour and form have survived the tests of time and are still able to inspire today.

This is a form of catechesis of which the cultured Luciani must have approved! January 1976 also witnessed the first publication in book form of Luciani's now-famous *Illustrissimi* – literally 'the Most Illustrious Ones'. Luciani himself later described the genesis of the work, and his method revealed typical imagination coupled with sober practicality:

When I preach in St Mark's, I have a hundred, a hundred and fifty, at most two hundred listeners. Half of them are tourists who don't understand Italian, and the other half are wonderful people but they are ... well, getting on in age. Then the editor of the Messagero di Sant' Antonio [of Padua] said to me: 'Write for us, and

---

[75] Yallop, pp. 50–1.

[76] Tiziano Vecelli, born c.1489, died in Venice, 27 August 1576, the leading painter of the Venetian High Renaissance. For the full Italian text of Pope Paul's letter, see *Acta Apostolicae Sedis*, LXVIII 1976, pp. 552–5. The following account is taken from the *Tablet*, CCXXX, 4 Sept 1976, pp. 865–6.

your audience will increase a thousandfold'. He convinced me.[77]

Illustrissimi consists of a series of forty letters to a variety of historical, literary and fictional characters. Each of the letters makes a moral point whilst commenting on aspects of modern life in a delightful, informal manner. Taken together, they form an invaluable insight into Luciani's mind and outlook on life, and demonstrate once again the apparent ease with which Luciani could communicate on a popular, yet still meaningful level. Based on experience, the book is firm on moral standards, but full of tolerance, sympathy and understanding, addressed to 'ordinary' people in ordinary language. His ability – and some of his views – was all the more unusual in a member of the Italian hierarchy.

Illustrissimi cannot be called a great work of literature, but it is a very good book and it is successful in its aim in that it communicates the Good News effectively by first engaging people's interest and then winning their hearts. It is relaxed and friendly in tone, being richly and intelligently anecdotal and conversational. Luciani left the writing of theological treatises to others; his letters are to characters that have become friends through long familiarity. The work is wide-ranging in scope: Luciani wrote comfortably and naturally on issues of relevance to ordinary people because he freely and easily mixed with such people in his own life. Likewise, *Illustrissimi* is contemporary in its language, whilst still firmly expressing fundamental Christian values like prudence, responsibility, humility, fidelity and charity.

The book shows much evidence of broad, reflective reading and thought on Luciani's part, despite its deceptively simple style. Thus, though there is genuine humour in it, there is also an underlying note of sadness in some parts. Luciani knew only too well the increasingly atheistic, materialistic trend in society, and yearned that Christian values should once again come to form the basis of that society. Perhaps he also realized that that was unlikely in the foreseeable future in some parts of the world. What of Luciani's choice of 'correspondents', and how 'progressive' are the views contained in his letters? Some of his choices are obvious, like Jesus and St Thérèse of Lisieux; some are surprising, like Giuseppe Gioacchino Belli, the nineteenth-

---

[77] Hebblethwaite, *Year of Three Popes*, p.107 (from *Il Tempo*, 27 August 1978). The letters first appeared between February 1971–December 1974.

century Roman poet; whilst others are obviously of Italian interest or note – few outside Italy would have heard of St Romedio's Bear![78] There were also some surprising ommissions; there were no letters to Antonio Rosmini, St Carlo Borromeo, Pope St Gregory the Great or Pope St Pius X.[79] With regard to his views, Luciani showed himself to be open-minded but, as always in his public statements, orthodox. Where he scored was in his generous interpretation of 'rules' in practice, paying attention to the spirit of the law not the letter. He recognized human weaknesses, made allowances, and with charity tried to help and offer advice. As with Pope John, sterile condemnations were not in his style.

Despite his increasingly 'centrist' political inclinations during his years in Venice, Luciani was still positive concerning the genuine improvements in society brought about by the Left. Thus in his first letter, to Charles Dickens, he wrote:

> The workers ... have become ... united by the trade unions and the various forms of socialism, which can undeniably claim to have been the main means of promoting their welfare almost everywhere.[80]

Luciani went on to note how the workers had advanced to achieve their economic and cultural goals and how, through the unions, they now had more say in their own fate. Further he stated, in forthright language: 'All this has come about through sacrifices, by overcoming opposition and obstacles'.[81] These were the 'abuses of capitalism, which was, and in certain cases still is, a wicked system';[82] strong words coming from Luciani, but he hadn't finished. He further criticized the rich nations for allowing poverty and insecurity, unemployment and deperson-

---

[78] Luciani's grandparents used to walk miles to get to the sanctuary of St Romedio, and Luciani himself visited it about November 1972: *Illustrissimi*, p. 133. St Romedio was a fourth-century hermit, who is honoured in the dioceses of Trent and Brescia. Pius X confirmed his cult in 1907. Feast Day, 1 October.

[79] *Time*, 112 4 September 1978, p. 8; Father Herbert Ryan, SJ states that Pope St Pius X was Luciani's 'favourite saint'. I can find no other authority that agrees with this, whilst Luciani himself is on record as saying that he had a personal devotion to Pope St Gregory the Great: see *The Teachings of Pope John Paul I*, p. 5. Whilst quoting Pius X in his sermons, Luciani was more interested in the former's personal sanctity and catechetical example than in his reactionary thought and intransigent policies.

[80] *Illustrissimi*, p. 17.

[81] Ibid., p. 17.

[82] Ibid., p. 18.

alization, 'the frantic rush to grow rich, and the exaggerated, crazy use of unnecessary things'.[83] His message was a plea for the unity and solidarity of peoples, the need to care for others and to trust in God.

In writing to G. K. Chesterton Luciani looked at their common belief that the world was becoming increasingly terrifying and separated from God. To those who would reply that the rationalist removal of God from the scheme of things brought 'progress', he had a ready answer:

> Yes, but this vaunted progress is not everything that was hoped: it also brings with it missiles, bacteriological and atomic weapons, the current process of pollution: things which – if provision is not made in time – threaten to bring catastrophe on the whole human race.[84]

Without the recognition of God, a human being risked becoming a machine possessed by machines, a number manipulating numbers ... Luciani thus emphasized the teaching of the Second Vatican Council that 'a Christian, precisely because he is a Christian, must feel more committed than ever to fostering progress, which is for the good of all, and to supporting social advancement, which is meant for everyone'.[85] True progress could only come through the practice of Christian values.

In his letter to the Members of the Pickwick Club Luciani warned against excessive pride, whether personal or group: 'From this flow the errors of racialism, parish pumpery, and imperialism, embraced by millions'.[86] Writing to Carlo Goldoni, in the letter already referred to in the context of abortion, he contrasted the 'feminist' Goldoni with the 'anti-feminist' Shakespeare, finding the former 'more human, more just, closer to the reality of then and of today, even if your 'feminism' now seems bland. Since your times, in fact, women have made some conquests! Conquests that, for the most part, are positive'.[87] In commenting on their improved social position Luciani expressed his wish 'that women may achieve new conquests, but just and lofty ones, developing everything the Lord has revealed about the true greatness of women'.[88]

Luciani wrote to St Teresa of Ávila as a practical, self-

---

[83] Ibid., p. 18.
[84] *Illustrissimi*, (US edn), p. 15.
[85] Ibid., p.16.
[86] *Illustrissimi*, p. 91.
[87] *Illustrissimi*, (US edn), pp. 241–2.
[88] Ibid., p. 246.

possessed woman 'worth twenty men', who had carried out a 'magnificent internal reformation' of her Order and influenced the whole Church with her work and writings. He observed:

> Women, in themselves that is, do not govern – that function belongs to the Hierarchy – but very often they inspire, they promote and at times they direct ... woman is more sensitive to religion and more able to give herself generously to great causes.[89]

Luciani also had perceptive comments to make, in a letter to St Bernard of Clairvaux, on the nature of principles and prudence:

> In 1815 the official French newspaper, *Le Moniteur*, showed its readers how to follow Napoleon's progress: 'The *brigand* flees from the island of Elba'; 'The *usurper* arrives at Grenoble'; '*Napoleon* enters Lyons'; 'The *Emperor* reaches Paris this evening.' What an amazing turnabout! This must not be compared with prudence, just as it isn't prudent to have a stubborn attitude and take no account of what is obviously real or to become excessively rigid and zealously upright, more royalist than the king, more papist than the pope.
> This happens. Some people seize on an idea, then bury it and guard it for the rest of their lives, defending it jealously without ever examining it again, without ever trying to check what has become of it after all the rain and wind and storms of events and changes.[90]

There is an interesting corollary to all this. On 13 July 1976 Luciani wrote to the eminent Swiss theologian Professor Hans Küng of Tübingen, thanking him for a personally dedicated copy of the Italian edition of *Christ Sein* ('Essere Cristiani', translated into English as 'On Being A Christian'). He wrote that, despite his imperfect knowledge of the language, he had already 'read it in part' in the German original. A copy of this had been given to him by Bishop Joseph Gargitter of Bolzano and Bressanone in the German-speaking South Tyrol.

Luciani wrote that 'I have found some very beautiful passages there. You have a gift for writing: you could be able to do much good. I confess that I have remained doubtful about some points (I'm not a specialist). About others I am in disagreement'. In return he sent Küng a copy of *Illustrissimi*, describing it, typically, as being 'a work of mine without pretensions'.

---

[89] Ibid., pp. 234, 235.
[90] *Illustrissimi*, p. 53.

Küng noted that 'This work of his surprises me: he is a theologian and a patriarch who knows how to write not only pastoral letters and devout sermons but real letters (almost encyclicals) to the great ones of the past in an elegant and very humane style. I have read with pleasure and enjoyment these collected letters of the book of the patriarch . . .'. Two years later, when Luciani was elected Pope, Küng wrote 'I am gladdened by your election and I like to hope that your pontificate [will] be able to respond to the urgent expectations of millions of men who have a thirst for God'. Further, he sent a copy of his latest book, *Existiert Gott?*, but sadly Luciani was dead before it arrived.[91]

From 24 August to 2 September the eighth meeting of ARCIC was held at the Casa Cardinale Piazza, Madonna dell 'Orto, Venice. This meeting produced the 'Agreed Statement On Authority In The Church' which was published on 20 January 1977. From 10 to 13 September Luciani presided over the commemorative celebrations for the millennium of Croatian Marian devotion at Split on the Dalmation coast of Croatia – then Yugoslavia – as the official representative of the Italian Episcopal Conference. He spoke of Fr Leopold Mandic, whom he had met so many years before as a young priest, and of his desire for reconciliation between Catholics and Orthodox.

From 30 October to 4 November the first ever congress of Italian Catholics was held in the imposing Palazzo dei Congressi in the EUR suburb of Rome, with the theme 'Evangelization and Human Promotion'. Luciani and his fellow Cardinal, Giovanni Colombo of Milan, 'as well as over half of the Italian bishops *deliberately stayed away*'. The congress, with its 1500 delegates and 120 bishops, met to consider a multiplicity of issues, including: the burgeoning dissident groups in Italian Catholicism, the splits caused by the divorce referendum, the growing self-awareness of the Italian Church as a *local* church, political links with 'Marxist-inspired' parties, their position on the forthcoming abortion legislation in the Italian Parliament, and much else. Luciani and the rest stayed away because it was self-evident that such a congress could never 'reaffirm the unity of Italian Catholicism' on so many fundamental matters, and any 'papering over the cracks' would inevitably, if unfairly, reflect badly on Pope Paul.[92]

---

[91] Translations from photocopies of the originals supplied by Professor Küng, translated by Dom Leander Hogg, OSB. My thanks also to Andrew Walby for pre-publication access to Küng's *Disputed Truth: Memoirs Vol. 2*, London, Continuum, 2008, especially pp. 392–4.

[92] Hebblethwaite, 'Paul VI', pp. 661–6, especially p. 664.

At this time Luciani got a new Private Secretary. Mario Senigaglia was named as a Monsignor – a *Cappellano di Sua Santita* – on 7 October, and left to take over the parish of Santo Stefano in Venice. As a replacement Luciani appointed Father Diego Lorenzi, a member of the Don Orione Fathers, who had studied theology in England and been ordained there in 1967. He had done his doctoral thesis on Cardinal John Henry Newman (1801–90) at the University of Padua, obtaining a *summa cum laude*. Lorenzi had first met Luciani in December 1973, having been assigned the task of establishing an institution for the handicapped at Chirignago. He was having trouble raising funds, and mentioned his problem to Luciani. The patriarch's immediate response was to auction his episcopal ring to raise money for the institute.[93] At the time Lorenzi joined Luciani he was still aged only thirty-seven. It was a 'meeting of minds'; the two men got on well together and soon became friends.

In May 1977 Luciani delivered a forthright homily, a masterpiece of condensed clarification, on the thorny issue of the intransigent, ultra-traditionalist Archbishop Marcel Lefèbvre and his beliefs. Lefèbvre – a reactionary monarchist deeply influenced by the anti-semitic *'nationalisme intégral'* of Charles Maurras' pre-war *Action Française* – had already been suspended *a divinis* on 24 July 1976 by the Congregation of Bishops. He and his supporters strongly opposed the conciliar teachings on Religious Liberty and Ecumenism which Luciani himself had been 'converted' by, and post-conciliar liturgical reforms, wishing to retain the Tridentine Mass celebrated in Latin. They looked to impose rigid certainties on a world requiring mature questioning and reflection, an essential element of the human condition.

Luciani's thoughtful, early-expressed opinion is interesting, coming as it did a full eleven years before events played out to their 'inevitable' conclusion, and should help dispel any lingering notion that he was naturally conservative himself in any perjorative sense of the word. His hopeful, inclusive approach was in direct opposition to Lefèbvre's peremptory, exclusive one.

Answering an imaginary interlocutor – a typical Luciani device – he denied that the Council's Declaration on Religious Liberty represented a 'surrender', whilst affirming that the

---

[93] J. L. Allen Jr., 'Word From Rome', *National Catholic Reporter*, vol. 2, no. 24, 7 February 2003.

Church had indeed changed course. Thinking back to the Inquisition's murderous campaign against the Cathars of southern France and similar cases, Luciani said that the Council had now 'humbly confessed' that in the Church of the past 'there have at times appeared ways of acting which were less in accord with the spirit of the Gospel and even opposed to it' (*Dignitatis Humanae*, 12). He continued: 'The Council, therefore, has admitted a series of not at all praiseworthy facts, it has deplored them, it has said they shouldn't be repeated; in this sense, it has changed'. One thing remained the same, however: the Church 'has kept safe and handed on the doctrine received from the Master and from the Apostles . . . no one is to be coerced into faith . . . ' (*Dignitatis Humanae*, 12).

Faith – or lack of – was a matter purely for the individual, standing before the eventual judgement of his or her God. There should be no coercion. The Council upheld 'social and civil freedom in religious matters', denying the right of any political power, Catholic or not, to interfere. Faith, Luciani said, 'supposes a free consent. And Jesus has never imposed his truths by force when he preached; he has never stopped the opposite opinion's propaganda. When James and John proposed to make the fire come down from Heaven over the Samaritans, He reproached them both and said: 'You don't know what kind of spirit you are of'.

There were, however, two important exceptions to this rule of non-involvement by the state in religious matters, as defined by the Council. The state should intervene, Luciani said, firstly 'when religious freedom is used by somebody in such a way [as] to endanger the freedom or the rights of others', and secondly 'regarding the common good and public order. The State, in fact, must be at the service of all, assuring a real peaceful existence in pluralism'.

In conclusion, Luciani stated that:

> The Council Fathers knew very well that the Church will always have adversaries. It was urgent for them to let everybody know the Church doesn't feel as an adversary of anyone; that it wishes to live the spirit of Christ, its Lord, who has declared Himself meek and humble, that He has come not to be served but to serve . . .[94]

Don Leandro Tiveron, SJ, Luciani's confessor, made the suggestion that Luciani should accompany the diocesan pilgrimage to

---

[94] 'Is Lefèbvre Right?', from *Gente Veneta*, May 1977.

the Shrine of Fatima in Portugal. Luciani was enthusiastic in his response: 'Yes, I will gladly go. It is a desire I have long had in my heart. It is a promise I have made the Madonna'. On 11 July 1977, accompanied by Lorenzi, Luciani celebrated Mass in the Church of the Carmelites in Coimbra. Whilst there, he spoke with Sister Lucia dos Santos, the surviving seer of Fatima, witness of the apparitions of Our Lady between 13 May and 13 October 1917. Luciani wrote about his conversation with Sister Lucia, which lasted nearly two hours, and about his view of the revelation of Fatima, in the Italian Blue Army magazine *Il Cuore Della Madre*, January 1978. Firstly, he rejected the argument that since Fatima is a private revelation, its message and implications can be safely ignored by believers:

> Someone may ask: so the cardinal is interested in private revelations. Does he not know that everything is contained in the gospel, that even approved revelations are not articles of faith? I know all that perfectly well. But the following is also an article of faith contained in the gospel: 'Signs will be associated with those who believe' (Mk 16:17). If it is the fashion today to examine the signs of the times . . . I think I may lawfully be allowed to refer to the sign of 13 October 1917, a sign to which even unbelievers and anti-clericals bore witness. And behind the sign itself, it is important to be attentive to the elements which this sign contains . . .[95]

Far from being ignored, the message of Fatima needed to be stressed with urgency. Troubled times called for all committed Catholics to participate in the work of expiation. Sister Lucia spoke animatedly and with conviction on the necessity for priests, religious and Christians 'with strength of mind, who must be as radical as the saints. It must be all or nothing if they want to belong seriously to God'.[96] Luciani further reflected on the nature and practice of everyday piety and reflection, of prayer in action. In writing of the place of the rosary in Marian devotion he used a simple, human analogy, in much the same way as he had done in *Illustrissimi*:

> Namaan the Syrian disdained the simple bathing in the Jordan. Some do as Namaan saying: 'I am a great theologian and a mature Christian, steeped in the Bible and in the liturgy through and

[95] F. Johnston, *Fatima: the Great Sign*, 1980, Augustine Publications, p. 2. On 13 October 1917, immediately after the vision of Our Lady, a 'miraculous solar phenomenon' took place, witnessed by an estimated 70,000 people.
[96] Johnston, p. 97, from *Soul* (special edition), US Blue Army magazine.

through, and they talk to me about the rosary'. Yet the fifteen mysteries of the rosary are also the Bible and so are the Our Father, the Hail Mary and the Glory – they are the Bible united to prayer that nourishes the soul. A Bible studied on the mere level of investigation could only nourish pride and empty it of its value. It is not rare for specialists of the Bible to lose their faith.[97]

To provide a focus for popular devotion to Our Lady of Fatima in his home country, Luciani asked Sister Lucia if she thought that Our Lady would be pleased if a Pilgrim Virgin was carried through Italy. Sister Lucia was enthusiastic, and so the statue was flown from Fatima to the Vatican, and just before Luciani – by now Pope John Paul I – died, 'it began a two-year journey through the country at the tomb of Padre Pio'[98] at San Giovanni Rotundo.

However, there was perhaps a little more to this meeting – held at Sister Lucia's request – than Luciani revealed at the time. According to a statement made by Edoardo, Luciani's brother, to the Italian Catholic weekly *Il Sabato*, published on 28 August 1993, Luciani came out of the meeting 'very upset':

> Every time when this meeting was mentioned in conversations with us, his face would go white. It was as if some dark thought disturbed him in his innermost self. He is [sic] quite convinced that on that day, the seer of Fatima told him something which concerned not only the Church but also his own life: the destiny that God had prepared for him.[99]

Edoardo further recalled his own last meeting with his brother, a few days before the latter's death, when the pope held him in a long embrace, 'as if it were a last goodbye'. Looking back, Edoardo said that 'everything is much clearer, when one puts together the hints given by my brother in various conversations'. Rather unhelpfully, he concluded: 'I could add other particular details, but I prefer to keep them to myself'. Others have been less reticent, it being alleged that Sister Lucia addressed Luciani as 'Holy Father', and that Luciani later confided to Venetian theologian Fr Germano Pattaro that the visionary had predicted his election.[100] At any rate, the impli-

[97] Johnston, p. 107, from *Il Cuore Della Madre*. Perhaps the 'Bible specialists' he had in mind were Döllinger, Renan and Passaglia.
[98] Johnston, p. 127.
[99] G. Leonard, 'Vision Of A Death Foretold?', *Universe*, 5 September 1993, p. 7.
[100] C. Bassotto, *Il Mio Cuore E Ancora A Venezia*, p. 116. Sr Lucia herself died on 13 February 2005.

cation is clear – Luciani was forewarned of his election to the papacy and of his early death. How much truth there is in this is hard to determine, but it is intriguing.

From 11 to 18 September 1977 Luciani attended the 19th Italian National Eucharistic Congress at Pescara, which had as its themes the Eucharist, mission and church unity. In the course of this Congress Luciani made several statements which are of interest in the light of subsequent events. Speaking on the theme of authority, he said:

> In the modern state authority comes from below, from the people. In the Church it is different. Christ alone confers authority on the pope and the bishops, and also makes clear how it should be exercised. Authority exists for the service of the faithful, entirely and solely for their good, so that they are more younger brothers of the pastors than subjects, responsible crewmen aboard the barque of the Church rather than mere passengers.[101]

He clearly showed that whilst being a democrat in political matters, when it came to the structure and life of the Church he was more traditional and indeed paternalistic. With Luciani as pope this would have presented few real problems, given the liberality and moderation of his views, his social concern and his personal humility. His comment on authority existing for the service of the faithful is a splendid echo of Pope St Gregory the Great's motto 'the servant of the servants of God'. However, with Pope Paul's reign palpably drawing towards its close, should some of those being spoken of as *papabile* amongst the cardinals become pope, then there would be trouble in store for the community of the Church.

In a sermon at the congress Luciani made an observation relating directly to the nature of the papacy itself: 'It requires three things especially: continuous and involved teaching, a dialogue unknown in previous times, and loyalty to the (Second Vatican) Council'.[102] So, whilst in Luciani's view the pope had supreme authority, it was an authority that should be tempered with humility, sympathy, consultation and service. All the evidence of his life and his own brief papacy point clearly in the direction that, had he been granted longer on the throne of St

---

[101] Hebblethwaite, *Year of Three Popes*, p. 110.
[102] O'Mahony, p. 84. When he became pope, Luciani regarded himself as 'the first amongst brothers', rather than as 'a father amongst sons' as Pope Paul had done.

Peter, he would have done his utmost to match his practice to his theory.

On 18 September Count Vittorio Cini, financier, philanthropist and friend of both John XXIII and Paul VI, died aged ninety-two. Officiating at the funeral Luciani said 'that since Cini had left a written statement that only the praises of God should be sung in Church, he could not sing Cini's praises. But the future pope had no hesitation in saying that with Cini he had always felt like a child before his father, whose behest must always be obeyed'.[103]

With barely a pause, Luciani had to attend the Fourth General Assembly of the Synod of Bishops, which met in Rome from 29 September to 28 October with the theme 'Catechesis In Our Time, with special reference to the catechesis of children and young people'. Preparatory texts had been circulated to all the bishops in April 1976, and in all two hundred and four participants took part. However, by this time a certain disillusionment with the effectiveness of the synod had set in, and the event caused little excitement. As at the previous synod, the issue of making the Church and its teaching accessible and relevant in the Third World came to the fore. This time the synod agreed with Asian and especially African prelates that to be effective, religious instruction should be adapted to specific cultures. Again, the synod refused to endorse a full 'theology of liberation', which could turn the Church into a political instrument, but equally rejected the conservative line that literal orthodoxy was more important than relevance.

Luciani himself made an interesting written intervention, bearing all his usual hallmarks of sympathy and broad understanding, distilled from many years of experience. He wrote:

> Catechesis must be concerned not only to transmit revealed truths, but to transmit them in such a way that the one who receives them will receive them with faith and be impelled to live them ... To interest and commit the young, particularly, catechesis will don Augustinian 'hilaritas'. They do not like a life bristling with 'no', bolted and padlocked, amid barriers of every kind ... They want to live, to grow, to conquer and to be protagonists ... Catechetical wisdom is to forbid them only what really cannot be permitted and fling them into action.

---

[103] Giulio Andreotti, *Lives: Encounters With History Makers*, 1988, Sidgwick & Jackson, p. 144.

He rightly declared that catechesis should begin with parents in the home, and that children could inspire companions in their peer group. Catechesis should also be realistically adapted to circumstance and social context:

> Culture should be understood here not in the classical humanistic sense of notions possessed by a few and at a rather high level, but as meaning the various people's ways of speaking, dressing, enjoying themselves, manifesting joys and sorrows, celebrating feasts, and so on.

This approach entailed taking some risks, making some innovations, but was in tune with Pope John's Opening Address to the Second Vatican Council.

Above all, Luciani felt that catechesis should 'stress that the Gospel is the News that makes people joyful . . . Let Morality be presented as man's magnanimous response to God's love; a response which cannot be made without God's help and which gives happiness not to him, but to us'.

As to the catechists themslves, they should be intellectually stimulating and fresh, readily adaptable to the capacity of their listeners, but firstly they must be morally sound. Luciani cited as the requisite moral gifts: 'holiness of life and piety (one preaches not only what one knows, but what one is; if I am not good, there comes from me, from my person, a denial of the words of goodness that come from my mouth); love for the Church and for the pupils'.[104]

In the event the synod was a 'moderate' one. Even its findings were not published, and, through circumstances, it fell to Pope John Paul II to eventually publish them in his Apostolic Exhortation *Catechesi Tradendae* on 16 October 1979 (the first anniversary of his pontifical election). In this document the Pope made revealing comments about his predecessor, claiming to take up his leads:

> Pope John Paul I, whose zeal and gifts as a catechist amazed us all, had taken them [reflections prepared by Paul VI, making extensive use of documents generated by the synod] in hand and was preparing to publish them when he was suddenly called to God. To all of us he gave an example of catechesis at once popular and concentrated on the essential, one made up of simple words and actions that were able to touch the heart.[105]

[104] *L'Osservatore Romano*, n. 41 (550), 12 October 1978, p. 3 (English edition).
[105] *Catechesi Tradendae*, CTS Do 513, p. 6.

After the Synod, Luciani wrote to his diocesan priests revealing a source of inspiration in his concern for the poor:

> When I went to the Synod of catechesis I brought with me – now don't laugh – the little old catechism of St Pius X which my mother made me read every night. There at paragraph 25 among the four sins crying out for God's vengeance was oppression of the poor and defrauding a worker of his wages.[106]

Cardinal Hyacinth Thiandoum of Dakar came to spend a couple of days with him. On All Saints Day (1 November) Luciani persuaded his African friend to preside at the ceremony, seated on the patriarchal throne. Thiandoum was deeply moved by this gesture of love and respect for the African Church. He was also highly impressed with Luciani's general popularity. 'When we walked in the streets or went in the gondolas or vaporetti, each time there were handshakes, smiles, manifestations of sympathy, which spoke much to me about the affection which the Venetian people felt for their pastor'.[107] Barely ten months later Thiandoum would consistently vote for Luciani in the conclave that placed him on the papal throne.

At this time Luciani also had cause, in common with other members of the Italian hierarchy, to speak out on matters of national interest and significance. Whilst the synod was still in session, Enrico Berlinguer, General Secretary of the Italian Communist Party,[108] put out peace-feelers to the Church by entering into a 'dialogue' with Bishop Luigi Bettazzi of Ivrea. Bettazzi had published an 'Open Letter' to Berlinguer on 6 July 1976 in the diocesan weekly *Il Risveglio Popolare*, seeking information on the Partito Comunista Italiano's (PCI) attitude to religious tolerance. Berlinguer's reply was published on 14 October 1977 in the PCI intellectual weekly *Rinascita*. Luciani, in one of his less enlightened statements, responded thus:

> At the time of Fascism people said, 'The difference between the Soviets and the Fascists is that if you have five cows, the Soviets

---

[106] *30 Days*, no. 9, 1993, p. 49.

[107] Seabeck, p. 40.

[108] Partito Comunista Italiano: with a then membership of 1.79 million, the largest communist party in Western Europe and, indeed, the largest non-governing Communist party in the world. It is ironic that Luciani grew away from the communists during the very period – from 1968 – when the Italian party had abandoned any remnants of Stalinism and adopted a progressive, democratic 'Eurocommunist' position. Many members were also practising Catholics.

take four and leave you one. The Fascists leave you all the cows, but they come and milk them all'. I'm afraid that tomorrow we'll be able to say something similar: 'The Communists of the Soviet Union rob you of almost all your freedom. The Italian Communists promise to leave you all of it, but in reality it's not so'.[109]

To the Christian Democrat-orientated review *Prospettive nel Mondo* Luciani stated 'I would like to remind my readers that Berlinguer forgot to say that article 5 of the statutes of his party obliges its members to profess nothing other than Marxism-Leninism'.[110] Relating back to the recent synod, he said

> In the Synod Hall, a bishop met me and referring to this 'dialogue', said, 'Be careful. The manoeuvre is classic. In Poland we know it well. They do everything in order to divide the bishops. If just one of you withdraws a little from the others and hints at even a reserved esteem for the Communist party, leftists everywhere will converge upon him through the press to take advantage of the situation. The Polish bishops have opposed this tactic with absolute unity.' The bishop in question was Cardinal Karol Wojtyla of Krakow, who, then as later, failed to appreciate the differences between the Polish and Italian psyche. Shortly afterwards Pope Paul, receiving Luciani in audience, said 'We thank you, Eminence, for what you did for us on that occasion.'[111]

In November Luciani publicly opposed the proposed new concordat between the Holy See and Italy, primarily because it would mean that religious studies would cease to be compulsory in State schools. He posed the question: 'By decapitating religious culture, will we not decapitate culture as well?'[112]

Another issue of immediate public concern in Italy in the late 1970s was that of domestic terrorism. Between 1969 and 1983 more than 14,000 acts of violence were committed by both left and right-wing 'urban guerillas', causing the deaths of 409 persons and injuries to 1,366.[113] This period was justly called the *anni di piombo*, the 'years of lead', and was over and above 'normal' Mafia-related activity.

Shortly after 9.00 a.m. on 16 March 1978, twelve members of

---

[109] *Time*, 112, 11 September 1978, p. 46.

[110] See L. Swidler and E. J. Grace, (eds), *Catholic – Communist Collaboration In Italy*, 1988, University Press of America, which also reproduces the texts of the Bettazzi – Berlinguer and related 'correspondence'.

[111] Seabeck, pp. 44–5, quoting article by Alberto Michelini, *'Prospettive nel Mondo'*, 43, January 1980.

[112] *Time*, 112, 11 September 1978, p. 46.

[113] F. Spotts and T. Wieser, p. 184.

the Red Brigades (*Brigate Rosse*) kidnapped Aldo Moro, the President of the ruling Christian Democrats and five times former premier of Italy, in Via Mario Fani in Rome, butchering his five bodyguards in the process. One of Italy's most respected and influential politicians, Moro was on his way to Parliament and the presentation of the new five-party government, in which the Communists, ostracized for thirty years, were represented.

The Italian government refused the terrorists demands to release their fifteen members being held for trial in Turin, and indeed refused any form of negiotiation for Moro's release. On 22 April Pope Paul made a bold and unprecedented personal appeal for the unconditional release of his friend in an open, handwritten letter, directly addressed to the 'men of the Red Brigades'. This humane approach was brutally rejected; on 9 May Moro was murdered – shot eleven times – and his body dumped in a red Renault 5 in Via Michelangelo Caetani off the Via Delle Botteghe Oscure in Rome, 'symbolically' midway between the Communist and the Christian Democrat headquarters. Moro had been virtually the sole architect of the 'historic compromise' (*compromesso storico*) between the Christian Democrats and Communists; the Red Brigades saw him as a cynical capitalist ensnaring Berlinguer and the Communist Party into 'betraying the revolution'.

On 13 May Pope Paul presided at the state funeral Mass in St John Lateran, upbraiding God for not heeding his prayers for Moro's safety. The Pope had written his own prayer that same morning: 'Lord, listen to us! You did not hear our plea for the safety of Aldo Moro, for this good, gentle, wise and innocent man, for this friend; but You, O Lord, have not abandoned his immortal spirit . . . For him, for him, Lord, listen to us!'.[114] Paul spoke for the nation, the *patria*. Naturally, Albino Luciani shared the universal revulsion created by this barbaric act. In a pastoral letter he condemned this 'cruel, cynical and terrifying deed. We are crushed, constrained to live in the midst of fear, insecurity, intimidation. Even the least traces of human compassion and fear of God are lacking'.[115] Moro's wife Eleonora and her family felt he had been abandoned by his Party, and resigned from the Christian Democrats in protest.[116]

[114] R. Katz, *Days Of Wrath: The Public Agony Of Aldo Moro*, 1980, Granada, p. 283.

[115] Dean, p. 9.

[116] For more details of the 'Moro Affair' see *Tablet*, CCXXXII, 1978, pp. 418, 480–81, 494; *Time*, 111, 27 March 1978, pp. 15–16; 1 May, pp. 8–15; 8 May, pp. 10–11; 15 May, p. 22; 22 May, pp. 8–13.

Speaking in more general terms, Luciani told a newspaper that 'the negation of God' was the root cause of such social distress.

> Tear God out of man's heart? Tell children that sin is only a fairy tale invented by their grandparents to make them behave? Print school textbooks that ignore God and deride authority? Then don't become amazed at what's happening. It's already an effort for those who believe in God to remain honest. Just imagine how it is if one no longer believes in God.[117]

Luciani looked for quiet in the eye of the storm, agreeing to give the Lenten sermons in his home village between 28 February-3 March. Don Cesare Vazza remembered a very simple, human, telling scene:

> It was Lent of 1978. In the silence of the church of Canale D'Agordo, Luciani, Patriarch of Venice, was kneeling, with the Rosary in hand, praying it. Perhaps he was alone, nearly hidden behind the column, to the right of the presbiterium, in that preferred place since he was a boy and a seminarist. (. . .) It would have been a sin to disturb that solitary prayer . . . but so I have been able to take with me the last alive image of Luciani (...) Just like a child, Luciani was there in church, kneeling with the Rosary in hand. Without moving, with head bowed, he seemed to see someone . . . in the intensity of a simple prayer, but contemplative . . .'.[118]

Despite the anguishing public events, Luciani never lost, at a personal level, his essentially warm, generous outlook, even with strangers. This was revealed on two occasions that give some insight into his life and character a few months before he became Pope, and therefore in what were sadly to be the last few months of his life. In April 1978 George Bull, visiting Venice to research material for books on Venice and on the Vatican, met Luciani in the patriarch's palace. Luciani had only been told the previous day that Bull was in Venice, but he made time and greeted his visitor most warmly. Much of the roughly thirty-minute conversation was conducted in French, and ranged over the history and beauty of Venice. Luciani talked gently 'about the materialism of the Venetians: about what was signified by the treasures of St Mark'.[119] The two men also talked about past patriarchs, and at the end of their conversation Luciani presented Bull with a large

---

[117] *Time*, 112, 11 September 1978, p. 46.
[118] Don Cesare Vazza, *The Solitary Prayer*.
[119] G. Bull, *Venice: The Most Triumphant City*, 1980, Folio Society, p. 82.

book on *The Life of St Lorenzo Giustiniani, First Patriarch of Venice*.[120] Foolishly – on his own admission – Bull neglected to ask Luciani to sign it! Then the Patriarch, with Diego Lorenzi, his secretary, showed Bull the State Rooms and the rooms of Pius X and John XXIII, on the first and second floors respectively. He spoke of the latter with particular warmth.

On taking his leave of Luciani, Bull conversed with Lorenzi on the subject of who would be the next pope, advancing the name of Cardinal Benelli as a possibility. Lorenzi spoke vehemently in favour of a pastoral and holy priest, leaving Bull with the distinct impression that he had his own patriarch in mind. Little did either of them know that Lorenzi's unspoken thought would soon become reality!

Luciani made a strong impression on Bull, who retained vivid memories of his host. He described him to me as being 'lively, not frail, but a delicate personality', having great charm, being shy, 'a great smiler', affable, gracious, 'someone overbubbling with friendliness and receptivity'. His 'sweetness of character was very evident', a slight figure, but one with whom one felt a 'great interpersonal reaction', one who showed eager interest in his visitor.[121] This is high praise from one who had met many ecclesiastics, but it is borne out by another person who – again, without preconceptions – met Luciani briefly at this time and came away much impressed.

On Sunday 2 July the Rural Dean of Shrewsbury, Reverend Ralph Lumley, was in Venice leading a party of English tourists, and they attended the feast of St Peter in the Church of San Pietro in Castello. The patriarch arrived by motor launch, and as he walked to the church from the canal Lumley took a photograph. Luciani stopped, and on finding that Lumley was English – and spoke no Italian – asked about him and his party. He then went into the church; the English party were put in the front row. Before the service started the group were invited to the Sacristy so that the patriarch could speak to them all.[122]

---

[120] *Vita B. Laurentii Justiniani Venetiarum Proto Patriarchae* by the Saint's nephew Bernardo Giustiniani. 1962, Rome, with Italian translation, Preface by Cardinal Giovanni Urbani.

[121] Information from interviews with the author 17 October 1986, 1 April 1987 and 8 June 1988.

[122] In a letter dated 9 February 1987 Rev. Lumley informed me that Luciani said, among other things, 'I have met your Archbishop Coggan'. However, in a letter dated 2 April 1987 Rev. Canon Christopher Hill, the Archbishop of Canterbury's Secretary for Ecumenical Affairs, informed me that 'no record at all of such a meeting' could be found, and that Archbishop Coggan had 'no remembrances' of it.

During the service representatives of the local fishermen brought a basket of fish to the altar, which the patriarch received, and it rested before the Nave Altar, which was being used, during the Mass. They also gave the patriarch a ring, and he presented them with one in return. During his service Luciani made special mention of the *'Anglicani Christiani'*, and, at appropriate intervals in his Italian, stated his main points in English: 'My God, I believe in Thee', 'My God, I hope in Thee', 'My God, I love Thee'. Besides being the main points of his sermon, Lumley perceptively made the point to me that they also served as the motto of Luciani's life, and that the three stars on his coat of arms stood for exactly those qualities of Faith, Hope and Love.

After the service, outside the church, the patriarch again stopped and said a farewell in English, before moving on to speak to the waiting fishermen. He blessed them and their boats; their pleasure, and Luciani's, is evident in the photographs taken by Lumley. Then, with a final wave to his new friends among the *'Anglicani Christiani'*, Luciani was whisked back to the patriachate in his motor launch.[123]

On 27 July Luciani named three priests to serve as episcopal vicars in charge of key apostolates. The three – Mgrs Antonio Meneguolo and Carlo Seno, and Don Antonio Agostini – were charged with coordinating the activities of the previously established regional and parish councils, developing a mass media apostolate and ministry to youth and workers, increasing contacts and cooperation with diocesan priests and overseeing charitable works, particularly those projects concerned with the elderly, the handicapped and the poor. The vicars were further instructed to meet on a monthly basis with senior officials of the already established federations of men and women religious, the workers' ministry team, the priests' council and the pastoral council, as well as the nascent laity council.[124]

Albino Luciani was very concerned with the quality of Catholic life within his diocese, and was not afraid to give problems a public airing. In July, from the pulpit of the Church of the Redeemer in Venice, he spoke bluntly to his congregation about clerical error: 'It is true that the Pope, bishops and priests do not cease to be poor men subject to errors and often we make errors.' He followed this general statement with a highly

---

[123] Information from letters to the author, principally that of 9 February 1987.
[124] Muthig, p. 170.

personal one: 'I am convinced that when Pope Paul VI destined me to the See of Venice he committed an error.'[125] Many of his audience, on reflection, might have agreed with his first statement. The majority probably disagreed with his second statement. None could know that he was soon to be elevated still higher, to the papacy itself.

As well as administration and preaching, Luciani kept up his flow of writing. On 25 July the Venetian newspaper *Il Gazzettino* published an article of his entitled 'Seeking God Through Everyday Work' on Opus Dei, the association of the faithful founded in Madrid on 2 October 1928 by Mgr José María Escrivá de Balaguer y Albás (1902–1975). By the time Luciani wrote his article for its fiftieth anniversary Opus Dei had spread to five continents, having over 70,000 members of eighty nationalities. It contains a tiny percentage of priests; the vast majority of members are lay men and women of the professional classes. Opus Dei's emphasis on the fact that for most people their growth in holiness should be through their own personal life and work, rather than through hours spent in formal prayer, and its success lies in the dedication and discipline of its members. This very success, and its undoubted influence in the secular sphere as well as in the Church, has led to considerable criticism, not all of it without foundation. The fact that it is on the ultraconservative wing of the Church has also inevitably made the association some enemies, it being maligned as 'The Holy Mafia' and 'Octopus Dei'.

Under Pope John Paul II Opus Dei's fortunes grew rapidly. On 19 February 1981 the Cause for the Beatification of Mgr Escrivá was presented in Rome. On 28 November 1982, in an unprecedented move, Opus Dei was elevated to the status of a 'Personal Prelature' by the apostolic constitution *Ut sit*, thereby removing it from the jurisdiction of local bishops. On 17 May 1992, Escrivá was beatified, and on 6 October 2002, only *twenty-seven* years after his death – a modern record – he was canonized!

In his article Luciani avoided controversy and concentrated on a brief historical outline of the association and comments on its basic spiritual concepts, underlining its practical approach. After quoting Escrivá's comments, made in 1967, about the nature and purpose of Opus Dei and its membership, Luciani continued:

---

[125] Yallop, p. 58.

Similar things had been taught more than 300 years earlier by St Francis of Sales. Escrivá de Balaguer, however, goes further than Francis of Sales in a number of aspects. The latter also advocates sanctity for all, but it would seem he teaches only a 'spirituality for the laity', whereas Escrivá proposes a 'lay spirituality'. Francis, in other words, almost always offers the laity the same means that the religious use, but with suitable adaptations. Escrivá is more radical. He speaks even of 'materialising' – in a good sense – the quest for sanctification. For him material work itself must be turned into prayer and holiness.[126]

Having established Opus Dei as being within the mainstream of the historical Church, Luciani made a statement of contemporary significance that linked with his sermon in the Church of the Redemptor on clerical error:

He [Escrivá] speaks also of a good and necessary 'anticlericalism', meaning that lay people should not take over the methods and roles of the priests and religious, nor vice versa ... How can a bricklayer, an architect, a doctor, a teacher, be a saint, if he is not also trying as best as he can to be a good bricklayer, a good architect, a good doctor, a good teacher? ... Faith and work competently done; for Escrivá the two go hand in hand. They are the two wings of sanctity'.[127]

Luciani went on to give an account of Escrivá's unceasing work amongst the sick and the young, and here we may see parallels with Luciani's own dedicated, practical approach, although in other ways the two priests were poles apart. Finally he gave his own, positive opinion of Opus Dei:

The extension, number and quality of the members of Opus Dei may have made some people imagine a quest for power, or some iron obedience binding the members. The opposite is true. All there is is the desire to make saints, but cheerfully, with a spirit of service and with great freedom.[128]

From 23 July to 5 August Luciani had to take a break from his work, having to spend time at the Stella Maris Institute on the Lido to counteract a possible reccurrence of gallstones, a condition for which he had previously been operated on in April 1964. His treatment at the Institute included being put on a

---

[126] *Tablet*, CCXXXII, 7 October 1978, p. 973.
[127] Ibid.
[128] Ibid.

bland diet and taking long walks morning and evening to alle-
viate the slight swelling in the ankles, and was successful.[129] A
medical showed no particular health problems.

Whilst still in hospital, Luciani made what was to be his last
public statement as Patriarch of Venice. At 11.47 p.m. on 25
July history was made when Louise Joy Brown, weighing in at
2.61 Kg (5 lbs. 12oz.), was born to Lesley and Gilbert Brown by
Caesarean section in Oldham and District General Hospital,
England. She was a perfectly healthy child. The only thing
special about her was the method of her conception: she was
the world's first 'test-tube baby'. The surgeons responsible for
this ground-breaking event were consultant gynaecologist
Patrick C. Steptoe and his associate Robert G. Edwards, a
Cambridge researcher into reproductive physiology. Lesley
Brown had a blockage of her fallopian tubes, having tried
unsuccessfully for a baby for nine years. On 10 November
1977 an egg cell was surgically removed from the mother and
fertilized *in vitro* with her husband's sperm. After two and a
half days the embryo was implanted in her uterus for normal
development.

Soon after news of the birth broke a journalist from the
review *Prospettive nel Mondo*, knowing of Luciani's interest in
reproductive concerns, telephoned to ask him for his opinion of
the matter. It was reported in advance by ANSA, the Italian
news agency, on 3 August.

Luciani began cautiously, stating that he was giving a personal opinion without being in possession of the full, scientific
facts, and that he awaited the authentic teaching of the
Church. He went on to give qualified enthusiasm for scientific
progress, noting that the development of atomic, bacteriologi-
cal and chemical weapons had been a disaster for humanity.
Having children *in vitro* brought great risks; the scientist might
become an 'apprentice sorcerer', who roused mighty forces
without afterwards being able to stem and control them. Also,
he expressed fears that 'baby factories' might develop, a new
industry feeding off financial greed and moral laxity, a matter
of regress rather than progress for the family and society.

These reservations expressed, Luciani continued on a
happier, more personal note:

> In imitation of God, who desires and loves human life, I too send
> my best wishes to the baby. As for her parents, I have no right to

---

[129] Yallop, pp. 242, 243.

condemn them: subjectively, if they have acted with honest intentions and in good faith, they may even have great merit before God
for what they decided and asked the doctors to carry out.

He then got down to the moral problem at issue, leaving good
faith out of consideration; is extra-uterine insemination, *in
vitro* or in the test-tube, permissible? In answering his own
question, Luciani noted the distinction made by Pius XII in
speaking of artificial insemination in marriage.[130] Medical intervention was permissible when it could be said to 'complete' the
sexual act by enabling it to reach its natural conclusion.
However, when conception resulted from the medical intervention in such a way that it became a substitute for sexual union,
then it was not permissible, because 'God has bound the trans-
mission of human life to conjugal sexuality.'
   This was perfectly orthodox teaching, albeit expressed
sympathetically. Luciani then made the point, obvious but very
often overlooked, that morality is concerned with human
actions; science is neither good nor bad, it is the manner in
which people use it that is good or bad. Next, he stated his
opinion which he held with regard to most moral problems, and
which may well have had a bearing on his attitude towards
Humanae Vitae:
   As for the individual conscience, we all agree: we have to
follow it always, whether it commands or forbids; the individual, however, must always strive to have a well-formed
conscience.' In conclusion Luciani explained that although the
conscience could not create the law, it had the capability to
inform our actions and judge them in the light of God's law, in
other words, that a man's conscience must command him, not
obey him.
   Luciani was the first Italian ecclesiastic to speak out, and the
only one of prominence to pronounce so favourably. Most were
either silent on the issue, or else condemned the birth and artificial insemination in general. Luciani had shown intelligence,
balance, pastoral sensitivity and open-mindedness. Firmness of
principle coupled with feeling for real people was a Luciani hallmark. He had simply expressed his own opinion, saying that he
found no reason to modify Pius XII's teaching; he did not

[130] The teaching of Pius XII is clearly and fully expressed in P. E. McKeever
'Artificial Insemination (Moral Aspect)' *New Catholic Encyclopedia*, vol.1,
pp. 922–4. Pius XII made two Addresses dealing with the subject, on 29
September 1949 and 29 October 1951 respectively.

suggest that no reasons could be found, nor did he suggest that some methods of artificial insemination might not be approved under Pius XII's principles. At any rate, his statement was soon to have repercussions.

On Sunday 6 August, the Feast of the Transfiguration of Our Lord, the fifteen-year reign of Pope Paul came to an end. He died at Castel Gandolfo at 9.41 p.m., three hours after suffering a heart attack whilst Mass was being celebrated by his bedside. The eighty-year old pope had known the end was near. On leaving the Vatican in July, Paul had said to Archbishop Giuseppe Caprio: 'We will go, but we don't know whether we will return to Rome . . . or how we will return'. On his deathbed, Paul was calm and at peace. Archbishop Gaetano Bonicelli of Albano remembered his last words: 'The death of a Pope is like that of other men. But it can always teach others something.'[131] Curiously, an old alarm clock that Paul had used ever since June 1923 when he had been briefly attached to the Nunciature in Warsaw, and which had rung at 6.30 that morning as usual and had not been rewound or reset, went off at the precise moment of his death.[132]

Almost immediately Cardinal Jean Villot, Vatican Secretary of State and now Camerlengo (papal chamberlain) for the duration of the *sede vacante*, arranged for all the cardinals to be notified by telephone or telegram. The telegrams, in Italian or French, were to the point: 'THE POPE IS DEAD. COME AT ONCE. VILLOT.' The telephone messages were equally brief. Paul's body lay in state at Castel Gandolfo until the Wednesday afternoon, when it was transferred to a spot before the Altar of the Confession in St Peter's.

Albino Luciani left Venice at 6.00 a.m. on Thursday 10 August, being escorted to the boat dock by Mgr Renato Volo, the chancellor of the archdiocese. Volo relates that Luciani wore 'a simple set of black clergyman's clothes that had been given to him as a gift by a local community of sisters for his saint name day (the *onomastico* that is still an important occasion for Italians)'.[133] He was then driven to Rome by his secretary, Don Diego Lorenzi, in his five-year-old Lancia 2000, a rather more modest car than those used by many cardinals.

[131] O'Mahony, p. 13.
[132] Pontiff, pp. 26, 111; Hebblethwaite, *Year of Three Popes*, p. 3.
[133] J. L. Allen Jr., 'Word From Rome', *National Catholic Reporter*, vol. 2, no. 22, 24 January 2003. St Albino, Bishop of Angers, died 560: his day is celebrated on 1 March.

Also, Luciani habitually sat beside Lorenzi, an indication of the personal and informal relationship between the two men. Before leaving for Rome he made another comment somewhat untypical of an Italian cardinal: to his former secretary, Mgr Mario Senigaglia, he said 'I think the time is right for a Pope from the Third World'.[134] The man he had in mind – and for whom he consistently voted in the conclave – was Cardinal Aloisio Lorscheider, OFM, the fifty-three-year-old Archbishop of Fortaleza, Brazil.

On arriving in Rome Luciani took up residence at the Augustinian Collegio Santa Monica at 25 Via Del Sant'Uffizio, to the left of Bernini's colonnade.[135] Two of his neighbours there were Cardinal James Freeman, Archbishop of Sydney, who had been created Cardinal Priest on the same day as himself, and Cardinal Reginald Delargey, Archbishop of Wellington.

The funeral Mass for Pope Paul took place at 6.00 p.m. on Saturday 12 August. For the first time in history a funeral Mass for a pope took place outdoors, in St Peter's Square, not in the Basilica, the much simplified ceremony taking place in front of an estimated 100,000 people. Cardinal Carlo Confalonieri, the eighty-five year-old Dean of the Sacred College, presided. The rest of the cardinals were paired according to seniority. Luciani was with Cardinal Timothy Manning, Archbishop of Los Angeles; the American instinctively liked the gentle Italian with the engaging smile.[136] After the Mass, Paul's body was quietly laid to rest near the tomb of John XXIII.

With Pope Paul buried the assembled cardinals now had to get on with the urgent business of running the day-to-day affairs of the Church and of organizing the conclave to elect his successor. The period between Paul's death and 25 August, the date set for the conclave to begin, was just one day short of the longest permissible time, and the longest in modern history. Referring to the cardinals who had to travel to Rome from different parts of the world, one wit remarked 'Too bad the Wright brothers couldn't make that thing fly'.[137] Nevertheless, the period was a busy one, with numerous formal General Congregations and informal meetings.

Luciani tried to consult with as many cardinals as possible,

---

[134] Yallop, p. 63.
[135] Hebblethwaite, *Year of Three Popes*, p. 113. The street was subsequently renamed Via Paolo VI.
[136] Pontiff, p. 161.
[137] Greeley, p. 111.

discussing ideas and exploring views. This was typical of him; in a more serious way conscientious preparatory work was as much a hallmark of his as the smile. It was a trait that he claimed made it much easier to reach the right decision in the end.

On 17 August Luciani paid a lunchtime visit to the Latin American cardinals who were staying at the Collegio Pio Latino on the Via Aurelia. Many of them were well known to him; Venetians had traditionally migrated to South America, and had often asked for his intercession concerning their initial problems in their new lands. As a fraternal gesture Luciani also took along signed copies of *Illustrissimi*, one for each cardinal. On his arrival his old friend Cardinal Juan Carlos Aramburú, Archbishop of Buenos Aires, led him inside to the college's main reception room where the entire contingent of Latin American cardinals awaited him. This impressive presence was a tribute to Luciani and the esteem with which he was held.

From a chair Luciani presented the books, showing obvious happiness at the pleasure with which the gifts were received. Aramburú, for the benefit of the others, asked Luciani how he came to write the letters in *Illustrissimi*. The reason he gave was simple but effective, and again showed his practical, pastoral approach. He explained that it was 'his way of bringing theology to the masses, to try and bolster their faith by relating the Gospel to people and events which everyone can grasp'.[138] Luciani's comments were well received, and at table much of the talk was about having *Illustrissimi* translated into other languages. Cardinal Aramburú's thoughts were that 'this fine and wonderful man could be a good Pope';[139] unwittingly, and completely unknowingly, Luciani had just put himself – as he would have seen the matter – in greater danger of obtaining the papacy.

Of the 131 members of the College of Cardinals only 115 were under eighty years of age and therefore eligible to vote in conclave under the ruling of Pope Paul VI's Apostolic Constitution Romano Pontifici Eligendo of 1 October 1975. Of these, Paul Yu Pin, the exiled Archbishop of Nanking, died suddenly in Rome after a heart attack on 15 August. Boleslaw Filipiak of the Curia, Valerian Gracias, Archbishop of Bombay, and John Wright, Prefect of the Congregation for the Clergy, were too ill to attend, and indeed Gracias died on 11 September and Filipiak on 12 October. Of the remaining 111

[138] *Pontiff*, p. 179.
[139] Ibid.

eligible cardinals only 55 were European – of whom 26 were Italians – whilst there were 56 non-Europeans. Thus, for the first time in history, the conclave would have a non-European majority, an accurate reflection of the demographic balance of Roman Catholicism in the world. It was also the largest conclave to date, equalled only by the one that elected Luciani's successor. The average age of the electors was 68.78 years. When not at the daily General Congregations and informal meetings, Luciani would walk and contemplate quietly in the Augustinian's gardens. The friars found him friendly, and it was noted favourably that when he was late back from the General Congregations he would sit at any available place at table. However, with his usual discretion, he refused to be drawn on the conclave. Two of the nuns persisted in asking him for his opinion on the newspaper stories of likely candidates and on where the journalists got their information. He would rather have made no comment, but they insisted that he could answer without breaking any confidentiality. Finally he said 'Journalists should learn to write less and to pray more',[140] advice some of those covering the conclave should have heeded.

Luciani was really still preoccupied with Venice. He received a visit from Mgr Giuseppe Bosa, his Vicar General, and they discussed future appointments. According to Diego Lorenzi he spent much of his free time preparing a retreat that he was due to give on 5 September.

The press, meanwhile, busied themselves with lists of cardinals considered to be *papabile*. Those who figured prominently were Giovanni Benelli, Sebastiano Baggio, Jan Willebrands, Sergio Pignedoli, Franz Koenig, Paolo Bertoli and Giuseppe Siri. Whichever cardinal was going to become pope was going to need 75 votes, two-thirds plus one of the number of electors. Few publications mentioned the name of Albino Luciani as a contender, only the *Daily American* (an English-language paper published in Rome), *Time* magazine, *The Irish Press*, and Peter Hebblethwaite's article in *The Sunday Times*, published on 27 August but written *before* the result was known.[141]

Luciani's attitude towards his chances was shown just days before the conclave when an NBC newsman in Rome telephoned him to ask for some biographical information. With

---

[140] Hebblethwaite, *Year of Three Popes,* p. 113.
[141] In July 1985 Hebblethwaite revealed his source 'Sotto Voce' to have been Fr Roberto Tucci, SJ.

self-effacing humour, Luciani observed: 'There is a Class A list of candidates, a Class B list of candidates, and a Class C list of candidates. I am surely on the Class C list'.[142] The Italian media largely agreed with him, and paid him only brief and peripheral attention. Vaticanologist Sandro Magister referred to him as 'the uncolourful Patriarch of Venice'.[143] Giancarlo Zizola, a man of great experience who had interviewed Luciani in depth in 1969, also misjudged the patriarch. A few days before the conclave he wrote a dismissive little biography entitled 'With the poor (not on the left)', in which he quoted an anonymous source who had stated:'The least you can say is that he is now the recognised leader of the ecclesiastical right, a Venetian replica of Cardinal Ottaviani'.[144]

On the day before the opening of the conclave Cardinal Hyacinth Thiandoum, Archbishop of Dakar, tried to sound Luciani out after the cardinals had finished their supper at the Roman convent.

'My Patriarch', he said, in oblique language alluding to the possibility, the desirability of Luciani becoming Bishop of Rome.

'I am the patriarch of Venice', Luciani replied.

'We're waiting for you', the Senegalese cardinal insisted.

'That's none of my business', concluded Luciani firmly. And there was no more to be said.[145]

Despite Luciani's opinion and that of the press another group, one whose opinion really mattered, were gradually reaching different conclusions; the cardinals themselves. As far back as 9 August Pericle Felici, the influential 66 year-old Administrator of the Patrimony of the Holy See and President of the Apostolic Signatura, had begun to think in terms of Luciani being a good compromise candidate. Carlo Confalonieri, at 85 years old, ineligible to vote but still an influential voice amongst the Italians in the General Congregations, also spoke of Luciani as 'a good and gentle man'.[146] Neither was Luciani as unknown as he had at first appeared; he was known to a number of the cardinals personally or by reputation, even though the fact that his visits abroad and meetings had been low-key affairs meant that he was little known to the outside world. As the *stranieri*,

---

[142] *Time*, 112, 4 Sept. 1978, p. 8.
[143] Yallop, pp. 69–70.
[144] Yallop, p. 70. The opinion was, of course, little short of ludicrous.
[145] C. Bernstein and M. Politi, *His Holiness: John Paul II And The Hidden History Of Our Time*, 1996, Doubleday, p. 158.
[146] Greeley, p. 105; *Time*, 112, 28 August 1978, p. 24.

or 'foreigners' as they were known by the Roman Curia, organized themselves, Luciani's candidacy strengthened, virtually without his knowledge.

Almost completely independently of each other different groupings – often, it may be noted with some amusement, opposed to each other – made the same assessments and coalesced around Luciani. Thus Benelli, no friend of Felici, also became convinced by 20 August that Luciani could be elected. Luciani fitted the 'description' for the next pope that was emerging from the cardinals' discussions. He had qualities that would appeal to the progressives, moderates and conservatives. For the former, there were the facts that he was 'collegial with his priests, simple in his personal life, a man of the poor, a whole life of pastoral work, a charming personality'.[147] For the latter, he was seen to be 'solid in doctrine, loyal on church discipline, firmly anti-communist':[148] truly a Man for All Seasons!

At this point Benelli decided to put together a dossier of Luciani's recent statements, including that concerning the birth of Louise Brown. It was distributed to influential cardinals in an effort to 'firm up' support for Luciani amongst the *stranieri*. The next day Leon-Joseph Suenens, another Luciani supporter, sounded out the Brazilians, the Dutch and the French, and discovered that they too were becoming more sympathetic to Luciani's candidacy. Virtually unstoppable forces had now been set in motion, and the reasons for the incredibly quick conclave become clear; a significant proportion of the electors had already settled on Luciani as their choice before they had even entered the conclave. In the first two ballots other candidates figured as votes were cast for favourite sons, out of loyalty, as marks of respect, or as the implacable conservatives tried to push their candidate Giuseppe Siri, but the issue had largely been decided several days beforehand. The outside world, in the main, remained in the dark.[149]

More to the point the object of all this intense debate and activity, Albino Luciani, also remained in the dark. Away from the meetings he continued to walk in the gardens of the Augustinian house, where he engaged Brother Clemente, perspiring as he worked among the flower beds, in conversation. Concerned that the outcome of the conclave would be for

---

[147] Greeley, p. 139.
[148] Ibid.
[149] For much of the last three paragraphs I am indebted to Greeley, pp. 105, 124–5, 139–40.

the good of the Church, Luciani recalled that he had worked in the fields as a boy. 'Then I had callouses on my hands. Now I have callouses in my brain'.[150] He was also still thinking of Venice. His car had developed engine trouble, and he told Lorenzi that he must get it repaired quickly. The voting in the conclave was due to start on Saturday 26 August. Luciani insisted that the car must be ready – and here Luciani obviously anticipated a short conclave – for the return journey to Venice the following Tuesday. He wanted to make an early start, because he had much to do on his return. On 24 August Luciani wrote to his favourite niece, Pia, in Caviola:

> Dear Pia,
> I write to you so that you can have the new stamps 'sede vacante' and also to congratulate you on the success of your first exam. We hope that the Lord will also help you with the rest. Today we have finished the pre-conclave with the last 'Congregatio Generalis'. Afterwards, the cells were chosen by lot and we went to see them. I have #60, a parlour made into a bedroom. It is like the seminary in Feltre in 1923, iron bed, mattress, a basin for washing. Cardinal Tomasek of Prague is in #61. Farther on, Cardinals Tarancón (Madrid), Medeiros (Boston), Sin (Manila), Malula (Kinshasa). Except for Australia there is a 'concentration' of the whole world.
> I do not know how long the conclave will last. It is difficult to find the person able to face so many problems, which are very heavy crosses. Luckily, I am out of danger. Even so, it is a very grave responsibility to vote in these circumstances.
> I am sure, that being a good Christian, you will pray for the Church at this time. Greet Francesco, papa and [mama]. I did not write to them as I have a bit to do at this time.
> Yours affectionately, Luciani.[151]

The next day, only a few hours before entering the conclave, he wrote in a similar vein to his sister Antonia:

> Dear Sister,
> I am writing to you shortly before going into the Conclave. These are heavy moments of responsibility, even if there is no danger for me, despite the gossip in the papers. Casting one's vote for a Pope in these moments is a heavy weight. Pray for the Church, and an affectionate greeting also to Ettore, Roberto and Gino.
> Albino Luciani.[152]

---

[150] Yallop, p. 70.
[151] Seabeck, pp. 52–3.
[152] Yallop, p. 71.

Giving his letter to his hosts to be posted, Luciani told them that he had left most of his belongings in his room. That morning he had celebrated a Mass 'for the Election of a Pope' with his brother cardinals. Now, carrying his overnight bag across St Peter's Square to the Sistine Chapel, cheerful Brother Clemente said to him: 'I don't know what to say, Your Eminence. Best wishes and *arrivederci*. If you are elected pope, come and see us some time. We are neighbours after all'.[153] Luciani gave him a shy smile. With all the cardinals assembled in the Sistine Chapel, Mgr Virgilio Noè, the Papal Master of Ceremonies, called '*Extra omnes*', the signal for all extraneous personnel to depart from the conclave area. Then the doors were slowly closed, not to be opened again until a pope had been elected. The time was 4.59 p.m.

---

[153] Hebblethwaite, *Year of Three Popes*, p.113.

Chapter Five

Pope 1978

No voting took place on that first evening in the already stuffy conclave area. Only eleven of the participating cardinals – about ten per cent – had taken part in a conclave before, although, as has been already noted, the sessions of the Synod of Bishops had provided a forum for personal contact and the exchange of ideas amongst them.[1] The atmosphere was one of controlled expectancy, but for the time being the cardinals had to sit through another reading of sections of the apostolic constitution, *Romano Pontifici Eligendo*, particularly those dealing with considerations of secrecy. After the reading, Villot, acting in his capacity as Camerlengo, required each cardinal in turn to swear the solemn conclave oath binding all present to acceptance of Pope Paul's conditions, to reject outside interference and to keep the deliberations secret. As we shall see, this last provision was not wholly adhered to. Finally, Villot addressed them on the importance of their deliberations and the need to keep the 'good of the Church' firmly in their minds, before concluding: 'May the Lord bless you all. Amen.' The assembled cardinals then dispersed to their 'cells' for the night.

Individual cardinals naturally reached different conclusions on the conclave arrangements. Cardinal Hume of Westminster said later that 'Many people could criticize the way a conclave is arranged, but it came to me that all these arrangements were symbolic – there was nothing between the cardinals and God. That seemed to me to be right'.[2] However, Cardinal Siri,

---

[1] The eleven were Giuseppe Siri, Stefan Wyszynski, Paul-Émile Léger, José Maria Bueno y Monreal, Franz Koenig, Bernard Jan Alfrink, Laurean Rugambwa, José Humberto Quintero, Juan Landázuri Ricketts, OFM, Raul Silva Henriquez, SDB and Leon-Joseph Suenens.

[2] Hebblethwaite, *Year of Three Popes*, p. 72.

veteran of the 1958 and 1963 conclaves, likened the experience to 'living in an airless tomb'. Cardinal Manning of Los Angeles who, like Hume, was at his first conclave, said that he felt 'like a schoolboy on his first day at school'.[3]

Catholics believe that it is the Holy Spirit who guides the deliberations of the cardinals in conclave towards electing the pope the Church of the time needs. In a sense the spirit of Pope Paul was also stamped on the proceedings: he had created so many of the cardinals present and had laid down such precise rules for the election of his successor (largely due to his own unpleasant experiences in the conclave of 1963).

The next morning – Saturday, 26 August – after the concelebrated Mass and a light breakfast, the cardinals moved to the glorious Sistine Chapel, built 1477–80 and named for Pope Sixtus IV, to begin the momentous business in hand.[4] The very setting itself inspired awe and solemnity. Covering the entire vault of the ceiling is Michelangelo's monumental fresco of the Creation (1508–12), whilst above the main altar is the stupendous Last Judgement (1535–41).

Amongst the cardinals themselves tension and a certain natural impatience after the lengthy preliminaries were now in evidence. First of all the voting cards were distributed by the master of ceremonies, before various electoral officials were drawn by lot. The upper half of each card contained the printed words '*Eligo in Summum Pontificem*' ('I elect as Supreme Pontiff'), whilst the lower half had a space for writing the name of the chosen candidate. Pope Paul's instructions even recommended each elector to disguise his handwriting so as to preserve complete anonymity. Once the card had been filled in it was designed to be folded in half.

In this fashion, then, after the various functionaries had left the chapel, the first ballot began. Once each cardinal had completed his card, they approached the altar in order of precedence. Each one knelt in prayer for a moment, before rising and pronouncing the oath, 'I call to witness Christ the Lord who will be my judge, that my vote is given to the one who, before God, I consider should be elected.' Then, before the gaze of the scrutineers, the card was placed on a plate, and tipped from the plate into a chalice on the altar. Tension grew as this lengthy process continued. Finally, when all the cardinals had voted, the cards were shaken up and counted. The

---

[3] Ibid.
[4] See Burns for a precise account of the electoral procedure as it then stood.

right number of cards being present, the first scrutineer opened a card, noted down the name, and passed it on to the second scrutineer, who did the same before passing it on to the third, who again noted the name whilst also announcing it so that the cardinals could keep their own records. The ballot cards were threaded together and prepared for burning, two ballots at a time.

So much for the procedure. What actually happened followed a pattern taken by no other twentieth-century conclave; a surprise candidate was elected within a single day. That the events can be described with a fair degree of accuracy is due to the various 'leaks' and 'indiscretions' that subsequently took place despite Pope Paul's exhortations for secrecy. Different authors have produced different figures – see Appendix C – but broadly speaking they are in general agreement. Unless the relevant material is ever released from the Vatican Archives – and at the current rate that would not be until the second quarter of this century – nobody except a few people in the Vatican itself will ever know exactly. For the moment I intend to broadly follow the thesis of Father Francis Xavier Murphy, the respected Redemptorist and long-term Vaticanologist. In close agreement with his figures are those of David Yallop. Neither author has revealed his sources – unsurprisingly – although Murphy has inferred that his sources were Italian cardinals.

On the first ballot the intransigent traditionalist Giuseppe Siri of Genoa got the most votes, closely followed by Albino Luciani, with Sergio Pignedoli, the most progressive of the curial cardinals, not far behind. Other cardinals got a scattering of votes. Luciani was bemused and a little worried, genuinely unable to understand how he had obtained so many votes. He frowned and shook his head as other cardinals nearby turned to smile at him, muttering something under his breath which a cardinal near him thought sounded like the word *'assurdo'* ('absurd').[5] The whole process had only taken an hour, though it must have seemed longer.

Who voted for Luciani in that crucial first ballot, the one that established the extent of the support for his candidacy before other cardinals 'jumped on the bandwagon'? Luciani's supporters were an influential and truly international group, and as far as can be determined they comprised the following individuals: Alfrink (Netherlands), Benelli (Florence), Colombo (Milan), Cooke (New York), Ekandem (Ikot Ekpene), Gantin (Benin),

[5] Greeley, p. 152.

Gouyon (Rennes), Höffner (Cologne), Koenig (Vienna), Lorscheider (Fortaleza), Malula (Kinshasa), Marty (Paris), Nsubuga (Kampala), Pellegrino (Turin), Poma (Bologna), Renard (Lyons), Sin (Manila), Suenens (Malines-Brussels), Thiandoum (Dakar), Ursi (Naples), Volk (Mainz), Willibrands (Utrecht) and Wojtyla (Krakow).[6]

The first ballot could be described as being an exploratory one, with some votes being cast in a complimentary way. The second one was more serious, and the tension rose again. Each cardinal now had an idea of the overall picture: which of the leading three candidates would pick up votes? In the event both Siri and Luciani increased their votes, with Siri still just ahead, whilst Pignedoli's vote dropped. Pignedoli's bid was blocked and Siri's support had peaked. Luciani recognized the signs, and was visibly upset by the turn of events. An insight into this moment was given by Luciani himself the next day at the start of his midday Angelus address from the central balcony of St Peter's, his lilting voice, a little hesitant and tremulous at first, gaining in strength and confidence:

> Yesterday – and here the almost imperceptible shrug of the shoulders drew a sympathetic laugh from the crowd – morning I went to the Sistine Chapel to vote tranquilly. Never could I have imagined what was about to happen. As soon as the danger for me had begun, the two colleagues who were beside me whispered words of encouragement. One said: 'Courage! If the Lord gives a burden, he also gives the strength to carry it.' The other colleague said: 'Don't be afraid; there are so many people in the whole world who are praying for the new Pope.' When the moment of decision came, I accepted.[7]

The first of these 'two colleagues' to offer his encouragement was Antonio Ribeiro, Patriarch of Lisbon, seated to Luciani's left. The second was his friend Jan Willebrands, Archbishop of Utrecht, seated to his right. The waiting crowds in St Peter's Square were disappointed to see black smoke rising from the Sistine chimney at noon, the signal that the cardinals had yet to elect a pope. Inside the conclave the mood was very different. As the cardinals left the Sistine Chapel for lunch the atmosphere was affable and purposeful. László Lékai, Archbishop of Esztergom and Primate of Hungary, remarked to

---

[6] Based on Murphy and Yallop's data. Murphy also advances the name of Pappalardo (Palermo).
[7] *The Teachings of Pope John Paul I*, p. 3.

Luciani: 'Your votes are increasing'. For his part, Luciani tried to pass this off with the comment: 'It's just a summer shower'.[8] Non-Italian cardinals got a better look at Luciani, who still looked a little dazed and unbelieving at what was happening to him. After lunch Luciani went back to his cell for a brief siesta, but was unable to sleep. All the cardinals were now confident that the issue could be settled that same afternoon; the conclave almost began to take on a momentum of its own.

At about four o'clock the cardinals began to reassemble in the Sistine Chapel for the third ballot. Many were in an almost joyful mood, believing that the Holy Spirit was inspiring their collective action. As he emerged from his cell, Luciani was given warm encouragement and congratulations by Joseph Malula of Zaire; Luciani's response was a sad shake of his head. 'A great storm is troubling me', he said.[9]

After about an hour the results were announced, and they were impressive. Luciani was now only a handful of votes short of the seventy-five required, whilst Siri and Pignedoli lost considerable ground. The final outcome could no longer be in doubt. In the third ballot many of the moderates and many of the conservatives, including the influential Pericle Felici of the Curia, had seen the signs and also swung behind Luciani as an acceptable candidate. Felici now approached Luciani, handing him an envelope with the comment 'A message for the new Pope'. Inside, the sheet of paper bore the words *Via Crucis*, a symbol of the Way of the Cross.[10]

Eager to press on to the by now obvious outcome, the cardinals dispensed with taking the oath each time they voted in the fourth ballot. At 6.05 p.m., the seventy-fifth Luciani vote was announced; the cardinals applauded enthusiastically in a burst of spontaneous acclamation, startling the Swiss Guard posted outside. Was it possible, a pope already? It was not only possible, it was a fact. By 6.20 p.m., when the last vote was announced, Luciani had been elected almost unanimously. Siri had maybe a dozen or so votes from diehard intransigents, whilst Lorscheider completed the course with one vote, that of Luciani himself.

Though he had been elected, it was by no means certain that he would accept his nomination. Luciani had had no wish for the papacy and had been reluctant even to consider the possibility.

[8] Hebblethwaite, *The Next Pope: An Enquiry*, p. 62.
[9] Murphy, p. 164.
[10] Yallop, p. 81.

Before he left Venice, Mario Senigaglia, his former secretary, had wished him luck and recommended that he take a selection of his speeches, in case the 'unthinkable' happened. Luciani had dismissed this suggestion: 'There is always a way out of it. You can always refuse'.[11] Once they had arrived in Rome, Diego Lorenzi, his current secretary, had also expressed the desire that Luciani should be the next pope. Again Luciani was dismissive. He reminded Lorenzi of Pope Paul's apostolic constitution governing conclave procedure. Referring to the moment when the elected cardinal is approached and asked if he accepts, Luciani smiled and said: 'And if they elect me I will say, "I'm sorry, I refuse"'.[12] To several other well-wishers before the conclave he had stated: 'You can't make gnocchi out of this dough'.[13]

Now the moment Luciani had dreaded had arrived. The doors of the chapel were opened and various masters of ceremonies entered to accompany the camerlengo, Villot, to Luciani. Luciani sat with head bowed as silence descended over the gathering. In careful Latin Villot asked the constitutionally prescribed question: 'Do you, Most Reverend Lord Cardinal, accept your election as Supreme Pontiff which has been canonically carried out?' Luciani paused, deciding, composing himself. Cardinal Luigi Ciappi, OP later described the moment: 'He was sitting three rows behind me. Even at the moment of his election he was hesitating; Cardinal Villot put the question to him and he continued to hesitate. Cardinals Willebrands and Ribeiro were clearly encouraging him'.[14] Others were also left with lasting impressions: Virgilio Noè noticed a 'shiny look' now in Luciani's eyes; Franz Koenig saw 'a certainty' that had not been present before; Bernardin Gantin sensed 'strength and resolve' whilst Jaime Sin was convinced that it was 'God's decision'.[15]

In this context, Luciani's response was stunning: 'May God forgive you for what you have done in my regard'.[16] Villot was

---

[11] Ibid., p. 77.

[12] Ibid.

[13] Yallop, p. 80. 'Gnocchi' are an Italian speciality, dumplings made of semolina pasta.

[14] Ibid., p. 82.

[15] Pontiff, p. 282.

[16] Luciani had a prodigious memory, which did not fail him even on this mind-numbing occasion. His remark was a slightly modified version of a comment written by St Bernard of Clairvaux to one of his monks on the latter's election as Pope Eugene III in 1145. Displeased with the younger man for accepting the papacy because he feared that it would cause problems for the monastic Orders, he had written 'May God forgive you for what you have done in this regard'. In fact, Pope Eugene proved to be a capable

taken aback at this unconventional response. Suddenly – and for the first time – Luciani smiled. '*Accepto* . . . in the name of the Lord.' In that instant, Luciani formally became pope. With obvious relief, Villot put the second question to Luciani that he was required to ask: 'By what name will you be known?' Luciani paused briefly, then, in a clear voice, announced 'I will be called John Paul the First.'

Thus did Luciani spring what was to be the first of many surprises in his pontificate, and the cardinals were delighted. Luciani was the 263rd pope of the Roman Church; in nearly two thousand years he was the first to take a double name, and indeed the first to take a new name of any sort since Pope Lando in 913–14.[17] Traditionally the name a new pontiff took upon his election signalled what the guiding principles of his reign would be.

John Paul's choice was innovative and encouraging, and just why he made this highly appropriate decision he himself revealed the next day during his first Angelus address:

> Then there was the question of the name, for they also ask what name you wish to take, and I had thought little about it. My thoughts ran along these lines: Pope John had decided to consecrate me himself in St Peter's Basilica; then, however unworthy, I succeeded him in Venice on the Chair of St Mark, in that Venice which is still full of Pope John. He is remembered by the gondoliers, the Sisters, everyone. Then Pope Paul not only made me a Cardinal . . . [but] . . . Furthermore, during his fifteen years of pontificate this Pope has shown, not only to me but to the whole world, how to love, how to serve, how to labour and to suffer for the Church of Christ. For that reason I said: 'I shall be called John Paul.'[18]

---

reformer. Luciani, typically, later apologized to the cardinals, explaining that he had meant no offence, and revealing the source of his quotation. However, it may well be assumed that the source and context of his statement escaped the majority of the cardinals at the time!

[17] It was also unprecedented for a pope to add a number after his name before there had been other popes of the same name. Luciani clearly felt – correctly – that there would be another John Paul after him.

[18] *The Teachings of Pope John Paul I*, p. 3. His sister Antonia has revealed that he very briefly thought of taking the name Pius XIII, out of respect for Pius XI. In the summer of 1931, at the height of Fascist persecution of Catholic Action, he had said to her that it was the popes called Pius who had suffered most. To link the name Pius with personal suffering on his reluctant acceptance of the papacy would have been psychologically consistent. However, he rejected the idea because of the divisive controversy it would cause in the Church. He was absolutely correct and he undoubtedly made the right decision. See S. Falasca, *La Speranza È Aspettare Qualcosa Di Bello Dal Signore*.

This brings us back to a fundamental question, and that is just why Luciani accepted the papacy that he so little wanted? Did his nerve fail him, was he overawed and afraid to decline? Yallop suggests that 'he was overwhelmed by the speed and size of the vote', stating that this was a common view 'perhaps best summarized by a member of the Curia who had a close, twenty-year friendship' with Luciani:

> He was distressed by it. If he had not been so overwhelmed by the sheer quantity, if events had moved more slowly, taken the Conclave into a second day, he would have had time to gather himself and refuse; and yet, if he had decided in that Conclave that he was not the man to become Pope he would have refused. He was one of the strongest men I have known in thirty years in the Curia.[19]

I suggest that it was this very strength of character, noted by many who knew Luciani well, that made him accept. On a purely internal, personal level, he naturally hesitated before the enormity of what lay ahead of him, as any man worthy of the office would. Beyond that, the reasons for – and the nature of – his acceptance of the papacy had close parallels with St Thomas More's reluctant acceptance of the Lord Chancellorship of England in October 1529. He grew in stature, accepted the will of the Holy Spirit so clearly manifested in the overwhelming opinion of his peers, and, with the desire to do all in his power for the good of the Church, took the burden on his shoulders. Bearing in mind Luciani's episcopal motto *Humilitas* there is one final point to consider, perhaps the most crucial one, and it is concisely put by Yallop in what is possibly the most genuinely insightful passage in his book:

> There is also the vital element of Luciani's personal humility. Describing the acceptance of the Papacy as an act of humility may appear to be contradictory. To equate the taking of supreme power with meekness is, in fact, entirely consistent, if the last thing you want on earth is supreme power.[20]

Immediately upon Luciani's acceptance, Cardinal Ciappi, the junior cardinal deacon, summoned Mgr Ernesto Civardi, the secretary of the College of Cardinals, and Mgr Virgilio Noè, the

---

[19] Yallop, pp. 82–3.
[20] Ibid., p. 83. The man was tried, tested and found worthy.

papal master of ceremonies, into the Chapel to notarize the documents certifying the election.[21]

Meanwhile, the new pope himself went to the Sacristy to be fitted out in his papal white cassock by tailor Anibaile Gammarelli.[22] Finishing touches were the zucchetto – the white papal skull cap – and red velvet slippers with gold crosses. At the same time – from 6.24 p.m. – the cardinals burnt their voting papers, adding the chemical that was supposed to produce white smoke – *sfumata bianca* – to signal the election of a pope to the outside world. In fact in their inexperience they added too much and for the next three-quarters of an hour it produced dense billows of smoke that varied from white to grey to black. Great confusion was caused, as the crowds in St Peter's Square tried to gauge what hue it was against the setting sun.

Inside the Sistine Chapel, Luciani emerged from the Sacristy and seated himself on a chair in front of the altar. There he received the obeisance of each cardinal who kissed his hand before being warmly embraced by the new pope. He had a friendly word for each one. Cardinal Suenens, who had played a large part in Luciani's election, said 'Holy Father, thank you for saying "yes".' Luciani smiled broadly at him, having a shrewd idea of the role he played: 'Perhaps it would have been better if I had said "no".' This ceremony over, the cardinals sang the *Te Deum*, the Hymn of Thanksgiving.

By 7.18 p.m. some people had begun to drift away, assuming that the conclave had still not produced a pope. Suddenly the massive public address system in the piazza crackled and the authoritative voice of Mgr Noè boomed out: '*Attenzione*'. A wave of excitement rippled through the waiting crowd, and those who had begun to leave hurried back. The big door of the Loggia Centrale, the main balcony of St Peter's, swung slowly open. Out came Cardinal Felici, the senior cardinal deacon, preceded by a cross-bearer and followed by assorted cardinals and monsignori.

Down amongst the crowd in the piazza was Diego Lorenzi, Luciani's secretary, as eager to learn the result as everyone else. Next to him stood a family from Sweden who had asked him what work he did. Lorenzi remarked, 'I am in Rome for a

---

[21] Murphy, p. 161.

[22] The House of Gammarelli, Sartoria Pontificia, have been tailors to the Holy See since 1797. Gianpaolo subsequently wrote to thank Gammarelli in one of the first letters of his pontificate. Pontiff, p. 657.

few days. I work in Venice',[23] before looking back towards St Peter's.

On the balcony, smiling broadly, Felici intoned his joyful news in the traditional Latin manner:
'*Annuntio vobis gaudium magnum: habemus Papam!*'.
Cheers greeted these words.
'*Eminentissimum ac Reverendissimum Dominum Albinum ...*'
The crowd fell silent.
'*... Sanctae Romanae Ecclesiae Cardinalem ...*'.
A pause. Then, ' ... LUCIANI!'
The crowd cheered wildly. At the mention of the name '*Albinum*', Lorenzi had turned back to the Swedish family. As tears began to run down his face he smiled and said proudly, 'I am the secretary of the newly-elected Pope.'[24]

Felici continued: '*Qui sibi nomen imposuit Joannem Paulum Primum!*'[25] A huge cheer greeted this final piece of information, and bedlam reigned in the piazza. The initial response was one of relief, of applause for the fact that the Church once again had a pope. The piazza was only about one-third full, and tourists made up a fair proportion of the crowd, many of the Romans being away on their annual holidays during the *ferragosto*. The name 'Luciani' thus meant little to many of those present. The more personal, enthusiastic response came when Luciani himself appeared on the balcony. Straight away, his audience -both those in the piazza and the millions watching on television – were touched by his smile, open, friendly, and infectious. The new pope clearly had a sense of fun. Obviously enjoying the moment, John Paul intoned his blessing '*Urbi et Orbi*' – 'to the City and the World' – before disappearing. Soon he returned to receive the salute of a battalion of Swiss Guards and Italian soldiers drawn up in the piazza. Then he was gone again. By 10.00 p.m. the great lights in the piazza had gone out.

To set the seal on some of the confusion that had taken place during the day, the first edition of *L'Osservatore Romano*, out less than half-an-hour after the election, carried a mistake that caused it to be withdrawn and become a collector's item worth over $100 on the open market.[26] Its front-page banner head-

23 Yallop, p. 84.
24 Ibid.
25 In translation, Felici announced: 'I bring you news of great joy: we have a Pope! He is the Most Eminent and Most Reverend Lord Albino Cardinal of the Holy Roman Church Luciani, who has chosen the name John Paul the First'.
26 See Lo Bello, pp. 126–7; *30 Days*, 1, no. 4, July-August 1988, pp. 76–7.

line announced: *HABEMUS PAPAM ALBINUM LUCIANI QUI SIBI NOMINEM IMPOSUIT IOANNEM PAULUM I*. To the amusement of others, and the embarrassment of the staff, the error was pointed out by the editor Valerio Volpini's high school son, who had just completed first-year Latin. Apologizing to his father for not being an expert in the language, he pointed out that the word *nominem* did not exist in Latin, and that the word should have been *nomen* ('name').

That evening Luciani kept the conclave in session, and sat down to dine with the cardinals in his previously assigned place. He also thought of the sixteen cardinals who had been excluded because they were over-age; they had already been notified of the result by telephone, now Luciani invited them in to the Mass that was to be celebrated in the Sistine Chapel at 9.30 a.m. the next morning. Still his humour did not desert him. Towards the end of the meal an American cardinal asked the new pope for permission to smoke, something contrary to protocol. 'The pope looked very solemn, he kept everybody waiting, while he gave the matter some thought; finally he said: "Eminence, you may smoke, on one condition: the smoke must be white!" Naturally there was much laughter'.[27]

Luciani also decided to deliver his televised message the next morning, immediately after the Mass and set the following Sunday as the date of his installation. Further, he took the document prepared by the Secretariat of State for his speech the next day, and retired to his cell, where he radically rewrote several key passages. What had initially been understandably rather vague statements on love, peace and war, became much more specific, bearing the Luciani hallmark.

The next morning, Sunday, 27 August, Luciani duly delivered his first message to the Church and to the world.[28] Given within sixteen hours of his election, it was to prove to be the most important of his pontificate. With its programmatic content, it could justly be said to stand as his last testament to the Church, and as such bears consideration in depth. In reflecting on this speech, however, the reader should try not to judge it too much in retrospect; when presented, this address stood at a new dawn of hope and joy, announcing policies that looked to the future. The speed with which the new pope delivered his

[27] Cardinal Suenens, *Memories And Hopes*, 1992, Veritas, p. 323.
[28] For various renderings of the full text see *The Teachings of Pope John Paul I*, pp. 37–44; *Tablet*, CCXXXII, 2 September 1978, pp. 856–8; *The Pope Speaks*, 23, no. 4, winter 1978, pp. 291–8; Greeley, pp. 281–6.

first address clearly emphasized his desire to share with the cardinals his vision of the direction that the Church should take, and as such was without precedent.

After some initial reflections on the 'awesome responsibility of the papacy', John Paul elaborated on the nature of the Church. The universal mission of the Church, he stressed, was to be 'at the service of the world'. He invited all Christians to pledge themselves to this service: 'The Gospel calls all of its children to place their full strength, indeed their life, at the service of mankind in the name of the charity of Christ'.[29] However, John Paul was at pains to point out that the service of the world did not mean conformity to it, did not remove the obligation of prophetic protest. The Church is in the world and for the world, but must not be of the world. He quoted extensively from the cherished Council constitution *Lumen Gentium*, which speaks of the Church entering into 'human history . . . advancing through trials and tribulations' to ultimately stand as 'the visible sacrament of this saving unity'.[30]

John Paul further underlined the 'uniqueness of the Catholic Church' with its 'tremendous spiritual power', so needed in the modern world. He echoed St Augustine in stating 'Only in the Church is salvation: *without it one perishes!*'[31] Ecumenists need not have worried over this apparently exclusively Catholic statement, because later the ecclesial reality of other denominations was implicitly recognized in the pope's comments on the 'constant and extraordinary advances' in the 'mutual relationships among the churches of the various denominations'.[32] In talking about the essential value of the Church and its irreplaceable relevance in dealing with the 'pressing problems of the day', John Paul developed a theme that had been a constant feature of his preaching in Venice:

> The world awaits this today: it knows well that the sublime perfection to which it has attained by research and technology has already reached a peak, beyond which yawns the abyss, blinding the eyes with darkness. It is the temptation of substituting for God one's own decisions, decisions that would prescind from moral laws. The danger for modern man is that he would reduce the earth to a desert, the person to an automaton, brotherly love to planned collectivization, often introducing death where God wishes life.[33]

[29] *The Teachings of Pope John Paul I*, p. 39.
[30] Ibid., p. 38; *Lumen Gentium*, 9.
[31] Ibid., p. 38.
[32] Ibid., p. 41.
[33] Ibid., p. 39.

Thus, he saw that the whole world needed evangelization, needed saving from dangers that humankind imposed upon itself, namely ecological ruin, nuclear war, abortion and the encroachment of too-powerful governments upon human rights. In guiding the Church and tackling these problems, John Paul promised to follow the example of his predecessors – going as far back as Pius XI (1922–39) – their 'lovable gentle ways bolstered by a relentless strength' and their 'great lessons of pastoral guidance'. Most of all, however, it was the pastoral plan of Paul VI that inspired him, who in turn had drawn strength from 'the great heart of John XXIII'. And so John Paul reached his programme: whilst containing no 'novel elements' it was sound and practical, wide-ranging and progressive, clear and logical. His order of priorities was interesting, moving as they did from the internal affairs of the Church to its external relationships.

Firstly, he stated his intention of continuing the work of putting 'into effect the heritage of the Second Vatican Council'. He urged caution against rash haste, but spoke equally strongly against 'an approach that is hesitant and fearful – which thus would not realize the magnificent impulse of the renewal and of life'.[34]

Secondly, he wished to 'preserve the integrity of the great discipline of the Church in the life of priests and of the faithful ... Throughout the ages, it has presented an example of holiness and heroism, both in the exercise of the evangelical virtues and in service to the poor, the humble, the defenceless'.[35] To achieve this, he placed priority on the revision of the two Codes of Canon law – the Oriental and the Latin – 'to assure the blessed liberty of [the] children of God'.[36]

Thirdly, John Paul reminded the 'entire Church that its first duty is that of evangelization'. He cited Paul VI's teaching, and exhorted 'all the sons and daughters of the Church ... to be tireless missionaries of the Gospel'.

Fourthly, he wished 'to continue the ecumenical thrust' which would be pursued in the light of Christ's great prayer: 'That they may all be one' (John 17:21). Despite his optimism and hope for the future, the new pope was realistic enough to note: '... yet division remains a cause for concern, and indeed a contradiction and scandal in the eyes of non-Christians and non-believers. We intend to dedicate our prayerful attention to

[34] Ibid., p. 40.
[35] Ibid.
[36] As noted in chapter three, this finally took place in 1983.

everything that would favour union. We will do so without diluting doctrine but, at the same time, without hesitance'.[37]

Fifthly, John Paul showed his resolve in pursuing constructive dialogue with all men, following Paul VI's basis for pastoral action as set out in his encyclical *Ecclesiam Suam*, namely, 'that men, as men, should know one another, even those who do not share our faith. We must always be ready to give witness of the faith that is ours and of the mission that Christ has given to us, "that the world may believe" (John 17:21)'.[38]

His sixth and final point was to express his 'support for all the laudable, worthy initiatives that can safeguard and increase peace in our troubled world'. Echoing John XXIII, he called upon 'all good men, all who are just, honest, true of heart' to act 'against blind violence which can only destroy and sow seeds of ruin and sorrow'. Still concerned with war and poverty, John Paul further called for mutual understanding in 'combining efforts that would further social progress, overcome hunger of body and ignorance of the mind and advance those who are less endowed with goods of this earth, yet rich in energy and desire'.[39]

In the last section of his address, John Paul sent his greetings to the various categories of people comprising his spiritual sons and daughters, and this gave him the opportunity to flesh out what he had already said in his 'six-point programme'. His greeting to the bishops allowed him to state that he placed high value on collegiality, continuing: 'We value their efforts in the guidance of the Universal Church both through the synodal structure and through the curial structure in which they share by right according to the norms established'.[40] He saluted those in the missionary Church 'in their outposts of evangelization' and gave encouragement: 'They should know that, among all who are dear to us, they are the dearest: they are never forgotten in our prayers and thoughts, because they have a privileged place in our heart'.[41]

Young people were hailed as 'the hope of tomorrow', whilst families, who play – as John Paul always recognized so clearly – such a vital role in the healthy formation of the young as tomorrow's adults, were greeted as the 'domestic sanctuary of the Church' and as a true, actual 'domestic Church'. Finally, he extended a particular greeting to 'all who are now suffering, to

[37] Ibid., p. 41.
[38] Ibid.
[39] Ibid.
[40] Ibid., p. 42.
[41] Ibid., p. 43.

the sick, to prisoners, to exiles, unemployed, or who have bad fortune in life ... to the tortured land of Lebanon ... to India, a land that is so tried'. None were left out; all unfortunates were included in John Paul's broad pastoral concern and sympathy. With some concluding exhortations for all – with 'no distinction as to race or ideology' – to cooperate towards making a better world under Christ, he imparted his 'first, most loving, Apostolic Benediction'.

With the conclusion of John Paul's address, the conclave was officially over, and the *sampietrini* – the skilled workmen whose normal job is the maintenance of St Peter's Basilica – began to dismantle the elaborate superstructures they had erected only two days earlier. With the portone cleared, the cardinals emerged from the conclave area into the Cortile di San Damaso. They had plenty to think about: the speed of the election, and the address that their new pope had just given. What impressions did they take away with them?

Obviously reactions to the election depended upon previous expectations; the disappointment of the grim-faced Giuseppe Siri, the first to emerge, was obvious as he brushed past those waiting outside and departed without comment. Cardinals Höffner, Guerri, Thiandoum, Gantin and Koenig expressed their delight at the outcome. Paolo Bertoli exclaimed *'Felicissimo! ...* A magnificent stroke ... it's a sin that we are not able to tell you what went on'.[42] Despite Bertoli's comment many what the Italians call 'indiscretions' would shortly be forthcoming, many more than were destined to follow the conclave that would elect Luciani's successor. Asked for his opinion Silvio Oddi replied 'I'd say it was definitely an inspiration. So many electors, from so many parts of the world; and *voilà*, all over in a few minutes.' Asked for Luciani's reaction he added 'Moved, greatly moved. But no, no, I did not see him cry'.[43]

Giovanni Benelli, who had played such a significant role in Luciani's election, agreed with Silvio Oddi's assessment: 'A striking manifestation of the unity of the church supported by the presence of the Holy Spirit ... The electors came from every part of the world, from every culture, and with very different mentalities and, in a single day, reached complete agreement'.[44] Basil Hume had also felt the presence of the Holy Spirit, commenting:

---

[42] Murphy, p. 164.
[43] Ibid.
[44] Greeley, pp. 159–60.

Seldom have I had such an experience of the presence of God ... I
am not one for whom the dictates of the Holy Spirit are self-evident.
I'm slightly hard-boiled on that ... but for me he was God's candidate.[45]

He added:

Once it had happened, it seemed totally and entirely right. The
feeling that he was just what we wanted was so general ... We felt
as if our hands were being guided as we wrote his name on the
paper![46]

Alone of all the cardinals, and despite his earlier assessment of
Luciani's personal qualities, only Juan Carlos Aramburú, the
conservative Archbishop of Buenos Aires, admitted that he had
not voted for the new pope.[47]

John Cody of Chicago was asked how it could be explained to
the American people that the pope's father had been a socialist. 'What's so difficult about that?' he answered, 'My father
was a fireman, and I'm a cardinal'.[48] Cardinal Suenens, another
enthusiastic supporter of Luciani's candidature, was questioned
over the pope's unique name: would he be more like John, or
more like Paul? He replied with a perceptive analogy: 'He will
be both in his own way. His manner is closer to John's but it is
like mixing oxygen and hydrogen – you get water, two different
elements producing a third substance'.[49] Cardinal Karol Wojtyla
of Krakow also had a comment to make on the elevation of his
friend Albino Luciani, little knowing that the latter's fate would
soon be his own:

Certainly he who has taken on his shoulders the mission of Peter –
pastoral responsibility for the entire church -has also taken on his
shoulders a heavy cross. We wish to be with him from the beginning
of his road, for we know that this cross – the pope's cross – is part
of the mystery of the world's salvation which has been accomplished in Jesus Christ.[50]

---

[45] Hebblethwaite, *Year of Three Popes*, p. 86.
[46] Cornwell, *A Thief in the Night*, p. 8.
[47] Hebblethwaite, *Year of Three Popes*, p. 84. Aramburú's admission appeared
in Il Giorno, 29 August 1978.
[48] Greeley, p. 160.
[49] Yallop, p. 87.
[50] K. Spink, *John Paul II In The Service Of Love*, 1979, Colour Library
International, p. 6.

Such, then, ran the cardinals' immediate thoughts on John Paul, but what did his relatives and friends make of his election, and what impact did he make on the rest of the world?

One of John Paul's first acts, taken the evening of his election and entirely typical of the man, was to telephone an old friend and colleague, Bishop Maffeo Ducoli of Belluno, his home diocese, 'to send greetings to his brother Edoardo, his sister Antonia, his nephews, nieces and friends'. The pope's opening line was 'Well, the fox may have lost his hair, but he still is a fox', implying that 'even though I may be pope, I'm still bothering you on the telephone'.[51] 'Holy Father', asked the astonished bishop eventually, 'can I tell people that I spoke to you on the telephone?' 'Of course you can,' said Pope John Paul, 'that is why I called you'.[52] Already he was 'lonely for my people':[53] such is the personal isolation of the papal office. Ducoli duly told the people of Belluno the next day. Later Luciani spoke to his brother Edoardo, saying: 'Now look what's happened to me'.[54] Edoardo himself, Chairman of the Chamber of Commerce of Belluno, formerly – for twenty years – Christian Democrat mayor of Canale d'Agordo and universally known as 'maestro Berto', soon found his new role as the pope's brother rather tiresome. At a special Mass of thanksgiving on the afternoon of Monday 28 August, he was ushered into the front row for the benefit of photographers. Afterwards he exclaimed feelingly:

> It's difficult to be pope – but it's even more difficult to be the pope's brother. I can't get any work done with all these journalists pestering me from morning till night. I would like to send them all to the devil, but what would my brother the pope say? He's landed me in a fine mess.[55] Their aunt, eighty years of age and wearing her black veil, said with simple insight: 'Poor Don Albino.'[56]

Toni Cagnati, the fifty-six-year-old communist mayor of Canale d'Agordo, had not attended church for more than twenty years, but that afternoon he became enthused with civic pride, putting out flags and later organizing coaches to take the citi-

---

[51] Fr Roberto Tucci, SJ quoted in Greeley, p. 172.

[52] Hebblethwaite, *Year of Three Popes*, p. 87; Murphy, p. 167, says the call occurred 'the morning after'.

[53] Yallop, p. 158.

[54] Ibid.

[55] Hebblethwaite, *Year of Three Popes*, p. 88.

[56] Ibid.

zens to the inauguration of the village's most famous son. The whole episode was quintessentially Italian, and well represents the warm response of the vast majority. One of the few dissenting voices to be raised over Luciani's election came from an eighty-year-old man of the village who grumbled: 'It's a scandal, this election of this Pope. He's a very good man, but his father burned crucifixes in his stove'.[57]

More seriously, Luciani himself was already troubled as the realization of his unique burden began to sink in. Only two days after his election he wrote to an Italian priest whose work he admired: 'I don't know how I could have accepted. The day after I already regretted it, but by then it was too late.'[58] Nonetheless, on the same day, in another letter written in his own hand, he found the time to write to Don Prospero Grech, OSA, Superior of Santa Monica, to thank his Augustinian hosts for their hospitality during his stay with them before the conclave, once again quietly displaying his almost incredible personal thoughtfulness.

Many journalists and reporters, as well as the onlookers in the piazza, had been caught off-guard at the speed of Luciani's election. One person who wasn't surprised was Cardinal Carlo Confalonieri. At eighty-five he had been excluded from the conclave, but as Dean of the Sacred College he had presided at the pre-conclave General Congregations. Interviewed on RAI, the Italian state television network, on the night of the election, Confalonieri was in an expansive mood, his pleasure at the result barely concealed. Asked whether the outcome was a surprise, he replied:

> It was certainly not a surprise for me or for the other cardinals. The name of Patriarch Luciani was one that had attracted the attention of the cardinal electors in the last days of the pre-conclave period. The press missed this altogether, perhaps because it was misled by the modest and reserved attitude of the Patriarch of Venice. I have to admit that, at the start, a number of cardinals did not know him well (*a fondo*), but this could no longer be said after the various daily meetings that were held under my presidency.[59]

Thus Confalonieri revealed that he too had played a part in

---

[57] *Time*, 112, 11 September 1978, p. 47. Whilst Giovanni Luciani had been an old school anticlerical socialist, it is entirely unproven that he burned crucifixes.

[58] Yallop, p. 158.

[59] Hebblethwaite, *Year of Three Popes*, p. 79.

advancing the cause of Albino Luciani, the man who he said was 'a bishop who reflects a lot, writes well and speaks well. The church has chosen well'.[60] Well, but not unexpectedly to Confalonieri. But how did it appear to others, those far removed from the inner workings of the conclave?

When John Paul emerged onto the balcony of St Peter's to give his Angelus address at noon – referred to earlier in this chapter – the day after his election, he was greeted by an enthusiastic crowd comprising about 200,000 people, about three times the size of the one that had seen his brief appearance the evening before. Countless millions more also saw the event on television. The pope waved to the crowd cheerfully, his white skullcap perched rather uncertainly on the back of his head, a somewhat unruly quiff of grey hair peeping out at the front. Cardinal Hume, astutely, was one of the first to pick up this 'kindly uncle' aspect of Luciani's appeal which, coupled with the soon-to-be famous smile, proved to be irresistible to people, men and women, young and old. Hume remarked: 'It is always a bit of a winner if you can have your skullcap slightly asquiff – it suggests a degree of incompetence that is not threatening'.[61] Some of the cardinals' feelings and the enthusiasm of the crowds were communicated to the media; the respected *Corriere della Sera* of Milan headlined with 'A GREAT POPULAR PERSONALITY'.[62]

Indeed, most people's reaction was one of optimism for the future. Cardinal John Wright predicted that John Paul would be 'a witty Pontiff who delights in combining love of literature with love of the words of God.'[63] On the evening of Luciani's election another member of the American hierarchy, who knew him well, made an equally accurate comment:

> He was a marvellous bishop in a small diocese. In Venice, he was uneasy and nervous, pressured by the problems of the city and by the decisions imposed on the Italian hierarchy by the Curia and the pope. Now that he's pope himself? It may sound crazy, but I've got a hunch that he may go back to being Don Albino, the country bishop.[64]

---

[60] *Time*, 112, 4 September 1978, p. 8.
[61] Hebblethwaite, *Year of Three Popes*, p. 114.
[62] *Time*, 112, 11 September 1978, p. 47.
[63] *Time*, 112, 4 September 1978, p. 8.
[64] Greeley, p. 157.

This early analysis proved to be entirely right, and at any rate was enough to make Father Andrew Greeley hopeful. The Chicago sociologist's own immediate assessment had been mediocre. He judged that 'He will probably not be an impressive pope; he does not seem to be the kind who will restore the impact of leadership in religion and morality around the world'.[65] To be fair to Greeley, he quickly realized his mistake on seeing John Paul's performance the next day and wholly revised his opinion. In fact, Greeley was vindicated in spectacular fashion. At 11.00 a.m. on Sunday 13 August, Greeley had held a conference in the Hotel Columbus on the Via della Conciliazione on behalf of the Committee for the Responsible Election of the Pope (CREP). As part of his sociological rationale, Greeley had asked that whoever was to be elected pope should be 'A hopeful holy man who can smile'.[66] This was exactly what the world needed, and, in the person of Albino Luciani, this was exactly what the world got. Gerald Priestland, Religious Affairs Correspondent for the BBC, compared the new pope to 'a rather tousled schoolmaster who has just been elected mayor of his village', catching Luciani's sense of unpreparedness for what had happened to him.[67] More seriously, Father Edward Schillebeeckx, OP, the distinguished and progressive Dominican theologian, stated: 'I have met Pope John Paul and he struck me as an open and humble man with a great love of the poor'.[68] It was noted by one Vatican observer that: 'He has no curial or international experience. But neither did Jesus'.[69]

Ecumenical reaction was also encouraging. Professor José Miguez-Bonino of Argentina, a Methodist liberation theologian and member of the Presidium of the World Council of Churches, said of John Paul: 'The name is of great importance. It shows that the new Pontiff is ready to continue with the program of reforms launched by the Vatican Council'.[70] A sign of the times was the sermon preached in Canterbury Cathedral the morning after John Paul's election, in which the Anglicans rejoiced with their 'Roman Catholic brethren throughout the world'.[71]

[65] Ibid.
[66] Greeley, pp. 87–9, 115–17, 263, 277–80.
[67] Hebblethwaite, *Year of Three Popes*, p. 183.
[68] O'Mahony, p. 30.
[69] *Tablet*, CCXXXII, 2 September 1978, p. 838.
[70] *Time*, 112, 4 September 1978, p. 10.
[71] For the full text, see A. M. Allchin, 'Pope John Paul I: A Sermon Preached In Canterbury Cathedral On Sunday, August 27, 1978', *One In Christ*, XIV, 4 1978, pp. 309–11.

Another indication of the fact that papal influence and importance now extended beyond the bounds of Roman Catholicism – the largest single body of Christians in the world by far – was given by Ecumenical Patriarch Demetrios I. He hoped that the new pontificate would be marked by a continuation of 'the spirit of Christian ecumenism', going on to say that: 'Given the present state of relations between the Orthodox Church and the Roman Catholic Church, the election of a new Pope is no longer merely a matter of inside concern to the Roman Church, but acquires an ecumenical dimension'.[72]

John Paul received many messages of congratulation on his election from religious and secular leaders all over the world, among them the heads of state of most Western European and Latin American countries. Reporting in the Eastern bloc showed a more varied response. The Soviet news agency, Tass, recorded the event in a mere three lines. The Chinese reported the election of John Paul and the death of Paul VI at the same time, and thereby broke a longstanding silence on Vatican affairs, and indeed on Christian affairs in general. It was the Polish news agency, PAP, who did best, supplying a full biography and stressing, with some justification, that John Paul was 'the first working-class pope', which in the 'post-Marxian' sense he was.

Generally speaking, the first few days after his election could be considered to be a 'honeymoon period', and John Paul largely got a good press. One dissenting voice was that of Andrew Young, the US Ambassador to the United Nations, who stated that he thought the appointment was a mistake, and that he would have preferred a cardinal from the Third World to have been elected.[73] Reporters and ordinary Catholics alike were in a hurry to uncover and study as much as they could about the background of this new and surprising pope. It was quickly reported that in Rome 'the stores around the city are getting his books out of the stock rooms and selling them like hot cakes'.[74]

The Romans found his name Giovanni Paolo rather unwieldy, and soon abbreviated it to the much more informal and friendly 'Gianpaolo'. That Luciani proved to be so popular so quickly with the hard-boiled Romans was an important and encouraging sign: first and foremost the pope is the Bishop of Rome, and the diocese had suffered some neglect during Pope Paul's

---

[72] *Tablet*, CCXXXII, 2 September 1978, p. 858.
[73] Hebblethwaite, *Year of Three Popes*, p. 119.
[74] Tablet, CCXXXII, 9 September 1978, p. 876.

declining years. Luciani himself liked his new nickname and happily used it to sign letters, 'only to have them returned by Secretary of State Villot for correction to the formal title'.[75]

Whilst the outside world probed into his background and speculated on the direction that his papacy would take, Luciani quickly – if a trifle haphazardly – set about establishing his personal household. Father Diego Lorenzi, his secretary in Venice, was naturally retained, as was Sister Vincenza Taffarel. Sister Vincenza, of the Sisters of Maria Bambina, had been housekeeper to Luciani since 1966 when he had been Bishop of Vittorio Veneto. Now aged in her fifties, Vincenza knew Luciani's ways and habits, and had become a valued confidante. In 1977 she had suffered a heart attack, and doctors had told her that she must give up manual work; this advice she had ignored and continued supervising domestic chores, reminding Luciani to take his medicine, and the like. Now she loyally came to the Vatican to augment the staff of nuns already serving in the papal household. Luciani had personally phoned her in Venice to ask if she would consider a move to the Vatican; Vincenza, overwhelmed, had only been able to whisper 'Sì'. An air of respectful friendship existed between the two: in their private conversation Vincenza always knew Luciani as 'Padre Albino', whilst from the earliest days Luciani always addressed her as 'my little Vincenza'.[76]

These two faithful helpers, Lorenzi and Vincenza, would be virtually Luciani's only link with his Veneto homeland during his brief papacy. When a man is elected pope he knows he will rarely see – and never live in – his home again. Added to this is the knowledge, as Yallop puts it, that 'when a man is elected Pope he immediately begins to live where he will, in all probability, die and, in all certainty, be buried'.[77] Yet, despite his yearning for the Veneto, Luciani gave no indication that he was about to staff the Vatican with Venetians; people would not be able to accuse him, as they had done his predecessor Pius X, that he had 'turned the barque of Peter into a gondola'.

Apart from Diego Lorenzi, Luciani needed a second personal secretary to cope with the volume and complexity of his paperwork and agenda. His choice fell on Father John Magee, a forty-one year old Irishman who had been secretary to Paul VI

---

[75] Yallop, p. 158.
[76] Largely derived from *Pontiff*, pp. 319–22, and Yallop, p. 179. Sister Vincenza died on 28 June 1983.
[77] Yallop, p. 179.

since December 1974. The two men had never met; how Magee came to enter Luciani's service is best told in his own words, as related in an interview given to Tommaso Ricci:

> The Monday after the election [28 August], I was in the study of the deceased Paul VI to organize and carry away his personal papers. At a certain point, at 10.30 a.m., I encountered the new pope. I had a box of books in my hand. I put them down immediately and I knelt. 'But you are Father Magee!' he exclaimed. 'Yes, Your Holiness.' 'Listen, can you do me a favour?' 'Yes, Your Holiness.' 'Do you know where the kitchen is? I need a coffee. I have a terrible headache.' 'Yes, Your Holiness.' And I ran to the nun and ordered a coffee. Paul VI had never asked me for even a drop of water. I returned to my work. The next day, when I was able to finish, I again met the Pope by chance. 'Ah, Father Magee, this time you will be scandalized by me.' 'Never, Your Holiness'. 'Yes, yes, because I need another cup of coffee.' Immediately after the coffee, he said to me, 'Come with me.' He closed the door of his study and said to me, 'Do you know this house well?' 'Yes, Your Holiness'. 'Do you know the Secretariat of State well?' 'Yes, yes.' The Pope confided to me that he had not yet oriented himself and that he needed help. 'Will it be possible for you to return here?' I didn't know what to say. 'Immediately, immediately.' But I was thinking to myself, how? I did not understand if he wanted me there as his secretary or only occasionally. 'You must come here as my secretary,' he said. 'Yes, Your Holiness.' Then he was relieved and said to me, 'Now go to the Secretariat of State and say to Monsignor Caprio that I have chosen my secretary'.[78]

Luciani also needed a personal confessor and, given his enthusiasm for the Jesuits whilst at the seminary at Belluno, his choice was interesting. He advised a friend, Father Bartolomeo Sorge, SJ, editor of *La Civiltà Cattolica* and influential in Christian Democrat circles, that he would like Father Paolo Dezza, SJ, also a Jesuit and long-time friend and confessor to Paul VI, to continue in the same capacity for himself. Many years before, Dezza had been Rector of the Gregorian University at the time of Luciani's graduation; now aged seventy-six, Dezza was more than happy to continue with the ministry that he had carried out for Paul VI. Within an hour of Luciani's request to Sorge, Dezza telephoned to make an

---

[78] *30 Days*, no. 5, September 1988, p. 12. On the death of John Paul I, Magee became secretary to John Paul II, thus gaining the unique distinction of having been secretary to three popes. After four years he was named as Papal Master of Ceremonies, before being consecrated on 17 March 1987 as Bishop of Cloyne by John Paul II himself.

appointment. The person who answered his call told him:

'I'm sorry, the Pope's secretary isn't here at the moment. Can I help?'

'Well, to whom am I speaking?'

'The Pope'.[79]

Dezza subsequently met Luciani many times in his private study. At their first meeting Dezza congratulated the new pope on his election after such a short conclave: '"The rapid consensus of the electors on you was a manifest sign of divine will!' I told him. He looked at me with that enchanting smile of his and replied, alluding to an important theological distinction: "his permissive will", at a loss to explain how he had been chosen by the consent of divine will'. Indeed, Luciani already had few illusions about the implications of his new office. When, on another occasion, Dezza tried to comfort the pope with the thought that many people were supporting him in his task with affection and enthusiasm throughout the world, he replied 'Wait a while, and you will see'.[80] Whilst considering such private acts, taken at the outset of his pontificate, it may be useful to outline the nature of what was to become Luciani's daily schedule, before returning once more to his public acts.

Luciani was a true *montanaro* – a man of the mountains – and so he slept with his windows open and the air conditioning system turned off. He loved the height at which his apartments were located; being on the third floor of the Apostolic Palace he wanted to enjoy both the view and 'the fresh air blowing in from the sea and down from the hills surrounding the Eternal City'.[81] In Paul VI's final years St Peter's Square had been closed to traffic from midnight and its fountains switched off in an effort to help the elderly, insomniac pope get some sleep behind his shuttered windows. Now, in Gianpaolo's time, both traffic and water continued to flow all night.[82] Gradually he became used to the distinctive *tufo* sound of Rome, an echoing hum produced as a result of the city being built on hardened volcanic ash – the *tufo* – just as he grew accustomed to the rolling syllables of the Roman accent, so different from his own lilting Veneto tongue.[83] Luciani had chosen to sleep in the bed that had been used by John XXIII rather than that used by Paul

[79] Yallop, p. 181. This incident has been denied, but I believe it to be authentic.

[80] *30 Days*, no. 2, May 1988, p. 43.

[81] Murphy, p. 173.

[82] *Pontiff*, pp. 23, 359.

[83] *Pontiff*, pp. 31, 359.

VI. Magee had told him that Paul had declined to sleep on John's bed 'because of his respect for Pope John'. Luciani's response had been simple: 'I will sleep in his bed because of my love for him'.[84]

In accordance with the habits of a lifetime, Luciani arose at 4.30 a.m. in response to a knock on his bedroom door by Sister Vincenza, informing him that a flask of coffee had been left outside. His bedside alarm clock was always set for 4.45 a.m., in case he overslept, but it was never needed. After his coffee, Luciani would shave and take a bath, before practising his English for half an hour with the aid of an instructional cassette; his reading knowledge of English was very good, and at the time of his election he had been studying conversational English for two years.[85] He might pause for a moment to take in the view from his windows and the new day, even exchanging a cheery wave with the policemen in the square, something unthinkable in the more formal days of Paul VI.

At 5.30 a.m. Luciani would go to his small private chapel, where he would be joined by Father Magee. The two would pray and recite the daily office from the Breviary together in English.[86] At 7.00 a.m. Luciani, having been joined by Father Lorenzi and the household nuns – Mother Superior Elena, Sisters Margherita, Assunta, Gabriella, Clorinda as well as Vincenza – would celebrate Mass. At this Mass another interesting aspect of Luciani's character was displayed and again the story is best told in John Magee's own words:

> He said to me, like he had that time when he asked me for a coffee, 'can you do me a favour?' 'Yes, Your Holiness.' 'Can you celebrate Mass for me tomorrow morning?' 'Yes, Your Holiness, I have often celebrated it for you.' 'Oh, no, I don't mean that. Tomorrow, you celebrate and I will be your altar server. I would like to serve at your Mass.' He made me celebrate in English, and he responded perfectly. I was understandably ill at ease: the Pope knelt before me and received from me the benediction. He understood that I was confused. 'You should not be afraid. I do this for my spiritual life. I need to do this. You will do this again for me. Allow me to do this. It's good for me, you know.' Three times in those thirty-three days he was my altar server. Once he said to me, 'When I serve at your Mass, I am certain that I am serving the person of Christ.' You can imagine how moved I was.[87]

[84] Yallop, p. 178.
[85] Yallop, p. 178; Murphy, p. 166.
[86] *30 Days*, no. 5, September 1988, p. 13.
[87] Ibid.

When Mass was ended at 7.30 a.m. Luciani and his two secretaries would have breakfast together, a meal which consisted of
caffe latte, freshly baked bread and a selection of fruit, jam and
cheese. For the pope, there was also a special bowl of nuts. In
between picking at his food, Luciani would read a selection of
that morning's international and Italian newspapers, interject-
ing comments on their contents. To the list of those papers
which were already delivered he had the Venetian daily *Il
Gazzettino* added. Some articles, those containing important or
topical points that he wanted to incorporate in his public
addresses, he would circle as an indication to his secretaries to
keep them.

Between 8.00 a.m. and 10.00 a.m. the pope would work in
his private study, preparing for the first of his audiences, which
took place on the second floor of the Apostolic Palace. On his
desk stood one of his few really treasured possessions, a
photograph of his parents, Bortola holding his baby niece Pia in
her arms, their home and snow-covered Dolomites in the background.[88] It was a reminder of happier, simpler times.

Between 10.00 a.m. and 12.30 p.m. Gianpaolo would meet
and converse with his visitors, whilst Monsignor Jacques
Martin, Prefect of the Pontifical Household, had the unenviable
task of trying to keep the pope's meetings moving according to
the schedule. Gianpaolo himself did not always help this
process, although things began to flow more smoothly as time
went by.

Lunch, served at around 12.30 p.m., consisted of minestrone
or pasta followed by whatever Vincenza had created for a
second course. This was an hour earlier than the time at which
Pope Paul had taken lunch; another 'innovation' was the fact
that the pope had female guests to his dinner table, albeit that
they consisted of his niece Pia and his sister-in-law. After
lunch, between about 1.30 p.m. and 2.00 p.m., Luciani would
have a short siesta.

This was usually followed by walks on the roof garden or in
the Vatican gardens; sometimes he was accompanied by
Cardinal Villot, but more often than not Luciani would take a
book and read. Apart from his Breviary, Luciani found quiet
enjoyment in the works of such authors as Mark Twain and Sir
Walter Scott, favourites since his youth. One afternoon, when
Luciani had taken some work onto the roof garden with him, a
problem occurred. Magee received a phone call in his office

---

[88] Yallop, p. 193.

about 3.00 p.m. from a security officer in the Cortile di Sisto Quinto, near the entrance to the IOR: 'Father, there's something strange happening. There are sheets of paper falling from the sky, and they're not in Italian. I've been collecting them all up.' Magee, intuiting what had happened, went up to the roof garden and found the pope, peering down into the courtyard in despair moaning *'O Dio mio! Dio mio! Cos'ho fatto'*. In order to take his handkerchief from his pocket, he had set down the papers for a minute and the wind had carried them away. The confidential pages were now scattered over three descending rooftops and in the gutters. Magee called up the Vatican fire brigade, the *pompieri*, who clambered over the roofs and managed to recover every sheet. The document was reassembled and given back to a very grateful pope, who had been genuinely upset by the incident.[89]

Soon after 4.00 p.m. Luciani would be back in his office studying the list, supplied by Monsignor Martin with a full briefing, of the visitors he would have to see the following day. At 4.30 p.m., over a soothing cup of camomile tea, he would receive the *Tabella* in his office. This was essentially his inner cabinet, composed of various cardinals, archbishops and secretaries of Congregations, which met to discuss the day-to-day organization of the Church.

The evening meal was served at 7.45 p.m.; at 8.00 p.m., while still eating, Luciani would watch the news – and, when possible, Formula One motor racing – on television in the company of his two secretaries and sometimes guests also. One such guest was Father Mario Ferrarese from Venice, who dined with Luciani on 5 September, the pope wishing to repay the hospitality that Father Mario had shown towards him in Venice. The meal, a typically simple one, was served by two members of the papal staff, Guido and Gian Paolo Guzzo. Luciani asked his guest for news of Venice, then quietly said, 'Ask the people there to pray for me because it's not easy being a Pope'.[90] Turning to the Guzzo brothers he said, 'As we have a guest we must serve him a dessert', and shortly bowls of ice cream were brought. For the others wine was available; Luciani drank mineral water. Early on in his pontificate Angelo Gugel, a former agent of the *Vigilanza*, was also appointed as the pope's valet, a position he retained under Luciani's successor.

[89] Cornwell, *A Thief in the Night*, pp. 185–6.
[90] Yallop, p. 180. Much of these paragraphs are derived from Yallop, pp. 178–80.

After dinner Luciani would do more preparatory work for the following day's audiences before saying the final part of his Breviary. Then, at approximately 9.30 p.m., he would retire for the night to read or work on papers whilst sitting up in bed. This, then, was his typical daily routine, but it was a routine that he would not infrequently change. More will be related of this later, but first we must return to his more public acts.

Pope Paul had explicitly admonished his successor not to reappoint any Vatican officials for the first three months of his pontificate; in dispensing with this ruling Gianpaolo signalled both his independence of mind and his desire to regularize the running of the Church as quickly as possible. Further, his move gave the Church a period of continuity and himself time to consider which people would best fill the various posts and help him move church affairs in the direction that he wished them to go.

On the evening of Sunday 27 August, Gianpaolo invited seventy-two year old Cardinal Jean Villot to dine with him. He asked Villot if he would be prepared to continue as Secretary of State, at least for the time being. Villot, who had fulfilled this role since May 1969, accepted. The appointment was confirmed in a chirograph – an autograph letter of the pope – the same day, in which Gianpaolo noted Villot's distinguishing 'gifts of mind and heart and of pastoral sensitivity and wisdom'. He assured Villot of his 'profound admiration and sincere appreciation', his 'paternal esteem', and looked forward to his 'robust support' in his pastoral work. Further, Villot was appointed Prefect of the Council for the Public Affairs of the Church, President of the Pontifical Commission for the State of Vatican City, and President of the Administration of the Patrimony of the Holy See (APSA).[91] The confidence shown in Villot was not without significance; it demonstrated that Gianpaolo was prepared to stand by a man who had a number of critics in the Curia, especially over the way he had performed his duties as Camerlengo before the conclave.

Having shown his personal confidence in Villot, the next day Gianpaolo reconfirmed the seventeen remaining heads of the dicasteries or curial departments. Thus Archbishop Giuseppe Caprio was reappointed as substitute Secretary of State (Sostituto), and Archbishop Agostino Casaroli remained as Secretary of the Council for the Public Affairs of the Church.

---

[91] Italian original, *Insegnamenti Di Giovanni Paolo I*, pp. 22–3.

Gianpaolo was criticized in the press for these reconfirmations. This revealed ignorance of several factors besides those already mentioned. Pius XII, John XXIII and Paul VI had all done the same thing. Furthermore, he was setting no irreversible precedent, having the power to alter any appointment at any time. Finally, whilst it should have surprised nobody that Gianpaolo did not emerge from conclave with a ready-made list of appointees having had no expectations or desire of being elected, there were other indications that the appointments could be regarded as being transitional. It was common knowledge in Rome that Cardinals Seper, Wright and Garrone had already expressed their wish to resign for health reasons, whilst Cardinals Baggio, Philippe, Pignedoli, Willebrands and Paupini had already exceeded the five-year-term laid down by Paul VI.[92] The nine remaining cardinals would have to offer their resignations within two to four years.

Another of Gianpaolo's early actions also drew criticism, this time from the Curia. By a long-standing tradition its members received the equivalent of an extra month's salary on the death of a pope, and again on the election of a new one. On the death of Paul VI the first instalment was paid as usual, but Gianpaolo, with the precarious state of the Vatican's finances already in mind, cut the second instalment by half. This meant that, at 1978 rates, each member only received the equivalent of about £125 or $250 instead of £250 or $500. This may sound little enough, but with around three thousand employees the two instalments combined cost the Vatican over £1 million or $2 million, about one half of the total cost of Pope Paul's funeral and the conclave to elect his successor. Subsequently, John Paul II, on his election, restored the practice of paying a month's extra salary.[93]

Gianpaolo was, as Peter Hebblethwaite noted with his usual concise perspicacity, 'a pope in a hurry'.[94] Desire for improvement in the Church was one factor; another, darker aspect of this sense of urgency in his pontificate will be seen later in the testimony of his secretary, Father Magee.

At 11.00 a.m. on Wednesday 30 August, Gianpaolo addressed the ninety-two cardinals still left in Rome in the Hall of the Consistory. Cardinal Confalonieri as Dean of the Sacred

---

[92] Hebblethwaite, *Year of Three Popes*, p. 123. It may be noted that John Paul II and Benedict XVI also reconfirmed all heads of dicasteries in their turn.

[93] Ibid.; Greeley, pp. 147, 264 n. 2.

[94] Hebblethwaite, p. 116.

College presented their greetings in rather grandiose style. However, Gianpaolo – 'the august pontiff' – as he was addressed, had already begun to tire of all this stiff ceremonial, and he largely discarded the speech prepared for him as being 'too curial in style' and 'too unctuous'. The prepared text, the one doggedly recorded in all official publications, proclaimed the indebtedness of the entire Church to the Roman Curia, who 'ensure in that organic way the exercise of legitimate autonomies, yet in the indispensable respect of the essential unity of discipline'.[95] Gianpaolo abandoned this and gave his own impromptu discourse from the heart; only Vatican Radio who recorded the pope's address was able to report parts of what he actually said in this closed audience. With refreshing honesty, he admitted his ignorance of the Curia's structure: 'As soon as I had a little time, the first thing I did on becoming pope was to get hold of the *Annuario Pontificio* and study the organization of the Holy See.'[96]

The evidence is here that Gianpaolo already had firm ideas on the nature of his papacy. The Curia was to be put in its proper place, that of administration. In one of his picturesque allusions he likened the Church to a clock, whose hands give guidance to the world. To function, the clock needs to be wound up, and that is the task of the Curia.[97] Further, Gianpaolo told the cardinals that he expected their full cooperation. 'This, he said "would require, at times, sacrifice and a change of viewpoint on their part"'.[98] To the curial cardinals in particular he stressed that he would determine policies and their implementation, not them. All this gives the lie to those in the Curia who, after Gianpaolo's death and for their own reasons, hinted that he would have been a weak and indecisive pope had he lived.

However, it should not be imagined that his address was a 'rebuke' to the cardinals or that his words were ill received. Much of his talk was concerned with promoting genuine collegiality; he would still value the cardinals' information, advice and help, even if many final decisions must be his ultimate responsibility: he said he would have 'great need of those bishops who are far from Rome'. Giving his final blessing, he said: ' Now I am blessing you, but it seems rather strange to

---

[95] *The Teachings of Pope John Paul I*, p. 46.
[96] Hebblethwaite, *Year of Three Popes*, p. 121.
[97] Ibid.
[98] Murphy, p. 167. What these 'changes' might have entailed will be discussed in the next chapter.

give you the apostolic blessing when all of you are, in fact, as bishops, the successors of the apostles.'[99] Then he spoke with each cardinal individually. Of eighty-three-year-old Cardinal Paolo Marella he asked simply 'Please say a Hail Mary for me.' To the fifty-six year-old Cardinal Bernardin Gantin of Benin – whose name means 'Tree of Iron' and who had been tipped as an outsider by some to become the first black pope of modern times – he said 'You are young. You will have plenty of strength and be able to help me.'[100]

One other factor was picked up in this address, as in his other statements; he consistently dropped the deadening, majestic 'We' that popes had used for centuries, and spoke using the familiar 'I'. This came quite naturally to Gianpaolo, but it certainly proved to be popular with the mass of the Catholic faithful and increased their receptivity to his message. His effectiveness as a communicator was beyond doubt. However, as noted previously, just as resolutely the Vatican Press Office and *L'Osservatore Romano* ignored his informal remarks and restored the pontifical 'We' to reports of his statements. Exactly the same thing had happened to Pope John, who had therefore taken to quoting himself, in the original non-edited version, in important speeches![101]

Within a week of his election the Romans had already begun to refer to Gianpaolo as 'the censored Pope'.[102] This impression was not helped by the fact that the 'official biography' of Gianpaolo published by *L'Osservatore Romano* was selective and inaccurate, presenting a dry portrait of a conservative Luciani who simply just did not exist in reality. The biography was supposed to be 'edifying' and 'proper', but it misfired, as it was increasingly exposed as being false. Furthermore, it was this concern with 'tidying up' matters, with presenting what 'should' have been said or done, that was to give conspiracy and murder theorists such an opportunity after Gianpaolo's subsequent death.

Meanwhile, on Thursday 31 August, the pope received in audience members of the Diplomatic Corps accredited to the Holy See. After greetings and congratulations had been

99 *Tablet*, CCXXXII, 9 September 1978, p. 879.
100 Ibid., p. 876.
101 Hebblethwaite, *John XXIII*, pp. 432–3.
102 *Tablet*, CCXXXII, 9 September 1978, p. 876; Hebblethwaite, *Year of Three Popes*, p. 121. Thus early on an exaggerated impression of 'the Pope versus the Curia' was formed in the popular mind.

presented by the Guatemalan Ambassador Signor Luis Valladares y Aycinena as Dean of the Diplomatic Corps, Gianpaolo addressed the assembly in French. This was naturally a rather more formal affair, but still one full of cordial warmth. The pope admitted his inexperience in the sphere of international politics, but offered his 'sincere collaboration in fostering 'understanding and peace'. He next went on to spell out the unique mission and competence of the Holy See:

> Obviously we have no temporal goods to exchange, no economic interests to discuss, such as your States have. Our possibilities for diplomatic interventions are limited and of a special character. They do not interfere with purely temporal, technical and political affairs, which are matters for your Governments. In this way, our diplomatic missions to your highest civil authorities, far from being a survival from the past, are a witness to our deep-seated respect for lawful temporal power, and to our lively interest in the humane causes that the temporal power is intended to advance.[103]

The role of the Holy See in international affairs was, he said, twofold. Firstly, it could, if invited, participate 'at the level of your Governments or of the international entities, in the search for better solutions to the great problems that see at stake détente, disarmament, peace, justice, humanitarian measures and aid, development, etc'.[104] Secondly, the Church could act also on a more specifically pastoral level. By this Gianpaolo meant the forming of consciences, '– chiefly the consciences of Christians but also those of men and women of good will, and through these forming a wider public opinion – regarding the fundamental principles that guarantee authentic civilization and real brotherhood between peoples'.[105]

The next day, Friday 1 September, the pope gave an audience in the Hall of Benedictions to over eight hundred journalists accredited to the Holy See and other reporters present in Rome to cover the recent events. Gianpaolo seemed more relaxed than he had been the previous day, and although he spoke from his prepared text he continually expanded it with other ideas and anecdotes. He thanked the assembled press for their efforts in covering the events of August, before commenting on the importance and influence of the modern news media. To do this he quoted the remark of Cardinal Mercier, the Belgian

---

[103] *The Teachings of Pope John Paul I*, p. 49.
[104] Ibid.
[105] Ibid., p. 50.

Primate during the First World War, to the editor of *La Croix*: 'Today, St Paul would be a journalist'. 'No', the editor had said, 'he would be the director of Reuters' (this produced some scowls from the representatives of UPI, AP and Agence France Presse). Gianpaolo continued: 'I think St Paul would not only be head of Reuters but would also ask for a little time on television'.[106]

Further, the pope commented on the difficulty in achieving balance in reporting, on concentrating on central issues and not just secondary 'colour'. This he illustrated by quoting the advice of Baldasarre Avanzini, editor of *Fanfulla* at the time of the Franco-Prussian War (1870–71), to his reporter about to interview Napoleon III: 'Don't worry about what the Emperor said to the King of Prussia. Find out the colour of his socks and what kind of cigars he smokes'.[107] Everybody laughed, but the point was made, enabling him to make the serious plea that his audience should 'be willing to contribute to the safeguarding in today's society of a deep respect for the things of God and for the mysterious relationship between God and each of us'.[108]

Also on this day Gianpaolo wrote an Apostolic Letter to mark the opening of the Third International Mariological Congress to be held from 16–24 September at Guayaquil, the biggest city in Ecuador – indeed, Latin America had become an increasing preoccupation in his life. The pope wrote:

> Ecuador for Christ through Mary! Beginning with this theme, develop your life and your apostolic action. Let Mary, the Mother of Christ and the most gentle Mother of each one of us, always be your model, your guide, your path towards the elder Brother and the Saviour of all, Jesus.[109]

The pope made what on first consideration seemed a surprising choice as his Legate Extraordinary for this mission, namely the highly conservative theologian and Scripture scholar, fifty-one year-old Cardinal Joseph Ratzinger, then Archbishop of Munich and Freising. However, the Archdiocese of Munich was twinned with the Diocese of Ecuador, and the local episcopate had

---

[106] Hebblethwaite, *Year of Three Popes*, p. 122.
[107] Murphy, p. 168.
[108] *The Teachings of Pope John Paul I*, p. 53.
[109] Meaolo, p. 225; for Ratzinger's letter of appointment, see *L'Osservatore Romano*, n. 40 (549), 5 October 1978, p. 2 (English edition).

already asked for Ratzinger to be appointed as Legate.[110] Therefore, Gianpaolo merely acceded to local sensibilities and agreed to the request.

Also, it is probable that the appointment came because the matter in hand was considered to be a 'safe', doctrinal one of finite duration, not directly involving social or political matters. However, Ratzinger used the occasion to mark his debut as a critic of liberation theology, as well as criticising Marxism and the extreme Capitalism of the USA. He decried the 'great rationalisms' of the age, saying that they had led the world into a deep crisis. In interviews with the German press shortly *after* Gianpaolo's death, he claimed that the pope had also been critical of liberation theology and that the next pope should maintain that position.[111] Gianpaolo's successor made Ratzinger Prefect of the Congregation for the Doctrine of the Faith on 25 November 1981 and approved his election as Dean of the Sacred College on 30 November 2002.

The following day was given over to preparations for his inauguration. The next day, Sunday 3 September, Gianpaolo made his second brief address before reciting the noon *Angelus* from the window of his study. It was the feast day of pope St Gregory the Great, a fact of some significance to Gianpaolo, who had a devotion to St Gregory. It was Gregory, pope from 590–604, who called himself 'the servant of the servants of God', a designation still used by popes. It sheds significant light on his conception of religious authority, one close to Gianpaolo's own conception of his ministry and his episcopal motto 'Humilitas'. Amongst other things, he commented on the saint's reluctance to accept his election to the papacy, quoting Gregory's observation to the Emperor's sister: 'The Emperor has wanted a monkey to become a lion'.[112] He sympathized with Gregory, and approvingly noted the latter's book *Pastoral Rule* suggesting, however, that he himself fell short of its ideals.

What happened that evening was quite revolutionary in papal terms, and perhaps marks the most visible and lasting symbol of Gianpaolo's papacy. At 6.00 p.m. he was simply 'inaugurated in his ministry as supreme pastor'.

---

[110] Ratzinger interviewed by G. Cardinale, 'The Lord Chooses Our Poverty', *30 Days*, no. 9, September 2003. The two men had met only once before, in August 1977 at the diocesan seminary of Bressanone, when Luciani had paid a courtesy call on the vacationing Bavarian.

[111] Allen, pp. 121–2, 148–9.

[112] *The Teachings of Pope John Paul I*, p. 5.

The coronation of John XXIII in 1958 had taken almost five hours. John was crowned with the triple-decked papal tiara in a traditional ceremony that included him being carried in procession in the *sedia gestatoria* – the portable papal chair – amidst uniformed officials, fans of ostrich plumes (*fabelli*) and fanfares of silver trumpets. Three times before the procession even reached the main altar of St Peter's, Franciscans touched flame to a ball of flax. As it flared and quickly burned itself out, the master of ceremonies intoned the ancient reminder that men are mortal and their works ephemeral: '*Pater sancte, sic transit gloria mundi*' ('Holy Father, thus passes the glory of the world').

In June 1963, Paul VI cut the ceremonial for his open-air coronation down to three hours, and never again wore the papal tiara after 13 November 1964. However, it was left to John Paul to sweep away all the time-honoured accretions and to truly and irrevocably alter the real meaning of the service. Gone now was any suggestion of temporal claims: what remained was the simplicity of a solemn Mass and the moving, spiritual significance of John Paul becoming supreme pastor of his flock.

If his radical simplification and reorientation of the ceremony surprised some, it was entirely consistent with his actions on becoming Patriarch of Venice, when he had abolished the traditional grand entry into that city. Some aspects of Gianpaolo's changes may seem relatively trivial, but compared with the outlook of the Roman Curia, which is said to 'think in centuries', they were as bold and profound as those of Pope John. His abolition of the crowning, for instance, broke with a tradition that dated back to the coronation of Pope Nicholas II in 1059.[113] Further, whilst Paul VI had been the first pope to have representatives from non-Catholic churches present at his coronation, including some from the Patriarch of Moscow, Gianpaolo's inauguration was the first time that the Soviet Union had ever been represented at a papal ceremony.[114] Gianpaolo's papacy accelerated a process that had begun with John XXIII and Paul VI, that of the growth in the spiritual standing of the Holy See in proportion to the diminution of its temporal ostentation.

It cannot be too strongly emphasized at this point that Luciani's actions were more than another unconscious demonstration of personal humility; they also formed another practical example of his method of catechesis. This time he was

---

[113] *Tablet*, CCXXXII, 9 September 1978, p. 878.
[114] *Catholic Herald*, no. 4821, 8 September 1978, p. 2.

making a statement on how he viewed the very nature of the Petrine office itself. The more theologically controversial titles like 'Vicar of Jesus Christ' and 'Supreme Pontiff of the Universal Church' were quietly dropped in favour of 'Bishop of Rome' and 'Supreme Pastor'.

Before the ceremony began Gianpaolo spent a while in silent prayer before the tomb of St Peter. Cardinal Pericle Felici 'greeted the pope while he was still at the tomb of St Peter with the liturgical expression that "the Lord would make him happy on earth". Smilingly he answered: "Yes, happy on the outside, but if only you knew what I felt like inside – *si scires*!"'.[115] What his thoughts and emotions were in those moments can only be imagined; perhaps more than any other pope in history he was acutely aware of the magnitude and diversity of the flock for which he was now personally responsible, and of the enormity and variety of the problems and dangers which beset them. That he must have prayed fervently for guidance and strength needs no elaboration.

At 6.00 p.m., and with the heat of the Roman day starting to abate, the ceremony began with a procession, the Holy Father, like everyone else, on foot. Crowded into the piazza were between 200,000 and 300,000 people, including over twelve thousand Italian police and carabinieri, a reflection on the times. Present were twelve Heads of State, with delegations from many more, while television carried the two-and-a-half hour event to millions of people in over fifty countries. Amongst the rather soberly dressed Heads of State, Queen Sophia, consort of King Juan Carlos I of Spain, stood out resplendently; by historic privilege Queens of Spain may wear white at papal ceremonies. Before the gaze of the world the cardinals venerated the open-air altar in pairs, according to the new liturgy devised by Mgr Virgilio Noè, newly reappointed Master of Ceremonies, and a commission of experts who had worked hard during the past week to prepare it.[116]

Spontaneous applause broke out as Cardinal Felici approached the seated pope for the most important part of the ceremony, the Imposition of the Pallium. Removing the pope's mitre, Felici placed the pallium, a circular band of white wool with a pendant hanging down the front and back and embroidered with six black Latin crosses, over Gianpaolo's shoulders, pronouncing a Latin benediction:

---

[115] Felici's sermon of 6 October 1978, quoted in Hebblethwaite, *Year of Three Popes*, p. 138.
[116] *Pontiff*, p. 316.

Blessed be God who has chosen you as Pastor of the whole Church, confiding to you the apostolic ministry. May you be able to shine gloriously for many years of earthly life so that when you are called by the Lord you may be clad with immortality as you enter the heavenly Kingdom. Amen.[117]

The pallium is an ancient symbol of Christian unity, having been presented to metropolitan archbishops of both East and West since the fourth century. In this context it became the ultimate symbol of the pope's pastoral ministry, the sign that he could now carry out his unique pastoral role to the fullness of his ability. Being placed over the shoulders, the pallium resembles a yoke and is a reminder that the service of unity and the People of God will not be easy, but that the Lord will lighten the burden. Further, it is presented as coming 'from the tomb of St Peter', and that all authority and stewardship in the Church derives from Christ through the founding Apostle.[118]

Immediately after the Imposition, and while the choir alternately sang *Tu es Petrus* and the *Benedictus Deus*, each one of the 104 cardinals present made their individual obedience to Gianpaolo, kissing his hand and receiving an embrace and the kiss of peace in return. For each one the pope had a few words; to Cardinal Hume he said 'Don't forget that I'm relying on the prayers of British Catholics'.[119] These personal acts of homage over, the Mass began, with the pope himself as chief concelebrant, accompanied by Gregorian chant. Italian and American seminarians from the Gregorian University in Rome served the Mass. The Gospel was sung in both Latin and Greek to symbolize the unity of the two rites, and the scriptural readings were given in nine languages, thus marking the universality of the Church.

Gianpaolo began his homily in Latin, still the official language of the Church, but he continued in his lilting Veneto Italian and then in French, before concluding in Italian again. He spoke simply about the origins, the nature and the significance of the Petrine office and of the responsibility that was now his. He thanked the people of Rome and throughout the world for their 'warm manifestations of affection' towards him since his election, and in turn sent his greetings to humankind everywhere, including both Catholics and those of 'other Churches and Ecclesial Communities'.[120]

---

[117] *The Teachings of Pope John Paul I*, p. 54.
[118] Hebblethwaite, *Year of Three Popes*, pp.125–6; *Pontiff*, p. 317.
[119] Hebblethwaite, *Year of Three Popes*, p. 126.
[120] For the full address, see *The Teachings of Pope John Paul I*, pp. 54–8.

By the end of the pope's address darkness was starting to fall, and the television lights became useful. When the time came to distribute Communion, members of the pope's own family and the people who had come in busloads from the dioceses of Belluno, Vittorio Veneto and Venice received the host from Gianpaolo's own hands. To distribute the host to the crowd, 200 priests were on hand. Finally, the ceremony drew to a close with the singing of the *Te Deum* and with the pope rising and walking into St Peter's.

With such unaffected yet epoch-making gestures did Gianpaolo mark his brief ministry. The new-style inauguration had been a resounding success, and yet the event had been somewhat marred by the intrusion of contemporary politics. Amongst the Heads of State present was Lt. General Jorge Rafaél Videla, the dictatorial President of Argentina. Such was that country's record on human rights that several activist groups had protested at Videla's participation; Amnesty International had gone so far as to send an open letter to the Holy Father.[121] Throughout the ceremonies Videla and his consort were escorted by Archbishop Agostino Casaroli 'in what seemed to be an obvious gesture of preventative goodwill'[122] by the pope. In the middle of Gianpaolo's address, angry shouts were heard, leaflets were scattered in the air and from several points around the piazza red balloons floated upwards, all bearing the legend *VIDELA – ASSASSINI!*. The police waded in, fights broke out with the demonstrators and 282 were arrested. Gianpaolo gave no sign of his awareness of what was going on, while the police gathered protectively about Videla.

After the events Gianpaolo was criticized for inviting such men as Videla, the Chilean Foreign Minister and the son of the President of Paraguay to his Inauguration. The criticism was ill-informed and misplaced. The Catholic Workers' Movement actually issued a statement expressing the hope that the pope *would* intervene with Videla on behalf of political prisoners in Argentina.[123] The fact of the matter was that the pope had not wanted these men to be present, and had expressed this wish to the Secretariat of State. However, he was too late, for the invitations had already been sent. When the criticism were made later, Gianpaolo could not respond without laying Cardinal Villot open for criticism, and this was not his way.

[121] Murphy, p. 172.
[122] Ibid.
[123] *Tablet*, CCXXXII, 9 September 1978, p. 881.

There was no point in prolonging the controversy and so he remained silent.

The next day the pope received in audience the heads of the 131 Official Missions who had been present at his inaugural ceremony. He dedicated himself to promoting international peace and understanding, whilst frankly admitting that he had no 'miracle solutions for the great world problems'. He also expressed the hope that the Christian communities in the countries represented at the audience would 'always enjoy the respect and freedom to which every religious conscience is entitled, and that their contribution in the pursuit of the common good will be given a just place'. His heart, he said, was 'completely open to all peoples'.[124]

A number of the leaders had private audiences as well. One was General Videla, and it was now that Luciani made his true feelings known, person to person, away from the glare of publicity. The audience lasted about fifteen minutes, and in that time Gianpaolo voiced his protest against the widely-reported injustices, torture and murders carried out by the general's regime, and in particular over the fate of '*Los Desaparecidos*', the thousands of political opponents who had 'disappeared' in Argentina. Videla must have wished that he had heeded the last minute pleas of Cardinal Aramburu and other Vatican officials to stay away.[125] At any rate, the general was very noticeably absent from Gianpaolo's funeral on 4 October, one month later.

A happier audience was the one granted to the Democrat Vice-President of the USA, Walter Mondale. Mondale gave Gianpaolo a book comprising the front pages of over fifty American newspapers announcing the new pope's election. On a more personal level, Gianpaolo was also presented with a first edition copy of Mark Twain's *Life On The Mississippi*; someone in the State Department had indeed done some timely research on the new pope.[126]

Tuesday 5 September was a day of mixed fortunes. During the day Gianpaolo met Frère Roger Schutz, the Swiss Protestant founder and Prior of the world-famous ecumenical community of Taizé in southern Burgundy.[127] Schutz commented: 'I said

---

[124] *The Teachings of Pope John Paul I*, p. 60.
[125] Murphy, p. 172; *Pontiff*, pp. 318–19; Yallop, p. 162. Videla retired in 1981; on Argentina's return to civilian rule he was convicted of murder and sentenced to life imprisonment in 1985.
[126] Yallop, p. 162.
[127] *Tablet*, CCXXXII, 7 October 1978, p. 958. Schutz (1915–2005).

to myself, this man has such humanity ... that at the risk of being torn apart he will try everything in order to keep hold of the two ends of the chain'.[128] But this auspicious occasion was overshadowed by a much grimmer occurrence, one of the saddest of Luciani's brief reign.

On the death of Paul VI the Holy Synod of the Russian Orthodox Church decided that its delegation to the pope's funeral should be led by Metropolitan Nikodim of Leningrad and Novgorod, Patriarchal Exarch to Western Europe. Forty-eight years old and a big, impressive man, Nikodim was very much in favour of contact with the Roman Catholic Church; he had played a leading role in negotiations to enable Russian Orthodox observers to attend the Second Vatican Council, and had frequently headed ecumenical delegations from Moscow to Rome. Also interesting was the fact that his doctoral thesis, completed in 1970, had been on the pontificate of John XXIII.[129]

In 1975 Nikodim had been elected President of the World Council of Churches. On 22 May the same year he had journeyed to the shrine at Fatima where he had celebrated a *moleben* in honour of the Most Blessed Holy Mother of God. Whilst in Rome for Paul VI's funeral, he made ecumenical history on 10 August by saying a *panikhida* – a Russian Orthodox prayer service – before the body of the dead pope as it lay in state at St Peter's. At Gianpaolo's inauguration he was seated in the front row of the ecumenical delegations.

On this Tuesday, the day when Gianpaolo received delegations from non-Catholic Churches and Christian Communities, the Russian Orthodox members – Metropolitan Nikodim accompanied by Archimandrite Lev Tserpitsky – were welcomed into the pope's private study at 10.00 a.m., having been allotted a full fifteen minutes. What happened next has been most ably told by Deacon Vladimir Rusak:

> Metropolitan Nikodim and Pope John Paul I greeted each other with brotherly affection. Metropolitan Nikodim conveyed to the Primate of the Roman Catholic Church cordial greetings on behalf of His Holiness Patriarch Pimen of Moscow and All Russia, the Holy Synod and the whole Plenitude of the Russian Orthodox Church and wished the new Pope many years of service in this office. He then

[128] Cornwell, *A Thief in the Night*, p. 9.
[129] *Journal of the Moscow Patriarchate*, no. 11, 1978, p. 15; no. 9, 1980, p. 62. Nikodim was awarded the degree of Magister of Theology for his dissertation 'John XXIII – The Discomforting Optimist'.

voiced the hope that the development of fraternal relations between our Churches, which began so well during the pontificate of Pope John XXIII and continued under Pope Paul VI, would proceed even further to the strengthening of mutual understanding between our Churches and their joint service in the cause of peace.

Pope John Paul I thanked the metropolitan for his good wishes and asked him, in turn, to convey to His Holiness Patriarch Pimen his wishes of good health and fruitful labours for the good of the Russian Orthodox Church. The Pope said he had always followed the ecumenical movement, in which Metropolitan Nikodim took an active part, and supported it with all his heart. He hoped that this cause would continue to make progress. Metropolitan Nikodim then presented Archimandrite Lev to His Holiness. It was at this moment that the fatal attack occurred. Metropolitan Nikodim turned very pale and slid off his chair onto the carpet. The doctor [Renato Buzzonetti], immediately sent for, gave the necessary injections and applied heart massage, but medicine was already powerless. Death was instantaneous as a result of heart failure.[130]

Gianpaolo, Cardinal Willebrands, Archimandrite Lev and Father Miguel Arranz SJ, Vice-Rector of the Russicum College in Rome who was acting as interpreter, fell on their knees by Nikodim's prostrate body. The pope, in Latin, said the prayers for the dying and for the remission of sins.

Initially he was stunned, repeating 'My God, my God, even this has to happen to me,'[131] but, to his credit, Gianpaolo quickly regained his composure and continued with his appointments. He also sent a telegram of fraternal sympathy to Moscow, which it will be worth noting here as it is sadly missing from the English translation of the official *'Insegnamenti di Giovanni Paolo I'*, which gives the telegram in its original French form:

To His Holiness Patriarch PIMEN:
Profoundly perturbed by the death of Metropolitan Nikodim during our conversation, we express to Your Holiness and the Holy Synod of the Russian Orthodox Church our feelings of great sorrow. We assure you of our prayers for the repose of the soul of this devoted servant of his Church and champion of the cause of deepening relations between our Churches. May the Lord receive him in His joy and peace.

Pope JOHN PAUL I.[132]

[130] Rusak, p. 13.
[131] Arranz, quoted in '. . . I Had Never Heard Such Fine Things', *30 Days*, June / July 2006.
[132] *Journal of the Moscow Patriarchate*, no. 11, 1978, p. 3.

At 5.00 p.m. on 7 September Gianpaolo met a delegation from Moscow in the same room in which Nikodim had died and he 'recounted with emotion the Russian hierarch's death, which had so perturbed him'.[133] The next day Nikodim's body was flown to Leningrad, and finally buried there in the brethren's graveyard of St Alexsandr Nevsky Lavra on 10 September with much honour. It was known that Nikodim's health was poor: he had suffered five previous heart attacks since March 1972, and he had, on medical advice, decreased his immense workload over the last few years. That morning he had shown signs of extreme fatigue. However, these facts did not stop a false, malicious rumour from circulating that Nikodim had drunk a cup of poisoned coffee that had been intended for the pope. Even the authors of *Pontiff* and *In God's Name* refute this,[134] but in the light of Gianpaolo's own subsequent death it shows the prevalent atmosphere and just what nonsense people were prepared to listen to. In retrospect, the rumour surrounding Nikodim's death could be seen as a sign of what was to take place after the unexpected death of the immensely popular, newly elected Gianpaolo.

The pontificate gathered pace. On Wednesday 6 September, the day after Metropolitan Nikodim's untimely death, Gianpaolo gave his first General Audience in the Nervi Hall. Opened on 30 June 1971 the huge auditorium, standing partly outside Vatican City territory, seating 6,300 people and equipped with glass-fronted booths for media commentators, is the work of Pier Luigi Nervi. Inside, behind the elevated platform at the western end, stands the largest bronze sculpture in the world, the Risen Christ, the creation of Pericle Fazzini. Commissioned in 1965 and unveiled on 28 September 1977 by Pope Paul, this stunning sculpture depicts 'the resurrection of Christ as if after atomic destruction on Earth'. Together, the hall – subsequently renamed the Paul VI Audience Hall – and its sculpture form the last major examples of papal patronage to date.

On this day an estimated twelve thousand people were crowded into the hall, including forty cardinals, nearly a hundred bishops, fifty or more television and still-cameramen and over two hundred reporters and broadcasters.[135] Gianpaolo was already held to be a most innovative, lively and quotable pope. He entered the hall on foot, and in the highly

[133] Rusak, p. 14.
[134] *Pontiff*, p. 344; Yallop, p. 224.
[135] *Pontiff*, p. 344.

emotionally charged atmosphere it took him half an hour to walk the length of the hall, shaking hands and exchanging greetings all the way, before seating himself on the throne beneath the Risen Christ.

At subsequent General Audiences, Gianpaolo was carried in on the *sedia gestatoria*. This in no way signified a change of heart on his part, but rather it was a result of another difference of outlook between himself and a section of the Curia. He detested the chair and its implications; feeling himself to be no better than other men, he did not wish to be carried on their backs. The traditionalists argued, however, that the faithful could not see him properly; the chair should return. Gianpaolo countered that he was seen frequently on television, and that he was clearly visible on the balcony when saying the noon *Angelus* every Sunday. Now the argument was advanced that he should practice true humility by being carried in the chair that he so disliked.

Gianpaolo's humility was transparently genuine – as the Curia well knew – and at this point he gave in, but still he never used the *sedia gestatoria* at solemn ceremonies. The episode forms a disgraceful comment on the worst kind of curial mentality, and how this outwardly trivial issue would have been resolved in the long term must remain as speculation. The mould was broken, however, as Gianpaolo's successor never used the chair, with no obvious signs of discontent from the faithful.

To return to Gianpaolo's address on 6 September, he held the rapt attention of his audience right from the start, when he introduced the cardinals and bishops present as 'my brothers in the episcopate. I am only their elder brother'.[136] This was such a simple, natural, disarming statement that its significance must be consciously thought out, especially now in the era of the 'post-Gianpaolo' papacy. John XXIII and Paul VI had reduced the exaggerated veneration of the person of the pope, and many progressive theologians before and since have argued for increased collegiality in the Church, but for a reigning pope to suggest, even by inference, a re-evaluation of the Petrine office was quite something. He acknowledged the catechetical example of Pope Paul in speaking to the people every Wednesday in the Hall, and added: 'I will try to imitate him, in the hope that I, too, will be able, somehow, to help people to become better'.[137]

---

[136] *The Teachings of Pope John Paul I*, p. 15.
[137] Ibid.

The purpose of his discourse was to expound the virtue of humility, but what touched and delighted people was the simplicity and directness of his speech. He was so readily understandable, making his points clearly, concisely and in an evocative way. His audience, both his immediate one and that communicated with via the media, quickly became eager to hear another of his modern parables, little stories illustrated with everyday events. They laughed with recognition and his point was made. A consummate narrator, Luciani had the gift of humour and impeccable delivery; he left flights of oratory and convoluted theology to others. 'Simplicity' can be merely the result of ill-conceived ideas, or it can be the product of a process of distillation in a highly intelligent and sensitive mind, and is not common. Luciani's 'simplicity' was of the second type, and that he struck a chord was shown in the almost universal response towards him of men, women and children from all walks of life.

After his introductory comments, the pope began his teaching:

> We must feel small before God. When I say, 'Lord, I believe', I am not ashamed to feel like a child before his mother; one believes in one's mother; I believe in the Lord, in what he has revealed to me. The commandments are a little more difficult to observe; but God gave them to us not to satisfy a whim, not in his own interest, but solely in our interest.[138]

Having established his subject, he proceeded to tell one of his illustrative stories:

> Once a man went to buy a motorcar from the agent. The latter talked to him plainly: 'Look here, it's a good car; mind that you treat it well: premium petrol in the tank, and oil for the joints; the good stuff'. But the other replied: 'Oh no, for your information, I can't stand even the smell of petrol or of oil; I'll put champagne, which I like so much, in the tank and I'll oil the joints with jam.' 'Do what you like; but don't come and complain if you end up in a ditch, with your car!' The Lord did something similar with us: he gave us this body, animated by an intelligent soul, a good will. He said, 'this machine is a good one, but treat it well'.[139]

---

[138] Ibid. Luciani's comment on being before God 'like a child before his *mother*' is interesting. It obviously seemed to him to be a more caring, intimate relationship. On 10 September he made an even more direct allusion to God's 'mother-like nature'.

[139] *The Teachings of Pope John Paul I*, pp. 15–16.

This produced great applause. When the crowd quieted, he observed that: 'If we were able to observe the commandments, we would be better off and so would the world'.[140] Gianpaolo then moved on to talk of particular examples of humility, of showing love and consideration for others, whether they be above us, our equals or below us. Above us, he said, are our parents: 'The pope must instill respect and obedience in children for their parents'.[141] To help him develop the point he called forward one of the altarboys from Malta, James DiMech di Bono, who had been serving Masses in St Peter's for a month. The circumstances must have been quite awe-inspiring for the ten-year-old boy, but the pope was good at making people feel at ease, and had a particularly sure way with children. This incident, and another similar one on 27 September at his last General Audience, showed another facet of Gianpaolo: 'Other world leaders were adept at picking up the young and kissing them. Here was a man who actually talked to them and even more remarkably listened and responded to what they had to say'.[142]

> He asked the boy his name, and the latter responded 'James'.
> James. And listen, have you ever been ill?
> No.
> Ah, never?
> No.
> Never been ill?
> No.
> Not even a temperature?
> No.
> Oh, how lucky you are! (The crowd was delighted; the pope patted the child's head.) But when a child is ill, who brings him a little broth, some medicine? Isn't it his mother? That's it. Afterwards you grow up, and your mother gets old; you become a fine gentleman, and your mother, poor thing, will be in bed, ill. That's it. Well, who will bring the mother a little milk and medicine? Who will?
> My brothers and I.
> (Gianpaolo beamed infectiously at this natural answer.) Well said! 'His brothers and he', he said. I like that. Did you understand?[143]

The crowd cheered and showed its approval. Gianpaolo continued, this time showing the other side of the coin; to do so, he

---

[140] Ibid., p. 16.
[141] Ibid.
[142] Yallop, p. 160.
[143] *The Teachings of Pope John Paul I*, p. 16.

drew on personal experience, subtly changing his voice to play both parts:

> But it does not always happen. As Bishop of Venice, I sometimes went to homes. Once I found an elderly woman, sick.
> How are you?
> Well, the food is all right!
> Are you warm? Is there heating?
> It's good.
> So are you content?
> 'No' She almost began to cry.
> But why are you crying?
> My daughter-in-law, my son, never come to see me. I would like to see my grandchildren.
> (In the hall, as the pope drew his moral from this, some people were actually crying.)
> Heat and food are not enough, there is the heart; we must think of the heart of our old people. The Lord said that parents must be respected and loved, even when they are old.[144]

Gianpaolo went on, mentioning the need for people to respect their superiors; here he smiled at James, gave him a final pat on the head, and sent him back to his place. He moved on to talk of how we are to treat our equals:

> And here, there are usually two virtues to observe: justice and charity. But charity is the soul of Justice. We must love our neighbour, the Lord recommended it so much. I always recommend not only great acts of charity, but little ones.[145]

To illustrate this, he repeated a little episode that he had read in Dale Carnegie's book *How to Win Friends and Influence People*, before drawing the conclusion for his audience: 'People work more willingly when their work is recognized. These are the little acts of charity. In our home we all have someone who is waiting for a compliment'.[146]

Finally, the pope spoke of 'those who are smaller than we are; there are children, the sick, even sinners'. With regard to the latter, he recommended mercy and humility. In doing so he made an exceedingly interesting statement that obviously came from deep within himself, and revealed the view that he

---

[144] Ibid., pp. 16–17.
[145] Ibid., p. 17.
[146] Ibid.

had always had of both himself and those who had been entrusted to his pastoral care:

> I run the risk of making a blunder [*uno sproposito*], but I will say it: the Lord loves humility so much that, sometimes, he permits serious sins. Why? In order that those who committed these sins may, after repenting, remain humble. One does not feel inclined to think oneself half a saint, half an angel, when one knows that one has committed serious faults. The Lord recommended it so much: be humble. Even if you have done great things, say 'We are useless servants'. On the contrary, the tendency in all of us is rather the contrary: to show off. Lowly, lowly: this is the Christian virtue which concerns ourselves.[147]

Gianpaolo had one other matter of great importance to raise that day. At the close of the audience he earnestly asked the crowd to pray for the success of the talks going on at Camp David between President Jimmy Carter of the United States, President Anwar Sadat of Egypt and Prime Minister Menachem Begin of Israel, and their efforts to secure peace for the Middle East.[148] He said earnestly, in language that, tragically, still has great contemporary relevance:

> This conflict, which has been going on for over thirty years on the land of Jesus, has already caused so many victims, so much suffering, both among the Arabs and among the Israelis, and like a bad disease it has infected neighbouring countries. Just think of Lebanon, a martyrized Lebanon, devastated by the repercussions of this crisis. For this reason, therefore, I would like to pray, together with you, for the success of the Camp David Meeting: that these conversations may clear the way for a just and complete peace. Just, that is, to the satisfaction of all the conflicting parties. Complete, without leaving any question unsolved: the problem of the Palestinians, the safety of Israel, the holy city of Jerusalem. Let us pray to the Lord to enlighten the leaders of all the peoples concerned, so that they may be far-sighted and courageous in making decisions that must bring serenity and peace to the Holy Land and to the whole of the Eastern world.[149]

The fate of the Middle East, and in particular the Lebanon,

---

[147] Ibid., p. 18.
[148] *Insegnamenti Di Giovanni Paolo I*, p. 54. This passage is not given in the English edition.
[149] *L'Osservatore Romano*, n. 40 (549), 5 October 1978, p.11 (English edition).

whose civil war had been escalating since 13 April 1975, was much on his mind; it was a subject to which he was to return at his noon *Angelus* address the following Sunday, and which he discussed on at least three other occasions during his short papacy, as will be seen shortly. At any rate, this first General Audience was a huge success, and was a far greater lesson in humility than any curial casuistry over the sedia gestatoria.

The following day, 7 September, Gianpaolo's thoughts moved closer to home when he met the priests of the Rome diocese for the first time in audience. He developed the theme of the 'great discipline of the Church' that he had mentioned when speaking to the cardinals in the Sistine Chapel on 27 August, and which he distinguished from the "little" discipline, which is limited to purely external and formal observance of juridical norms'.[150] The great discipline, he said, 'exists only if external observance is the fruit of deep convictions and the free and joyful projection of a life lived deeply (in intimacy with) God'.[151] The soul needed to continually master its bad inclinations, which required 'continued, long and difficult effort'. Here he was back to what he had written in February 1976, when he had quoted from Sadhu Sundar Singh in order to point out that Christianity should penetrate, live within and change people for the better, and not be merely an external show, an act of hypocrisy.

The pope said he wanted to speak to his audience with 'brotherly familiarity' and the whole tone of his address was informal, that of a priest speaking to fellow priests in the light of shared experience. Naturally he sympathized with their problems because he too had experienced them; what was remarkable was the way he let them know this. In continuing his theme he related another of his stories taken from life:

> The 'great' discipline requires a suitable atmosphere; and, in the first place, meditation. At Milan station I once saw a porter, who, with his head resting on a sack of coal propped against a pillar, was sound asleep ... Trains left whistling and arrived with clanking wheels, the loudspeakers continually boomed out announcements; people came and went in confusion and noise, but he – sleeping on – seemed to be saying: 'Do what you like, but I need to be quiet'. We priests should do something similar: around us there is continual movement and talking, of persons, newspapers, radio and television. With priestly moderation and discipline we must say: 'Beyond certain limits, for me, who am a priest of the Lord, you do

---

[150] *The Teachings of Pope John Paul I*, p. 61.
[151] Ibid.

not exist. I must take a little silence for my soul. I detach myself from you to be united with my God.[152]

Many people, Gianpaolo went on, wanted to feel that their priest was 'habitually united with God', that God was acting through their priest, which would indeed be the case if the priest was a true pastor. The model of the true pastor, he said, after quoting from St Gregory the Great's *Regula Pastoralis*, should be the local bishop, who presided through service:

> Our presidency is just if it consists of service or takes place for the purpose of service, with the spirit and style of service. This episcopal service would be lacking, however, if the Bishop did not wish to exercise the powers received.[153]

It was for this reason that the Second Vatican Council's *Lumen Gentium* stated that: 'Bishops govern ... by their counsel, exhortations and example, as well, indeed, as by their authority and sacred power.'[154]

The pope departed from his text – although, once more, this fact is totally ignored in all official versions – to speak of the late Metropolitan Nikodim, who had died in his presence only two days before. He cited him as an example of a priest deeply united with God and close to his fellow men, and paid tribute to him as one 'who suffered much for the Church and did a great deal to further the cause of unity'.[155] He assured his listeners that 'never in my life had I heard such beautiful words for the Church. I cannot repeat them; that is a secret'.[156]

Gianpaolo then moved on to another element of priestly discipline, that of having love for one's own job. He faced realities:

> It is not easy, I know, to love one's job and stick to it when things are not going right, when one has the impression that one is not understood or encouraged, when inevitable comparison with the job given to others would drive us to become sad and discouraged. But are we not working for the Lord? Ascetical theology teaches: do not look at whom you obey, but for Whom you obey.[157]

---

[152] Ibid., p. 62. This last statement strongly echoes the 'self-regulatory' ideas expressed in various places in Pope John XXIII's famous *Journal of a Soul*.

[153] Ibid., p. 63.

[154] Ibid.; LG. 27/351.

[155] *Tablet*, CCXXXII, 16 September 1978, p. 901.

[156] A. Santini, *A Thousand Years Of Faith In Russia*, 1987, St Paul Publications, p. 124. He later said of Nikodim to a friend that he was '*un vero santo!*', 'a true saint!': Quoted in Seabeck, p. 64.

[157] *The Teachings of Pope John Paul I*, p. 63.

Again he recommended 'reflection' and added that having been a bishop for twenty years, on several occasions he had 'suffered because I was unable to reward someone who really deserved it; but either the prize position was lacking, or I did not know how to replace the person, or adverse circumstances occurred'.[158] Some ideas from St Francis de Sales on the restlessness of the human spirit rounded off this train of thought, before he made his concluding comments to this unusual but friendly papal introduction to the Roman clergy:

> I have spoken simply and I apologize for it. I can assure you, however, that since I have become your Bishop I love you a great deal. And it is with a heart full of love that I impart to you the Apostolic Blessing.[159]

The next really noteworthy event of Gianpaolo's pontificate was the noon *Angelus* address, already alluded to, that he gave to the faithful gathered in St Peter's Square on Sunday 10 September. In the event it generated some mild controversy. The pope returned to the topic of the Camp David summit, which took place from 5–17 September. He spoke for many, also showing his personal concern, when he said:

> All men are hungry and thirsty for peace, especially the poor who pay more and suffer more in troubled times and in wars; for this reason they look to the Camp David meeting with interest and great hope. The Pope, too, has prayed, had prayers said, and is praying that the Lord may deign to help the efforts of these politicians.[160]

He said that he was 'very favourably impressed' by the fact that the three leaders 'wished to express their hope in the Lord publicly in prayer', before continuing his discourse:

> Also we who are here have the same sentiments: we are the objects of undying love on the part of God. We know: he always has his eyes open on us, even when it seems to be dark. He is our father; even more he is our mother. He does not want to hurt us; he wants only to do good to us, to all of us. If children are ill, they have addi-

---

[158] Ibid.

[159] Ibid., p. 64.

[160] Ibid., p. 7. The summit led to negotiations and a peace treaty, which was signed on 26 March 1979 and ratified on 26 April 1979. Camp David is in Maryland, USA.

tional claim to be loved by their mother. And we too, if by chance we are sick with badness, on the wrong track, have yet another claim to be loved by the Lord.[161]

With these words Gianpaolo concluded, asking for prayers 'for the Middle East, for Iran, and for the whole world'. His statement about God – '*He is our Father; even more he is our mother*' – caused a certain amount of confusion and controversy, until the pope himself settled the matter by simply stating that the concept was the Prophet Isaiah's, not his own. He was happy that the popular imagination had been stimulated. After his sudden death, however, the remark 'gave the cartoonists the chance to show him streaking happily heavenward, shouting "Mamma!"'.[162]

In actual fact, Gianpaolo had firm theological precedents and support from tradition for speaking as he did. Apart from Isaiah (Is 49:15), St Gregory of Nyssa (*Contra Eunomium*, 2), St Anselm (*Prayer To St Paul*), Dame Julian of Norwich (*Showings*, ch. 61), St Teresa of Ávila (*The Way Of Perfection*, ch. XXXI), amongst others, all used powerful images of the nuturing, maternal nature of God and our relationship with the Divinity. Père J-P De Caussade, SJ, whom Luciani read whilst a seminarian, referred to God as 'that mother of love who is calling us', and to the faithful as being 'like children playing in their mother's lap'.[163] Whilst still a seminarian himself Angelo Roncalli, later John XXIII, wrote in his diary about God's care for him: 'He took me ... and with the affection of a loving mother he has given me all I needed ... and he still cares for me without respite, day and night, more than a mother cares for her child' (*Journal Of A Soul*, 10–20 December 1902).[164] The Trappist spiritual writer and social activist Fr M. Louis Merton, OCSO – Thomas Merton – in explaining about *Hagia Sophia* in a private letter to a Catholic friend dated 14 May 1959, wrote: 'God is not only Father but a Mother', referring to this belief as 'a very ancient intuition of reality'.[165] Gianpaolo's 'innovation', then, although he had no opportunity to develop his ideas, was to give the concept

---

[161] Ibid., pp. 7–8.
[162] Nichols, p. 218.
[163] J-P De Caussade, *The Sacrament Of The Present Moment*, 1981, tr. K. Muggeridge, Fount, pp. 52, 118.
[164] For a sensitive treatment of this subject see M. Hebblethwaite, *Motherhood And God*, 1984, Geoffrey Chapman.
[165] M. Furlong, *Merton: A Biography*, 1995 (rev. edn), Liguori, p. 218.

such widespread publicity and the stamp of papal authority.

On 30 November 1980 John Paul II issued his encyclical *Dives In Misericordia* in which he confirmed his predecessor's teaching. He analyzed the various words the Old Testament uses to describe God's mercy; one is '*rahamim*', or maternal love. Then he too quoted Isaiah 49:15.[166]

The situation in the Middle East, and in the Lebanon in particular, remained in the pope's mind. Before many others he saw the potentially explosive situation building in that troubled land. He discussed the problem with Archbishop Agostino Casaroli, and informed him that he wished to visit Beirut before Christmas 1978, then less than four months away.[167] This statement was quite astonishing coming from a newly elected pope, but Gianpaolo was perfectly serious. He wanted to *do* something and he talked at length about that country's problems and his desire to intercede personally before disaster struck.

However, it must be said that Gianpaolo's inexperience concerning the complexity of Vatican diplomacy nearly caused a diplomatic incident in that very area of the world that seemed to cause him most anguish. When he had settled into office he wrote a personal note of thanks to, amongst others, the Israeli President Yitzhak Navon, thanking him for his good wishes on his accession to the throne of St Peter. He had also written the envelope himself, concluding the address 'Jerusalem, Israel'. Horrified aides in the Secretariat of State intercepted the letter before it was posted. The implications of this innocent act, one so easily made, have been concisely told by Paul Hofmann:

> The address, in the papal handwriting, would have been tantamount to a Vatican acknowledgement that Jerusalem was the capital of the Jewish state. Ever since the end of World War II the papacy had advocated a special international status for Jerusalem, and had never recognized Israel's claim, after the 1967 war, to exclusive and sovereign jurisdiction over the Holy City.[168]

Another, relatively minor error was committed when, addressing a group of Spanish pilgrims, Gianpaolo cheerfully exclaimed '*¡Arriba España!*', clearly not realizing that this was a Falangist slogan, discredited in the democratic Spain that had arisen

---

[166] *Dives In Misericordia*, Pt.III, ch. IV, para. 9 & Ft. 52.
[167] Yallop, p. 184.
[168] Hofmann, p. 121.

since the death of General Franco in November 1975.[169]

On Wednesday 13 September, Gianpaolo gave the second of his General Audiences, speaking for about forty minutes without a prepared script in his hand. He drew on Pope John for his inspiration, and proposed to illustrate one of what his predecessor had called 'the seven lamps of Sanctification' at successive audiences. By these he meant the seven virtues of faith, hope, charity, prudence, justice, fortitude and temperance. He lived long enough only to speak on the first three; John Paul II paid him the unusual tribute of continuing with the other four and thus 'completing his programme', albeit in different style.

Citing the example of St Paul on the road to Damascus, he said faith meant surrendering to God and transforming one's life. It meant responding to the Lord generously, and to illustrate this he used another anecdote from his own life:

> My mother used to tell me when I was a boy: 'When you were little, you were very ill. I had to take you from one doctor to another and watch over you whole nights; do you believe me?' How could I have said: 'I don't believe you, Mamma?' 'Of course I believe, I believe what you tell me, but I believe especially in you.'
>
> And so it is in faith. It is not just a question of believing in the things that God revealed, but in him who deserves our faith, who has loved us so much and done so much for our sake.[170]

The pope went on to say that the truths of faith were of two kinds, 'some pleasant, some unpalatable to our spirit'. It was, for example, 'pleasant to hear that God has so much tenderness for us, even more tenderness than a mother has for her children, as Isaiah says'.[171] This further reference to the maternal qualities of God went largely unremarked; this time Gianpaolo was careful to name his source. Next he mentioned the other side of the coin, that some truths were hard to accept, that if we resist God and refuse to repent we may be punished by him.

Another difficulty that Gianpaolo explored in some depth was the Church itself, and in view of the fact that he was now Supreme Pastor of this earthly, human organization, his views on the subject were both important and interesting. He agreed with St Paul on the nature of the Church:

[169] Hebblethwaite, 'God's Appointment', p. 139.
[170] *The Teachings of Pope John Paul I*, p. 20.
[171] Ibid.; Isaiah 49:15.

> It is clear that Jesus and the Christians, Jesus and the Church are the same thing, indissoluble, inseparable ... Christ is the Head, we, the Church, are his limbs. It is not possible to have faith and to say, 'I believe in Jesus, I accept Jesus but I do not accept the Church'. We must accept the Church, as she is. And what is this Church like? Pope John called her 'Mater et Magistra' [Mother and Teacher].[172]

In words that he would echo to Cardinal Gantin on the last day of his life, he said that the sole purpose of the clergy, from highest to lowest, was to present the doctrine of Christ: 'It is not our doctrine, it is Christ's; we must guard it and present it'.[173] Once more he invoked the name of Pope John, and spoke of the message of hope for the future that the Second Vatican Council had engendered. He agreed with what Pope John had meant when he had said that with the Council the Church would take a leap forward. The truths of the Church in themselves were 'certain and immutable', but, he said to his audience, 'we must walk along the way of these truths, understanding them more and more, bringing ourselves up-to-date, proposing them in a form suited to the new times'.[174] In his approach, he was, of course, practising exactly what he was preaching. In the spirit of the Council he wanted a more mature faith; he tried to stimulate people to think ideas through for themselves.

Gianpaolo went on to speak of the Church as a mother, and what an individual's response should be towards her imperfections:

> If she continues Christ, and Christ is good, the Church too must be good; good to everyone. But if by chance there should sometimes be bad people in the Church? We have our mother. If mother is sick, if my mother by chance should become lame, I love her even more. It is the same in the Church. If there are, and there are, defects and shortcomings, our affection for the Church must never fail.[175]

The Catholic Church, he continued, was possessed of the means to salvation, but it remained the individual's responsibility to make active use of these means, which he likened to a cleansing soap:

---

[172] Ibid., p. 21.
[173] Ibid.
[174] Ibid.
[175] Ibid., pp. 21–2.

The gospel read and lived; the sacraments celebrated in the right way; prayer well used, would be a marvellous soap, capable of making us all saints. We are not all saints, because we have not used this soap enough. Let us try to meet the hopes of the Popes who held and applied the Council, Pope John, Pope Paul. Let us try to improve the Church, by becoming better ourselves. Each of us and the whole Church could recite the prayer I am accustomed to recite: 'Lord, take me as I am, with my defects, with my shortcomings, but make me become as you want me to be.[176]

Gianpaolo concluded with some gentle words of encouragement to groups of the sick and of newly-weds who were present, his whole address his usual sure and effective blend of realism and idealism, the personal and the general, the light and the serious. He presented his vision of the postconciliar Church, ever-old, ever-new, in the same, simple, catechetical manner that he always had, only now his audience was the whole world. The nature and import of his teaching will be discussed in more depth in the final chapter.

On the morning of 15 September, Gianpaolo received in audience Cardinal Gabriel-Marie Garrone, Prefect of the Sacred Congregation for Catholic Education. Garrone had come to discuss with the pope a document entitled *Sapientia Christiana*, the proposed apostolic constitution giving directives for the governance of all Catholic ecclesiastical universities and faculties throughout the world. The conciliar declaration *Gravissimum Educationis* (1965) had called for a review; thus mandated by the Council the Congregation had promulgated the *Normae Quaedam* (1968) in the interim. Meanwhile, the Congregation had consulted with the universities and faculties themselves, then with departments of the Roman Curia and other interested bodies. Finally a commission of experts had been established which, under the direction of the Congregation, had carefully reviewed the legislation concerning ecclesiastical academic studies. At length, in April 1978, the work was complete and the document was presented to Pope Paul. He had approved it, but before it could be issued Paul was dead.[177]

As is well known, any initiative that is unproclaimed at the time of a pope's death immediately becomes void, unless his successor approves it. Garrone must naturally have hoped and

---

[176] Ibid., p. 22.
[177] *Sapientia Christiana*, CTS Do 511, esp. pp. 13–15; *Tablet*, CCXXXIII, 2 June 1979, p. 537.

prayed that Pope Paul's successor would do just that with *Sapientia Christiana*, after so much time and effort. He needn't have worried on that score. Gianpaolo told Garrone that he had spent most of the previous day studying the document, and now gave evidence of his excellent memory and analytical mind. This he did by discussing the topic at length and in great detail without referring to a copy. Garrone is said to have sat 'astonished at the Pope's grasp and understanding of such a highly complex document'.[178]

At the end of the audience the pope advised the cardinal that he approved the document, and that it should be issued on 15 December. Returning to his office a somewhat awed Garrone happened to meet Mgr Tiziano Scalzotto of Propaganda Fide and remarked: 'I have just met a great Pope'.[179] Of course, in the event Gianpaolo also died before the constitution could be issued, and it was left to John Paul II to finally promulgate it on 15 April 1979, with Garrone's congregation bringing out the Norms of Application on 29 April.

With hindsight, a poignant note was struck later on in the day of his meeting with Garrone. Gianpaolo entertained his brother Edoardo to dinner; it would be the last meeting with a member of his family that the pope would ever have.[180] Already his pontificate had only a fortnight to run.

This was, of course, unforeseen, and the pontificate continued at full pace. Most of the world's problems – problems of all kinds, not just religious ones – pass across the pope's desk at one time or another, and a tragic example of this occurred on 16 September. On that day an earthquake measuring 7.7 on the Richter scale, the most powerful in the world in 1978, shook the villages of Tabas and Firdaus in eastern Iran, killing at least 25,000 people and leaving thousands more homeless. Immediately the pope sent an undated telegram 'in haste' via Cardinal Villot to Mgr Annibale Bugnini, CM, the Apostolic Pro-Nuncio to Iran:

Nuncio Teheran
Holy Father deeply moved on hearing of catastrophic earthquake that has struck East region Iran raises fervent prayers for so many deceased victims and charges you with expressing his condolences

---

[178] Yallop, p. 184. *Sapientia Christiana* is complex; the Constitution is composed of a Foreword and 94 Articles, many sub-divided, whilst the Norms of Application run to 64 Articles and 2 Appendices.
[179] Yallop, p. 184.
[180] Ibid., p. 195.

to the Iranian Authorities and his deep sympathy to the many wounded and victims so sorely tried for whom he asks God to grant consolation in their grief by bringing forth outbursts of solidarity to bring them brotherly and effective assistance.
Cardinal VILLOT.[181]

On Sunday 17 September Gianpaolo had the much more congenial task of giving another of his popular *Angelus* addresses, and he used the opportunity to extend his 'heartiest good wishes both to teachers and to scholars', as the new term began the following Tuesday. Once again, therefore, he tailored his comments to suit the circumstances and thus ensured maximum receptivity on the part of his audience, and as a former seminary teacher himself he spoke with some authority. To the adults he rightly maintained that 'Italian teachers have behind them classic examples of exemplary attachment and dedication to the school',[182] and cited Giosuè Carducci as one such. His message to them was simple, true, if not always possible to achieve: 'To teach John Latin, it is not enough to know Latin, one must also know and love John', and: 'the value of the lesson depends on the preparation'.[183]

He tried to inspire the primary school pupils with the example of Pinocchio, 'who took a liking to school, to such an extent that every day, for the whole academic year, he was the first to enter the classroom and the last to leave it'.[184] The effect this statement had on subsequent attendance is not recorded; it was probably beyond even Gianpaolo's persuasive powers to influence this!

However, the pope reserved his 'most affectionate wishes' for the 'pupils of the secondary schools, especially senior ones'. They were faced, he acknowledged, not only with immediate school problems, but also with what to do when they left school. Looking beyond his immediate audience he said:

> Both in Italy and in other nations of the world, today, when they have their diploma or their degree and leave school ... they cannot find work, and they cannot get married. These are problems that the society of today must really study and try to solve.[185]

---

[181] *L'Osservatore Romano*, n. 39 (548), 28 September 1978, p.12 (English edition).
[182] *The Teachings of Pope John Paul I*, p. 9. Giosuè Carducci (1835–1907), Italian poet and scholar.
[183] Ibid.
[184] Ibid.
[185] Ibid., pp. 9–10.

Having made his point, he lightened his tone a little and spoke of himself with some gentle, knowing irony:

> The Pope, too, was a pupil of these schools: junior high school [*ginnasio*], senior high school [*liceo*], university. But I was thinking only of youth and the parish. No one came to tell me: 'You will become Pope'. Oh! If only they had told me! If they had told me, I would have studied more, I would have prepared myself. Now, on the contrary, I am old, there is no time.[186]

His young audience, on the other hand, had, he said, all the advantages of time, youth, health, memory and brains, and they should 'try to exploit all these things'. They would form the 'ruling class of tomorrow', and so they should prepare themselves so as to gain the 'necessary competence' to fulfil this important function. He cited the example of the Duke of Wellington, concluding: 'And so I say to you, dear boys and girls: you will have battles in life ... but if you want to win them, you must begin now, prepare now, be assiduous in study and at school now'.[187]

The virtue of Hope was the subject of the pope's General Audience address on Wednesday 20 September, and it was, he said, a virtue 'which is obligatory for every Christian'.[188] In saying this he did not mean 'that hope is ugly or hard. On the contrary, anyone who lives it travels in an atmosphere of trust and abandonment'.[189] All those who lived in a spirit of hope, whatever their circumstances, could have the words of St Paul on Abraham applied to them: 'In hope he believed against hope' (Rom 4:18). This could be so because of three truths, Gianpaolo said:

'God is almighty, God loves me immensely, God is faithful to promises. And it is he, the God of mercy, who kindles trust in me; so that I do not feel lonely, or useless, or abandoned, but involved in a destiny of salvation, which will lead to Paradise one day'.[190]

Interestingly, in paraphrasing a passage from St Augustine, he defined hope as 'starving love' [*l'amore affamato*], before developing his theme through another of his anecdotes from life:

---

186 Ibid., p. 10.
187 Ibid.
188 Ibid., p. 24.
189 Ibid.
190 Ibid., p. 25.

'Someone will say: what if I am a poor sinner? I reply to him as I replied to an unknown lady, who had confessed to me many years ago. She was discouraged because, she said, she had a stormy life morally. "May I ask you," I said, "how old you are?"'

'Thirty-five.'

'Thirty-five! But you can live for another forty or fifty [years] and do a great deal of good. So, repentant as you are, instead of thinking of the past, project yourself into the future and renew your life, with God's help'.[191]

Our failings, the pope continued, give 'to us an opportunity to remain humble and to understand and to sympathise with our neighbour's failings.'[192] It was an opportunity that he personally had always made full use of, but he was aware that not everyone shared his sympathy for the virtue of hope. Nietzsche had called it the 'virtue of the weak', while others spoke of 'alienation', which, they alleged, turned the Christian 'away from the struggle for human advancement'. Gianpaolo rejected these calumnies and turned to one of his favourite sources of inspiration to do so: 'the Christian message', the Council said, 'far from deterring men from the task of building up the world . . . binds them, rather, to all this by a still more stringent obligation'.[193]

This did not mean that Christians were entirely blameless, however, and here he was talking in the long term. It is worth giving this section in full, because it shows Gianpaolo's historical sense, one possible explanation behind his own frequent smile, and another anecdote:

In the course of the centuries there have also appeared, from time to time, affirmations and tendencies of Christians that were too pessimistic with regard to man. But these affirmations were disapproved of by the Church and were forgotten, thanks to a host of joyful and hardworking saints, to Christian humanism, to the ascetic teachers, whom Sainte-Beuve called 'les doux', and to a comprehensive theology. St Thomas Aquinas, for example, puts among the virtues *jucunditas* or the capacity of changing things heard and seen into a cheerful smile – to the extent and in the way appropriate.[194] This kind of cheerfulness, I explained to my pupils,

---

[191] Ibid.
[192] Ibid.
[193] Ibid. *Gaudium et Spes*, n. 34, cf. nn. 39 and 7; cf. 'Message to the World' of the Council Fathers on 20 October 1962.
[194] St Thomas Aquinas, *Summa Theologiae*, II-IIae, q.168, a.2.

was shown by that Irish mason who fell from the scaffolding and broke his legs. He was taken to hospital and the doctor and Sister nurse rushed to him. 'Poor thing', the latter said, 'you hurt yourself falling'. But the patient said: 'Mother, not exactly falling, but reaching the ground I hurt myself.'[195]

Only Gianpaolo could talk of the theology of St Thomas Aquinas and tell a funny Irish story almost with the same breath, and as such he is unique in papal history, and likely to remain so for some time. His was a very personal catechetical style. But underlying his comments were firm foundations; as he himself pointed out, St Thomas' theory 'was in agreement with the "glad tidings" preached by Christ, and with the *hilaritas* recommended by St Augustine'.[196]

The pope then told a story from the life of Andrew Carnegie, the multi-millionaire, in order to point out the joy that could be obtained even from the simple things in life. However, he maintained a sense of proportion, reminding his audience that such joys, 'though good and encouraging, ... serve as a means, they are not the supreme purpose', being transitory in nature. Christ himself had already said: 'Seek first of all the kingdom of God' (Matt 6:33).

Gianpaolo next addressed the question of hope and how it was related to the Church in the contemporary world. In doing so he gave his audience an insight into his social thinking from the time of the Council, and generated some more controversy in the process:

> I would like to refer to a hope which is proclaimed Christian by some people, and on the contrary is Christian only up to a certain point: Let me explain. At the Council, I, too, voted for the 'Message to the World' of the Council Fathers. In it we said: the principal task of *divinizing* does not exempt the Church from the task of *humanizing*. I voted for *Gaudium et Spes*. I was moved and enthusiastic when *Populorum Progressio* came out.[197] I think that the Magisterium of the Church will never sufficiently insist in presenting and recommending the solution of the great problems of freedom, justice, peace, development; and [the] Catholic laity will never fight sufficiently to solve these problems. It is wrong, on the other hand, to state that political, economic and social liberation coincides with salvation in Jesus Christ, that the *Regnum Dei* is identified with the

---

[195] *The Teachings of Pope John Paul I*, p. 26.
[196] Ibid.
[197] *Populorum Progressio:* Pope Paul VI's landmark social encyclical on 'Fostering the Development of Peoples', promulgated on 26 March 1967.

Regnum hominis, that *Ubi Lenin ibi Jerusalem* ['*where Lenin is there is Jerusalem'*].[198]

It was this final dictum that caused the controversy. The periodical *Newsweek* thought that Gianpaolo was condemning the theology of liberation outright, and continued that: 'since Luciani had been elected pope with the considerable support of the progressive cardinals in Latin America, his remarks were widely seen as a rejection of the Third World efforts to liberate the poor through church-based social action'.[199] This was too strong and simplistic a statement even when based solely on the pope's *reported* remarks; it was still more the case when his important qualification is added, a qualification that was omitted due to 'over-zealous editorship' at *L'Osservatore Romano*. After his dictum, Gianpaolo had carefully added: 'There is some coincidence but we cannot make a perfect equation'.[200]

Needless to say the pope had not rejected the Latin American cardinals, none of whom, of course, was Marxist, and none of whom could be considered radical liberation theologians. He had not even rejected liberation theology '*up to a certain point'*. What he had done was to reject the *complete* equation of politics and Christianity: they could be complementary, but never identical. Sterile condemnations were no more in Gianpaolo's style than they had been in John XXIII's. His usual approach was to try as hard as he could to find common ground and honest compromise, without ever giving ground where Church doctrine was concerned. The whole episode was an object lesson in simplistic press reporting, and also in the undesirability of curial 'censorship' of the pope's actual words.

To conclude his remarkable address, Gianpaolo mentioned the eighty-fifth *Katholikentag*,[201] which had been held in Freiburg from 13 to 17 September, and its subject, 'the future of hope'. In speaking of hope for individuals' souls, he said, we must also speak of 'eternity': 'This is a Christian hope; this is what Pope John intended ...[202] In this address, Gianpaolo showed a distinct lack of complacency about how Christians acted in the world: it was unprecedented, in that he criticized

---

[198] *The Teachings of Pope John Paul I*, p. 27.
[199] Greeley, p. 162.
[200] Yallop, pp. 197, 231.
[201] German Catholic Congress, which had been attended by some 28,000 people. See *Tablet* CCXXXII, 30 September 1978, pp. 952–3.
[202] *The Teachings of Pope John Paul I*, p. 28.

Christians – and here he clearly meant Catholics – for being too pessimistic in the past, and for not doing enough in the present. It can only serve as an indication of what great social teaching he might have given had he lived.

Pausing to speak to special groups attending the audience, in particular participants in the Third World Conference of Therapeutic Communities, Gianpaolo earnestly gave his support to drug rehabilitation initiatives amongst young people.

On the same day the pope sent an important Address to the Presidents of the Episcopal Conferences of Argentina and Chile, Cardinals Juan Carlos Aramburú of Buenos Aires and Raul Silva Henriquez SDB of Santiago. A state of acute tension existed between the two predominantly Catholic countries, centred ostensibly on disputed territorial claims over the three small islands of Pictón, Lennox and Nueva in the Beagle Channel. The dispute actually dated back to the 1840s, but had reached a peak between the two military juntas then in power, the real issue at stake being control of the Antarctic and Cape Horn, and thus potential reserves of fish, krill, minerals and petroleum. Relations had deteriorated badly since 25 January, when Argentina officially rejected a ruling by an international court of arbitration awarding the three islands to Chile. Since then a sixth round of talks had begun in Santiago on 13 September, but had made little progress.

Gianpaolo hoped to be able to play a role in helping to calm the air of rising tension. Given the gravity of the situation, and the fact that the Address does not appear in the official *Teachings*, it is worth quoting in full as an example of his thought in his new role of world intermediary for peace:

Venerable Brothers in the Episcopate:
In these moments in which, faced with the situation existing between your respective countries, your responsibility as pastors has urged you to ask your faithful to work and pray for peace, we desire to express our mind as Supreme Pastor and common Father in order to support your efforts in such a meritorious task.

In effect, the present circumstances, with their tensions and threats, call for our attention and induce our proposal to bring them to the awareness of all our sons and daughters and all persons of good will, in order that the open differences not exacerbate spirits and lead to unforeseen consequences.

Without entering into technical aspects, which are outside our purpose, we wish to exhort you, with all the moral force at our disposal that you work for peace, encouraging all, governors and governed, towards the goals of mutual understanding and generous appreciation of those who, above national barriers, are common members of the human family, sons and daughters of the same Father, united to Him by identical religious ties.

It is necessary to create a general climate in which, all warlike attitudes and animosity set aside, reasons of concord prevail over forces of hate and division which only leave trails of destruction behind them.

We recommend these intentions to the Prince of Peace in prayer, with which we are sure that you and your faithful will associate themselves. Upon all who collaborate in this wonderful work of peace we beg, with our Apostolic Blessing, the reward from the Lord.

J. P. PP I'.[203]

Gianpaolo was granted no time to do more. By the end of the year the situation had reached crisis proportions, the armed forces of both countries being put on alert. On 23 December Gianpaolo's successor appointed Cardinal Antonio Samorè, Librarian and Archivist of the Holy Roman Church and a noted expert on Latin American affairs, as his personal envoy to mediate the dispute. It was patient work, but disaster was avoided; the three islands were finally awarded to Chile by a treaty that became effective on 2 May 1985.

On Thursday 21 September, Gianpaolo received in audience the archbishops and bishops of the US Twelfth Pastoral Region, on the occasion of their *ad limina* visit.[204] Mgr Cornelius M. Power, Archbishop of Portland in Oregon, offered the loyal congratulations of the assembly, and stated that ' . . . we see in Your Holiness a Shepherd who will be 'a man for all seasons', a pastoral Pontiff' . . .[205]

The pope replied by warmly greeting his 'Dear Brothers in Christ' in English and continued by claiming a natural unity with the 'wise teaching' of Paul VI. He went on:

Although I am new in the Pontificate – just a beginner – I too want to choose topics that deeply touch the life of the Church and that will be very relevant to your episcopal ministry. I believe that the Christian family is a good place to start. The Christian family is so important, and its role is so basic in transforming the world and in

---

[203] Spanish original in AAS, LXX, 30 September 1978, p. 762; I am indebted to Dom Leander Hogg, OSB for the translation.
[204] *visitatio ad limina apostolorum*: obligatory five-yearly visit to Rome by every residential bishop to report on the status of his diocese.
[205] *Insegnamenti Di Giovanni Paolo I*, p. 80. An inspired tribute.

building up the Kingdom of God, that the Council called it a 'domestic Church' (*Lumen Gentium*, II).[206]

The family was a 'community of love', he said, and should always be proclaimed as such. Naturally, he also took an interest in the educational aspect of family life:

> ... We must encourage parents in their role as educators of their children – the first catechists and the best ones. What a great task and challenge they have: to teach children the love of God, to make it something real for them. And by God's grace, how easily some families can fulfil the role of being a *primum seminarium* (*Optatum Totius*, 2): the germ of a vocation to the priesthood is nourished through family prayer, the example of faith and the support of love.[207]

There is a strong suggestion here that Gianpaolo was paying tribute to those who inspired and sustained him in his early desire to be a priest: his devout, caring mother Bortola, and his father Giovanni, who allowed him to go to the seminary despite his anti-clerical convictions.

The pope said that families could help to bring about the 'sanctification of the world'. By this he meant mutual sanctification between the individual members of the family, and also that 'by the loving witness of their lives, families can bring Christ's Gospel to others'. Further, he specifically emphasized the importance of the role of the laity in the modern Church, noting approvingly:

'A vivid realization of the sharing of the laity – and especially the family – in the salvific mission of the Church is one of the greatest legacies of the Second Vatican Council. We can never thank God enough for this gift'.[208]

Gianpaolo then spoke of the clergy's responsibilities in 'supporting and defending the family – each and every family'. These were 'to preach the word of God and to celebrate the Sacraments', for it was from these that the faithful drew their 'strength and joy'. The clergy also had the role 'of encouraging families to fidelity to the law of God and the Church'. In doing so, the clergy need have no fear in proclaiming 'all the exigencies of God's word, for Christ is with us and says today as

---

[206] *The Teachings of Pope John Paul I*, pp. 65–6. I have restored his use of 'I' where relevant.
[207] Ibid., p. 66.
[208] Ibid.

before: 'He who hears you hears me' (Luke 10:16).[209]

The pope spoke in this context about divorce – although he did not actually use the word itself – naturally, it was this section that made all the papers:

> In particular, the indissolubility of Christian marriage is important; although it is a difficult part of our message, we must proclaim it faithfully as part of God's word, part of the mystery of faith. At the same time we are close to our people in their problems and difficulties. They must always know that we love them.[210]

Having made this statement, Gianpaolo immediately went out of his way to express his 'admiration and praise' for all those trying to make a success of Christian family life, and for all those priests and religious 'trying to support and assist them' in preserving the family 'as God made it, as God wants it'.

What the pope was driving at was that for Christianity to really take root and transform people, those people must truly *live* according to the precepts of Christ, obeying his teaching *willingly* in their day-to-day activities, especially in relation to those around them. Quite simply, the collective faithful *are* the Church, the 'Mystical Body of Christ'. This is what he meant when he concluded:

> The holiness of the Christian family is indeed a most apt means for producing the serene renewal of the Church which the Council so eagerly desired. Through family prayer, the *ecclesia domestica* becomes an effective reality and leads to the transformation of the world. And all the efforts of parents to instil God's love into their children and to support them by the example of faith constitute a most relevant apostolate for the twentieth century. Parents with special problems are worthy of our particular pastoral care, and all our love.[211]

Helping the Christian family, the Christian laity, to fulfil themselves was, as he himself said, where Gianpaolo's priorities lay. He took the papal appellation 'Servant of the Servants of God' seriously. The address itself was more narrowly conceived than some of his public ones and was largely unremarkable, though stamped with his hallmark of pastoral concern. The image of the family that he projected was an idealized one, as he himself

---

[209] Ibid., p. 66. Luke 10:16, Christ instructing the 72 disciples.
[210] Ibid., pp. 66–7.
[211] Ibid.

would have been aware, but it was still an ideal worth striving for. An *ad limina* address was not the place to delve deeply into minutiae; here he was outlining general principles for approaching contemporary problems. Had he lived we can be sure that his ideas would have been translated into social encyclicals of the calibre of his two predecessors.

In emphasizing the traditional aspects of the address, the press ignored Gianpaolo's innovation. At the end of the formal address, the pope asked all the functionaries, including the translator, to leave. Alone with the American bishops, and getting one of their number to translate, he said 'Now it's your turn to ask questions'. In all this session of genuine dialogue lasted for nearly an hour. Gianpaolo admitted that he did not have all the answers, adding: 'After all, I am only a bambino pope'. The bishops asked him whether his first encyclical would concern the priesthood: he replied that he would like it to, but that he felt largely committed to treating the subject of catechesis first, as this had been the last issue tackled by the Synod of Bishops. In doing so he showed a commendable adherence to collegiality.[212]

Saturday 23 September marked what was in retrospect a symbolic and rather sad landmark in Gianpaolo's pontificate, and that was his first and only appearance outside the Vatican. On that day he took possession of his cathedral as the Bishop of Rome, the Archbasilica of St John Lateran. Typically, the Pope scaled down the pomp of the event. Unlike many of his predecessors on the same occasion, he was not carried across Rome on the *sedia gestatoria* with a magnificent cortege, but travelled the five kilometres or so journey in an open car with only one or two other cars and a few police outriders in attendance. Accompanying him was Cardinal Jean Villot, Secretary of State, and Cardinal Carlo Confalonieri, Dean of the Sacred College.

Following the precedent set by Paul VI, Gianpaolo stopped at the Capitol en route to meet the Mayor of Rome, Professor Guilio Carlo Argan – an internationally known art historian – and members of the city council. A Communist Administration presided over the troubled city for the first time in its history, and the mayor addressed the pope on the issues of intolerance, violence and poverty, before saluting the stand of the Bishops of Rome for world peace and social justice.[213]

---

[212] Greeley, pp.164–5,168. Greeley's source was 'Father Carter' (a pseudonym).
[213] *Insegnamenti Di Giovanni Paolo I*, pp. 91–2.

In replying, Gianpaolo expressed his deep gratitude for the 'respectful and sincere expressions . . . kindly addressed' to him by Signor Argan. He said the meeting had special significance for him 'because it enables me to have a first direct contact with those in charge of civic life and its sound organization. It is, therefore, a propitious opportunity to extend to them my cordial greetings and good wishes'.[214] The pope continued that he was particularly concerned about the problems of Rome 'because of their urgency, their seriousness and, above all, the hardships and human and family dramas of which they are not infrequently the manifest sign'.[215] Then, on behalf not only of himself but also of all the members of the 'Church of God here in Rome', he made a declaration of commitment, cooperation and action:

> As Bishop of the City, which is the original See of the pastoral ministry entrusted to me, I feel these painful experiences more acutely in my heart, and am urged by them to availability, collaboration, and to that contribution of a moral and spiritual nature, corresponding to the specific nature of my service, in order to be able at least to relieve them.[216]

Here was a pope pledged to the cause of relieving human suffering, regardless of the 'niceties' of the Italian domestic political situation, or of the fact that the Municipal Administration was Communist. There were no doctrinal differences here; just plain humanitarianism. From the denunciations of communism on theoretical grounds that had become more common in his later years in Venice, faced with human need, Albino Luciani, now pope, refused to stay aloof, and returned to the practical working relationship with communists of 'good will' that he had had in Belluno in the 1950s. He had reminded the Administration and all the citizens of Rome that he was *Bishop of the City*, and that Rome was the *original See of the pastoral ministry* entrusted to him. This was another title that he clearly took seriously, and he stated his intention of getting involved in the affairs of the See. In fact there are indications that he intended making weekly visits to the parishes of Rome, but death forestalled him. Once again, it would be left to his successor to take up and bring to fruition

---

[214] *The Teachings of Pope John Paul I*, p. 68.
[215] Ibid.
[216] Ibid., pp.68–69.

his initiative. Gianpaolo backed up his previous statement by picking up the note of hope contained in Signor Argan's address. It was, as he had recalled at the General Audience the previous Wednesday, 'an obligatory virtue' for Christians, and 'an elect gift of God'. He concluded by trying to make this a rallying point, an area of common ground:

> May it serve to reawaken energies and resolutions in each of us and, as I trust, in all fellow citizens of good will; may it serve to inspire initiatives and programmes, in order that these problems may have a suitable solution and Rome may remain faithful, in actual fact, to those unmistakeably Christian ideals which are called hunger and thirst for justice, an active contribution for peace, the superior dignity of human work, respect and love for brothers, and unfailing solidarity with regard to the weakest.[217]

After this important meeting Gianpaolo continued on his way to St John Lateran. On arrival he was met by about twenty cardinals, members of the diplomatic corps, representatives of the Italian Government, and numerous others. Here the pope conceded to tradition and popular demand by being carried into the basilica on the *sedia gestatoria*, so that people could see him better. Once inside, Cardinal Ugo Poletti, Vicar General of the City of Rome and District, welcomed him to his cathedral and then, before formally presenting the pope with the keys, gave him the equivalent of about £70,000, 'which had been collected from the people of the diocese in order that a church could be built in Castel Giubileo, one of the poorest districts on the outskirts of the city'.[218]

Following the ceremony of Gianpaolo taking possession of his cathedral, Mass was celebrated at 6.00 p.m. After the gospel of the Mass, the pope delivered his homily. First of all he gave his 'heartfelt thanks' to the Cardinal Vicar and members of the diocese for 'the devotion and the intentions of effective collaboration' expressed to him in the Cardinal Vicar's address. Then, 'truly touched', he thanked them for the donation for the new church. The papal Master of Ceremonies, Mgr Virgilio Noè, had chosen the three lessons that he judged to be suitable for the solemn liturgy; Gianpaolo accepted his choice, but proceeded to explain them in his own way.

The first lesson concerned Rome itself, the see through which the pope, as Bishop of the City, acquires authority over the

[217] Ibid., p. 69.
[218] *Tablet*, CCXXXII, 30 September 1978, p. 951.

whole Church. With illustrations from the prophet Isaiah he cited the importance of Rome as the visible centre of the Catholic Church, whilst immediately adding that what was 'an honour' was 'also a responsibility'. With this in mind, Gianpaolo desired that, with God's help, pilgrims would find Rome to be 'a model of a true Christian community'.

In developing his theme, the pope said that Professor Argan's earlier address had reminded him of one of the prayers that he had recited as a child with his mother:

> It went like this: 'the sins that cry for vengeance in the presence of God are ... to oppress the poor, to defraud the workers of a just wage'. In his turn, the Parish Priest questioned me at school on the Catechism: 'Why are the sins that cry for vengeance in the presence of God among the more grievous and harmful?' *Reply*: ... 'Because they are directly contrary to the good of mankind and are most hateful in as much as, more than others, they provoke the chastisements of God. (*Catechism of Pius X*, no.154)[219]

Thus, Gianpaolo concluded, God is honoured 'not merely with a multitude of the faithful in the churches, not merely with private life that is lived morally, but also with love for the poor', those whom St Lawrence had called 'the true treasures of the Church'.[220]

The poor must be helped, the pope insisted, 'by those who can, to have more and to be more'. Here he was clearly thinking in material and spiritual terms, and proposing action in the liberal north Italian tradition of progressive social action coupled with dogmatic clarity. In fact he emphasized the point, so that there should be no room for misunderstanding: the poor must not be 'humiliated and offended by ostentatious riches', money must not be 'squandered on futile things', but rather should be invested 'in enterprises of advantage to all'.[221] The old socialist, Giovanni Luciani, would surely have approved of his son's stirring words.

Gianpaolo now moved onto the second lesson which, he said, could be applied to the faithful of Rome. In mentioning its subject a moment of hesitancy crept in, as if he still could not quite conceive of himself as the pope. Reminding his audience

[219] *The Teachings of Pope John Paul I*, p. 71.
[220] Ibid. St Lawrence, Roman deacon and martyr, died in Rome, 258 (Source of quote: St Ambrose, *De Officiis Ministrorum*, Bk. II, ch. XXVIII, written c.391).
[221] *The Teachings of Pope John Paul I*, p. 71.

that the Master of Ceremonies had chosen the subject of the lesson, he said: 'I confess that when it speaks of obedience it places me in a slight embarrassment. Today, when personal human rights are confronted with rights of authority and of the law, it is so difficult to convince!'[222] Regaining his stride, he illustrated the dilemma by portraying liberty as a warhorse, and authority as a prudent rider: 'To reconcile the horse and the rider, liberty and authority, has become a social problem'.

The issue of liberty versus authority was also, of course, an important one within the Church, and it had become especially so since the time of the Second Vatican Council. Gianpaolo was only too aware of the problem, and he tried to offer some guidelines by quoting from the fourth chapter of one of his favourite Conciliar decrees, *Lumen Gentium*. First, he gave the Conciliar indications for the 'rider':

> The sacred pastors know very well how much the laity contribute to the welfare of the whole Church. They know that they them-selves were not established by Christ to undertake alone the whole salvific mission of the Church to the world, but that it is their exalted office to be shepherds of the faithful and to recognize the latter's contribution and charisms in such a way that all, in their measure, will with one mind cooperate in the common task.
> *(LG* 30)[223]

Further, it was noted that the pastors were also aware that 'in the decisive battles it is at times from the front that the happi-est initiatives begin' (*LG* 37, note 7). This latter point was something that Gianpaolo himself had often – though not always – found in his own pastoral experience, and it was precisely because he knew how difficult it could be 'at the front' that he had often been prepared to be lenient and forgiving with penitent sinners.

However, there was also a conciliar indication for the 'high-spirited warhorse', that is, for the laity: 'the faithful should acquiesce to the bishop as the Church to Jesus Christ and as Jesus Christ to the Father'(*LG* 27). This of course raised the age-old problem: should the laity *always* 'acquiesce'? What of their initiatives and contributions? It is, of course, insolu-ble, for the situation will always be in flux, according to the circumstances pertaining at the time. Gianpaolo asked for prayers 'that the Lord will aid both the bishop and the faith-

---

[222] Ibid.
[223] Ibid, p. 72.

ful'. In other words, he wanted to see a spirit of generous understanding and cooperation emanating from both parts of the Church.

Returning specifically to the subject of the Diocese of Rome, the pope mentioned the 'numerous catechists' and others who devoted themselves to the faithful, and prayed that through this service Rome would become 'a living and active Christian community'. This was no idle comment: in the years since Rome had become the capital of the newly unified Italian state in 1870 the city had undergone a tremendous process of secularization. Much of it was virtual mission territory, with the number of baptisms, marriages celebrated in church and Mass attendances falling annually, and with a corresponding rise in illegitimate births, civil marriages and divorces. Further, Rome was totally failing to provide itself with enough new priests, and many were having to be 'imported' from outside.[224] In 1978 the diocese only produced *seven* ordinands!

Gianpaolo explained that he had been quoting from the fourth chapter of Lumen Gentium precisely because it was the chapter on 'ecclesial communion', the life of the Christian community, and that what he had said had 'special reference to the laity'. Priests, and men and women religious, were, he said, in a special position, as they were bound 'either to the promise or to the vow of obedience'. He spoke of his own experience:

> I recall, as one of the solemn points of my existence, the moment in which, with my hands in those of the bishop, I said 'I promise'. From that time, I considered myself bound for my whole life, and never have I thought that it was a matter of an unimportant ceremony. I hope that the priests of Rome think likewise.[225]

From the subject of the Roman clergy finding God through obedience, Gianpaolo moved on to this third lesson, that of his own duties as the Bishop of Rome. The first of these duties was 'to teach, proposing the Lord's word with fidelity both to God and to the listeners; with humility, but with fearless sincerity'.[226] The pope spoke of two of his predecessors, Bishops of Rome and also Doctors of the Church, namely St Leo the Great

---

[224] For a concise account of this development see Hebblethwaite, *In The Vatican*, ch. 2, 'From Sacred To Secular City', pp. 12–23.
[225] *The Teachings of Pope John Paul I*, pp. 72–3.
[226] Ibid., p. 73.

and St Gregory the Great.[227] He said that he did not feel able to match the very high theological thought and outstanding Latin style of the former; rather, he would try to imitate the latter.

We have seen already that Gianpaolo had a special devotion to St Gregory the Great. Now he praised the guidelines given in the third book of Gregory's *Regula Pastoralis* on how a pastor should instruct, guidelines which Gianpaolo himself had taken to heart. Gregory's advice was both practical and adaptable, he said, in that it took account of 'the various circumstances of social conditions, age, health and moral temperament of the hearers. Poor and rich, cheerful and melancholic, superiors and subjects, learned and ignorant, cheeky and shy, and so forth; all are there in this book, it is like the Valley of Jehoshaphat'.[228] Further, the pope claimed that the 'pastoral approach' introduced by the Second Vatican Council, how pastors meet people's needs, anxieties and hopes, was not new. Rather, it had, he said, 'already been applied many centuries earlier by Gregory, both in preaching and in the government of the Church'.[229]

The pope moved on to his second duty, which he explained was expressed in the word 'baptize' and which referred 'to the sacraments and to the whole of the liturgy'. He made reference to the fact that the Diocese of Rome, in common with the other dioceses of Italy, had been following the programme of the Italian Bishops Conference (CEI) entitled 'Evangelization and Sacraments'. He endorsed the 'great concept' of its teaching wholeheartedly: evangelization prepares for the sacrament, the sacrament draws him who has received it to live in a Christian way'.

The next part of Gianpaolo's discourse, following on from this, attracted some criticism, and is worth presenting in full:

> I should like also that Rome should in fact give a good example of Liturgy celebrated devoutly and without ill-placed 'creativity'. Certain abuses in liturgical matters have succeeded, through reac-

---

[227] St Leo (Pope 440–461; declared Doctor 1754); St Gregory (590–604; 1295). 'Doctors of the Church' are proclaimed as such by a pope or general council for their orthodoxy of doctrine and holiness of life, and for the eminence of their learning and excellence of their teaching. At present their number stands at 33, only 3 of whom are female.

[228] *The Teachings of Pope John Paul I*, p. 73; 'the valley of Jehoshaphat' is the site of Jehovah's apocalyptic judgement upon the nations.

[229] Ibid.

tion, in favouring attitudes that have led to a taking up of positions that in themselves cannot be upheld and are in contrast with the Gospel. In appealing with affection and with hope to the sense of responsibility of everyone, before God and the Church, I should like to be able to give an assurance that every liturgical irregularity will be diligently avoided.[230]

Such criticism as there was was largely unfounded;[231] there was little in his statement that was unreasonable, and it was not a subject that he dwelt on. Gianpaolo now came to his final episcopal duty: '"to teach and to observe"; it is the *diakonia*, the service of guiding and governing'.[232] He claimed, humbly, that in twenty years as a bishop he had not yet 'learned the job' well. Once more he looked to the example of St Gregory the Great, and quoted extensively from the latter's *Regula Pastoralis* on how a pastor should relate to his flock. The pastor should, with compassion, consider himself on a level with those in his spiritual care, whilst not fearing 'to exercise the rights of his authority against the wicked'. Further, the pastor should have humility, and not become corrupted by earthly power. Gianpaolo pledged himself to act according to these precepts whilst pope.

His explanation of the lessons finished, the pope added an important point. True Christianity must include right intention with right action: 'it is God's law that one cannot do good to anyone if one does not first of all wish him well'.[233] Thus, in conclusion and very much in the spirit of the Gregorian motto 'servant of the servants of God', Gianpaolo assured the clergy and faithful of the diocese of Rome 'that I love you, that I desire only [to] enter into your service and to place the poor powers that I have, however little they are, at the disposal of all'.[234]

The day after his landmark trip outside the Vatican, Sunday 24 September, Gianpaolo delivered what was to be the last of his *Angelus* addresses. As usual on these occasions, his theme was a topical one, the power of love against violence. Acts of violence and terrorism were a problem in many European countries in general in the 1970s, but particularly so in Italy, as we have seen. As examples of the 'many cases of violence which

---

230 Ibid., p. 74.
231 For instance, in Hebblethwaite, *Year of Three Popes*, p. 127.
232 *The Teachings of Pope John Paul I*, p. 74.
233 Ibid.
234 Ibid.

are continually afflicting this poor and restless society of ours', the pope cited the case of a Roman student killed in cold blood for a trivial reason, and that of Luca Locci, a seven-year-old boy who had been kidnapped three months before. These acts, however, did not lead Gianpaolo to become pessimistic about society as a whole. He denied that society generally was fatally flawed:

> People sometimes say: 'We are in a society that is all rotten, all dishonest'. That is not true. There are still so many good people, so many honest people. Rather, what can be done to improve society? I would say: let each of us try to be good and to infect others with a goodness imbued with the meekness and love taught by Christ.[235]

Evidently Luca Locci's kidnappers listened to Gianpaolo's profound words, because *at midnight the very same day* the boy was left at the door of his home, unharmed. Days later he and his grateful parents attended the pope's funeral.

In his address, the pope went on to recommend that people should follow the teaching and example of Christ in their general efforts to improve the quality of life:

> Christ's golden rule was: 'Do not do to others what you do not want done to yourself. Do to others what you want done to yourself'. And he always gave. Put on the cross, not only did he forgive those who crucified him, but he excused them. He said: 'Father, forgive them for they know not what they do'. This is Christianity, these are sentiments which, if put into practice, would help society so much.[236]

As an example of Christian faith and love being maintained in the face of terrible odds, Gianpaolo cited the sixteen Carmelite nuns of Compiegne, martyred during the French Revolution and beatified by Pope Pius X in 1906:

> During the trial they were condemned 'to death for fanaticism'. And one of them asked in her simplicity: 'Your Honour, what does fanaticism mean?' And the judge: 'It is your foolish membership of religion'. 'Oh, Sisters,' she then said, 'did you hear, we are condemned for our attachment to faith. What happiness to die for Jesus Christ!'[237]

---

[235] Ibid., p. 11.
[236] Ibid.
[237] Ibid., p. 12.

Taken from the prison of the Conciergerie to the guillotine, each one in turn renewed the vow of obedience kneeling before the Prioress. They sang *Veni Creator*, the sound becoming weaker as each sister was executed. The Prioress, Sister Theresa of St Augustine, was the last to die. In concluding his address, Gianpaolo recounted her last words and his agreement with them:

'Love will always be victorious, love can do everything.' That was the right word, not violence, but love can do everything.

Let us ask the Lord for the grace that a new wave of love for our neighbour may sweep over this poor world.[238]

'What happiness to die for Jesus Christ!' 'Love can do everything!' How apt and applicable these words were to Gianpaolo as he neared the end of his life. In fact, this address actually changed the course of one man's life. Philip Gannaway, chairman of the Bristol local branch of the extreme-right National Front, announced his resignation because of the effect that Gianpaolo's words had on him while he was on holiday in Rome. 'There was something about the Pope of tremendous warmth and sincerity which touched me. It was then I decided to resign. I realised demonstrations do not achieve anything.'[239]

Three days later, on Wednesday 27 September, the pope gave his final General Audience address on the third of Pope John's 'lamps of sanctification', namely charity. So popular had Gianpaolo's General Audiences become that for the first time in his pontificate this one was 'divided into two sessions to accommodate the large crowds'.[240] Despite this measure, Andrew Greeley, who was lucky enough to be present on this occasion near the front, estimated that there were still 'perhaps sixteen thousand people'[241] packed into the hall. Most of the seats to the rear of the hall had been removed so that more people could get in. As Greeley noted, Paul VI never filled the hall in quite the same way, though it must be admitted that there was always a slight element of 'novelty' attached to Gianpaolo's handful of audiences.

The pope saw a large number of German people in St Peter's before the General Audience; when he finally came in he was about twenty minutes late. He began his address simply, with a

---

[238] Ibid.
[239] *Tablet*, CCXXXII, 14 October 1978, p. 1007; see also *Catholic Herald*, no. 4825, 6 October 1978, p. 7.
[240] John Paul I, *The Pope Speaks*, p. 326.
[241] Greeley, p. 169.

prayer that he said his mother had taught him, and which he said he recited 'several times a day even now':

> My God, with all my heart above all things I love you, infinite good and our eternal happiness, and for your sake I love my neighbour as myself and forgive offences received. O Lord, may I love you more and more.[242]

Gianpaolo well knew that his audience – both those in the hall and those worldwide – incorporated a wide spectrum of people and so, as always, he pitched his explanation of the prayer at a level that all could understand, 'word by word, as a parish catechist would do'. It was effective.

Andrew Greeley has recorded his impressions of this last public address of Gianpaolo's, and before examining the pope's detailed explanation of his initial prayer, it will be of value to 'set the scene' by relating some of these eyewitness observations. They illuminate aspects of Gianpaolo's character and approach, and largely conform to a general pattern by now familiar. Of the pope's address, then, Greeley has written:

> His talk was about love – simple, declarative sentences delivered in a rather low, somewhat timid voice, but with a great deal of conviction, charm, and, of course, the famous smile, which just dazzles people. You get the impression that he likes his job and – my travelling companions thought this too – that he's a little bit uncertain about what to do, somewhat overwhelmed by it all, but pleased, particularly when he's able to talk to people. One had the impression that he was fairly hemmed in by the monsignors who accompanied him and that at times he would have liked to break away from them and go over to shake hands with people – really work the crowd – but was almost afraid to do so. He read a summary of his talk in English, the first time he's done that, and his English pronunciation is excellent – some people said better than Paul VI. His rapport with crowds, no matter what the language, is also better than Paul VI's because of the simplicity and the timid charm of his manner. His voice leaves something to be desired, but it's made up for by his smile. He really turned the crowd on – I mean, they just cheered wildly . . .[243]

Greeley's comments contain a number of concise, largely self-explanatory points, the more valuable because he recorded them at the time, and set them down largely unaltered when

[242] *The Teachings of Pope John Paul I*, p. 29.
[243] Greeley, pp. 169–70.

later compiling his book *The Making of the Popes*. It is true that Gianpaolo did not fully capitalize on his incredible rapport with crowds by 'working them' as much as he might: it was left to John Paul II to take his predecessor's initiative to its logical conclusion, and finally break the 'monsignorial strait-jacket' separating pope and people, a move that was to prove to be both popular and dangerous.

To return to Gianpaolo's address, Greeley had a few more significant statements to make on the abilities and qualities of the man before him, with whom he was delighted:

> So you have this simple, kindly man, smiling and giving a simple catechetical talk to smiling and cheering people. It almost seems utterly spontaneous, until you realize that Don Diego, his tall, bespectacled secretary, is up there flipping the pages of the text as he talks. The pope is speaking from memory, but his secretary has the exact text, and according to those who have listened to him on tape and seen the text afterwards, he doesn't deviate from the final text (which he has revised himself by hand before he uses it). So, on that stage one had a sort of symbol of everything, a man hemmed in, a man uncertain, but also a smart man with a tremendous memory, one who has not been stopped from doing what he wants to do by the people around him now. All in all, it was a virtuoso performance.[244]

This is praise indeed from Greeley, not noted for his ready approbation of the achievements of the Catholic hierarchy. As noted, Gianpaolo stuck faithfully to his own text – the product of much effort on his part whilst Vatican sources gave their own version. However, it is obvious that even the pope couldn't know exactly what was going to be said when he asked a child to come forward and speak with him. On this occasion, he called a young Roman boy, Daniele Bravo, to him. Altering the microphone to the boy's height he asked: 'Do you always want to be in the fifth grade?'. Daniele answered: 'Yes, so that I don't have to change teachers'. This got a laugh, as did Gianpaolo's reply: 'Well, you are different from the Pope. When I was in the fourth grade I was worried about making it to the fifth'.[245] Later the boy recalled only that 'I was very frightened',[246] presumably of the circumstances rather than the pope, for in photographs of the event he is smiling happily enough.

---

[244] Ibid., p. 170.
[245] *Time*, 112, 9 October 1978, p. 11.
[246] John Paul I, *The Pope Speaks*, p. 326.

Needless to say, the event does not figure at all in official texts.

In his explanation of the prayer Gianpaolo began simply with the phrase *I love,* and in so doing referred back to his own days as a student, as he had done on several occasions in previous addresses:

> In the philosophy class the teacher would say to me: You know St Mark's bell tower? You do? That means that it has somehow entered your mind: physically it has remained where it was, but within you has imprinted almost an intellectual portrait of itself. Do you, on the other hand, *love* St Mark's bell tower? That means the portrait, from within, pushes you and bends you, almost carries you, makes you go in your mind towards the bell tower which is outside. In a word: to love means travelling, rushing with one's heart towards the object loved.[247]

To love God was therefore, the pope stated, to make a wonderful journey with one's heart to God, and outstanding examples of such journeys could be found in the lives of the saints. The journey could involve making sacrifices, the pope said, but these must not stop us: 'Jesus is on the cross: you want to kiss him? You cannot help bending over the cross and letting yourself be pricked by some thorns of the crown which is on the Lord's head'.[248]

Gianpaolo thus reminded his listeners that the sacrifice that Jesus had already made for them was far greater than any that they might make for him. Furthermore, he said that the journey was a mysterious one, in that we cannot even start unless God takes the initiative first. As Jesus himself said: 'No one can come to me, unless the Father who sent me draws him'.[249] Referring to St Augustine's theories, the pope said that God respects human freedom by drawing people to himself in ways that they themselves want and even enjoy.

Gianpaolo moved on in his explanation of the prayer to the phrase *With all my heart,* stressing the adjective 'all'. He also clearly showed the difference in his approach to politics and religion, stating 'Totalitarianism in politics is an ugly thing. In religion, on the contrary, a totalitarianism on our side towards God is a very good thing.'[250] He firmly backed this opinion with the commandments of Deuteronomy (6:5–9): 'You shall love

---

[247] Ibid., p. 29.
[248] Ibid., p. 30; cf. St Francis De Sales, *Oeuvres,* ed. Annecy, t.XXI, p. 153.
[249] Ibid., p. 30; John 6:44.
[250] Ibid.

the Lord your God with all your heart, and with all your soul, and with all your might.'[251] He elucidated further: 'That "all" repeated and applied insistently is really the banner of Christian maximalisim'.[252] Christians, the pope implied, should not be half-hearted in their faith; such is the greatness of God, being infinite good and the source of eternal happiness, that the things of this world are fragmentary and fleeting in comparison. It is therefore not wise for people to give so much of themselves to the world and so little to Jesus.

Next Gianpaolo focused on the phrase *Above everything else.* In speaking of the approach to be taken towards God and man, towards God and the world, he said: 'We must love "both God and man": the latter, however, never more than God or against God or as much as God. In other words: love of God, though prevalent, is not exclusive.'[253] To illustrate this he quoted the biblical example of Jacob, loved by God, working for seven years to win Rachel as his wife; and, as the Bible so beautiful-ly has it, 'they seemed to him but a few days because of the love he had for her'.[254] Jacob's love of Rachel was complemen-tary to his love of God, not contrary to it.

The pope now drew out the meaning of the phrase *And for your sake I love my neighbour*. In many ways what he had to say about this was stating the obvious, but his words were still expressed with simple, compassionate clarity:

> It is easy to love some persons; difficult to love others; we do not find them likeable, they have offended us and hurt us; only if I love God in earnest can I love them as sons of God and because he asks me to. Jesus also established how to love one's neighbour: that is, not only with feeling, but with facts. This is the way, he said. I will ask you: I was hungry in the person of my humbler brothers, did you give me food? Did you visit me, when I was sick?[255]

Ever the advocate of practical action allied with personal compassion, he recognized the enormity of the problems facing the modern world. Of the 'seven corporal works of mercy and the seven spiritual ones' listed in the Catechism, he said bluntly: 'The list is not complete and it would be necessary to update it. Among the starving, for example, today, it is no

---

[251] Ibid.
[252] Ibid., p. 31.
[253] Ibid.
[254] Ibid.; Genesis 29:20.
[255] Ibid., pp. 31–2; cf. Matthew 25:34ff.

longer a question just of this or that individual; there are whole peoples.'[256] Gianpaolo quoted extensively from Paul VI's great encyclical letter of 1967, *Populorum Progressio*, specifically the sections on world hunger (n. 3), private property (n. 22) and the 'intolerable scandal' of the arms race (n. 53). When promulgated, the encyclical had been attacked in certain quarters for being 'warmed-over Communism', a sure testament to its fundamental truth and accuracy. 'To all men of good will', however, as it is addressed on its title page, it remained – and remains – a rallying point, and Gianpaolo endorsed it wholeheartedly. As he put it: 'In the light of these strong expressions it can be seen how far we – individuals and peoples – still are from loving others "as ourselves" as Jesus commanded'.[257]

The pope dealt with the self-evident words *I forgive offences received* briefly, opining merely that: 'It almost seems that the Lord gives precedence to this forgiveness over worship'[258] and quoting Matthew 5:23–24 on the importance of being reconciled with others before offering prayers to God.

He concluded his explanation with the last words of the prayer: *Lord, may I love* you *more and more.* This he put in terms of obedience to a commandment of God, 'who put thirst for progress in our hearts'. He spoke of mankind's technological advances, and of peoples' desire to travel more rapidly and more distantly. But, as he had shown, to love God was also to make a journey, and it was one that God wanted to be 'more and more intense and perfect'. That meant, Gianpaolo concluded, 'to love God not a little, but so much; not to stop at the point at which we have arrived, but with his help, to progress in love.'[259] To Gianpaolo, then, his prayer was one of perpetual renewed commitment and desire for improvement, his love of God a never-ending journey.

The audience was over by about 11.30 a.m.; such was the popularity of Gianpaolo's audiences by now that tourist buses were still causing traffic problems in the Piazza San Pietro and Via della Conciliazione nearly an hour later.[260]

Thursday 28 September 1978 was 'a cool, clear, crisp day'[261] in Rome. It was also the last day of Albino Luciani's life. Some

256 Ibid., p. 32.
257 Ibid.
258 Ibid.
259 Ibid., p. 33.
260 Greeley, p. 170.
261 Ibid.

of the details of that day's events – and those of the next day – are still unclear, with sometimes contradictory accounts being given. Information is deficient for various reasons; confidentiality, the death of principal players, the fading of memory, and the protection of personal positions amongst them. However, the main outline is clear and can be set down with confidence.

The pope's last day on earth was a typically busy one for him, with thirteen official audiences scheduled, apart from the routine administration, briefings and so on.[262] At 9.00 a.m. Gianpaolo received his first visitor of the day, Maximos V Hakim, the seventy-year-old Patriarch of Antioch of the Greek-Melkite Catholics. After a fraternal embrace, Hakim presented Gianpaolo with some gifts whilst Luigi Felici, the papal photographer, captured the happy moment on film. The pope was 'genuinely delighted with the gifts of icons of Christ and the Virgin Mary, and a Damascene tablecloth',[263] telling the patriarch that the icon of the Virgin was a worthy companion to one – that he had brought with him from Venice. Typically, though, he maintained that the fine tablecloth was too good for him, a grin revealing the easy naturalness of his words and robbing them of possible offence. On Hakim's gentle insistence that he use it, however, he graciously gave in, promising to use it as a reminder of his visitor. These moments were probably among Gianpaolo's happiest on this sad day.

After the greetings, Gianpaolo and Hakim discussed alone the worsening situation in the Middle East until 9.15 a.m. Patriarch Hakim knew the problems well; patriarch since November 1967, and normally resident in Damascus, his flock were scattered across both the invaded Lebanon and the invading Syria. For his part, Gianpaolo discussed with Hakim his projected visit to the Lebanon.[264] It should be noted here the seriousness of the pope's intent, and the anticipation and gratitude that his personal interest aroused in the Lebanon itself. After Gianpaolo's untimely death the Maronite Patriarch of Antioch, Antoine Pierre Khoraiche, normally resident in Beirut, made a statement on Vatican Radio in which he confirmed that the pope had 'planned to make a trip to the Lebanon in order to plead for a return of this strife-ridden country to peace'.[265] The secular authorities also voiced their appreciation; in his

---

[262] Lo Bello, p. 59; *Pontiff*, p. 367.
[263] *Pontiff*, p. 370.
[264] Yallop, p. 204.
[265] *Tablet*, CCXXXII, 14 October 1978, p. 1002.

telegram of condolence President Elias Sarkis said that ' ... Lebanon in particular will preserve an unforgettable memory of the great interest and solicitude that the illustrious deceased has constantly shown to it ...'[266] What the outcome of a personal intervention by Gianpaolo in the Lebanon would have been is open to speculation: what is known is that his much-travelled successor did not reveal his 'inner imperative' to visit that country until August 1989, a period of nearly eleven years during which time the Lebanon's problems had grown immeasurably worse.[267]

A little later the pope received Cardinal Bernardin Gantin and Father Henri de Riedmatten, OP, the President and the Secretary of Cor Unum respectively. Also present was the Secretary of Justicia et Pax, Father Roger Heckel, SJ. They discussed Third World problems, Gianpaolo acknowledging material needs whilst emphasizing the importance of evangelization. The pope told Gantin: 'It is Jesus Christ alone we must present to the world. Outside of this, we have no reason to exist, we will never be heard'.[268] At the end, and to the cardinal's amazement, the pope personally rearranged the chairs for a group photograph. De Riedmatten was favourably impressed: 'It was the first time I had met him privately and I found that he was the hearty happy man everybody was talking about. We left the room filled with joy'.[269]

Further meetings followed, amongst them private audiences with the Apostolic Nuncio to Brazil, Mgr Carmine Rocco, the Apostolic Pro-Nuncio to the Netherlands, Mgr John Gordon, and with the editor of *Il Gazzettino*, from Venice, Dr Gianni Crovato. Next Gianpaolo received Cardinal Julio Rosales, Archbishop of Cebu, and nine bishops from the Philippines who were making their *ad limina* visit. He addressed them in English, his words following the theme he had developed earlier with Gantin, that of evangelization. To begin, he quoted from a homily that Paul VI had given on 29 November 1970 during his visit to the Philippines. It was a passage concerning Christ that had, he said, struck him 'forcefully': 'I must bear witness to his name: Jesus is the Christ, the Son of the living God ... he is the King of the new world; he is the secret of history; he is the key to our destiny.'[270] For his part, Gianpaolo

---

266 AAS, LXX, 1978, p. 881. The original telegram is in French.

267 *Tablet*, CCXLIII, 19 August 1989, p. 954; 2 September 1989, p. 1006.

268 Cornwell, *A Thief in the Night*, p. 254.

269 *Catholic Herald*, no. 4825, 6 October 1978, p. 5. De Riedmatten, a Swiss Dominican, died suddenly of a heart attack in Rome on 9 April 1979.

270 *The Teachings of Pope John Paul I*, p. 75; Breviary, 13th Sunday of the Year.

said that he hoped to sustain, support and encourage them in their great episcopal mission of proclaiming Jesus Christ and evangelizing his people.

The pope then went on to outline the nature and importance of this mission of the episcopate in the modern world:

> Among the rights of the faithful, one of the greatest is the right to receive God's word in all its entirety and purity, with all its exigencies and power. A great challenge of our day is the full evangelization of all those who have been baptized. In this, the Bishops of the Church have a prime responsibility. Our message must be a clear proclamation of salvation in Jesus Christ.[271]

Both by natural inclination, and very much in the spirit of the Second Vatican Council, Gianpaolo wanted a church of believers who had a mature, deep faith, who consciously understood what they believed in and why, not a group of people who blindly followed dogmatic rules. He thus spoke in clear, specific terms on the nature of evangelization 'For us, evangelization involves an explicit teaching about the name of Jesus, his identity, his teaching, his Kingdom and his promises. And his chief promise is eternal life. Jesus truly has words that lead us to eternal life'.[272]

It was this element of 'eternal life' that Gianpaolo was convinced that he needed to emphasize to complete his message and model his teaching on that of Jesus. In imitation of the Lord, he said, 'the Church is irrevocably committed to contributing to the relief of physical misery and need'. However, the Church's pastoral charity would be incomplete if it did not tend even 'higher needs'. In making his point, Gianpaolo referred once more to Paul VI's visit to the Philippines:

> At a moment when he chose to speak about the poor, about justice and peace, about human rights, about economic and social liberation – at a moment when he also effectively committed the Church to the alleviation of misery – he did not and could not remain silent about the 'higher good', the fullness of life in the Kingdom of heaven.[273]

The pope stressed that, 'more than ever before', the episcopacy must help the faithful to fully realize the importance of Jesus

[271] Ibid.
[272] Ibid., pp. 75–6.
[273] Ibid., p. 76.

Christ as their Saviour, 'the key to their destiny and to the destiny of all humanity'.[274] How the latter part of his statement would be received by those of other faiths and those of no faith at all is questionable, but it is perhaps unfair to highlight this out of context. Gianpaolo was a convinced ecumenist and believer in toleration. There are many different paths leading up the mountain to God; for Gianpaolo the *best* and the *surest* way was obviously the Catholic Christian one, both for himself and others, and his comment should be seen in this light.

The pope said that he felt 'spiritually close' to all the many efforts that his brother bishops were making regarding evangelization, and that he greatly esteemed all their 'endeavours on behalf of the Kingdom of God'. One such endeavour he selected for special mention, continuing: 'In particular, I fully support the affirmation of the missionary vocation, and earnestly hope that it will flourish among your youth'.[275] This comment underlines an interesting point about Gianpaolo's whole address, and that is why it was that he chose to speak to the Filipino bishops about evangelization. The population of the Philippines were 84.1% Catholic,[276] having the highest percentage of Catholics of all the countries of Asia. Indeed, it is the only predominantly Christian country in Asia. However, it is a fact that aspects of traditionalist belief are still held by many of the people, alongside – and sometimes incorporated into – their Christianity. This issue is a common one in many Latin American and African countries as well. It may well have been this need to underpin the integrity of the faithful's belief that was in Gianpaolo's mind, for in numbers the Church could hardly have been much stronger, on a percentage basis standing higher than most European countries. As many observers have noted, Catholicism is growing faster in the Third World than in Europe, and it is Europe that is becoming missionary territory in need of evangelization.

The pope obviously believed that the Filipinos had the faith and vigour to meet this challenge of continuing the evangelization of their people and those of other nations. This he demonstrated in his next comments:

> I am aware that the Philippines has a great vocation in being the light of Christ in the Far East: to proclaim his truth, his love, his

[274] Ibid.
[275] Ibid., p. 76 (first person restored).
[276] *World Christian Encyclopedia*, p. 562. Another 10.2% professed allegiance to other Christian denominations (figures given are for mid-1980).

justice and salvation by word and example before its neighbours, the peoples of Asia. I know that you have a privileged instrument in this regard: Radio Veritas. It is my hope that the Philippines will use this great means to proclaim with the entire Church that Jesus Christ is the Son of God and Saviour of the world.[277]

Gianpaolo sent his greetings to the bishops' local churches, 'especially to the priests and religious', concluding by imparting to his brothers his 'special Apostolic Blessing' and invoking upon them 'joy and strength in Jesus Christ'. In the grief and despair following the pope's death that same night, the content of this address was naturally rather overlooked, but it was not without significance. In it Gianpaolo had stressed the importance of thorough evangelization in the modern world – the theme of the 1974 Synod of Bishops. He had endorsed his predecessor's teaching, and in so doing he had effectively reaffirmed the Church's concern and commitment on two fronts, the spiritual and the material, but with primacy staying with the former. Finally, he had given his firm seal of approval to modern means – broadcasting – in propagating the Faith, and a clear signal of his confidence in the Asian hierarchy in leading their Churches into the next century.

Photographs of Gianpaolo with the Filipino bishops and shaking hands with Cardinal Rosales were the last ones to be taken of him in life, but this meeting was far from being the pope's last duty of the day. There was yet more on the agenda. A lot more. Another person who had an audience with the pope was Cardinal Sebastiano Baggio, the sixty-five year old Prefect of the Congregation for Bishops. Gianpaolo had several important matters to discuss with him concerning the world hierarchy, the first being the issue of Cardinal John Cody, the embattled and rather controversial Archbishop of Chicago.[278] The pope's chief concern was the terrible state of relations between Cody and the clergy of his archdiocese, amid allegations of financial misdemeanours. He informed Baggio that Cody should be given the opportunity to retire on the grounds of ill-health. This was reasonable; the seventy-year old Cody was indeed ill, his eventual death on 25 April 1982 being attrib-

---

[277] *The Teachings of Pope John Paul I*, pp. 76–7 (first person restored). Radio Veritas is based in Manila, reaching throughout East Asia and beyond. It is owned and operated by the Philippine Radio Educational and Information Centre, a non-profit making organization with 7 Filipino bishops as board members. See *World Christian Encyclopedia*, p. 566.

[278] Greeley, p. 172; Yallop, pp. 204–5.

uted to 'severe coronary artery disease'.[279] If Cody declined to retire then a coadjutor was to be appointed. Again, this would not be an unusual move; Cody had himself acted in the same capacity in New Orleans earlier in his career. Either way, a potentially delicate situation would be resolved.

If Gianpaolo and Baggio were agreed on this matter, it is not clear that they agreed on the second issue that the pope raised, namely who was to fill his recently vacated Patriarchal See of Venice. It has been asserted that Gianpaolo offered Baggio himself the position, and that Baggio angrily rebuffed the Holy Father, on the grounds that he wanted to stay in Rome at the centre of the decision-making process.[280] This assertion was officially refuted, however, in a Vatican Memorandum supplied to Episcopal Conference, dated June 1984 and entitled 'The death of Pope John Paul I'. Point Number 5 of this document reads:

> It is not true that Pope John Paul I wished to send Cardinal Baggio to Venice as his successor. He had just confirmed the Cardinal's appointment in the Congregation for Bishops, and in the presidency of the [Conference of the] Latin American episcopate scheduled for Puebla. Cardinal Baggio has himself directly denied the theory, saying 'Not only did he not ask me, but if he had asked me, I would have gone there – flying.[281]

What is more likely is that the pope proposed the name of Bishop Marco Cé, the general ecclesiastical assistant of Italian Catholic Action, as his successor in Venice, a proposal he was to make again later in the day to Cardinal Villot.[282] The idea obviously found favour, for after Gianpaolo's death his successor as pope, John Paul II, promoted Cé to Venice on 7 December 1978 and created him a cardinal on 30 June 1979. Baggio, at any rate, stayed in Rome, and on 25 March 1985 was named as Camerlengo.

At 12.30 p.m. the pope had lunch with his two secretaries, before taking his customary short siesta. Then, because of the chill wind that day, Magee warned Gianpaolo about going up on the roof garden. The pope's reply was significant: 'I won't go up because in fact I'm not feeling too good. I just don't feel myself.' At this, Magee said that he would like to

---

[279] Yallop, p. 299. For accusations against Cody, see Greeley, pp. 89–92.
[280] Yallop, pp. 205–6; Murphy, p. 191.
[281] Cornwell, *A Thief in the Night*, pp. 282–3.
[282] *Pontiff*, p. 372; Cornwell, *A Thief in the Night*, pp. 191, 255.

call the pope's personal doctor, Renato Buzzonetti, but the pope replied: 'Oh, no, no, no. No need to call the doctor. I'll walk in the house'.[283] And so saying, he began to walk round and round the salone next to the secretaries' room, quietly saying his rosary. However, he could not put aside his work for long. For one thing, he was 'very busy' reading the relevant material on the forthcoming Third General Assembly of the Latin American Bishops' Conference, CELAM III, that was to be held at Puebla, Mexico on 12–28 October.[284] Early on in his pontificate, Gianpaolo had confirmed both the dates and the officers of the meeting who had been named by Paul VI; the three presidents were to be Cardinals Sebastiano Baggio and Aloisio Lorscheider and Archbishop Ernesto Corripio Ahumada, and the General Secretary was to be Bishop Alfonso López Trujillo.

In fact Gianpaolo had been approached by Baggio and Lorscheider whilst still in conclave, less than an hour after his election. During this discussion he had 'astonished both Cardinals with his knowledge and grasp of the central issues which would be explored at Puebla',[285] the main theme of which was to be 'Evangelization in Latin America Present and Future'. The Puebla conference itself promised to be crucial, being a follow-up to the famous one held at Medellin, Colombia in 1968, and whose 'Manifesto' had proved to be the launch-pad for the 'theology of liberation'. Naturally enough, the Latin American bishops wanted Gianpaolo to visit Puebla. After all, Paul VI had visited Medellin. However, early in his pontificate, Gianpaolo announced that he would not be attending the conference,[286] although it is obvious that he continued to interest himself closely with developments until the day he died. In a long audience he expressed to López Trujillo particular interest in the issues of lay ministers, religious and catechists, and announced he was preparing a television message for the conference.[287]

One reason for his not attending could simply be that he felt that he had too many other pressing problems to deal with in the Vatican to justify an engagement abroad at that time. However, another, more ominous reason, has subsequently

---

[283] Cornwell, *A Thief in the Night*, p. 187.
[284] *30 Days*, no. 5, September 1988, p. 13.
[285] Yallop, p. 171.
[286] *Tablet*, CCXXXII, 9 September 1978, p. 880.
[287] G. Cardinale, 'First Stop, Puebla', *30 Days*, no. 1, Year XXII, January 2004.

presented itself, and that is the distinct possibility that the
pope had premonitions of his own imminent death. Other
instances of this will be given in their due place, but with
regard to his attendance at CELAM III, Magee states:

> [Gianpaolo] confided to me that he would not go, that he did not
> feel like going. To tell the truth, he said even more. On the day of
> his first general audience [6 September], a group of Mexicans had
> handed to him a facsimile airplane ticket for Mexico as a public sign
> of invitation. After the audience, he gave it to me and said, 'Perhaps
> it would be of use to you. To me, no. As Pope, I will never travel.'[288]

No modern pope after Paul VI, the 'Pilgrim Pope' who made
nine ground-breaking foreign trips, including visits to the Holy
Land and India in 1964, would say *'I will never travel'* without
concrete reason. John Paul II travelled to virtually every part of
the world, making an unprecedented total of 104 trips outside
Italy to 129 countries and territories. Certainly after
Gianpaolo's death his successor quickly announced the new
dates of 27 January – 12 February 1979 for the conference,
and duly attended its opening. One last indicator as to
Gianpaolo's involvement with CELAM III surfaced in December
1978, when the London-based *Tablet* reported that:

> Commentators in the United States have drawn attention to the fact
> that the names of 12 bishops, a number of them known for their
> conservative outlook or their association with Latin American mili-
> tary regimes were added recently to the list of episcopal delegates.
> It has been suggested that the twelve were 'probably chosen by
> Pope John Paul I during his short reign' since there is no indication
> that the present Pope either added to or subtracted from the names
> on the list.[289]

In the middle of the afternoon of his last day, Gianpaolo made
telephone calls to Cardinal Felici in Padua, where Felici was
about to attend a spiritual retreat, and to Cardinal Benelli in
Florence.[290] He also sent what was to be the last letter of his
life to Mgr Hugo Aufderbeck, the Apostolic Administrator of
Erfurt-Meiningen in the German Democratic Republic, on the

---

[288] *30 Days*, no. 5, September 1988, p. 13.
[289] *Tablet*, CCXXXII, 23/30 December 1978, p. 1268. In the event, whilst
   almost inevitably not as 'radical' as Medellin, Puebla was largely a success
   in that it reaffirmed the need for a 'preferential option for the poor'.
[290] Yallop, pp. 202, 206.

seven-hundredth anniversary of the founding of the Church of San Severus.[291]

During the afternoon Cardinal Villot telephoned Magee in order to make an appointment with the pope that evening. Magee went to inform the pope, who was clearly upset, saying: 'Oh! Cardinal Villot again! But I've no document to read'.[292] Magee's comment on Gianpaolo's reaction is more than a little interesting in the light of subsequent events. As he explained to John Cornwell: 'You see, he [Gianpaolo] thought that Villot was always chasing him for things he should have read, and he was really perturbed'.[293] Nonetheless, it was arranged that Villot would see the Pope at 6.30 p.m. The pope, meanwhile, resumed his walking around the salone.

Shortly after this, Magee, next door in the secretaries' room, heard Gianpaolo 'making a sort of harsh coughing noise'. Magee rushed into the salone and found him standing near the table. The pope said: 'I have a pain! Send Sister Vincenza to me. She knows what to do.' Magee suggested that it would be better to call the doctor, but Gianpaolo insisted that Magee should not call him. Magee pressed him: 'Holy Father, it might be something serious.' However, the pope was adamant, and retired to his room, while his secretary went to the kitchen to see Sister Vincenza. Magee's news did not seem to unduly alarm the nun, who simply said: 'Oh yes, this has happened before.' Then, in Magee's words:

> She took some medicine and went off to see the Pope. For her this was quite normal, although it wouldn't have been for any other nun. She had been infirmarian in Venice and evidently had this rapport with him.[294]

All this took place at about 5.30 p.m. An hour later, as arranged, Cardinal Villot arrived and had an audience alone with the pope in the latter's private study. Nobody knows for certain the exact details of what was discussed between the two men before Villot re-emerged at 7.35 p.m. Various Vatican 'sources' would later claim that the meeting was 'acrimonious, charged with emotion'.[295] However, there is no proof of this, and neither man appeared to be notably ill-tempered after-

[291] *Insegnamenti Di Giovanni Paolo I*, pp. 103–4.
[292] Magee in Cornwell, *A Thief in the Night*, p. 189.
[293] Ibid.
[294] Ibid., p. 190.
[295] Ibid., pp. 255, 248.

wards. In all likelihood the conversation simply concerned – as Magee maintains – the appointment of a new patriarch for Venice.[296] It is also possible that the issue of Cardinal Cody was discussed, and whether Archbishop Tomas O Fiaich of Armagh, Primate of All Ireland, should be elevated to the Sacred College of Cardinals.[297] Some of these issues would certainly have been problematical to Gianpaolo – as he stated to Magee later that evening – but this in itself does not prove that there was undue tension between the pope and the Cardinal Secretary of State on this occasion.

At this point in the story there is a discrepancy between the accounts of the two principal eye-witnesses to these events, John Magee and Diego Lorenzi. It is not merely a question of degree, but a major contradiction of facts, and one which is both important in relation to the pope's subsequent death, and as an indicator of the less than satisfactory organization of the papal household at that time.

According to Magee, he informed Lorenzi about the pain that the pope had had earlier. He too is said to have wanted to call the doctor. Despite this agreement, it is notable that neither secretary did so. At any rate, after Cardinal Villot had departed, and as the pope and the two secretaries prepared for supper, Magee says that he asked the pope how he was. ''*Sto bene! Sto bene! Eccomi!'* he cried, pummelling his chest. *'Andiamo!* Those tablets of Sister Vincenza are miraculous. Let's go to supper!'[298]

Diego Lorenzi's account presents a rather different picture of events. Interviewed on Italian television and by author John Cornwell, he has spoken of:

> ... the symptoms of a heart attack which the Pope had experienced on 28 September 1978. At about quarter to eight, or ten to eight, he came to the door of his study and said that he had had a dreadful pain, but that it had passed. And I said to him that we should call a doctor, but he absolutely forbade me to do this. And I obeyed, for one should obey the Pope.[299]

Leaving aside the rather sobering implication that Lorenzi would obey the pope even to the latter's detriment, Lorenzi has gone further; according to him John Magee has previously

[296] Ibid., p. 191.
[297] O Fiaich was created a cardinal by John Paul II on 30 June 1979.
[298] Cornwell, *A Thief in the Night*, p. 190.
[299] Ibid., p. 74. See also *Catholic Herald*, no. 5290, 9 October 1987, p. 1.

acknowledged that this version of events is accurate. As Lorenzi recalled:

> In January 1979 I went to Naples and on the way back I called Father Magee, who was now the new Pope's secretary, and I said, 'Look, John, you remember when the Pope told us at ten to eight that he had a pain?' And he said, 'Yes, I do'. Then I said, 'Don't you think that we had not done enough of certain things in order to save his life?' 'Oh,' he said, 'forget all about it'. I was not very pleased with this answer he gave me. I didn't like it. Anyway, he had not forgotten. The problem was that the Pope would not let us call anybody. He kept saying he was now feeling OK.[300]

If Diego Lorenzi's account is true, the pope complained of feeling ill three times between 2.00 and 7.50 p.m., yet none of the pope's household staff called either Dr Buzzonetti or Dr Da Ros in Venice. There are no grounds for suspecting malicious intent, but this fact does perhaps betoken a confusion of responsibilities.

At 7.50 p.m. Gianpaolo, Magee and Lorenzi sat down to a dinner of veal, vegetables and salad served by Sisters Vincenza and Assunta. John Magee has given a detailed account of the conversation held during this meal, which gives a valuable insight into the pope's state of mind on this last evening. This state was not one of fear, rather one of calm preparation, of expectant resignation, an intuition of imminent death. Magee relates that:

> During supper he ate well and he was in good form. I used to ask him certain questions, because he was always anxious lest he forget certain things he had to do. I asked him, 'Holy Father, have you chosen the person to give the Vatican retreat next Lent?'
> He said, 'Yes, I have'. Then he immediately said, 'The type of retreat I would like at this moment would be for a good death'.
> He was constantly talking of death, constantly reminding us that his Pontificate was to be of short duration, constantly saying that he was to go so that he would be replaced by 'the foreigner'. All of this was a great enigma to us then. I said to him, 'Oh Holy Father, not again! Coming again to that morbid subject! You're only beginning your Pontificate'. Now Don Diego, who was at the end of the table, said, 'That reminds me of a prayer we Italians have all learned, which we say when we go to bed at night. It was composed by St Alphonsus Liguori and it goes something like this: *0 Lord, grant me the grace to accept the death which you will send me, and wherever it will come from*'.

---

[300] Cornwell, *A Thief in the Night*, p. 75.

The Pope immediately intervened and said, 'That's not correct. It was not written by St Alphonsus, and it goes like this: *Lord, grant me the grace to accept THE DEATH BY WHICH I SHALL BE STRUCK DOWN*'. The Italian would be – *dammi la grazia di accettare la morte nel modo in cui mi colpira*.

I said, 'My God! What kind of a subject are we talking about?' That was almost exactly to the second at about a quarter past eight.[301]

It will be noted that for the first twenty minutes or so Gianpaolo was in 'good form'; it was only Magee's question that brought the pope's underlying feeling to the surface, and that even then his language was calm and measured.

When the meal was finished the pope asked Lorenzi to put a call through to Cardinal Giovanni Colombo in Milan. Whilst Lorenzi went to place the call, Gianpaolo turned to Magee as they sat alone at the dining table and told him why he wanted to consult Colombo: 'We have a problem that Cardinal Villot brought up this evening as to whom we should appoint as the new Patriarch of Venice'.[302] Magee asked the pope how he was feeling; the pope said he 'felt fine'. They got up, and Gianpaolo said grace, before going into the kitchen to greet the sisters, as was Gianpaolo's habit. As the two men emerged into the corridor, Lorenzi called from the far end, 'Cardinal Colombo on the line'. The time was around 8.45 p.m. According to Magee:

'The Pope then took off down the corridor at such a speed I was worried he would slip and fall on the marble floor. I couldn't believe the speed he went down there. He went straight in and took the call, which lasted about fifteen to twenty minutes.'[303]

It has been cogently argued by John Cornwell that this vigorous act on Gianpaolo's part triggered a major embolus, and that this is what killed the pope later that evening. This theory will be discussed in the next chapter. As to the content of the conversation between Gianpaolo and Colombo, this can be reconstructed quite clearly.

Earlier in September Colombo had visited Boston, in the United States, where he had found that people were already enthusiastic about the new pope. Now, talking on the telephone, with the Holy Father, Colombo immediately said: 'When

---

[301] Ibid., pp. 190–1; See also *30 Days*, no. 5, September 1988, pp. 13–14.
[302] Cornwell, *A Thief in the Night*, p. 191.
[303] Ibid.

I was in Boston I made a promise to the people there: that you would visit them. In response, they gave me a gift [a valuable enamelled watch] for you'.[304]

If Colombo's account is accurate and complete at this point, then it is interesting to note that Gianpaolo neither accepted nor rejected the suggestion, calmly responding: 'Now let's talk about more serious things'.[305] He mentioned his schedule, that he retired to bed early in order to rise early next day. The implication could be that the pope did not wish to take Colombo's suggestion seriously: we will never know. His successor, John Paul II, visited Boston on the first day of his trip to the United States on 1–7 October 1979.

As to the main subject of conversation between Gianpaolo and Colombo, Diego Lorenzi concurs with John Magee, whilst adding more detail:

> I came to know what he said through other people. The only truth is this: the Pope was concerned about his successor in Venice, because over a month had passed since he vacated the See and he was trying to put in there a Salesian who was the Provincial of the order. And this man had refused to accept the job, and to my mind Luciani was trying to get in touch once again, through the Cardinal of Milan, with this man in order to get him to accept.[306]

What comments or suggestions Cardinal Colombo had to make on the issue are unknown, but there is no evidence for believing that the conversation was anything other than friendly. Colombo later recalled:

> He spoke to me for a long time in a completely normal tone from which no physical illness could be inferred. He was full of serenity and hope. His final greeting was 'pray'.[307]

After his talk with Colombo, Gianpaolo recited Compline in his chapel with John Magee. Then he bade his staff good night, using his common expression: '*Buona notte! A domani, se Dio vuole!*' – Good-night! Until tomorrow, if God is willing![308] God,

---

[304] *30 Days*, no. 1, January 1989, p. 80.
[305] Ibid.
[306] Cornwell, *A Thief in the Night*, p. 75.
[307] Yallop, p. 211.
[308] Cornwell, *A Thief in the Night*, p. 192; Yallop, p. 211. There appears to be no truth in the story given widespread circulation – in, for instance, Greeley, p.172; Lo Bello, p. 60; *Time*, 112, 9 October 1978, p. 9; Hebblethwaite, *Year of Three Popes*, p. 128 – that the pope was upset

however, had his own plan. It was about 9.30 p.m. when Gianpaolo shut the door to his room: he would never be seen alive again.

---

shortly before he retired to bed by a report that a left-wing youth had been ambushed and killed in Rome by right-wing extremists, and that he lamented 'They kill each other – even the young people'. It is probably a conflation with the case of the murdered student he mentioned in his *Angelus* address of 24 September.

Chapter Six

Message and Legacy

The next morning – Friday 29 September – Sister Vincenza arose at 4.00 a.m. as usual. At around 4.30 a.m. she quietly performed her first task of the day, leaving a tray of coffee on a small table outside the pope's bedroom door.[1] This done, she returned to the kitchen where some of the other nuns were starting to prepare breakfast. At about 5.20 a.m. Vincenza returned to collect the tray. To her surprise it was untouched, something she could not recall ever happening in all the time that she had worked for 'Padre Albino'. He never overslept. Unwilling simply to remove the tray, Vincenza listened at the door. There was no sound from within. Uncertain of her own fears, Vincenza knocked gently on the door. There was no response. She tried again, more insistently this time. Still no reply. With rising concern and alarm Vincenza knocked harder. Silence.

Reaching a decision, Vincenza opened the door and entered the pope's bedroom. What she saw made her stop in her tracks. The reading light was on, and Gianpaolo was sitting up in bed. His head was tilted slightly to the right, and he stared sightlessly through his glasses, which had begun to slip down his nose. His lips were drawn back over his teeth in an unnatural rictus. The pope's knees were drawn up, and in his oddly clenched hands was a sheaf of papers, some of which had fallen and scattered across the bed.

The pope was clearly dead.

---

[1] Unless otherwise indicated, in detailing the events of the morning of 29 September I have followed the basic chronology established by John Cornwell. However, it should be noted that even Cornwell's extensive researches have not resolved all the small discrepancies between the accounts of, say, Magee and Lorenzi.

Horrified, Vincenza turned and rushed to rouse John Magee. 'The Pope is dead,' the nun informed Magee, still startled from having been shaken awake. Quickly, he got up, buttoned a soutane over his pyjamas and ran to the pope's room. The time was now around 5.30 a.m. Knowing what he must find, but as yet unable to comprehend the situation, Magee entered the pope's room just as Vincenza had done. He called the pope. There was no response. Magee took hold of Gianpaolo's hands in a desperate but futile attempt to wake him up; the pope didn't move, and his hands were cold and stiff. As Vincenza and the other nuns came to the door of the room, Magee was finally hit by the enormity of what had happened. As he has since related that moment: I fell on my knees. I buried my head in the quilt. It was very soft. I shouted into it, my voice muffled, 'Oh God! No! Why? Why? Why?' And it suddenly came across me what to do. I was the only one in the world, apart from the sisters, who knew that the pope was dead. I remained for a moment; then I stood up and looked at him ... I really loved that man. I turned round and the sisters were distraught. I said, 'Yes, sisters, he's dead. Now one of you go and call Don Diego. The others remain here and pray'.[2]

Quickly, Magee went to his desk in the office two doors away; the time was now about 5.40 a.m. As he phoned the private apartment of Cardinal Villot, the Secretary of State and Camerlengo, Magee wondered how he could break the news to him, knowing that the cardinal had heart problems. From the pope's room Magee could hear the nuns praying and the voice of Lorenzi as the latter arrived on the scene. After a delay, the cardinal's secretary put Magee through to Villot, who was still in bed. Magee got a surprisingly cordial response for the hour of day. As he has related, Villot responded amiably:

'Oh, good morning! How are you at this hour of the morning? It's a beautiful morning!' I interrupted him: 'Eminence, the Pope.' 'What is it? The Pope does not want me at this hour, does he?' 'No,' I said. 'The Pope is dead'. He shouted into the telephone: 'It isn't true, it's impossible, I was with him yesterday evening, it's impossible.' And I: 'He is dead.' 'No, no.' 'He is dead.' He didn't want to believe me. I said to him: 'You've got to come.' 'Okay, I'm coming now.' 'Meanwhile, I'll call the doctor'.[3]

[2] Cornwell, *A Thief in the Night*, p. 195.
[3] *30 Days*, no. 5, September 1988, p. 15. Concerning the events surrounding Gianpaolo's death, Magee gave essentially the same information to Tommaso Ricci of *30 Days* and to John Cornwell, but with different emphasis of detail in each case.

Immediately, at 5.42 a.m.,[4] Magee called Dr Renato Buzzonetti, who lived in Piazza Adriana, only a few hundred metres from the Vatican next to the Castel Sant'Angelo. Buzzonetti was very tired, and he also had trouble believing Magee's incredible statement that the pope was dead. He later confided to Magee that halfway on his short drive to the Vatican he nearly turned back because he thought he had been dreaming, but he came anyway to see.

Villot and Buzzonetti arrived at the papal apartments almost simultaneously, and with Magee they entered the pope's bedroom together. It was now approximately 6.00 a.m. Dr Buzzonetti made a brief examination of the body, and pronounced his verdict that the pope had died of an acute myocardial infarction – a heart attack – at about 11.00 p.m. the previous evening.[5]

Whilst Cardinal Villot considered how to release the incredible news to the outside world, Diego Lorenzi made two important phone calls. The first he made about 5.55 a.m., and it was to Gianpaolo's niece Pia, the member of his family who had probably been closest to him. Thoughtfully, Lorenzi felt that the family should hear the news personally rather than hearing it on the radio. Informing Pia that her uncle was dead, Lorenzi said: 'Look, Pia, you need a great deal of faith. I found, him this morning, about ten minutes ago'.[6] Pia, her husband and two children, dressed and drove to their parish church in Canale d'Agordo. The priest, Don Rinaldo Andrich, had just finished saying Mass and the congregation of thirty was still present. Pia whispered to him: 'Uncle Albino is dead' – *'Zio Albino è morto'*. Andrich, unable to think of anything else to say, turned to his congregation and said simply: 'They tell me the Pope is dead'.[7] By 7.20 a.m. the bells of the little church were tolling in mourning.[8]

The second of Lorenzi's phone calls, made at about 6.05 a.m., was to Dr Antonio Da Ros in Venice, Luciani's doctor since 1959. During those years he had generally seen his patient on a weekly basis. Da Ros had visited Luciani in the Vatican on 3, 13 and 23 September, routinely taking his blood pressure. All

---

[4] Cornwell, *A Thief in the Night*, p. 170; Buzzonetti himself logged the time.
[5] For a reproduction of the 'Death Certificate of John Paul I', see Cornwell, *A Thief in the Night*, p. 281.
[6] Ibid., pp. 73–4.
[7] Hebblethwaite, *Year of Three Popes*, p. 129.
[8] Yallop, p. 220.

he had noticed was some 'slight swelling up' of Luciani's ankles.[9] The doctor's reaction to the news was much the same as that of many other people on that fateful day, one of shocked disbelief. As Lorenzi told it:

> He couldn't believe what I was saying. He had seen the Pope the previous Sunday afternoon and he found him in very good health. And I thought that the doctor couldn't accept the truth. He found himself somehow defeated by this sudden death. He couldn't accept it, of course. I know that he tried to get a seat on a plane from Venice to Rome, but he couldn't. So he drove all the way from Veneto to Rome and he arrived in the Vatican around three o'clock. So it is silly to say as some people do that the Pope the previous night had phoned his doctor.[10]

From then on the pace quickened as senior curial officials were contacted before the public release of the news. Cardinal Confalonieri, the Dean of the Sacred College, was told, as were Archbishop Casaroli and Archbishop Caprio, who was in Montecatini Terme to take the waters and was awakened by a telephone call at 6.00 a.m.[11] Cardinal Benelli, who had been so instrumental in Gianpaolo's election, heard the news in Florence by telephone at 6.30 a.m.: 'Grief-stricken and openly crying, he immediately retired to his room and began to pray'.[12] He did not emerge until 9.00 a.m., when he was surrounded by reporters. Still crying, Benelli spoke for many when he said: 'The Church has lost the right man for the right moment. We are very distressed. We are left frightened. Man cannot explain such a thing. It is a moment which limits and conditions us'.[13]

At 7.15 a.m. Father Roberto Tucci, SJ, the Director of Vatican Radio, was informed of the pope's death.[14] At 7.27 a.m., a mere two hours after Gianpaolo's body had been found, Tucci broadcast the news to the world. However, the content of the official statement was to cause endless trouble for the Vatican, and the responsibility for this must lie with Cardinal Villot. Believing that the concept of a nun finding the pope dead in his bed would create a scandal, he had decided to give a version of

[9] Da Ros, interviewed by A. Tornielli in *Il Giornale*, 27 September 2003.
[10] Cornwell, *A Thief in the Night*, p. 74. See also *30 Days*, no. 9, 1993, pp. 50–2.
[11] Interview with *30 Days*, no. 9, 1993, p. 45.
[12] Yallop, p. 220.
[13] Ibid., p. 222.
[14] Greeley, p. 175.

the events that departed from the truth in several essentials. In the pressure of the moment Villot made a grave error, for his old-fashioned, rather naive sense of decorum was to have a devastating effect, and has given grist to the mill of conspiracy theorists ever since. The bulletin briefly stated that:

> This morning, September 29th 1978, about 5.30, the private Secretary of the Pope, contrary to custom not having found the Holy Father in the chapel of his private apartment, looked for him in his room and found him dead in bed with the light on, like one who was intent on reading. The physician, Dr Renato Buzzonetti, who hastened at once, verified the death, which took place presumably towards eleven o'clock yesterday evening, as sudden death that could be related to acute myocardial infarction.[15]

At 7.30 a.m. Tucci offered a Latin Requiem Mass for the repose of the late pope's soul. Simultaneously, Father Romeo Panciroli, MCCI, the Director of the Vatican Press Office, telephoned the same statement that Tucci had read out on the radio to major foreign and Italian news agencies in Rome.[16] Later, Vatican Radio bulletins specified that the secretary in question was Father John Magee, and that the pope had been reading *The Imitation of Christ*, the early fifteenth-century devotional work generally attributed to Thomas à Kempis.

This last piece of information – broadcast at 2.30 p.m.[17] – was completely false, and was indeed retracted by Vatican Radio on 2 October at the 'suggestion of the Secretariat of State'.[18] However, despite the 'inventive' assertions of conspiracy theorists to the contrary,[19] Cardinal Villot was not responsible for this particular fabrication. The researches of John Cornwell have put this beyond reasonable doubt; the story was not an official Vatican 'plant', but an innocent – if rather unthinking – invention by journalists in the Vatican Press Office which had been picked up by Vatican Radio, which has some capacity for independent news gathering.[20]

What Gianpaolo was actually reading was explained by Vatican Radio in its correction broadcast on 2 October:

---

[15] Yallop, p. 220.
[16] *Pontiff*, p. 390.
[17] Cornwell, *A Thief in the Night*, pp. 14, 151.
[18] Ibid., pp. 14, 159; Yallop, p. 221.
[19] *Pontiff*, p. 382; Yallop, pp. 220–1.
[20] Cornwell, *A Thief in the Night*, pp. 151, 180, 234.

After the necessary enquiries, we are now in a position to state that the Pope, when he was found dead on the morning of September 29th, was holding in his hands certain sheets of paper containing his personal writings such as homilies, speeches, reflections and various notes.[21]

Only four people were really in a position to know the truth. Villot and Vincenza are dead. Both Lorenzi and Magee are adamant that what the pope was holding in his hands were indeed homilies and sermons:[22] not lists of changes to be made to Vatican personnel, not a disciplinary speech due to be made to the Jesuits, not a copy of *The Imitation of Christ* or secret lists of Vatican Freemasons.

To return to the Friday; as the news spread, people everywhere reacted with stunned amazement and grief. In Rome itself, many Romans ran to the Vatican, where flags were flying at half mast and the massive Bronze Doors leading into the Apostolic Palace were half closed in mourning.[23] By noon *L'Osservatore Romano*, framed in a black band, and special editions of several Italian newspapers, were on the streets.[24] At noon bells throughout Rome tolled, as they were to do at noon and dusk for two days.[25] Inside the Vatican, Gianpaolo's death certificate was drawn up and signed by Dr Buzzonetti, and witnessed by Professor Mario Fontana, the Director of the Vatican Health Service and an experienced pathologist.[26] The pope's body was blessed by Bishop Petrus Canisius Jean Van Lierde, OSA, the long-serving Vicar General of Vatican City. It was then prepared and vested in the papal garments by Buzzonetti, Lorenzi, Magee, Mgr Noè – the papal Master of Ceremonies – and a religious of the Order of St John of God, from the Vatican Pharmacy.[27] At 11.00 a.m. the body was removed, *unembalmed*, to lie in state in the Sala Clementina, a hall of Renaissance splendour.

At noon the doors were opened to admit the public: 'Romans and tourists formed a mile-and-a-half queue that wound around St Peter's Square to pay their respects to the Pope'.[28]

---

[21] Yallop, p. 233.
[22] Cornwell, *A Thief in the Night*, pp. 72, 196.
[23] Muthig, p. 165.
[24] Greeley, p. 176.
[25] *Catholic Herald*, no. 4825, 6 October 1978, p. 2; Greeley, p. 175.
[26] Professor Fontana himself died in 1979.
[27] Cornwell, *A Thief in the Night*, p. 171.
[28] *Time*, 112, 9 October 1978, p. 11.

Two nuns, overcome, rushed, forward to kiss the dead pope's hands as he lay on the bier, and had to be gently restrained by Vatican ushers.[29] Many of the mourners wept openly; Gianpaolo's body seemed small and vulnerable isolated in the great hall, and many noted with poignancy that his papal red slippers showed scarcely any signs of wear.[30] Present also was Father Andrew Greeley, who found the whole occasion distasteful and reflected on 'The frailty of all things human.'[31] One estimate claims that up to 250,000 people filed past the body on that Friday alone, before the doors were closed at 6.00 p.m.[32]

Other people, outside Rome, grieved too. In Belluno, Gianpaolo's old friend Bishop Maffeo Ducoli said: 'People are crying in the streets and in the shops as if someone in their family had died'.[33] Cardinal Willebrands, who, like Cardinal Benelli, had worked hard to promote Luciani's candidacy in the conclave held such a short time before, said feelingly:

'It's a disaster. I cannot put into words how happy we were on that August day when we had chosen John Paul. We had such high hopes. It was such a beautiful feeling, a feeling that something fresh was going to happen to our church.'[34]

More philosophically, Willebrands then put the event into perspective by placing it in the general scheme of all human existence:

'His death reminds us how small and how weak man is, that life and death are mysteries, that we are in God's hand. That is why we also have faith'.[35]

Luciani himself would have undoubtedly approved of the lesson that Willebrands drew. But how were ordinary people, Catholics and many non-Catholics alike, to come to terms with this sudden, seemingly incomprehensible loss? What meaning could such a brief pontificate have, that showed such bright promise only to be extinguished after a mere thirty-three days? For a shorter papacy it was necessary to go back 373 years to 1605 and the twenty-seven day reign of the frail, sixty-nine year-old Medici Pope Leo XI who died after catching a chill.

It is fair to say that Gianpaolo's death was felt more forcibly

---

[29] *Time*, 112, 9 October 1978, p. 11.
[30] Hebblethwaite, *Year of Three Popes*, p. 128.
[31] Greeley, p. 176.
[32] Yallop, p. 222.
[33] *Time*, 112, 9 October 1978, p. 11.
[34] Ibid., p. 9.
[35] Ibid.

and profoundly than that of Pope Paul, simply because it was so much more unexpected. Paul's death after a fifteen-year pontificate was not a surprise, whilst that of Gianpaolo was, and, coupled with the fact of Gianpaolo's warmer rapport with the crowds, this made it all the harder to bear. Peter Hebblethwaite commented that: 'It was as though a vision of hope and reconciliation had been tantalizingly glimpsed and then suddenly dashed to the ground'.[36]

During the day all nineteen rooms of the Papal Apartments had been cleared of Gianpaolo's possessions, the more personal items to be returned to the family. At 6.00 p.m., in accordance with tradition, Cardinal Villot sealed the Papal Apartments, which were to remain unopened until the election of a successor.[37] Lorenzi, Magee and the nuns left to take up temporary residence in a house run by the Sisters of Maria Bambina.

Not for nothing is a pope's secretary referred to as the 'pope's widow' on the death of his employer, although as we have seen Magee was, uniquely, to serve in the capacity of a papal secretary for a third time.

There remained one more important job to be completed before this sad day was ended. Shortly after 6.00 p.m., with the doors now closed to the public, Gianpaolo's body was temporarily removed from the Sala Clementina to the Sala dei Forconi, the Hall of the Preachers. There it was undressed again and, in Dr Buzzonetti's words:

> The body was treated for hygienic preservation without the removal of organs, intestines or blood. The reason was to ensure as far as possible the feasibility of exposing the body to the faithful for some days, taking the climate and so on into consideration.[38]

Injections of formalin and other preservatives were made into the body through the femoral arterial and vein passages,[39] the entire process taking from about 7.00 p.m. to about 3.30 a.m. the next morning, when the body was dressed again ready for exposition.[40] In charge of the team was Professor Cesare Gerin, Director of the Istituto di Medicina Legale at the State University of Rome. Gerin was assisted by Professors Fucci, Mariggi and Maragin, with one of the Signoracci brothers, Ernesto and

---

[36] Hebblethwaite, *Year of Three Popes*, p. 128.
[37] Yallop, p. 224.
[38] Cornwell, *A Thief in the Night*, p. 171.
[39] Yallop, pp. 225–6.
[40] Dr Buzzonetti, in Cornwell, *A Thief in the Night*, p. 172.

Arnaldo, on hand as technical assistant. All were chosen for the task by Professor Fontana.[41] At 11.00 a.m. the next morning – Saturday 30 September – whilst mourners continued to stream past Gianpaolo's body, Cardinal Confalonieri presided over the first meeting of the Congregation of Cardinals. Only twenty-nine, mostly Italian, were present, but this minority quickly made some key decisions. Gianpaolo's funeral was set for the following Wednesday, 4 October, and in the meantime, in order to accommodate the large number of people wishing to pay their last respects, it was decided that the pope's body should be transferred into St Peter's that evening. This duly took place at 6.00 p.m., the procession being watched by huge crowds in St Peter's Square and by millions more on television.

The assembled cardinals also made two more important deci-sions. After the death of Paul VI they had allowed themselves nearly the longest constitutionally acceptable time before enter-ing conclave to elect his successor. The time the cardinals reversed that decision completely, and, conscious of the sense of crisis and the emotional and financial cost to the Church, set the earliest possible date: Saturday 14 October. The other decision arrived at was that there was to be no autopsy performed on the body. Gianpaolo's death was sudden, unexpected, tragic and apparently senseless. Faced with such circumstances, with such shock, the human mind is often at first uncomprehending. As a process of recovery takes place with time, incomprehension is replaced by emotion and rationalization, the search for reasons and meaning, as the mind attempts to come to terms with the event and make it acceptable and understandable, limiting its power to shock and hurt. This process is in itself, of course, neutral: the rationale arrived at may be right or wrong, depend-ing upon the fullness and correctness of information available.

On Gianpaolo's death all too many people were prepared to believe that 'they' had somehow killed the people's hero. It offered an explanation and comfortably vague scapegoat for the inexplicable, without the need to provide a shred of evidence. Once started, the rumours were infectious and rapidly spread, encouraged by the inevitable sensationalists. Already on the Saturday Greeley was noting 'the cynicism of the Romans over in the Trastévere section of the city who darkly hint at poison', and that 'many Italians believe that Pope John Paul I was murdered'.[42]

---

[41] Cornwell, *A Thief in the Night*, p. 172.
[42] Greeley, pp. 177, 179. The Trastévere, adjacent and to the south of Vatican City, is the most 'Roman' quarter of Rome.

It was against this background that the cardinals decided against an autopsy. Conspiracy theorists would have ignored the findings of such an autopsy anyway, or claimed that they were false. However, a grave error was made when the Vatican declared that there was no precedent for a papal autopsy, and that anyway Article 17 of Paul VI's apostolic constitution *Romano Pontifici Eligendo* of 1975 implicitly ruled them out.[43] Firstly, Pope Paul's constitution made no reference to papal autopsies. Secondly, at least *four* popes have had autopsies performed on them.

Pope Clement II died suddenly on 9 October 1047 at the Abbey of San Tommaso, near Pesaro, aged about forty-two, after a reign of only nine months, during which he had convoked the reforming Council of Rome, which dealt with abuses such as simony. It was soon rumoured that he had been poisoned by a rival for the papacy, the violent and licentious Benedict IX, who quickly reappeared in Rome and installed himself as pope on 8 November. Clement's tomb, in Bamberg Cathedral, Germany, was opened on '3 June 1942 and the remains subjected to an exhaustive examination which disclosed that he probably died of lead poisoning'.[44] The five German scientists were, however, unable to determine the *circumstances* in which the poisoning took place, for although the presence of lead sugar was detected, this was not proof of assassination, as it was often used as a cure for venereal diseases at the time.

The Franciscan Pope Alexander V died suddenly on 3 May 1410 at Bologna aged about seventy-one. Elected by the Council of Pisa on 26 June 1409, his election to the papacy was an attempt to end the Great Schism of 1378–1417. However, although he retained the greatest share of allegiance, two other claimants still held considerable support and today he is rather unfairly considered to be an anti-pope. At the time of his death there was a suspicion, probably unfounded, that he had been poisoned by Cardinal Baldassare Cossa, who succeeded him as pope John XXIII, who is also now regarded as an anti-pope. The cardinals demanded an autopsy, no light matter at the time, and Alexander was eviscerated and embalmed by Milanese physician Pietro D'Argellata, whose findings were inconclusive.[45]

---

[43] Lo Bello, p. 61; see AAS, LXVII, 1975, p. 618.

[44] Kelly, p. 146; see also Lo Bello, p. 63.

[45] M. N. Alston, 'The Attitude Of The Church Toward Dissection Before 1500', *Bulletin Of The History Of Medicine*, 16, 1944, pp. 221–38; [pp. 235–6]. D'Argellata, who died in 1423, left a description of the autopsy in his *Cirurgia*, first published in 1480.

On 22 September 1774 Pope Clement XIV died aged sixty-eight. Clement's final year was one of depression, morbid fear of assassination, and torment caused by a scorbutic skin ailment. After his death his body decomposed so rapidly that his face had to be covered with a mask for the solemn exequies at St Peter's, fuelling rumours of poison. The main suspects were the Jesuits, whose Society Clement had suppressed by the breve *Dominus Ac Redemptor Noster* (21 July 1773); it was alleged that Clement had ceased kissing the feet of Christ on a particular crucifix for fear that it had been coated with poison. In the event, the autopsy, performed by Clement's physicians Natale Saliceti and Pasquale Adinolfi in front of many spectators, ascribed death to scorbutic and haemorrhoidal dispositions of long standing, aggravated by excessive labour; more recent medical interpretations of their reports ascribe death to oedema and possible gastric carcinoma.[46]

On 30 November 1830 Pope Pius VIII, regarded as being something of a liberal, died following 'frequent convulsions' aged sixty-nine after a pontificate of only twenty months. Poison once again being suspected, Prince Don Agostini Chigi, the Marshal of Conclave, recorded in his diary that the evening after the pope's death an autopsy was secretly performed upon the body. Again death was found to be from natural causes; apart from some weakness in the lungs all the organs were found to be healthy.[47]

Meanwhile rumour and speculation began to harden, in the face of Vatican silence, into specific accusations and demands. Franco Antico, secretary of the small but vocal traditionalist Catholic organization Civiltà Cristiana, which in August had plastered Rome with posters demanding 'ELECT A CATHOLIC POPE', formally petitioned the Vatican authorities to undertake not just an autopsy but a full judicial investigation to determine 'the true reasons for John Paul's death'.[48]

More seriously, on Sunday I October, one of Italy's most respected newspapers, *Corriere della Sera* of Milan, ran a front page article headlined 'Why Say No To An Autopsy?' The article was written by Carlo Bo, who pointed out that there were no Vatican rules forbidding papal autopsies, and cited the case of Pope Pius VIII as a precedent for them. Whilst being confident

---

[46] NCE, 3, p. 942; L. von Pastor, *History Of The Popes*, 38, pp. 533–7; Cornwell, *A Thief in the Night*, p. 25.
[47] Yallop, p. 235; *Time*, 112, 16 October 1978, p. 72; *Pontiff*, p. 406.
[48] Lo Bello, p. 60; see also Yallop, pp. 234–5.

that the 'era of crimes at the Vatican' was long past, Bo felt that curiosity concerning the unexpected death of Gianpaolo was quite understandable, especially as none of the fifteen doctors attached to the Vatican Health Service would make any comment on the matter. Bo made a good case: in calling for an autopsy, he argued cogently that:

> The Church has nothing to fear, therefore nothing to lose. On the contrary, it would have much to gain ... Now to know what the Pope died of is a legitimate historical fact, it is part of our visible history and does not in any way affect the spiritual mystery of his death. The body that we leave behind when we die can be understood with our poor instruments, it is a leftover: the soul is already, or rather it always has been, dependent on other laws which are not human and so remain inscrutable. Let us not make out of a mystery a secret to guard for earthly reasons and let us recognize the smallness of our secrets. Let us not declare sacred what is not.[49]

Whilst none of the Italian newspapers went so far as to suggest that the pope had actually been murdered, this may in part have been due to the stringency of the libel laws concerning the Vatican and the Catholic Church in Italy before the revised Concordat of 1984. *La Stampa* of Turin, Italy's second-most important daily, did however opine that the Vatican's decision to refuse to hold an autopsy was untenable and made 'the situation appear suspicious'.[50] What was becoming apparent, as Vittorio Zucconi accurately observed in *Corriere della Sera*, was that: 'Behind the doubts about the Pope's death lies a vast dissatisfaction with 'official versions'.[51] In the 'post-Watergate era' people's reluctance to automatically believe all they were told was unsurprising and indeed healthy, but sadly it also left them open to equally undesirable manipulation from other quarters.

By Tuesday 3 October, the 'poison theory' was common currency in Rome and was becoming widespread in the rest of the world as well. People continued to stream past the body at the rate of some twelve thousand an hour; many were heard to complain that their pope had been killed by the Curia, whilst

---

[49] Yallop, p. 232; see also Lo Bello, pp. 60–1. Bo's words echoed those of Pope Leo XIII, who, on opening the hitherto secret archives of the Vatican to scholars, declared that the Church had nothing to fear from historical truth (1883, 'Letter To Three Cardinals').

[50] Lo Bello, p. 61.

[51] Yallop, p. 234.

some screamed out: 'Who did this to you, who did this to you?'–•
That evening, around 7.45 p.m., a brief examination was made
of the body to check its state of preservation. Naturally, some
claimed that a partial autopsy had been performed, but no –
evidence has been produced.[52]

To jump ahead briefly in our story, the Vatican made its final
public statement on the issue on Thursday 12 October, through
Father Romeo Panciroli, in rather quaint but still self-evident
terms:

> At the end of the 'Novendiales', when we enter a new phase of the
> Sede Vacante, the director of the Press Office of the Holy See
> expresses words of firm disapproval for those who in recent days –
> have indulged in the spreading of strange rumours, unchecked,•
> often false and which sometimes have reached the level of grave
> insinuations, all the more grave for the repercussions they may
> have had in those countries where people are not accustomed to
> ¬excessively casual forms of expression. In these moments of
> mourning and sorrow for the Church one expected greater control
> and greater respect.

He repeated that 'what happened has been faithfully reported in
the communiqué of Friday morning, 29th September, which
maintains its full validity and which reflected the death certificate
signed by Professor Mario Fontana and Dr Renato Buzzonetti
so faithfully as to render its publication unnecessary'.

He also noted with satisfaction, 'the rectitude of many
professionals who in such a difficult moment for the Church,
showed loyal participation in the events and informed public
opinion with considered and objective reports'.[53]

To return to our sequence of events, as Wednesday 4 October
dawned it was raining heavily, as it had done for four straight
days. It was the feast of St Francis of Assisi, the patron saint of
Italy, and also the day of Gianpaolo's funeral. This seemed
somehow apt; two men full of simplicity, humility, charity, two
men loved by all. What David Yallop has rightly called the
'dialogue of love that Albino Luciani had inspired between
himself and the people'[54] continued to the end. By the time the

---

[52] Yallop, p. 236; Greeley, p. 182; Cornwell, *A Thief in the Night*, pp. 235–6.
[53] Yallop, p. 239. The *Novendiales* are the nine days of official mourning. One
publication that lacked 'rectitude' was the satirical magazine *Male*, which
suggested that Cardinal Benelli, of all people, had poisoned the pope.
Greeley, p. 182.
[54] Yallop, p. 237.

coffin was closed at noon it was estimated that between 750,000 and 850,000 people had filed past his bier.[55] In view of this, and despite the weather, it was decided that the rites should be the same as those held for Paul VI, and that once again an open-air Mass should be held in St Peter's Square.

In the event more people attended Gianpaolo's funeral than that of any previous pope, with estimates of up to 100,000 being present, including delegations from other Christian churches and organizations, and representatives from 117 states and international bodies. Thirty-one countries took live television pictures from the piazza. However, the diplomatic representation was more low-key than it had been for Pope Paul's funeral, the Secretariat of State having let it be known that it did not expect statesmen to disrupt their schedules for the third time within two months. Rather, it was hoped that they would come for the inauguration of the new pope when he was eventually elected.

The funeral service began at 4.00 p.m. The sky was dark and leaden, with drizzle and occasional downpours; it was said that 'even the heavens wept'. This, together with the more profound sense of grief amongst the crowd, made it 'much grimmer, much more melancholy, but also much more real than the August funeral'.[56] Once again, as at Pope Paul's funeral, Carlo Confalonieri was chief celebrant amongst the ninety-five cardinals present.

The triple coffin of cypress wood, lead and oak was borne from the Basilica on the shoulders of twelve *sediari*, and placed on a carpet on the ground in front of the altar. It was flanked by a tall paschal candle, denoting the resurrection and life hereafter, which flickered in the wind and the rain: the pages of the Bible, lying open on the coffin and sodden with water, stayed open at the Gospel of St John. The Sistine Chapel choir and Roman seminarians sang psalms associated with the funeral Mass, including Gregorian chants.

Cardinal Confalonieri truly rose to the occasion, delivering an inspired and moving funeral oration, in which he spoke of Gianpaolo with genuine warmth and insight:

> We have scarcely had the time to see the new Pope. Yet one month was enough for him to have conquered hearts – and, for us, it was a month to love him intensely. It is not length which characterises

---

[55] *Catholic Herald*, no. 4825, 6 October 1978, p. 2.
[56] Greeley, p. 182.

a life in a pontificate, but rather the spirit that fills it. He passed as a meteor that unexpectedly lights up the heavens and then disappears, leaving us amazed and astonished . . . we were quickly struck and fascinated by his instinctive goodness, by his innate modesty, by his sincere simplicity in deed and word.[57]

The cardinal then discoursed on the late pope's particular gift:

What emerges even more in his loving gift of self was his manner of teaching. He knew well how to translate with ease and joy the lofty theological doctrine into the more accessible language of a catechist. He taught with clarity the way of Christian formation . . . All understood that he was speaking in order to reach their soul. This was true even when, with wonderful humility and the wisest psychological intuition, he spoke directly to children 'in order that they might help the Pope' (as he so graciously put it). Everybody understood that he was speaking to the little ones in order that the adults would hear and understand. That delicacy, so evident to all, drew from his listeners both attention and action.

Confalonieri spoke of the devotion of all those who had paid their last respects to the deceased pope, and summarized the feelings of many when he said: '. . . before a world submerged in hatred and in violence, Pope John Paul has been himself, personally, a message of goodness'.[58] He then began the canon of the Mass, which was concelebrated by the Cardinals present, with 150 priests taking the host to the people. Interestingly, the rain stopped just in time for communion. In conclusion, the Sistine Chapel Choir chanted *In paradisum deducant te Angeli*.

At 5.50 p.m., the public ceremony at an end, the twelve frock-coated *sediari* bore the coffin back into the Basilica; the largely Roman crowd burst into applause, clapping smartly four times in a traditional tribute of respectful gratitude,[59] the much more expressive Latin equivalent of Anglo-Saxon silence. Then, as the people solemnly dispersed into the gathering evening, the private ceremony of sealing the coffin and entombing it in the catacombs took place, with only the immediate family and close friends in attendance. Gianpaolo was the 147th pope to — be buried in the catacombs beneath St Peter's.[60] His sarcophagus has a beautiful simplicity, consisting of gleaming slabs of

---

[57] J. Oram, *The People's Pope: The Story Of Karol Wojtyla Of Poland*, 1979, Bay Books, p. 154.

[58] Ibid., p. 155.

[59] Seabeck, p. 72.

[60] *Catholic Herald*, no. 4825, 6 October 1978, p. 2.

pale grey, striated marble, situated so appropriately opposite that of Marcellus II, plainly inscribed *Ioannes Paulus PP.I* above the Monogram of Christ. On the two front ends of the sarcophagus are yellowed marble angels in bas-relief, arms crossed on their breasts. The angels once belonged to a fifteenth century tabernacle in the Vatican Basilica that contained the relics of the Holy Lance.

With Gianpaolo buried, the demands for an autopsy were largely buried too: the storm quickly blew itself out, for it had been without the essential driving force of evidence. On 14 October the cardinals once again duly entered conclave, but this time they found it harder to make a choice. It was not until the eighth ballot, held on Monday 16 October, that they managed to elect a pope, but when it came their decision was both surprising and momentous. The new pope was Cardinal Karol Wojtyla, the fifty-eight-year-old Archbishop of Krakow, Poland, and he took the name John Paul II because, he said, of his 'reverence, love and devotion to John Paul and also to Paul VI, who has been my inspiration, my strength'.[61] He was the first Slav pope and the first non-Italian elected since the Dutchman Adrian VI in 1522, 456 years before.

Curiously, in 1848 the great Polish Romantic poet and playwright Juliusz Slowacki (1809–49) had written a prophetic poem foretelling the coming of a strong Slav pope during times of trouble. Wojtyla would have known of this poem since his childhood.[62] He was also the youngest pope elected since Pius IX in 1846, the health of the new pope being an obvious consideration in the minds of the cardinals.[63] Following his predecessor's inspiration, John Paul II was simply inaugurated into his ministry as 'universal pastor of the church' on 22 October in St Peter's Square.

Having completed the story of Albino Luciani's life, some assessment must now be made concerning his character, the nature of his thought and actions, and the impact that he has had on both individuals and on the Church as a whole.

So, first of all, what of Gianpaolo's teaching? In the strict

---

[61] *Greeley*, p. 220.

[62] For the poem and commentary, see *Tablet*, CCXXXIII, 20 January 1979, pp. 63–4.

[63] 'Pio Nono', elected aged 54, reigned for 31 years 7 months 23 days. St Peter is traditionally reckoned to have reigned as head of the church for 34–37 years. John Paul II became the third longest reigning pope in history, serving for 26 years 5 months 17 days. Gianpaolo, by contrast, had the eleventh shortest reign.

sense it was, of course, totally orthodox. It is clear that the pope did not enter the Vatican, planning a 'revolution from without'. However, a detached look at the evidence of his statements and actions from his years in Vittorio Veneto up to his death shows that, when he had crystallized his ideas and had the power to implement them, he clearly came to believe in the need for some form of 'revolution from within'. In this he showed distinct signs of going beyond the work of Pope John nearly twenty years before; the Church needed to *continue* to renew itself. His was to be not a revolution in the sense of creating more new layers, but in the sense of stripping away the unnecessary, and returning the Church to the simplicity and immediacy of its early centuries. For this he has been called a 'reactionary nostalgic', albeit one with 'some remarkably progressive ideas'.[64]

'Revolution' is an emotive word, conjuring up images of convulsive disruption. However, the word itself is neutral, merely meaning profound change, whether for good or ill. Whether a person considers an idea or action to be revolutionary is subjective, and depends on several factors: how previous historical developments and the existing situation are viewed, and what opinion is held of the nature of the proposed changes and their likely effects.

Further, something does not have to be complex to be revolutionary; often it can be fundamentally simple. Neither John XXIII nor John Paul I was a revolutionary in the classic sense, but they were unconventional in their means and to some extent in their ends. They were catalysts, and the results were noteworthy and far-reaching; people listened, saw, were affected and acted accordingly.

Gianpaolo worked within 'the system', but he suffered under no illusion that the Church, that is the contemporary human members of the Body of Christ, was perfect. It was not an ossified museum specimen, as the followers of Archbishop Lefèbvre would have had it, but a living, breathing, evolving entity. Yes, some members were bad, but that did not invalidate its existence or the ideal. In fact, it specifically underlined the need for the Church: are not all mortals sinful and in need of spiritual succour? Gianpaolo wanted to make the existing edifice more efficient, not to pull it down or enlarge it. It was in this light that he had seen the Second Vatican Council.

Certainly Gianpaolo had the strength of mind to carry out

---

[64] Yallop, p. 54.

sustained reform, albeit at great personal cost, as the independent testimony of a number of witnesses who knew him well shows. Even early on in his career Bishop Giuseppe Carraro, his predecessor in Vittorio Veneto, had said to members of his diocesan curia 'When necessary, Don Luciani knows how to be strong and resolute ... You'll see'.[65] Father Roberto Busa, SJ, who knew Luciani from his seminary days in 1928, observed: 'His mind was as strong, as hard and sharp as a diamond. That was where his real power was. He understood and had the ability to get to the centre of a problem. He could not be overwhelmed. When everyone was applauding the smiling pope, I was waiting for him *'tirare fuori le unghie'*, to reveal his claws. He had tremendous power'.[66]

Cardinal Benelli made a similar assessment of Gianpaolo's determination: 'With Pope Luciani, you laid out the facts, made your own recommendation, then gave him time and space to consider. Having absorbed all the available information, he would decide and when Pope Luciani decided, nothing, and understand me on this, nothing would move him or shift him. Gentle, yes. Humble, yes. But when committed to a course of action, like a rock'.[67]

Archbishop Caprio found Gianpaolo self-assured, natural, clear and precise. He later wrote:

> His understanding of men and his ability to face situations were far more superior than his humility would admit ... We must not be deceived by his smile. He listened, he asked for information, he studied. But once he made a decision, he did not go back on it, unless new facts came to light ... the Pope had no intentions of deviating from what had been his rule of life and the direction of his pastoral action; fatherly, yes, but absolutely firm in the guidance of the souls entrusted by God to his care.[68]

Mgr Ausilio Da Rif, who had known Luciani since 1936, concurred:

> From Cardinal Villot down they all admired Papa Luciani's way of working. His ability to get to the root of problems, to make decisions quickly and firmly. They were very struck with his ability to carry out his tasks. It was clear that he was a man who took deci-

---

[65] Saez, 2nd edn, 1991, p. 105.
[66] Yallop, p. 163.
[67] Ibid., p. 174.
[68] Seabeck, pp. 65–6.

sions and stuck to them. He did not give way to pressure. In my own personal experience this ability to stick to his own line was a very remarkable feature of Albino Luciani.[69]

Bishop Gioacchino Muccin, another intimate, stated 'In spite of his fragile physical constitution, he always showed great endurance in his work and an incredible strength of will which is rarely met with in healthy, robust persons'.[70]

During his papacy, Archbishop Agostino Casaroli, Secretary of the Council for the Public Affairs of the Church, put before Luciani seven important questions regarding the Church's relations with the communist countries of Eastern Europe. Casaroli, a long-term exponent of the Vatican policy of 'Ostpolitik', was much impressed when the pope gave him five prompt, decisive answers, merely asking for a little time to consider the other two.[71] French author Georges Huber put it bluntly.

> One can see that Albino Luciani was not an inert and powerless spectator in his palace while 'the assassins of the faith' came and threatened the doctrinal and moral integrity of the priests and faithful entrusted to his care. He did not belong to the category of pastors who became 'dumb dogs' for fear of losing popularity. Nor did he belong to those who defend truth but without charity.[72]

Those who subsequently implied that Gianpaolo lacked the necessary *mental* strength and resolution to carry through his papal responsibilities were either simply deluded or motivated by different agenda, thrown off the scent by his natural humility and courtesy.

On 7 September Gianpaolo had given a private audience to his friend Vittore Branca and his wife Olga. Branca, Professor of Italian Literature and Vice-President of the Cini Foundation in Venice, expressed his concern about the weight of the papacy. In replying Gianpaolo unwittingly confirmed these witnesses testimony, revealing his simple but unshakable core:

> Yes, certainly I am too small for great things. I can only repeat the truth and the call of the Gospel as I did in my little church at home. Basically men need this, and I am the keeper of souls above all. Between the parish priest at Canale and me there is a difference

---

[69] Yallop, p. 206.
[70] Seabeck, p. 33. Muccin was talking in 1980.
[71] Greeley, p. 164.
[72] Seabeck, p. 35.

only in the number of faithful but the task is the same, to remember Christ and his word.[73]

Gianpaolo had also revealed his ideal working methods in *Illustrissimi*, in his October 1971 letter to St Bernard of Clairvaux. In writing about the prudence that those in authority should exercise, he said it should be dynamic, inspiring action. He further believed that it consisted of three stages: deliberation, decision, execution.

> *Deliberation* means seeking out means to the desired end: it is based on reflection, advice asked, careful examination ... *Decision* means picking out one of the various possible means after having studied them ... *Execution* is the most important of the three stages; here prudence is associated with strength in not allowing discouragement in the face of difficulties and obstacles. This is the moment when one is proved a leader, a guide.[74]

A number of commentators made comparisons between the pontificate of Gianpaolo and that of Marcellus II, and indeed the parallels are close enough to be worth reflecting on. Marcello Cervini (1501–1555) was elected after a short conclave at a difficult time for the Church, being the successful candidate of the reform party. Exceptionally, he kept his baptismal name on election. 'Few elections have aroused such eager hopes as Marcellus's':[75] created a cardinal in 1539 by Pope Paul III, he had been an energetic reformer in his episcopal sees of Reggio Emilia then Gubbio, a co-president at the Council of Trent and a member of Paul's reform commission. On being elected – on 9 April 1555 – Marcellus immediately gave signs of his desire for reform; he reduced the cost of his coronation to a minimum, cut the size and cost of his court, kept his relatives away from Rome and insisted that justice be impartially administered. He also proposed to promulgate a comprehensive reform bull.

However, after only twenty-two days, Marcellus died of a stroke on 1 May, his frail constitution worn out by ceaseless activity and the burden of his responsibilities. His successor, Paul IV, did not continue his reform programme. It was for Marcellus that Giovanni Pierluigi da Palestrina, composer to the Cappella Sistina, wrote his beautiful *Missa Papae Marcelli*,

---

[73] Yallop, p. 196. Branca (1913–2004).
[74] Luciani, *Illustrissimi*, (US edn), p. 38.
[75] Kelly, p. 264.

published in 1567 but composed somewhat earlier. This he did in memory of the late pope's directions to his singers on Good Friday 1555 that the music for Holy Week should be more in keeping with the occasion, and that as far as possible the words should be clearly understood.

Luciani's personal and spiritual outlook was one of patient realism, one of pastoral concern in the fullest, deepest sense. In both his private and public actions his gentle, unassuming commitment to real, practical Christian love was transparent. He was also prepared to share his human faults and weaknesses publicly with others, always a good indicator of genuine humility. In his wide grasp of the realities of ordinary people's lives, in his approachability, and in his great personal generosity and charity, Gianpaolo may fairly be compared to Benedict XV, the great, open-hearted but modest pope of the First World War.

With his personal warmth, simplicity, dislike of bureaucracy and his appeal to 'all men of good will', Gianpaolo was most like the hugely popular John XXIII. He also shared a similar philosophy of history with John regarding his concept of the Church. The Church must have deep, authentic roots but be of genuine contemporary relevance.

> [This] involved the paradox of saying that the Church must go back in order to go forwards, that it is new because it is ancient, youthful because it is old. Tradition is not the dead hand of the past weighing down on the present; it is the guarantee of continuity in a living organism, made young by the abiding and dynamic presence of the Holy Spirit.[76]

Regarding his humility, his tendency to caution and deliberation, his attempts always to accommodate others if possible, and in his ecumenical concern, Gianpaolo most closely paralleled his predecessor, the intellectual, intense Paul VI. With these qualities he brought to the papacy his own gift of catechesis and his infectious smile, along with his concern for the poor, the Third World and the environment. With Gianpaolo, the 'Good News of the Gospel' was good news indeed: to those like Lefèbvre, who wanted another 'Prince of Power' as Pius XII had been, he was a disappointment, to the rest of the world he was a delight.

One person who was inspired by Gianpaolo was Oscar

---

[76] Hebblethwaite, *John XXIII*, p. 181.

Romero, Archbishop of San Salvador. On 3 October 1978 he presided at a packed Funeral Mass for the late pope, and later recorded the following taped diary entry:

> In the homily I emphasized three concepts in honor of the Holy Father. How during his brief pontificate, he was a luminous response from God, showing forth these three concepts of the Church: its hierarchical nature ... but the hierarchical nature is subordinated to service to the Church, in the same way that the Church is subordinated to service to the Kingdom of God and to the world as a whole.
>
> And because of this (the second concept), that hierarchy and the Church must be, above all, Christian. And this is the great lesson left us by Pope John Paul, because his humility, his poverty, his disregard for the vanities of life, the sureness of his teaching, a discipline not based on legalism but on conviction and on love, are all expressions of a pope at the apex of the hierarchy in the service of the Church, but, above all, of a Christian who, like Paul, can say: 'Be imitators of me as I am of Christ' [1 Corinthians 11:1].
>
> And therefore the third concept: devotion to Mary. I pointed out the affection that the pope showed for the Virgin and I ended reading the brief message that the pope addressed to the Third Marian Congress in Ecuador, his only radio message addressed to Latin America.[77]

Mother Teresa of Calcutta, with her vast experience of working with those suffering from intense poverty and disease, also testified movingly to Gianpaolo's special love for the poor:

> He has been the most beautiful gift of God. A ray of the sunshine of God's love that shines upon the darkness of the world. He was like the hope of eternal happiness. A burning flame of God's love. A proof that God loves the world always and, for the Church, that Christ is still with her and that Christ is living always in the Church. For the poor and the marginalised he represented hope. Also our people, in India, considered him like a father. Some Hindu people when they have known the character of John Paul I, have said 'This is a pope who is close to the heart of Mother Theresa because he is full of love for the poor.'
>
> His death is a mystery which we must accept; human explanations are not for us. His passage through life has given a witness to the vitality of the Church.
>
> He was a person always full of joy and love. He has not spoken much, he has smiled and has conquered the world. John Paul I

---

[77] O. Romero, *A Shepherd's Diary*, 1993, CAFOD/CIIR, p. 82.

succeeded in inspiring love. Also just looking at his picture one was led immediately to love him; one was, as it were, pushed to a complete surrender, to give him one's own love, to commit oneself completely to him.[78]

In mentioning Gianpaolo's wide grasp of the realities of ordinary people's lives and his success at communicating his sympathy and understanding of their problems to these very people, his audiences, it must also be noted that this empathetic process did not meet with universal approval. Curial critics sniped, and this attitude was taken up by some writers who had not only been taken totally by surprise by Luciani's election, but who were also uncomprehending as to the nature of the man and his instant success. Now they tried to cover themselves by belittling him after his death, doing the dead Pope a great injustice. Thus Robert Solé, Vatican correspondent for the French leftist intellectual daily *Le Monde*, opined that Gianpaolo's audiences had:

> attracted the immediate sympathy of the public but had disappoint- ~
> ed and sometimes worried church officials. The Pope expressed a
> philosophy of existence that recalled on occasion the *Reader's
> Digest*: common sense, a little simple at that, which broke with the
> grand theological flights of oratory of Paul VI. Visibly, he did not
> have the culture and the intellectual training of his predecessor.[79]

Solé was simply wrong. Luciani's anecdotes had been deft parables for the times, springing from his natural comprehension of the human condition.

Further, without detracting from Paul VI's own many great talents and abilities, his mind was broader-based and his imagination richer than Paul's. It was these very qualities which enabled him to be 'simple', to convey exactly what he wanted to say and be clearly understood. It was time for a break from 'grand theological flights of oratory', just as it had been when John XXIII had followed Pius XII. Archbishop Manuel Menéndez, the head of Caritas in Argentina, underlined this when he reported: 'The other day on a street in Rome a little boy was asked if he loved the Pope and he said yes. He was

---

[78] Testimonianza Di Madre Teresa Sul Papa Giovanni Paolo I, p. 325; translated from the Italian by Dom Leander Hogg, OSB. Mother Teresa (1910–1997) was beatified on 19 October 2003.

[79] *Time*, 112, 9 October 1978, p. 11.

asked why. 'Because I understand everything he says'.[80]

Commonweal, the New York based political, religious and literary review, managed to totally miss the point about Gianpaolo's openness about himself, his honesty, the genuineness of his simplicity, and about the fact that it was these qualities that endeared him to people. Concerning this 'unknown pope', the editors revealed that:

> We followed first with eagerness, then with a growing sense of the ridiculous, his generous efforts to discover who he was. He smiled, his father was a socialist, he rejected the tiara for a simple stole, he spoke informally at his audiences.[81]

Sadly even the very experienced Peter Nichols, Rome correspondent for *The Times* since 1957, failed fully to comprehend Gianpaolo's impact. Writing in this instance in the *Spectator*, he compared the pope to a popular Italian comedian of yesteryear, who had merely to appear before the populace to receive an ovation. He did not explain why the newly elected Gianpaolo had been such an immediately popular figure, or why Paul VI had not been so rapturously applauded. To do Nichols justice, however, his obituary of Gianpaolo for *The Times* was sympathetic and thoughtful.

Linking Gianpaolo's personality and his death, we now come to the distinct possibility, alluded to in the previous chapter, that he foresaw both his own imminent death and the identity of the one who would succeed him as pope. There have been many pious tales told down the centuries concerning papal 'visions' and the like, but Gianpaolo's does seem to have been rather definite and specific. Foreseeing his own death, and that death's actual occurrence, may be put down to either coincidence or some psychosomatic process; accurately indicating his successor and the name he would assume – an unlikely choice from 127 cardinals – is harder to explain.

Diego Lorenzi has gone on record in stating that:

> In a sense, at the end of 1977 and the beginning of 1978, Luciani was fed up with this world. He wanted only one thing – to die and to enjoy the presence and the goodness of God. He told me once – we had come home from a pastoral visit, and we were at the table, and he said – 'Sometimes I ask the Good Lord to come along and take me away' ... And I think that this prayer of his 'God, please

[80] Ibid.
[81] Greeley, p. 163.

take me away' – was said thousands of times during that month of his Papacy. Although, mind you, he told us many times, 'I am enjoying a deep peace of mind. I am light as a feather. I am not overburdened. I am not unhappy'.[82]

That those who are aware of their impending death may experience, on one level at least, a feeling of tranquility, is well known. But in the *30 Days* interview between Tommaso Ricci and John Magee already quoted from several times, the following conversation ensued:

That pontificate was marked by warning signs of its brevity. Can you cite some of them?

MAGEE: I would not know how to define them. I can only relate them. Two nights before he died, in the evening when he was at the table, he spoke about his election. He still had not succeeded in understanding why the cardinals had chosen him. 'There were others better than me, who could have been chosen,' he said. 'And Paul VI had already indicated his successor. He was right in front of me in the Sistine Chapel during the conclave. But he will come, because I am going away.' I tried to unravel the meaning of this. Certainly I thought about who that person could have been, because Paul VI has never named any names in that regard. But I did not ask anyone who was sitting in the conclave in front of Cardinal Luciani.

So you never knew?

MAGEE: Only four years later, when I was named Master of Ceremonies for John Paul II. In my first meeting with the masters of ceremonies, some of whom were present in that August conclave, I learned that it was Cardinal Karol Wojtyla who had sat in front of Cardinal Luciani'.[83]

Diego Lorenzi has come close to implying that Gianpaolo was too good for the world in stating that: 'The good Lord had given him to us; and he has taken him away from us. We did not deserve him'.[84] Within a few years of the pope's death petitions containing many thousands of signatures had been collected in Italy urging that the process for his canonization should be initiated. If the Roman Catholic Church moves in the direction that Gianpaolo wished it to go – as, in the present author's opinion, it *must* do to survive – then his canonization, as a man of personal holiness, as a teacher, and as a champion of peace

---

82 Cornwell, *A Thief in the Night*, p. 78.
83 *30 Days*, no. 5, September 1988, p. 13; Cornwell, *A Thief in the Night*, p. 201.
84 Cornwell, *A Thief in the Night*, p. 211; Greeley, p. 177, reached an almost identical conclusion.

and of the poor is not at all unlikely sometime in the early twenty-first century. The Church must not let him become just a smiling 'plaster saint' however: he was a man firmly grounded in hard realities, and his precious priestly ministry cost him and his health dear over the years. Victory was not achieved without struggle. Pictures of Gianpaolo still sell well: it is also important that people continue to keep his example and teaching in their minds.

One unfortunate aspect of Gianpaolo's continued popularity has been the production of a stream of populist books concerning him, chief amongst these being David Yallop's *In God's Name*, published in June 1984, which claimed that the pope was murdered because he was a threat to various people involved in financial corruption. Yallop's standards of accuracy are rather poor, complex issues being over-simplified, and the source and context of quotations are often lacking, even on non-controversial points. His conclusions have been ably disproved by Cornwell, Hebblethwaite, D'Orazi and Willi, and it is not necessary to discuss them at length here. Cornwell in particular has set the record straight on most of Yallop's main points, namely as to who found the body and when, at what time the papal embalmers were called, and the whereabouts of Gianpaolo's will and personal effects.[85]

Yallop relied on the fact that it is hard to prove a negative, that the pope was *not* murdered. His work is compellingly written, but it is mostly insinuation, without conclusive evidence to support such a definitely stated allegation as murder. Certainly much of the information that he gives about the Mafia, the illegal masonic lodge P2 and various financial institutions is true, but it all has nothing to do with the manner of the pope's death. It is theoretically possible to murder anyone on earth, but the onus is on the accuser to prove that a murder has occurred and the identity of the murderer. The sober fact is that Yallop failed, despite all his 'inside contacts', to conclusively prove either the 'who', 'how', or even the 'why', let alone all three. He pointed at no less than six people who *may* have killed Gianpaolo and said how the deed *may* have been committed, but there his argument petered out.

There is no need to postulate a murder theory; the sheer workload alone was enough to kill a man of Gianpaolo's health, temperament and age, at a time of life when most people have

---

[85] Cornwell, *A Thief in the Night*, pp. 229–36. Gianpaolo's personal effects are held by his sister Antonia.

retired. Death from stress-enhanced natural causes is not romantic, exciting or mysterious, but in this case it was the simple truth. Had Luciani not been elected pope, and died in Venice, nobody would have batted an eyelid. Such a death is not surprising anyway: many other prelates have died before their years have reached 'three score and ten'. Indeed, early death, especially from a heart attack, seems to be almost an occupational hazard of high ecclesiastical office. In January 1922 Pope Benedict XV died unexpectedly aged sixty-seven of influenza that developed into pneumonia. In September 1969 Cardinal Urbani, Luciani's predecessor in Venice, died following a heart attack, aged sixty-nine. As we have seen, Metropolitan Nikodim died of a heart attack in Gianpaolo's presence in September 1978 aged only forty-eight, and in October 1982 Cardinal Benelli died in Florence of a heart attack aged only sixty-one. In June 1983 Cardinal James Knox died aged sixty-nine after suffering a heart attack in May. These are just a handful of examples; nobody has ever seriously suggested that any of them were murdered!

Luciani, whilst far from being frail, had never enjoyed really robust health. As he himself said to a group of sick and handi-capped people during his last General Audience on 27 September: 'Remember your Pope has been in hospital eight times and had four operations'.[86] Briefly, the facts of Luciani's medical history are as follows: a military doctor cured him of a serious pulmonary when he was six, he had his tonsils removed aged eleven, and his adenoids at fifteen. Twice in 1947 he was admitted to a sanatorium with suspected tuberculosis; each time tests proved negative and the pulmonary illnesses were diagnosed as bronchitis. In April 1964 he was operated on for gallstones and a blocked colon by Professor Amadeo Alexandre at the Pordenone hospital, and again in August for haemor-rhoids. In December 1975 Luciani was treated for an embolus (blood clot) in the retinal artery of the left eye – caused by a depressurization in the aircraft when returning from Brazil the previous month – by Professor Giovanni Rama of Mestre; recovery was almost immediate and was complete. His low blood pressure, normally around 120/80, also aggravated an occasional swelling in his ankles. In July-August 1978 he spent a fortnight in the Stella Maris Institute on the Lido to counter-act a possible recurrence of gallstones.[87] He once also had to

---

[86] Yallop, p. 226.
[87] Yallop, pp. 242–3; Dr Lina Petri in Cornwell, *A Thief in the Night*, p. 242.

have surgery 'to set a broken nose after a fall'.[88]

As mentioned in the previous chapter, Cornwell has made a convincing case that Gianpaolo 'almost certainly died of a pulmonary embolus due to a condition of abnormal coagulability of the blood',[89] triggered by his running down the corridor to speak to Cardinal Colombo on the telephone on the last evening of his life. His theory has the support of Dr Joaquín Navarro-Valls, Director of the Vatican Press Office from 1984–2006 and a medical doctor in his own right, Dr Lina Petri, the pope's niece and also a medical doctor, and Dr C. Francis Roe, a highly experienced cardio-vascular specialist formerly of Harvard and Yale.[90] Dr Renato Buzzonetti's hurried, catch-all verdict of myocardial infarction as the cause of Gianpaolo's death was reached without his ever having seen his 'patient' in life, without ever having seen Gianpaolo's medical file, without seeking a second opinion, without questioning the secretaries about the pope's recent symptoms, and without an autopsy. This perhaps betokens a certain lack of 'method', but is no indication of malicious intent. Whatever the exact cause of Gianpaolo's death, it was definitely natural.

Finally, we come to the subject of Gianpaolo's legacy 'to the Church and to the World', to the influence that he has had on the subsequent development of the papacy and the Church as a whole, and to the question of what would probably have occurred had his pontificate lasted longer. Gianpaolo did not leave a will in the sense of a detailed spiritual testament intended for publication such as the one left by Paul VI. He had no time to prepare one as pope; his will, dating from his time in Venice, was a brief, personal document in which he left everything to a seminary in the Veneto.[91] Rather, his legacy is contained in his words and actions in life, and in the reactions they have provoked in others since his death.

Considering the brevity of his reign, Gianpaolo's pontificate was of significant influence in shaping that of his successor, John Paul II. It will be remembered that the then Cardinal Wojtyla voted for Luciani right from the first ballot in the August conclave. Upon his own election in October he unhesitatingly followed Gianpaolo in both his papal name and in the manner of his simple inauguration as supreme pastor. Further,

---

[88] Oram, p. 14.
[89] Cornwell, *A Thief in the Night*, p. 265.
[90] Ibid., principally pp. 37, 242–3, 251–3.
[91] Ibid., p. 235; Yallop, pp. 247–8.

as stated in the previous chapter, in his first four General Audiences he completed, in his own way, Gianpaolo's talks on the 'Seven Lamps of Sanctification'. Gianpaolo had covered the three theological virtues of Faith, Hope and Charity; Papa Wojtyla completed the programe by speaking of the four cardinal virtues of Prudence, Justice, Fortitude and Temperance.

Like Gianpaolo, John Paul II used the first person singular, and never used the *sedia gestatoria*. More robust than his predecessor, he took Gianpaolo's love of personally getting amongst the people to its fullest extent, and made regular trips all over the world. Gianpaolo was still partly hemmed in by officious curial monsignori. Early on his successor determined that he would impose his own independence of action:

'They told my predecessor [John Paul I] what he should do and when', the pope said to one of his Polish friends. 'This may have led to his early death. They will not tell me what to do or when. I will decide. They will not kill me.'[92]

In promulgating *Sapientia Christiana* and *Catechesi Tradendae*, the Polish pope was setting forth the work of Paul VI and Gianpaolo as much as his own, a debt he freely acknowledged. His genuine devotion to his predecessors was shown after the attempt on his life by Mehemet Ali Agca on 13 May 1981. After convalescence at the Policlinico Agostino Gemelli, he returned to the Vatican on 14 August: his first act was to pray at the tombs of John XXIII, Paul VI and Gianpaolo in the crypt of St Peter's, to give thanks that his life had been spared.

Furthermore, John Paul II spoke warmly of Gianpaolo on a number of occasions in tones that made his personal admiration plain. Even before his own election as pope, Wojtyla spoke emotionally of Gianpaolo at a Mass in St Mary's Basilica in Krakow on 1 October:

We expected so much, hoped so much from him. He seemed to answer those expectations with his entire human, sacerdotal, episcopal, papal personality. So quickly did he become whom he was to have become by virtue of his calling to the papacy ... Everybody says he inaugurated a new pastoral style at the Holy See. A style full of great simplicity, modesty, respect for man. He had inherited that style from his predecessors, John and Paul, but from the very first minute he gave it an aspect that was his own ... Did the Pontificate of John Paul I fulfill itself? Let us ask rather: is ever a man's life, whoever he may have been on this earth,

92 Oram, p. 208.

fulfilled, in the dimensions of time, between the hour of his birth and the hour of his death? Faith tells us ... that a man's life is fulfilled only in God. That is why the Easter candle tells us of passing from unfulfilment to fulfilment ... And when our thoughts and reflections now follow the deceased Pope, with all our human powerlessness and hopelessness, let us have hope. If Christ wanted him to be the Pastor of His Church here on earth for such a short time only, we can only accept that inscrutable will of Providence. Answers to our questions will, perhaps, be given by time, by history. Or rather no answer could be the full one. We too must wait for that meeting towards which we are all going, for which we are all living.[93]

In his broadcast address from the Sistine Chapel on the morning of 17 October 1978, the day after his election, Wojtyla went out of his way to approvingly remind the cardinals and the world that only recently both he and they had:

... heard Pope John Paul speaking at the very beginning of his ministry, from which one might have hoped much. Both on account of the memory that is yet fresh in the mind of each one of us and on account of the wise reminders and exhortations contained in the allocution, we consider that we cannot overlook it. That same address, as in the circumstances in which it was given, is truly apposite and clearly maintains its validity here and now at the start of this new pontifical ministry to which we are bound.[94]

Further on in his address, after elaborating on the topics of the Second Vatican Council, collegiality and the Synod of Bishops, the pope spoke of his predecessor's personality in glowing terms:

What warmth of charity, nay, what 'an abundant outpouring of love' – which came forth from him in the few days of his ministry and which in his last Sunday address before the Angelus he desired should come upon the world. This is also confirmed by his wise instructions to the faithful who were present at his public audiences on faith, hope and love.[95]

Again in his homily during his inaugural Mass in St Peter's Square on 22 October he spoke of Gianpaolo at several points and firmly endorsed his decisions, for instance in rejecting the

[93] Oram, p. 151.
[94] Greeley, p. 287.
[95] Ibid., p. 290.

papal tiara. In his first encyclical, *Redemptor Hominis*, given at St Peter's on 4 March 1979, the pope paid further tribute to Gianpaolo and his other two immediate predecessors, and reaffirmed their influence on his own pontificate:

> I chose the same names that were chosen by my beloved Predecessor John Paul I. Indeed, as soon as he announced to the Sacred College ... that he wished to be called John Paul ... I saw in it a clear presage of grace for the new pontificate. Since that pontificate lasted barely 33 days, it falls to me not only to continue it but in a certain sense to take it up again at the same starting point. This is confirmed by my choice of these two names. By following the example of my venerable Predecessor in choosing them, I wish like him to express my love for the unique inheritance left to the Church by Popes John XXIII and Paul VI and my personal readiness to develop that inheritance with God's help.[96]

On 22 August 1979, addressing a crowd of some 20,000 people in St Peter's Square, the pope spoke of the forthcoming promulgation of *Catechesi Tradendae*, saying that it could be said to contain Gianpaolo's testament. He continued that although 'death did not allow this great Pope to publish his exhortation on this key theme for the life of the Church', he himself 'left a special mark on Rome and on the universal Church', and 'demonstrated and affirmed by his own example what catechetics is and what it means in the life of the Church of our times'.[97]

On the following Sunday, 26 August, the first anniversary of Gianpaolo's election, the pope made a special visit to Canale d'Agordo and to Belluno in honour of his predecessor. In Canale d'Agordo he celebrated Mass with Cardinal Marco Cé -Luciani's successor as Patriarch of Venice – Bishop Maffeo Ducoli of Belluno and Feltre, and Don Rinaldo Andrich, the local parish priest. During his homily he talked especially of Gianpaolo's love for and dedication to the Church:

> As parish priest, as bishop, as patriarch and as pope he did nothing but dedicate himself totally to the service of the Church, right up to the moment when he drew his last breath: that is how death caught him, on the ramparts, as it were, in true and vigilant service. Thus he lived and thus he died, dedicating himself utterly to the Church with disarming simplicity, but also with unshakeable determination,

---

[96] *Redemptor Hominis*, CTS Do 506, p. 6.
[97] *Tablet*, CCXXXIII, 8 September 1979, p. 882, 'A Living Example'.

which knew not fear, because it was based on the clarity of his faith
and on the promise made by Christ to Peter and his successors.[98]

Such was John Paul II's avowed assessment of Gianpaolo. In a
sense he owed his very election to the success of his predecessor's pontificate, the cardinals seeking, as they saw it, another
pope in a similar mould to Gianpaolo, who had been such a
popular choice. However, despite the influences and statements mentioned, in practice John Paul II often proved to be in
many ways a very different pope. Here we may just consider a
few speculative thoughts on what a longer Gianpaolo papacy
may have brought forth.

When electing the sixty-five year-old Luciani in August 1978,
the cardinals must reasonably have hoped to have been electing a pope for at least ten to fifteen years, and one who had the
vigour to tackle the many difficult issues which faced the
Church. Gianpaolo, whether or not he thought that the cardinals had been mistaken in electing him, would not have ducked
the challenge, whatever the personal cost. Like Paul VI he
might have considered resignation at the age of seventy-five,
which he would have reached in October 1987, but, again like
Paul, a sense of unique duty would have kept him at his post.[99]

It is improbable that he would have called another
Ecumenical Council, given that he felt that the Second Vatican
Council had not yet been fully absorbed into the Church.
Nevertheless, he would have encouraged the Church to explore
and develop more deeply the teachings of that Council, teachings that would have been reinforced by great social encyclicals
of his own. These would have been in the tradition of John
XXIII and Paul VI, but in his own less formal, more anecdotal
style.

With regard to Paul VI's contentious legacy *Humanae Vitae*,
whilst being unable to ignore his predecessor's encyclical, it is
likely that Gianpaolo would have left no stone unturned in his

---

[98] Ibid. See also AAS, LXXI, 1979, pp. 1021–38. In June 1985 the pope visited
Venice and the surrounding area for three days, recalling Pius X, John XXIII
and Gianpaolo. *Tablet*, CCXXXIX, 29 June 1985, p. 677.

[99] The precedent setting Pope St Celestine V remains unique in papal history
in having voluntarily resigned the papacy, which he did on 13 December
1294. Dante placed Celestine at the entrance of Hell for his abdication and
alluded to the Pope as 'him, who to base fear yielding, abjured his high
estate' (Inferno, canto III, lines 56–7). In 1976 Pope Paul considered
resigning the papacy to become a Benedictine monk at the Abbey of Monte
Cassino.

efforts to ameliorate the worst consequences of that document and pushed for a more generous, pastoral interpretation of it when priests were confronted with people's very real problems. On the issue of 'test-tube babies' Gianpaolo would have remained positive in his loving concern for the children and parents involved, whilst being increasingly concerned to protect against the abuses of peripheral 'medical research', already touched on in his original interview.

He most certainly, after due probing and careful considera-tion, would have taken a firm line in sorting out the tangled web of Vatican finances. After Paul VI's death Cardinal Villot, as Camerlengo, had ordered some pre-conclave reports on diverse subjects to be prepared for the cardinals. One was devoted to the financial situation of the Holy See, prepared by Cardinal Egidio Vagnozzi, Prefect for the Economic Affairs of the Apostolic Holy See. It did not include the IOR as it was not part of the Holy See's administration.[100]

Also, within a few days of his election Gianpaolo met Cardinals Felici and Benelli 'who had compiled a thick dossier on [the] IOR's involvement in the Sindona affair, and urged the Pope to oust Marcinkus. Before he could act on their suggestion – and it is believed that he would have – he died'.[101] A state-ment by Father Francesco Farusi, Vatican Radio news editor at the time, confirmed that 'Marcinkus was in difficulty after the new Pope's [Gianpaolo's] election'.[102] Under Gianpaolo's successor, Marcinkus remained for another eleven years, as we have seen, although reforms in the accounting procedures were gradually introduced.

Gianpaolo would also naturally have been concerned to main-tain a Christian primacy of focus amongst members of religious orders 'in the field'. On 30 September he was due to have deliv-ered a speech to the Congregation of Procurators of the Jesuits, then meeting in Rome. These were eighty Jesuits elected from all the Society's Provinces, delegated to decide on the appropri-ateness of calling a General Congregation. The contents of the speech were revealed on the following 8 December and it must be said that, as written, it displayed a certain harshness.

Gianpaolo recalled that Paul VI 'had so loved, had prayed, done and suffered so much for the Society of Jesus', adding his own love too. He then made recommendations that were

---

[100] B. Lai, *Les Secrets Du Vatican*, 1983, Hachette, pp. 135–9.
[101] Gurwin, p. 175.
[102] *30 Days*, no. 9, 1993, p. 49.

'barely disguised reprimands', admonishing them not to get involved with economic and political problems, to maintain discipline and to cultivate a spiritual life:

> You may well know and justly concern yourselves with the great economic and social problems which trouble humanity today and are so closely connected with the Christian life. But in finding a solution to these problems may you always distinguish the tasks of religious priests from those of the laymen. Priests must animate and inspire the laity to fulfil their duties, but they must not take their place, neglecting their own specific task of evangelisation.[103]

Warningly, Gianpaolo continued: 'Do not allow Jesuit teaching and publications to become a source of confusion and disorientation ... This naturally presupposes that a sound and solid doctrine be taught in the institutions and universities training young Jesuits'.[104] He concluded by insisting that they avoid secularizing tendencies and stay true to their founder's intentions.

On the subject of clerical celibacy, Gianpaolo would most certainly have strictly pursued traditional doctrine, tempered with sympathy for the individuals involved. Where leeway existed, he made use of it. For instance, he was prepared to sanction the laicization of priests according to Paul VI's relatively compassionate Norms of 13 January 1971. Paul himself had granted, with a 'heavy heart', 31,324 dispensations out of 32,357 applications:[105] during his short pontificate Gianpaolo signed some 200 petitions from priests to return to the lay state and marry within the Church.[106]

Finally, there are two last 'footnotes' to complete this narrative on the life of Albino Luciani, all attesting – in different ways – to his continuing popularity.

Firstly, there are the marks of popular affection shown for Gianpaolo. One representative story concerning reactions to Gianpaolo's death is worth relating as it is told with a humour which I believe the pope would have appreciated. Sr Mary Joseph McManamon, OSB, at that time a nun of St Scholastica's Priory, Petersham, MA, remembers:

---

[103] Yallop, p. 211.
[104] A. Woodrow, *The Jesuits: A Story Of Power*, 1995, Geoffrey Chapman, p. 236.
[105] J. Kwitny, *Man Of The Century: The Life And Times Of Pope John Paul II*, 1997, Little, Brown, p. 318.
[106] Murphy, p. 195.

On the morning of 29 Sept 1978, we Sisters awoke early and walked across the yard to our chapel for the Office of Readings which began around 5.30 am. It was a chilly, clear New England morning and the sky was bright with stars, but only a handful of the nuns bothered to look up to admire the sky – the early birds who somehow manage to wake up, full of life at 5.00! The rest of us, the 'night people', had a hard enough time just making it to the chapel at that 'ungodly' hour. Taking time to star gaze in the early morning was unthinkable. We rushed past the Sisters who were gazing up into the heavens, and crowded into our warm chapel before the morning chill had time to settle into our bones.

The reading at the Liturgy that morning, the Feast of the Archangels, was about the Woman who appeared in the sky with a crown of stars around her head. There was a bit of shuffling of cowls and pointed looks among some of the Sisters (the star-gazers) which were completely lost on those of us who hadn't stopped to look at the sky. At the end of the Liturgy, our Prioress announced to us the sad news of the death of the Holy Father, John Paul I. We were shocked at the news and saddened to have lost such a holy Pope whom we had come to love in the short period of his pontificate. As we left the chapel, the Sisters began whispering among themselves and it was then that we learned that the star-gazers weren't just looking up at a pretty, star-studded sky on their way over to the chapel. There had been a shower of shooting stars and the Sisters were awed at the celestial display. Shooting stars appear quite often in New England, but this had been more than the usual one or two. How the rest of us wished we hadn't been so intent on rushing to chapel, but had taken the time to look at what the others had stopped to admire. Now we realized why there had been a stir during the reading of the biblical passage at Office. We were quite certain the display of shooting stars had been a 'sign' of the arrival in heaven of our dear Pope John Paul I.[107]

On Gianpaolo's death poet Paolo Pesci of the Centro Trilussa in Rome, penned a brief but affectionate poem in the Romanesco dialect capturing the popular esteem in which the late pope was already held. Entitled *'Addio, Giovanni Paolo I'*, it runs:

> Er Papa der soriso se n'è annato.
> Trentatré giorni, er numero de Cristo,
> Ma er monno già ce s'era affezionato,
> e' stato n'imprevisto ...
> Pe' li romani, poi, Papa Luciani
> L'aveva abbracicato de sorpresa
> co' li più belli verzi de Trilussa,

[107] Personal Communication, 24 September 2007.

'na simpatia indiscussa
e noi t'aringraziamo, Omo de Chiesa.
Er popolo de Fede s'inginocchia
ar Prete contadino de Parrocchia.
Un moccoletto, un fiore,
'na lagrima precipita dar còre
de tutti li romani.
Addio, Papa Luciani! . . .[108]

In 1984 *Humilitas-Papa Luciani*, a review journal dedicated solely to all matters relating to the late pope, was launched by the Centro Papa Luciani in S. Giustina (Belluno). On 17 December 2000 the 'Amici Di Papa Luciani' was founded by Massimiliano Piovesan in Cadoneghe (Padua), the first time that a pope has had a fan club! The organization has a growing, worldwide membership. Between May and October 2006 it is recorded that 35,000 faithful visited San Giovanni Battista in Canale D'Agordo to see the place where Gianpaolo was baptized. On 27 April 2007 a well-received new play, Roger Crane's *The Last Confession*, premiered at the Chichester Festival before transferring to London, in which a dying Cardinal Benelli reflects on the lost promise of Luciani's papacy.[109]

Secondly, when considering Gianpaolo's posthumous popularity, is the fact of the serious moves to have him proclaimed as a Saint of the Roman Catholic Church. In the Diocesan Archives of Belluno lies a petition signed by over 300,000 people calling for the initial stage, Beatification, to take place. The documents for the Diocesan Process for his Cause were duly sent to Rome on 11 January 2002. On 26 August 2002, after Mass at San Pietro in Canale D'Agordo, Bishop Vincenzo Savio, SDB of Belluno-Feltre announced the opening of the preliminary investigation to establish evidence for the 'heroic virtue' of Albino Luciani leading, it was hoped, to the eventual Beatification of the humble Servant of God. The Cause was formally opened on 28 September 2003, the twenty-fifth anniversary of Luciani's death, the Postulator being the Salesian Don Pasquale Liberatore, SDB[110] of Rome, the Vice-

[108] Nicolini, 1979, pp. 182–3. Luciani had addressed a letter to Trilussa in *Illustrissimi*.
[109] R. Crane, *The Last Confession*, 2007, Oberon Books.
[110] Sadly Don Pasquale died on 31 October 2003, and Bishop Vincenzo on 31 March 2004 (aged only 59). On 9 December 2003 Don Enrico Dal Covolo, SDB was nominated as the new Postulator. A native of Feltre, his paternal uncle, Mgr Antonio Dal Covolo, had been Dean of the seminary of Belluno when Luciani was Vicar-General of the Diocese.

Postulator being Mgr Giorgio Lise, the rector of the Centro Papa Luciani. A solemn ceremony was held in the Cathedral of Vittorio Veneto on 23 November 2003.

On 11 November 2006 the diocesan phase was formally completed, with initial investigation of the reported 'miraculous' cure of an Italian man from Puglia suffering from a tumour, now in remission for fourteen years, being carried out. Luciani's formal biography and 190 witness testimonials were then forwarded to the Congregation for Saints Causes in Rome, who opened their phase of investigations on 3 January 2007. On 14 May 2007 Mgr Mario Paciello, Bishop of Altamura (Bari), signed the Decree constituting the Tribunal for the Diocesan Inquiry into the presumed healing miracle, the first session sitting on 26 May.

On 9 June 1990 bishops from Region-East 2 (Brazil), on their *ad limina* visit, presented John Paul II with the 'Petition for the Beatification of Pope Luciani from the Brazilian Episcopal Conference'. It was signed on 15 April 1990 by 226 bishops, including four Cardinals: Paulo Evaristo Arns, Lucas Moreira Neves, Aloisio Lorscheider and Eugênio de Araújo Sales. The bishops wrote of the 'luminous wake of faith and holiness' that the late pope had left behind him through his smiling persona, his humility and his striving after the theological virtues of Faith, Hope and Charity. He was the embodiment of a Good Shepherd, whose powerful intercession was already leading many of the faithful to receive special graces, and whose greatness was inversely proportional to the length of his papacy.

John Paul II died aged eighty-four at 9.37 p.m. on 2 April 2005 from complications arising from advanced Parkinson's disease. He died during the Octave of Easter, when by old Polish tradition he would go straight to Heaven, riding on the back of Christ Himself. Naturally there was much sympathy for his long suffering, but much of the creative energy, hope and goodwill that had marked his accession to the papacy had inevitably long since dissipated in largely unfulfilled expectations.

On 19 April the 115 cardinals in conclave elected his seventy-eight year-old right-hand man and Dean of the Sacred College Joseph Ratzinger on the fourth ballot. Ratzinger took the name Benedict XVI; he was the oldest cardinal to become pope since Clement XII was elected in 1730, also aged seventy-eight, and the first German since Victor II in 1055–57. His outlook has been in many ways the antithesis of Luciani's, but there are signs of the stern 'policeman' already becoming the smiling pastor.

At the final pre-conclave Mass on 18 April he warned grimly against building 'a dictatorship of relativism'. On the other hand, at a General Audience given on 27 April Benedict announced that he had chosen his name 'to create a spiritual bond' with the great Pope Benedict XV, who worked so tirelessly for peace and reconciliation between peoples during the First World War. The further spiritually symbolic simplification and broadening of the ceremony of his Inauguration on 24 April was another hopeful sign. Benedict put forward no 'programme of governance'. Instead, he spoke movingly of his own duty to 'listen, together with the whole Church, to the word and the will of the Lord', and of the 'desert of poverty, the desert of hunger and thirst, the desert of abandonment, of loneliness, of destroyed love' in the world.

On 24 September Benedict had a four-hour meeting at Castel Gandolfo with Hans Küng, at the latter's request. John Paul II had refused such a meeting for nearly twenty-seven years. Thus, although the two men avoided doctrinal issues, their conversation was reported by both as being amicable, a great step forward. The work initiated by John XXIII and Gianpaolo has taken firm root: the language of papal dominance and triumphalism within the Church has been broken forever, to be eventually followed by its undue practice.

Further, regarding Luciani's Beatification, it is noteworthy that the then Cardinal Ratzinger said in an interview published in September 2003

> Personally I'm altogether convinced he was a saint. Because of his great goodness, simplicity, humility. And for his great courage. Because he also had the courage to say things with great clarity, even going against current opinions. And also for his great culture of faith ... He was a man of great theological culture and of great pastoral sense and experience. His writings on catechesis are precious.[111]

What is more, on 16 October 2004 Ratzinger travelled to the Centro Papa Luciani to launch his book *Faith, Truth, Tolerance: Christianity and the Religions of the World*. Whilst there he said 'I pray every day for this beatification; Pope Luciani is an example for all. He is a figure I have loved much.' He continued 'I was impressed by Luciani's goodness and great humility. I

---

[111] Ratzinger, *30 Days*, no. 9, September 2003. Benedict is himself a distinguished theologian.

remember when I was a very young archbishop of Munich and Luciani came to see me, with great simplicity, to Bressanone, where I was spending a brief holiday. His goodness of heart made a great impression on me.' Describing him as a 'man of great faith' and 'great loftiness', the soon-to-be pope went on 'His book *Illustrissimi* shows how much he read, how much he reflected. Luciani also had thorough theological learning. Speaking with him, one perceived that he was an essential man – that he focused on the simple, but was in no way simplistic.[112]

Looking ahead, it is entirely possible that the *next* pope may come from Latin America, which now has the largest Catholic population on earth. Gianpaolo himself consistently voted for the Brazilian Aloisio Lorscheider in the August 1978 conclave; this may yet prove to have been of prophetic significance. If a Latin American *is* elected, then Gianpaolo's own Cause of Beatification is likely to be advanced ...

What Luciani's attitude to his own beatification might have been is of course ultimately unknowable, but a good clue is given by the following, written in Venice in 1973, in what can be seen as a form of 'preferential option for the poor and undervalued':

> Lived holiness is very much more widespread than officially proclaimed holiness. The Pope canonizes, its true, only genuine saints ... If we here on earth make a kind of selection, God doesn't do so in Heaven; coming into Paradise, we will probably find mothers, workers, professional people, students set higher than the official saints we venerate on earth.[113]

Regarding essential change in the Church, Gianpaolo was a man always willing to listen and to learn, to let ideas percolate and mature, and then to act decisively. Like John XXIII he also did much to give the papacy a human face, to make it less mysterious and more accessible. It is tempting to view Gianpaolo as an ecclesiastical forerunner of Mikhail Gorbachev, President of the USSR and architect of *glasnost* (public openness, accountability) and *perestroika* (radical societal restructuring). Both men were of honest heart, intending gradual, yet far-reaching, meaningful reform, whilst actually, through inopportune circumstances, paving the way for

---

[112] Cardinal Ratzinger Prays For Beatification of John Paul I (Zenit 20/10/04).
[113] *Opera Omnia*, vol. 6, p. 16.

quicker, but flawed, more superficial change. Such people's thought is often over-simplified, and thus overlooked, ignored, denigrated or misunderstood.

On 22 June 1633 the astronomer Galileo Galilei, after being forced by the Holy Office to abjure his correct proposition that the earth is not fixed, but orbits around the sun, is said to have whispered '*Eppur si muove*' . . . 'But it does move'. The Church did not acknowledge its error and rehabilitate Galileo until the statement of John Paul II on 31 October 1992. The Church too needs to move and it will take a pope of the stature of Albino Luciani to sheperd it.

At any rate, Gianpaolo was a man of huge potential. As Mgr Loris Capovilla, former Private Secretary to John XXIII, said 'There was more in his shop than he put in his window'.[114] As for the brevity of his reign, let the last words be from an apt dictum of St John of the Cross: 'The least act of pure love is of more value to the Church than all other works put together.'[115]

---

[114] Nichols, p. 90.
[115] 'Spiritual Canticles' ('*Cántico Espiritual*'), Commentary on Strophe XXIX, 1584.

Appendix A

Select Chronology

1912	17 Oct.	Born in Forno di Canale (Canale d'Agordo since 1964).
	19 Oct.	Baptism formalized in San Giovanni Battista, Forno di Canale.
1918	26 Sept.	Confirmed.
1919	Oct.	Begins elementary school.
1923	18 Oct.	Enters the minor seminary at Feltre.
1929	11 Feb.	Lateran Pacts, including Concordat, between Holy See and Italian Government.
	Sept.	Enters the major seminary, the Gregorian, at Belluno.
1934	8 July	Ordained sub-deacon.
1935	2 Feb.	Ordained deacon.
	7 July	Ordained priest in San Pietro, Belluno.
	8 July	Celebrates his first Mass.
	9 July	Named curate of Forno di Canale.
	18 Dec.	Named curate of neighbouring Agordo and instructor of religion at the local Technical Institute of Mining.
1937	July	Appointed Vice-Rector of the seminary at Belluno, teaching dogmatic and moral theology, canon law, and sacred art (until 1947).
1941	27 Mar.	Obtains a dispensation, signed by Cardinal Maglione, from attending classes at the Pontifical Gregorian University in Rome. Enrolls as student in November.
1942	16 Oct.	Obtains *lizenziato* with marks of nine out of ten.
1946	23 Nov.	Defends his doctoral thesis on 'The Origin of the Human Soul According To Antonio Rosmini. Exposition and Criticism'.

1947	27 Feb.	Graduates magnum cum laude, becoming Doctor of Sacred Theology – STD (HONS).
	summer	Twice in Sanatorium with suspected TB. Tests negative.
	Nov.	Appointed Pro-Chancellor of the Diocese of Belluno.
	15 Dec.	Created a Monsignor.
1948	2 Feb.	Appointed Pro-Vicar General of the Diocese of Belluno.
	2 Mar.	Death of his mother Bortola Luciani.
1949		As Director of the Catechetical Office he organizes the Diocesan Eucharistic Year and Congress at Belluno.
	Dec.	First publication of *Catechetica In Briciole*.
1950	4 Apr.	First publication of his doctoral thesis.
1952	9 Jan.	Death of his father Giovanni Luciani.
1954	6 Feb.	Appointed Vicar-General of the Diocese of Belluno.
1956	30 June	Becomes Canon of the Cathedral.
1958	15 Dec.	Appointed Bishop of Vittorio Veneto by Pope John XXIII on the recommendation of Bishop Girolamo Bortignon, OFM Cap., Bishop of Padua.
	27 Dec.	Consecrated by Pope John in St Peter's Basilica.
1962	Aug.	Looks into the case of two priests of his diocese who had become involved with a speculator.
1962 – 1965		Participates in the four sessions of the Second Vatican Council. He makes an address on Our Lady at Verona and submits a written intervention on Collegiality. Both are largely unnoticed. Initially has difficulty with the declaration On Religious Liberty, but on reflection comes to support it. For him the Council is a time of spiritual rejuvenation.
1966	16 Aug.– 1 Sept.	Visits Ngozi in Burundi, the diocese with which he had twinned that of Vittorio Veneto. Member of the doctrinal commission of the Italian Bishops Conference (CEI).
1968	Apr.	Submits report to Pope Paul VI on behalf of the Veneto diocese on the subject of birth control.
	25 July	Publication of the encyclical *Humanae Vitae*.
	10 Sept.	Response, which Luciani had helped to draft, of the Italian Bishops Conference to *Humanae Vitae*.

1969	15 Dec.	Appointed Archbishop of Venice by Pope Paul.
1970	14 Jan.	Becomes President of the Episcopal Conference of the Triveneto.
	8 Feb.	Enters the city – having dispensed with the traditional ceremonies – and takes the title of Patriarch of Venice.
		Violent strikes in Mestre and Marghera, concerning which he urges negotiation and conciliation.
	21–28 Sept.	Second meeting of ARCIC is held in Venice, producing working papers on the Eucharist, Ministry and Authority.
1971		270 workers made redundant at SAVA factory; again he calls for a 'negiotiated solution' but satisfies neither side.
	12–14 June	Pastoral visit to Switzerland, returning via Haute-Savoie.
	22 Oct.– 6 Nov.	Nominated by Pope Paul to take part in the Second General Assembly of the Synod of Bishops, which has as its themes 'Justice in the World' and 'The Priestly Ministry'. He suggests that rich churches should donate 1% of their income to Vatican aid organizations.
1972	summer	Involvement in Banca Cattolica del Veneto controversy.
	12–17	Elected Vice-President of the Italian Bishops Conference, holding this position until 2 June 1975.
	June	Pope Paul publicly – before 20,000 people –
	16 Sept.	confers his stole upon Luciani in St Mark's Square, Venice.
		Attends Italian National Eucharistic Conference in Udine.
1973	5 Mar.	Created Cardinal Priest by Pope Paul, his titular church being that of St Mark adjoining the Piazza Venezia, Rome.
1974	Apr.	Enters into controversy with the student group of San Trovaso (FUCI) over their pro-divorce position.
	12 May	National Referendum on Divorce in Italy; 59.1% vote to retain legislation.
	27 Sept.– 26 Oct.	Attends the Third General Assembly of the Synod of Bishops, which has as its theme 'Evangelization of the Nations'.
		Attends a conference on the environment.

1975		Holy Year; Venice's role is to portray the religious aspects of Italian culture.
	18 May	Pastoral visit to Mainz in Germany.
		Holds meeting with Jewish leaders in Venice.
	30 Sept.	Becomes member of Congregation for the Sacraments and Divine Worship.
	6–21 Nov.	Visits Brazil. Receives degree of *honoris causa* from State University of Santa Maria a Rio Grande do Sul.
1976	Jan?	Attends Italian Bishops Conference in Rome.
	Jan.	First publication – in book form – of *Illustrissimi*. He sends a copy to Hans Küng in return for copy of *On Being A Christian*.
	Feb.	Writes article in diocesan magazine urging sale of church jewels to benefit the poor and the sick.
	14 July	Pope Paul writes to Luciani to mark the quatercentenary of Titian's death (27 August) in Venice.
	24 Aug.–2 Sep.	Eighth meeting of ARCIC is held in Venice, producing the 'Agreed Statement On Authority In The Church'.
1977	11 July	Meets Sister Lucia dos Santos, visionary of Fatima, at Coimbra, Portugal.
	11–18 Sept.	Attends 19th Italian National Eucharistic Congress in Pescara; makes an observation on the nature of the papacy.
	29 Sept.–28 Oct.	Attends the Fourth General Assembly of the Synod of Bishops, which has as its theme 'Catechesis In Our Time'.
	Nov?	Attacks the proposed new Concordat between the Holy See and Italian Government primarily over educational issues.

1978	May	Condemns the murder of ex-Italian Premier Aldo Moro.
	25 July	*Il Gazzettino* publishes his article on Opus Dei.
	3 Aug.	Interview reported by ANSA in which he congratulates the parents of Louise Brown (born 25 July), the first 'test-tube baby'; he is the first Italian bishop to speak out.
	6 Aug.	Death of Pope Paul VI at Castel Gandolfo.
	10 Aug.	Leaves Venice at 6.00 a.m. for Rome, and stays at the Augustinian house of Santa Monica, 25 via del Sant' Uffizio.
	25 Aug.	Enters conclave, the first with a non-European majority.
	26 Aug.	Papal election; Luciani is elected pope on the fourth ballot, taking the name John Paul I. He is the 263rd pope, the first with a double name.
	28 Aug.	Reappoints all the heads of the nine Vatican Congregations.
	29 Aug.	Breaks with papal tradition by refusing to be carried in the *sedia gestatoria*; he makes his way to St Peter's on foot.
	3 Sept.	Dispenses with the traditional coronation; instead he is 'inaugurated'.
	5 Sept.	Meets Frère Roger Shutz of Taizé. Russian Orthodox Metropolitan Nikodim of Leningrad dies of heart attack in his presence during an audience given to the Delegations of Non-Catholic Christians.
	23 Sept.	Makes his only journey outside the Vatican during his papacy, visiting the Communist Mayor of Rome Guilio Carlo Argan at the Capitol, and taking possession of St John Lateran.
	28 Sept.	Dies, unattended, about 11.00 p.m.
	4 Oct.	Buried in the crypt of St Peter's opposite Pope Marcellus II.

Appendix B

The Luciani Family

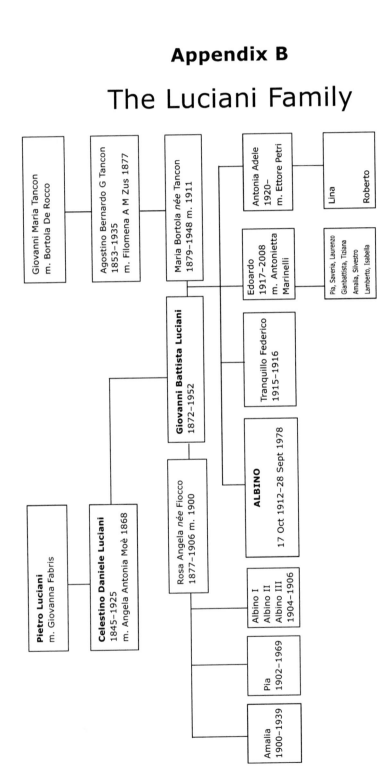

Appendix C

Ballots in Papal Conclave, 26 August 1978

Siri	25	Luciani	55	Luciani	69 or 70	Luciani	90
Luciani	23	Siri	25			Siri	20
Pignedoli	<20	Pignedoli	15			Lorscheider	1
Baggio	<10	Lorscheider	12				
Koenig	<10						
Bertoli	<10						
Pironio	<10						
Lorscheider	2						
Felici	2						

Greeley, pp.151–3

Siri	25	Luciani	56	Luciani	>90	
Luciani	23	Pignedoli	15	Pignedoli	17	'Election is secured
Pignedoli	18	Lorscheider	12	Lorscheider	1	at the third ballot,
Baggio	9	Baggio	10			but a forth confirm-
Koenig	8	Felici	8			ing ballot is not
Bertoli	5 or 6	Cordeiro	4			excluded by these figures (Cardinal
Pironio	4					Höffner had said
Felici	2					that the name of
Lorscheider	2					Luciani was the only one read out)'.

Hebblethwaite, p. 82

Siri	25	Siri	33	Luciani	>65	Luciani	>90
Luciani	23	Luciani	31	Siri	c.12	Lorscheider	1
Pignedoli	18	Pignedoli	15	Pignedoli	c.12		
Baggio	12	Lorscheider	12	Lorscheider	c.12		
Koenig	9	Baggio	10	Koenig	c.12		
Bertoli	6	Felici	8				
Pironio	4	Cordeiro	4				
Lorscheider	2						
Felici	2						

Murphy, pp.160–1

Siri	26	Luciani	46	Luciani	66	Luciani	96
Luciani	23	Pignedoli	19	Pignedoli	21	Pignedoli	10
Pignedoli	18	Lorscheider	14	Lorscheider	1	Lorscheider	1
Baggio	9	Baggio	11				
Koenig	8	Felici	9				
Bertoli	5	Bertoli	4				
Pironio	5	Hume	1				
Felici	2						
Lorscheider	2						
Hume	1						
Pappalardo	1						

Thomas, Morgan-Witts, pp. 273–82

Siri	25	Siri	35	Luciani	68	Luciani	99
Luciani	23	Luciani	30	Siri	15	Siri	11
Pignedoli	18	Pignedoli	15	Pignedoli	10	Lorscheider	1
Lorscheider	12	Lorscheider	12				
Baggio	9						

Yallop, pp. 78–82

Appendix D

Mementos of John Paul I's Papacy

Pontifical Medal: 1978[1]
Commemorative Set in gold, silver and bronze.
Profile of John Paul I, head left.
Reverse, pontifical crest beneath motto 'HUMILITAS'.

Coin: 1978[2]
1000 Lire (Ag).
John Paul I, head and shoulders, facing left.
Reverse, pontifical crest, value.

Stamps: 11 December 1978[3]
Commemoration of Pontificate, multicoloured.
Issue: 1,450,000 Complete Series.
70 Lire :   The Pope seated on throne.
120 Lire :   The Pope smiling.
250 Lire :   The Pope in Vatican Gardens.
350 Lire :   The Pope giving blessing (horizontal format).

11 October 1979
Fiftieth Anniversary of Foundation of Vatican City State, multi-coloured.
Issue: 1,200,000 Complete Series.
250 Lire: Coat of Arms and Effigy of Pope John Paul I (horizontal format).

---

[1]   See H. E. Cardinale, *Orders Of Knighthood, Awards And The Holy See*, 1983, 1984 revised, Gerrards Cross, Ed. P. Bander Van Duren, Van Duren, pp. 78–9.
[2]   See G. Schön, *World Coin Catalogue: Twentieth Century*, 1987 Sixth edition, London, B. A. Seaby, p. 1602.
[3]   See *L'Osservatore Romano*, N.47 (556) (23 November 1978), p. 9; N.39 (600) (24 September 1979), p. 12 (English editions).

Bibliography

Minor references are given in full in relevant footnotes to the text. References in footnotes without page details are from one of the listed Websites.

ABBOTT, W.M., (ed.), *The Documents Of Vatican II*, London, Geoffrey Chapman, 1966.

ALLEN, J. L., Cardinal *Ratzinger: The Vatican's Enforcer Of The Faith*, London, Continuum, 2000.

ANDREOTTI, G. A., *Ogni Morte Di Papa – I Papi Che Ho Conosciuto*, Milan, Rizzoli, 1980.

ANNUARIO PONTIFICIO, Città Del Vaticano, Libreria Editrice Vaticana, various editions.

L'ATTIVITÀ DELLA SANTA SEDE Città Del Vaticano, Libreria Editrice Vaticana, 1978.

BARRETT, D. B., (ed.), *World Christian Encyclopedia*, Oxford, Oxford University Press, 1982.

BINCHY, D. A., *Church And State In Fascist Italy*, London, Oxford University Press, 1941, 1970.

BOLLETTINO ECCLESIASTICO DELLA DIOCESI DI VITTORIO VENETO, n. 46 (1958) – n. 58 (1970).

BOLLETTINO ECCLESIASTICO INTERDIOCESANO DI BELLUNO E FELTRE , n. 14 (1935) – n. 49 (1959).

BULL, G., *Vatican Politics At The Second Vatican Council, 1962–5*, London, Oxford University Press, 1966.

—— *Inside The Vatican*, London, Hutchinson, 1982.

BURNS, C., *The Election Of A Pope*, London, CTS, H468, 1978.

CASTELLI, M., 'The Church In Italy', *Pro Mundi Vita Bulletin*, 66 (May-June 1977).

CATHOLIC HERALD, August-October 1978, London.

CORNWELL, J., *A Thief In The Night: The Death Of Pope John Paul I*, London, Viking, 1989.

—— *The Pope In Winter: The Dark Face Of John Paul II's Papacy*, London, Penguin Viking, 2004.

DA ROS, I., *L'Africa Di Albino Luciani E Dei Missionari Vittoriesi*, Vittorio Veneto, Grafiche De Bastiani, 1996.

DEAN, S., *Pope John Paul I*, London, CTS, B501, 1978.

DE ANASAGASTI, P., 'La Dimensione Missionaria In Giovanni Paolo I', *Il Missionario Francescano*, 54, no. 10 (1978) [Rome].

DE LA CIERVA, R., *La Diario Secreto De Juan Pablo I*, Barcelona, Planeta [Colección Fábula 262], 1990. [*Well researched, factually based 'novel' purporting to be Luciani's private diary*].

DE ROSA, G., 'Learning The Hard Way: The Referendum On Divorce In Italy', *Month*, CCXXXV (August 1974).

DELHAYE, P., 'Adieu Au Pape Jean-Paul Ier. Textes Et Commentaires', *Esprit Et Vie*, 48 (1978).

DIETSCHY, H., '"Gott Ist Vater Und Mutter": War Johannes Paul I Ein Ketzer?' *Reformatio*, 30 (July-August 1981).

D'ONOFRIO, A., *Giovanni Paolo I 'Il Papa Del Sorriso'; Profilo Biografico, Discorsi, Fioretti, Pensieri Spirituali*, 3rd edn., Rome 1978. 1989.

D'ORAZI, L., *Impegno All'Umilta: La Vita Di Papa Luciani*, Rome, Edizioni Logos, 1987.

—— *In Nome Di Dio O Del Diavolo? La Morte Di Papa Luciani*, Rome, Edizioni Logos, 1988.

FERRARO, G. 'La Catechesi Nel Ministero Di Paolo VI E Di Giovanni Paolo I', *Rassegna Di Teologia*, 19 (1978) [Naples].

FLANNERY, A. (ed.), *Vatican Council II: The Conciliar And Post Conciliar Documents*, Tenbury Wells, Fowler Wright, 1975.

—— *Vatican Collection, Volume II: Vatican Council II: More Post Conciliar Documents*, Leominster, Fowler Wright, 1982.

GANTIN, B., 'Il Concilio Vaticano II Nelle Scelte Pastorali Di Albino Luciani' *Dolomiti*, 1–2 (1989).

GERLIN, M., *Illustrissimo: Il Segreto Di Papa Luciani*, Vittorio Veneto, Grafiche De Bastiani, 1989.

GREELEY, A. M., *The Making Of The Popes: The Politics Of Intrigue In The Vatican*, London, Futura, 1979.

HEBBLETHWAITE, P., *The Year Of Three Popes*, London, William Collins, 1978.

—— 'God's Appointment: Finding The Right Pope' *The Way*, 19 (April 1979).

—— *Introducing John Paul II: The Populist Pope*, London, Fount, 1982.

—— *John XXIII Pope Of The Council*, London, Geoffrey Chapman, 1984.

—— *In The Vatican*, London, Sidgwick and Jackson, 1986.

—— *Paul VI The First Modern Pope*, London, HarperCollins, 1993.

—— *The Next Pope: An Enquiry*, London, Fount, 1995.

HOLMES, J. D., *The Papacy In The Modern World 1914–1978*, London, Burns & Oates, 1981.

HUBER, G., *Jean-Paul Ier, Ou La Vocation De Jean-Baptiste*, Paris, Editions SOS, 1979.

HUMILITAS–PAPA LUCIANI 1984 – [Centro Papa Luciani, Sartena Alta 1, 32035 S. Giustina, Belluno, Italia]

INCITTI, L., *Papa Luciani: Una Morte Sospetta*, Rome, Gremese, 2001.

INFIESTA, J., *Juan Pablo I: Alegria De Los Pobres*, Madrid, Ediciones Paulinas, 1978.

ITALIAN EPISCOPAL CONFERENCE: *Commission For The Teaching Of The Faith And Catechesis. Parents, God And The Under-Fives: A Catechism For The Very Young*, tr. WOOD-HALL, R., Slough, St. Paul Publications 1975.

JOHN PAUL I (See also LUCIANI, A.) n. 10, 23 Septembris 1978; n. 11, 30 Septembris 1978; n. 12, 31 Octobris 1978.

Acta Apostolicae Sedis; Commentarium Officiale, LXX (1978), Città Del Vaticano, Typis Polyglottis Vaticanis.

—— 'Pope John Paul I', *The Pope Speaks: The Church Documents Quarterly*, 23, no. 4 (winter 1978).

—— *Insegnamenti Di Giovanni Paolo I*, Città Del Vaticano Libreria Editrice Vaticana, 1979.

—— *The Teachings Of Pope John Paul I*, Città Del Vaticano, Libreria Editrice Vaticana, 1979.

—— 'St Alphonsus de Liguori: Model Of Sheperds', *Christ To The World*, 29 (November–December 1984).

—— 'Homily At A Marian Shrine In Brazil Says That Mary's Assumption Attests To Christ's Victory Over Death', *L'Osservatore Romano*, n. 44 (1012) (2 November 1987) (English edition).

JOHN PAUL II, 'Discourse To The Faithful Of The Diocese Of Vittorio Veneto Speaking About The Humanity And Consistent Firmness Of John Paul I', *L'Osservatore Romano*, n. 30 (896) (29 July 1985) (English edition).

KAISER, R., *Inside The Council: The Story Of Vatican II*, London, Burns & Oates, 1963.

—— *The Encyclical That Never Was: The Story Of The Pontifical Commission On Population, Family And Birth, 1964–66*, London, Sheed & Ward, 1987.

KELLY, J. N. D., *The Oxford Dictionary Of Popes*, Oxford Oxford University Press, 1986.

KUMMER, R., *Albino Luciani, Papa Giovanni Paolo I: Una Vita Per La Chiesa*, Padua, Edizioni Messaggero, 1988.

KÜNG, H., *On Being A Christian,* London tr. QUINN, E., William Collins, 1974, 1977.

LAZZARINI, A., *Johannes Paul I, Der Papst Eines Neuen Morgens,* Freiburg, Herder, 1978.

LO BELLO, N., *The Vatican Papers,* London, NEL, 1982.

LORENZO, D., 'Gli Insegnamenti Di Giovanni Paolo I Sulla Pastorale Della Predicazione', *Seminarium,* 19 (January–March 1979).

LUCIANI, A., (See also JOHN PAUL I) *Catechetica In Briciole,* Belluno, Tipografia Vescovile, 1949; 2nd edn, Rome, Edizioni Paoline, 1953.

—— *Catechesis In Easy Stages,* London, 1949.

—— *Nuove Briciole Di Catechetica,* Vittorio Veneto, L'Aedi Editore, 1961.

—— *L'Origine Dell'Anima Umana Secondo Antonio Rosmini. Esposizione E Critica,* Belluno, Tipografia Vescovile, 1950.

—— *L'Origine Dell'Anima Umana Secondo A. Rosmini. Esposizione E Critica;* 2nd edn, Padua, Gregoriana Editrice, [pp.152], 1958.

—— 'Cardinal Warns Journalists Against Traps In Reporting', *Our Sunday Visitor,* 64, no. 2 (15 February 1976).

—— *Illustrissimi,* Padua, Grafiche Del Messaggero Di Sant' Antonio, 1976.

—— *Illustrissimi: The Letters Of Pope John Paul I,* London tr. QUIGLY, I., William Collins, 1978.

—— *Illustrissimi: Letters From Pope John Paul I,* Boston and Toronto, tr. WEAVER, W., Little, Brown, 1978.

—— *La Figlia Inglese Della Provetta, Prospettive Nel Mondo* (August 1978).

—— *Il Magistero Di Albino Luciani: Scritti E Discorsi,* Padua, ed. CATTABIANI, A., Edizioni Messaggero, 1979.

—— *Albino Luciani, Il Buon Samaritano: Curso De Esercizi Spirituali,* Padua, ed. TOLLARDO, G., Edizioni Messaggero, 1980.

—— et al. *Giovanni XXIII, Papa Di Transizione,* Rome, ed. CAPOVILLA, L. F., Storia E Letteratura, 1979.

—— *Un Vescovo Al Concilio: Lettere Dal Vaticano II,* Rome, Città Nuova, 1983.

—— *Maria: La Donna Dalla Quale Gesu' Volle Nascere,* Venice, ed. BASSOTTO, C., Camillo Bassotto, 1988.

—— *Opera Omnia*
   1 Catechetica In Briciole; Thesis; Illustrissimi
   2 Vittorio Veneto, 1959–1962
   3 Vittorio Veneto, 1963–1966

4 *Vittorio Veneto, 1967–1969*
5 *Venezia, 1970–1972*
6 *Venezia, 1973–1974*
7 *Venezia, 1975–1976*
8 *Venezia, 1977–1978*
9 *Roma, 1978; Buon Samaritano; Letters; Index* 9 vols., Padua Edizioni Messaggero, 1988–1989.
—— *Il Mio Cuore È Ancora A Venezia* Venice, ed. BASSOTTO, C., Tipolitografia Adriatica, 1990.
LUCIANI, A. and DE ROCCO, S., *Don Filippo Carli (1879–1934)*, Canale D'Agordo, Parrochia Di Canale D'Agordo, 1982.
LUCIANI, A., *Mio Fratello Albino: Ricordi E Memorie Della Sorella Di Papa Luciani*, Venice-Mestre, ed. FALASCA, S., Libreria edn, Paoline, 2003.
LUCIANI, P., *Une Prete Di Montagna: Gli Anni Bellunesi Di Albino Luciani (1912–1958)* Padua, Edizioni Messaggero, 2003.
MACEOIN, G., *The Inner Elite: Dossiers On Papal Candidates*, Kansas City, Sheed, Andrews and McMeel, Inc., 1978.
McSHEFFERY, D. F., 'John Paul I Taught Us To Hope Again', *Priest*, 48 (November 1992).
MAGISTER, S., *La Politica Vaticana E L'Italia 1943–1978*, Rome, Editori Riuniti, 1979.
MARTIN, J., *Mes Six Papes. Souvenirs Romains Du Cardinal Jacques Martin*, Paris, Marne, 1993.
MEAOLO, G., *La Catechesi Mariana Di Papa Luciani*, Padua, Edizioni Messaggero, 1987.
MUCCIN, G., 'Testimonianze E Riflessioni Su Albino Luciani' *Dolomiti*, 1–2 (1989).
MURPHY, F. X., *The Papacy Today*, London, Weidenfeld and Nicolson, 1981.
MUTHIG, J., 'The Life Of Pope John Paul I', *Official Catholic Teachings: Update 1978*, 1980, Wilmington, N. C., McGrath (A Consortium Book) (As reprinted in *Origins*, 8, no. 17, 1979).
NAPOLI, C. and MARCUCCI, E., *Giovanni Paolo I: Papa Per 33 Giorni*, Bologna, Cappelli, 1978.
NEW CATHOLIC ENCYCLOPEDIA; Supplement; Supplement: Change In The Church, 17 vols, Washington, D.C., Catholic University Of America 1967, 1974, 1979. (O'BRIEN, T. C., 'John Paul I', Pope vol. 17).
NICHOLS, P., 'Obituary: Pope John Paul I: Premature End To A Pontificate Which Promised The Common Touch', *The Times*, no. 60420 (30 September 1978).

—— *The Pope's Divisions: The Roman Catholic Church Today*, London, Faber and Faber, 1981.

NICOLINI, G., *Trentatré Giorni Un Pontificato*, Rovigo, Istituto Padano Di Arti Grafich, 1979.

—— *Papa Luciani*, Bergamo, Edizioni Velar, 1995.

NIERO, A., 'A Venezia. Gli Anni Del Patriarcato, in Papa Luciani 1912–1978. Itinerario Di Una Vita' *Gente Veneta*, nr. Unico (1979).

—— 'Il Postconcilio Nel Patriarcato Di Venezia (1965–1978)' *Rivista Del Clero Italiano*, 71, n. 1 (1990).

O'MAHONY, T. P. *The New Pope: The Election, The Man And The Future*, Blackrock, Co. Dublin, Villa Books 1978.

L'OSSERVATORE ROMANO (semi-official daily newspaper of Vatican City. Weekly English edition, 1968–).

PUES, L., *Het Augustusconclaaff Van 1978 De Verrassende Keuze Van Johannes–Paulus I*, Licentiate Thesis, Faculty of Theology K. U. Leuven, 1982.

RICHARDS, M., 'The Message Of John Paul I' *Clergy Review*, LXIII (November 1978).

RIVISTA DIOCESANA DEL PATRIARCATA DI VENEZIA n. 54 (1969) – n. 63 (1978).

ROSMINI, A., *The Five Wounds Of The Church*, tr. WATSON, T. and CLEARY, D., Leominster, Fowler Wright, 1848, 1987.

RUSAK, V., 'The Funeral Of Metropolitan Nikodim', *Journal Of The Moscow Patriarchate*, no. 11 (1978).

RYNNE, X., *Letters From Vatican City; The Second Session; The Third Session; The Fourth Session*, London, Faber and Faber, 1963, 1964, 1965, 1966.

SACRA CONGREGAZIONE PER L'EVANGELIZAZIONE DEI POPOLI 'DE PROPAGANDA FIDE', *Annuario 1978*, Rome, Urbaniana University Press, 1979; 'La Pastorale Missionaria Del Vescovo E Patriarca Luciani'; 'Testimonianza Di Madre Teresa Sul Papa Giovanni Paolo I'.

SAEZ, J. L., *Se Pedira Cuenta: Muerte Y Figura De Juan Pablo I*, Madrid, Origenes, 1990.

SCALTRITI, G. A., 'Papa Paolo VI Montini E La Sintesi Savonaroliana Dopo Papa Giovanni Paolo I Luciani E All'Inizio Di Papa Giovanni Paolo II Wojtyla', *Palestra Del Clero*, 58 (1978), 172–89, 217–30, 284–99 [Rovigo].

SCHALL, J. V., 'Divorce In Italy', *Month*, CCXXXV (September 1974).

SCHRAÜWEN, L., *Le Mystère Jean-Paul I, Pape Pour Quelches Jours, Un Règne Éphémère*, Alleur, Marabout Editions, 1995.

SCOPELLITI, N. and TAFFAREL, F., 'Lo Stupore Di Dio': *Vita Di*

Papa Luciani, Milan Edizioni ARES, 2006.

SEABECK, R. and L. (eds), *The Smiling Pope: The Life And Teaching Of John Paul I,* Huntington, IN, Our Sunday Visitor, 2004.

SENIGAGLIA, M., 'Le Radici Della Spiritualita Di Giovanni Paolo', *Dolomiti,* 1–2 (1989).

SERAFINI, L., *Albino Luciani: Il Papa Del Sorriso,* Padua, Edizioni Messagero, 2005.

SILVESTRINI, E., *Albino Luciani E L'Humanae Vitae,* Milan, Ancora, 2003.

SPACKMAN, P., 'The Poet And The Pope: G. K. Chesterton And John Paul I' *Chesterton Review,* XXVII, no. 3 (August 2001).

STELLA, G., *Giovanni Paolo I: Il Messaggio Dell' Umilta,* Venice, Edizioni Turismo Veneto, 1995.

TABLET, August-October 1978, vol. CCXXXII London.

TAFFAREL, F., *Papa Luciani: Un Pensiero Al Giorno,* Padua, Edizioni Messaggero, 1990.

THIERRY, J. J. (pseud.), *Lettres De Rome Sur La Singulier Trépas De Jean-Paul I,* Paris, Pierre Belfond, 1981.

—— *La Vraie Mort De Jean-Paul Ier,* Paris, Jean-Cyrille Godefroy, 1983.

30 DAYS, 1988–91, vols I–4, San Francisco, Ignatius Press, 1992– Newton, NJ, Italcoser Corp.

THOMAS, G. and MORGAN-WITTS, M., *Pontiff,* London, Granada, 1983.

TIME: The Weekly Newsmagazine, August-October 1978, vol. 112, New York, ('Europe' edition).

TORNIELLI, A. and ZANGRANDO, A., *Papa Luciani: Il Parroco Del Mondo,* Udine, Edizioni Segno, 1998.

—— *Papa Luciani: Il Sorriso Del Santo,* Casale Monferrato, Edizioni Piemme, 2003.

VALENTINI, N. and BACCHIANI, M., *Il Papa Buono Che Sorrideva,* Milan, Sperling & Kupfer, 1978.

VIAN, G. M., 'Giovanni Paolo I', *Enciclopedia Dei Papi,* III (2000).

WILLI, V. J., *Im Namen Des Teufels?,* Steim-am-Rhein, Christiana, 1987.

WITHERS, K., 'Pope John Paul I And Birth Control', *America,* 140 (24 March 1979).

YALLOP, D. A., *In God's Name,* London, Jonathan Cape, 1984; Rev. edn, London, Constable & Robinson, 2007.

WEBSITES
www.albino-luciani.com/
www.amicipapaluciani.it/
www.johannes-paulus1.web-uno.org/
www.johnpaul1.com/
www.papaluciani.com/
www.papaluciani.it/
www.vatican.va/holy-father/john-paul-i/index-it.htm

Index

Lightning Source UK Ltd.
Milton Keynes UK
20 May 2010

154456UK00001B/149/P